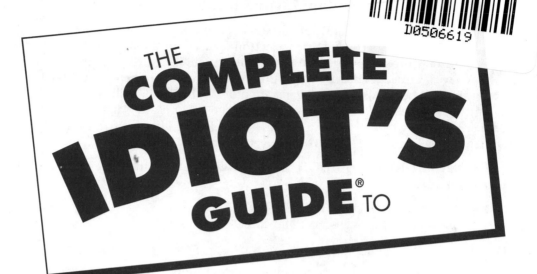

THE COMPLETE IDIOT'S GUIDE® TO

Jewish History and Culture

by Rabbi Benjamin Blech

alpha books

A Pearson Education Company

International Standard Book Number: 0-02862711-3
Library of Congress Catalog Card Number: LOC 98-89886

03 02   8 7 6

Interpretation of the printing code: the rightmost number of the first series of numbers is the year of the book's printing; the rightmost number of the second series of numbers is the number of the book's printing. For example, a printing code of 98-1 shows that the first printing occurred in 1998.

Printed in the United States of America

Grateful ackowledgement of permission to use the "blood libel" and Shabbetai Zevi illustrations from *Heritage: Civilization and the Jews*, by Abba Eban. Copyright © 1984 by Abba Eban. Reprinted by permission of Summit Books.

Contents at a Glance

Contents

Foreword

What makes Jews the Chosen Ones? Is it that they have not only survived, but prospered?...through thousands of years and thousand of places; through destructive war and saddening exile; through long wanderings and hasty disguises. Of course, Jews have also survived plates of *kishke* and *kugel*, the all-knowing Jewish mother, and the ever-embarrassing yenta. And, as less than one quarter of one percent of the world's population, the Jewish people have made quite an impact.

So why is this people different from all other people? It is said that a Jewish mother could take care of a hundred children, yet a hundred children couldn't take care of her. It is also said that the astounding number of Jewish doctors comes not from wanting to impress their Jewish mothers, but from a desire to fix the world. And as for Jewish comedians, Jackie Mason, Woody Allen, and Jerry Seinfeld are laughing proof that Jews are funny people.

This book is about a people who came from Israel and expanded in every direction, from the Bronx to Ethiopia. Some went west, some went to Miami, and others returned to Israel. They share a religion tested by history and, despite assimilation across geographical boundaries and melting pots, their culture is still solid and intact.

Rabbi Blech, well versed in Jewish culture and tradition, has created a piece of art in which the two intertwine. He discusses the persecution and alienation that have challenged Jews not to suffer but to succeed, on the field and in the theater. Starting at the beginning with Adam and Eve, he traces the evolution of Jewish history through the Crusades and the Inquisition to the Holocaust, arriving at the present day. The text thoroughly examines the future of Judaism and its relationship to other religions.

This book is for the Jew who, like the Wise Son, wants to know the meaning in all of this. For those who are familiar with Jewish history and culture, it offers fascinating trivia and insight. And for the Gentile who has always wanted to know but was afraid to ask, it is an engaging text that eases the guilt of not knowing. This book is also a tool for Jews with non-Jewish relatives and non-Jews with Jewish relatives.

The information is presented in an intriguing way, leaving memories of monotonous Biblical lessons far behind. Sidebars explain little-known facts about Judaism and the symbolism in tradition. *The Complete Idiot's Guide® to Jewish History and Culture* teaches the reader that a Jew is supposed to question, and that here, within these pages, are the answers.

—Larry King and Rabbi Irwin Katsof

LARRY KING, host of *Larry King Live* on CNN, began his career in 1957 at a small radio station in Miami. His show, the only live phone-in television talk show, airs on over 325 stations worldwide. Named "Best Radio Talk Show Host" by the *Washington Journalism Review*, he is the author of several books, including *Best of Larry King* and *How to Talk to Anyone Anytime*. He is also author of *Powerful Prayers* (with Rabbi Katsof). King is the head of the Larry King Cardiac Foundation, which awards grants to individuals suffering from heart disease to help pay for medical treatment.

RABBI IRWIN KATSOF, an inspiration to celebrities and business leaders exploring their Jewish roots, is creator of the *Twentysomething Seminar* and *Let My People Know*, the largest-ever international satellite broadcast in the world. Ordained in 1992, he is an Orthodox rabbi with an unorthodox approach that provokes people to accept the spiritual challenge he offers. He has co-authored *Powerful Prayers* with Larry King, a book that explores the private spiritual lives of well-known celebrities and politicians.

Introduction

Try this experiment on your friends: Ask them to guess how many Jews there are in the world. Next, ask them what they imagine the percentage of the total Jewish population is to that of the entire world.

Based on the accomplishments of individual Jews, Nobel Prize winners and heroes of modern culture, as well as the amount of attention Jews get in the media, you'd never believe the correct answers: There are little more than 13 million Jews in the world, comprising less than 1/4 of 1 percent of the world's population!

So few in number, yet so great in ability. There's no doubt about it, Jews must have special gifts. They have the gift of survival: they are the oldest of any people on earth still around with their national identity and cultural heritage intact. The gift of talent: talent in every field of human endeavor. And perhaps most important of all, the gift of memory. It is the Jews who have given the world an understanding of the importance of history.

Henry Ford was famous for his belief that, "history is bunk." The Ford Motor Company is also famous for producing the Edsel. And both were probably equally stupid blunders. History is the only way we can learn from the past. History allows us to grow by standing on the shoulders of giants. Make a mistake once, and you're human. Never learn from what happened before, and you're dumb. That's why it's so important to heed the words of American philosopher George Santayana: "Those who do not learn from the past are condemned to repeat it."

The *idea* of history is a Jewish invention. It's called *The Bible*. It speaks in the language of "remember." Remember what happened there. Remember what your ancestors taught you. Remember what the Lord did for you. Remembering will make you better. Remembering will make you smarter. Remembering will transform you from a people of history to a people of destiny. That was the message Jews took from God and attempted to teach the world.

The past is history and the future is mystery. The time we live in right now is a gift from God—that's why it's called the present. And to make the most of a present, we've got to try to use the insights gleaned from the past to create a better future.

The reason I tell you all this is to explain why a book like this is so important. We know how horrible it can be to live without an awareness of events that came before. For an individual we have a name for it that fills us with terror: Alzheimer's. And it's a disease we wouldn't wish on anyone. Strangely enough, we don't have a similar word for the condition that describes ignorance of our collective past. Knowing what preceded us is almost as important in an historic sense as it is in a personal one. Only by knowing our past can we truly get to know ourselves.

And whether you're Jewish or not, Jewish influence on world events, on Western civilization, and on modern-day culture have been so overwhelming that the story of the Jews has to be a part of the universal heritage. That's why this book and the information it has to share with you are so important. The style is purposely light. We don't want you to be intimidated even if you are a complete idiot. Not an idiot in general—then you wouldn't have been smart enough to buy this book—but an idiot about the subject matter. There's no previous information expected of you. You should never feel shy about not knowing something before. The only really stupid thing to do is to maintain ignorance and not seek to learn more.

Throughout these pages I'm going to try very hard to entertain you as well as to educate you. I'm going to—hopefully—make you laugh. But the humor will really be the sugar coating for a very important medicine: a medicine for your mind and for your soul that will help you to more fully understand the past in order to better comprehend the present and prepare for the future.

And Here's What You'll Find

This book is divided into eight sections that will explore Jewish history and culture from the beginning of time to the present day:

Part 1, Who Are the Jews? is the introduction to the Jewish people. You'll learn the difference between the words Hebrew, Israelite, Jew and Israeli. You'll find out whether Jews are a race, a nation, a chosen people—or none of the above. You'll get an understanding of some of the more typical Jewish characteristics. You'll find out why there are so many Jewish doctors, as well as Jewish comedians. And you'll discover the relationship between Jews and their "homeland" of Israel—even if they don't live there.

Part 2, In the Beginning picks up the story from the beginning of creation and takes it through all the major events recorded in the *Torah*, the five books of Moses. You'll meet God, the Creator, and find out if He is really Jewish. You'll discover how old the world is according to Jews. You'll meet Adam and Eve and learn whether men and women are equals according to the Bible. (Bet you can't wait for the answer!) You'll get to know the heroes of the Bible and travel with Moses from Egypt to the Promised Land.

Part 3, Judges, Kings, Prophets—Those Were the Days will delight you with the later tales of the Bible, from Deborah (the Jewish Joan of Arc) to David and Solomon, as well as to the prophets Elijah, Isaiah and Jeremiah.

Part 4, Confronting Empires: Babylonia, Persia, Greece, and Rome shares with you Jewish confrontations with the major empires of ancient times: Babylonia, Persia, Greece and Rome. You'll find out all about the good times that gave the Jews the holidays of Hanukkah and Purim. And then you'll learn about the days when Rome came to conquer and to crucify—and helped to transform a Jew named Jesus into some people's vision of Messiah and God. The birth of Christianity and the completion of the *Talmud* make this one of the most exciting and important eras of Jewish history.

Part 5, The Crescent and the Cross explores the relationship of the Jews with the Arab, as well as with the Christian, world in the early Middle Ages. The irony, from a modern perspective, of Muslim friendship and Christian hatred deserves to be fully analyzed. The Jewish responses to persecution by way of mysticism, Messianism, Hasidism, as well as the pursuit of scientific study, leave us with significant legacies to this day.

Part 6, Emancipation and Enlightenment carries us close to modern times with the breakthrough movements that led to Jewish emancipation and enlightenment. Here we will see how Jews cope with the challenge not of foes, but of friends. How can Jews live apart, maintaining their own separate identity, when the world is finally ready to accept them? The answers of French, German, English, and American Jews are highly instructive as they are different. It is in this section that we will discover the uniqueness of America and its very special relationship with the Jewish people.

Our overview of Jewish communities around the world will include not only the *Fiddler on the Roof "shtetel"* existence of Polish and Russian Jewry, but also the esoteric Jews in such far-flung and remote areas as South Africa, New Zealand, Yemen, India, China—and even the "Jews in caves."

Part 7, Death and Rebirth: The Twentieth Century focuses on the great tragedy as well as the great miracle of modern times. Nazi Germany's attempt at the "Final Solution," the genocide of the Jews, was followed by the "Final Return." We'll learn about Zionism as a dream, and Zionism fulfilled with the birth of the State of Israel and its fifty-year history of incredible achievements. This will be a prelude to the last chapter in this section, which summarizes the gifts of the Jews to the world and to Western civilization.

Part 8, The Hall of Fame: A Jewish Who's Who closes the book with a short synopsis of Jewish "giants" in four major categories: *Welcome to Hollywood* reviews the tremendous influence and impact of Jews on the movie industry; *Let Me Entertain You* is a brief look at the famous comedians, stars of radio, TV, theater, music, and sports who have brought their Jewish genius to impact on these cultural mediums; *The Doctor Is In* will familiarize you with the incredible roles Jews have played in medicine and psychology; and the broad category of *Changing The World* is where you'll be given a good idea of the scope of Jewish contributions to science, literature and the arts, and philosophy.

As a Bonus

To make reading this book an even more enjoyable experience, you'll find boxes of extremely interesting and helpful information throughout these pages. These include:

Yenta's Little Secrets

A *yenta* is a Yiddish word for a gossip, and gossips sometimes have very important things to tell us. They are the little asides that didn't make it into the text but deserve to be told because they're interesting, entertaining, and contain a "little secret" you just might want to pass on to other people.

Pulpit Stories

Well, you don't really need a pulpit to tell them, but they're the cute, funny and fascinating stories that any speaker would use to powerfully illustrate an idea. Like I always say, people might forget a fact, but they'll never forget a story.

Listen to Your Bubbe

A *bubbe* is a Yiddish word for a grandmother. Actually, it's more like granny than grandmother, or even grandma—it has a very affectionate tone to it. And a *bubbe* always gives good advice to her grandchildren. Listen to what's in these boxes for tips or warnings.

Aha, That's It

Definitions explaining words you might never have heard of.

Sage Sayings

Quotes from famous people that powerfully summarize an idea in a way that makes it memorable and "quotable."

Be sure to look for these boxes as you're reading the book. And now, don't waste another minute. Go start on your journey!

Acknowledgements

Somewhere in this book you have to learn that the word "Jew" comes from a Hebrew root that means thankfulness. The very name of a people makes clear their recognition of the need to express gratitude. How could I, as a proud Jew, not close this introduction with an all-important acknowledgment of thanks to all those who helped bring this book to fruition?

Special thanks to my dear friend, Rabbi Dr. Jacob Reiner, for carefully reading the manuscript and making important suggestions and comments. He proved to me why he has such a reputation for scholarship as well as being a master teacher—a professor of history at Yeshiva University with two doctorates, from Dropsie University as well as the Bernard Revel Graduate School of Yeshiva University.

Thanks also to my extremely able editor, Carol Hupping, whose stylistic improvements are visible throughout the book; to Gary Krebs, Editorial Director of the CIG series, for his unstinting support; to my tireless secretaries, Eileen Greeley and Shelly Kitsberg, who miraculously managed to keep up with the ever-present deadlines; and to all the people behind the scenes who do one heaven of a job in producing the beautiful product you hold in your hands.

Finally, I want to dedicate this book about the past to my future—my children and grand-children—as well as to my beautiful wife Elaine who is responsible not only for them but for every blessing of my life.

Benjamin Blech

Part 1
Who Are the Jews?

Not a day goes by that you don't read something about them. For good or bad, they are at the center of the world's stage in spite of their remarkable, rather small number.

Jews are a conundrum, a riddle of history wrapped in an enigma. They are funny; they are wise; they are successful; they are different; they are unique; they are a group unto themselves. They have made contributions to the world far in excess of their population, and they have been an object of the world's hatred far more than any other people.

They are the oldest people alive, and they've created one of the youngest states in modern history. To understand them better is to gain an insight into the contemporary civilized world.

Part I introduces you to the Jews. Get to know who they are. What they're like. Their characters, personalities, and temperaments. Understand the cultural and religious baggage they have carried with them throughout the centuries that makes them what they are today.

Chapter 1

That's Funny, You Don't Look Jewish

In This Chapter

➤ Defining "who is a Jew" by discarding popular misconceptions

➤ The roles of race, nation, and "chosenness" for Jewish identity

➤ The diversity of religious differences among Jews

➤ What makes you "in" and what makes you "out"

For thousands of years, the world has had a love-hate relationship with the Jews. Okay, more hate than love. Jews have been harried and hunted, cursed and condemned, exiled and slaughtered. Yet, strangely enough, they've also been respected and envied, admired and emulated, and universally acknowledged as the source of many of the major religions of the world.

One more remarkable thing about them: They were able to do what no nation, no empire, no other people has ever done in the course of all of history—survive! The Persians, the Greeks, and the Romans have been stripped from the earth. But a small tribe, whose origin preceded that of those great nations, still exists. Mark Twain spoke for countless people when he asked the obvious question: "All things are mortal but the Jew; all other forces pass, but he remains. What is the secret of his immortality?" To find out how the Jew has survived, we must first ask ourselves, who is he really?

Sage Sayings

"We have not taught our young people how to explain the Law of Return, one of the great human rights documents of the twentieth century. They think it's an exclusionary, apartheid-type of legislation when in fact it is the ultimate affirmative action to the world's failure to open its doors to the Jews."

—Alan M. Dershowitz

Aha, That's It

The Knesset is Israel's governing body, also known as the Parliament of Israel. It consists of 120 politicians who meet together regularly to shout, yell, and insult each other while passing laws.

Who Is a Jew?

It's funny when you think about it. Almost a decade after the state of Israel was established, a cabinet crisis broke out in the *Knesset,* Israel's governing body. The newly created nation had passed a bill called the Law of Return. It guaranteed automatic citizenship and right of entry to every Jew around the world. But one thing they neglected to spell out clearly: Who is a Jew?

Imagine: A people survives for more than three thousand years. It finally manages to make it back home. And then at last it begins to question its own identity!

The best answer they could come up with was in the Israeli government's decision of July 20, 1958: "Anyone declaring in good faith that he is a Jew, and who does not profess any other religion, shall be registered as a Jew." In other words, if you *say* you're Jewish, that's good enough for us! Of course that really begs the question. After all, what would declaring that you are a Jew mean if we haven't agreed on the definition of the word?

Jewish by Ancestry

So, in 1960, Israel's Supreme Court tried to clarify: "For purposes of this Law (of Return), a Jew is someone born to a Jewish mother, or converted (to the Jewish faith) and (s)he is not a member of another religion." Now go ahead and think about that one for a minute. At the same time, give me the answer to the age-old question: Who came first, the chicken or the egg? What the court did was to throw the definition back a generation. You're a Jew if your mother was Jewish. And how was your mother determined to be Jewish? Oh...!

What they must have had in mind was that Jewish identity is first and foremost decided by ancestry. Jews are descendants of common parents. They are "the children of Abraham, Isaac and Jacob" as opposed to simply the sons of Adam and Eve. A unique set of ancestors made them special even as it set them apart.

And right now you're saying to yourself, "Who are these people—Abraham, Isaac and Jacob? And what made them different? And why should their children think of themselves as a group apart from the rest of mankind?" Good questions. But like the man who prayed, "God, please give me the gift of patience—and I WANT IT NOW," you've got to have a little more patience in order to really understand. There's just too much to squeeze in at once. Look, it took almost 6,000 years for the Jews to get where they are now so you'll have to wait at least until you get to Chapter 5, "At Last the Jews:

From Abraham to Moses," to learn the historic background. In the meantime, have faith—another Jewish trait—that as you continue to read it will all become clear.

You must have noticed that in the first part of the Court's ruling, the one based on biology, the standard used was the religion of the mother. The reason for that was that traditional Jewish law had for centuries based religious identity on matrilineal lines: You are what your mother is. And that opened the first can of worms. Because within Judaism we're going to learn (just a little of this will be coming up later in this chapter, a lot more in Chapter 20, "When the Walls Came Tumbling Down: Germany," and even more than that in Chapter 22, "America the Beautiful") there are different denominations. The most important ones are Orthodox, Conservative and Reform. (Remember what I told you about being patient. I promise you'll find out the most significant ways they differ—and why.)

But for now, it's enough to know that even though Judaism is monotheistic, it's not monolithic. There are major disagreements about a host of fundamental issues. One of them is what we are going to mention right now. Reform Judaism has within the recent past adopted patrilineal descent as equally valid for determining Jewish status. That means according to Reform Jews, as long as *either* parent is Jewish, the child is a Jew as well. And that is something the Israeli Supreme Court in its ruling did not accept.

Clearly, by siding with the Orthodox and Conservative views based on tradition rather than a more recent modern interpretation, the stage has been set for major conflict. A Jew for some isn't a Jew for all. So the issue of "Who is a Jew?" is the source of a great deal of controversy—a controversy which, because of the strong feelings involved on both sides, isn't likely to be resolved in the near future.

Jewish by Conversion

Compounding that (and you thought it couldn't possibly get any more difficult) is the second half of the Courts ruling: "or converted." Yes, but converted by whom? Orthodox Judaism has very rigid standards for conversion, Reform is very liberal, and Conservative Judaism—as is the case in so many of the issues we'll be discussing—is somewhere in the middle.

To get an idea of the wide range of possibilities, consider this: For an Orthodox conversion, there is a lengthy period of study required of at least a year, if not more, followed by a firm commitment on the part of the proselyte to live by the laws of Judaism (resting on the Sabbath, not eating certain foods, observing all the holidays, etc.). Then, for the conversion to "take" there must be a circumcision for males and an immersion in special waters (known as the *mikveh*)—a procedure later adopted in somewhat altered form by Christianity as baptism—for men and women.

Reform Judaism compromises on many of these requirements and Conservatives on a few. So what is considered a "proper conversion" for one group is wholly insufficient by another. Once again you can have someone recognized as a Jew in some circles but not in others. Is (s)he or isn't (s)he? Not even his or her hairdresser knows for sure! And the Court's phrase "or converted" isn't clear enough to give us an answer.

It's probably true that the phrasing was purposely left unclear. The Court didn't want to be drawn into theological controversy. But in leaving the matter unsettled, it left room for the inevitable consequence. The issue is still a subject of intense debate to this day. And as is so often the case, if you want to know what most Jews think about this, try asking ten of them. You'll probably get eleven answers!

Maybe that in itself is the first definition of a Jew. Jews love to argue, to analyze, and to see three sides to every question. Could be it's their exposure to Talmudic thinking that emphasizes fine and subtle distinctions. Or maybe it's because they've been around longer than anybody else and have come to realize there are no easy answers to any questions, even the most basic one of all—the one that asks you to come to grips with defining who you really are. But we can't let it go at that. Jews, at the very least, deserve their own definition.

What Jews Are Not

Jews have their own ways of answering a question. The most famous, of course, is to answer a question with a question. Ask me why, and I'll ask you. Why not?

Perhaps that tendency is rooted in the realization that there are no definitive answers possible, sort of the Jewish confirmation of the philosophic Uncertainty Principle. What can be done easily, however, is to respond with a negative: To the question "Is she beautiful?" the Jewish answer is "Well, she's not ugly." Knowing what something is not is a good start. So let's begin with some observations about what Jews aren't.

Jews Aren't a Race

To speak of a Jewish "race" is to perpetuate a myth propagated by Adolf Hitler and the Nazi regime. In their fanatical quest to carry out a final solution, the total extermination of the entire Jewish people, the standard was "Jewish blood," going back countless generations. Even the smallest trace of Jewish ancestry was sufficient to warrant execution.

But to speak precisely, in the language of the anthropologists, there is no such thing as a "Jewish race." It is true that the Jews sprang from the Mediterranean subdivision of the Caucasoid race. Over the course of centuries, however, and as the result of migrations round the globe, Jews developed a multitude of different physical characteristics because of their fusion with other racial blends wherever they lived. Although, unlike Christianity, they never actively missionized, Jews have readily accepted sincere converts into their fold.

An Aside: Meet Ruth

The story of Ruth is not only a remarkable demonstration of this truth but also a powerful witness to the respect and warm welcome accorded to those who voluntarily choose to enter into the covenant of the Lord. Ruth was, according to Jewish tradition, a Moabite princess—as distinguished from a Jewish American princess on two counts: She wasn't American and she wasn't Jewish. Yet, she ended up having a book of the Bible named after her because of her greatness of character. She married a Jew while still a Moabite. Yes, there were intermarriages even then. But her husband died—some commentators would have it as punishment for marrying out—and Ruth was left childless and penniless.

Her mother-in-law, a woman as gracious as her name, Naomi (which in Hebrew, by coincidence, means "pleasant") decided to return to Israel, her original homeland. Ruth felt the strong pull of both love and of duty. She just couldn't forsake the woman who had been so kind to her all the years. More, she was so deeply impressed by Naomi's character that she wanted to emulate her by joining her faith. "I, too, wish to become a Jew," she insisted. Her mother-in-law warned her of the difficulties. Do you know how hard it is to follow the strict demands of Jewish law? Do you realize you are going to become part of a people who are almost universally despised? Do you understand the difficult life you are choosing? To all of which Ruth replied, "Nevertheless, that is my will. Your people are my people, your God is my God."

Her perseverance makes her a true Jewish heroine. The fact that she was a convert, far from diminishing her stature, makes her all the more noble. For what she did was rewarded by God. The Bible tells us she was given the gift of having as a descendant the greatest king the Jewish people would ever have, King David. (And look forward to reading all about him in Chapter 9, "Father and Son: David and Solomon"). And from King David, as Jewish tradition has it, will eventually come forth the Messiah. Quite a job for a nice Jewish boy descended from someone who wasn't even born Jewish!

No one can change their race, but people can and have, through the ages, chosen to share their lot with the Jewish people. Which means quite clearly that the Jews are not a race.

Jews Aren't a Nation

In the aftermath of the French Revolution, Napoléon considered granting French Jews equal rights with all other citizens. But he was troubled by one nagging thought: Could Jews indeed be considered Frenchmen if they themselves thought they possessed a different national identity? So he convened a modern-day *Sanhedrin*, a Jewish assembly of seventy members, to whom he submitted a series of questions. Among them were the following.

In the eyes of Jews, are Frenchmen considered their brethren? Are they considered strangers? Can Jews born in France and treated by the laws as French citizens consider France their country? Are they

Aha, That's It

Sanhedrin is the Biblical Supreme Court comprised of seventy elders, which disbanded with the destruction of the Temple. A council of rabbis with this designation was reconvened by Napoléon after the French Revolution.

bound to defend it? Are they bound to obey the laws and conform to the dispositions of the civil code?

The answer was concise and pointed: "There is no Jewish nation, but only Germans, Frenchmen, Englishmen who profess the Jewish religion."

A nation has its own land, its own government. The Jews have survived with neither for countless centuries. During all that time they have been good and loyal citizens, praying for the welfare of the land in which they resided.

If Jews do speak of themselves as a nation, they mean it in a different sense than the way the word is commonly used. A Jewish nation implies shared borders of the spirit—ideas, values and heritage, rather than geographic location. It is a "nation" of mutual responsibility—one for another—that transcends common land or government. That's why Jews *can* be Jews and Americans—or any other citizens for that matter—without any schizophrenic feelings. The descriptives simply refer to two wholly different categories.

Jews Aren't Even the Chosen People

The famous ditty by William Ewer feigns surprise:

> How odd
> of God
> to choose
> the Jews.

The anonymous Jewish response is not so well known:

> It's not so odd.
> The Jews chose God.

Aha, That's It

Midrash is a compilation of aphorisms, Biblical commentaries, and rabbinic insights into life, religion, and history by sages of the first century C.E.

It might be comforting to believe that Jews were selected from among all other peoples as some kind of divine acknowledgement of their excellence. But Jewish sages tell the story somewhat differently. In the *Midrash,* God goes to all the nations of the world and asks them whether they would be willing to accept His commandments. Every one of them asks first for the details. What does He demand from them? When given specifics—things such as not stealing, killing, and adultery—they beg off; such laws would interfere with their lifestyles. Only the Jews were willing to accept. That, say the rabbis, makes them not the *chosen people,* but rather the *choosing people.*

And Jews Don't All Buy Wholesale

All right. I just threw this one in to cover all the other stereotypes. And Jews don't all have long noses—even the ones who couldn't afford plastic surgery. Nor is every New Yorker a Jew in disguise who gives away his identity because he says *hutzpah, goniff,* and *schlep.*

Yenta's Little Secrets

The Yiddish words *hutzpah, goniff, schlep* don't just have a meaning, they've also got an "attitude." *Hutzpah* is not just nerve. This is someone who kills his parents and asks for mercy because he's an orphan. *Goniff* means business partner. And *schlep,* as in: The Queen sends her chauffeur for her purchases, explaining she'd rather "not have to schlep them back to the palace" (because even the Queen speaks Yiddish when no other word will do as well).

So Do Jews All Share the Same Religious Beliefs?

You've got to be kidding. Who hasn't heard of the shipwrecked Jew who was finally found after many years alone on a desert island. He had managed to make a home for himself and even built two synagogues for his spiritual needs. "Why in the world do you need two synagogues?" his rescuers asked him in bewilderment. "Simple," he said, "One is the shul I built to pray in regularly. The other is the one I will never ever set foot into."

It's hard for Jews to agree on almost anything—and religion is surely important enough to warrant disagreement. What is a Jew supposed to believe in?

Aha, That's It

Shul is the name commonly used to describe a synagogue, from the German/Yiddish word for school, emphasizing its main function as a house of study.

From Orthodox to Atheist

1. Ask an Orthodox Jew and he'll tell you: Religion demands total adherence to Torah—to all the laws, traditions, and doctrines as received from the past, going all the way back to Mount Sinai. Orthodox Jews are the "fundamentalists" of the faith.

2. Ask a Reform Jew, and he will tell you that the Bible is not the literal word of God but rather divinely inspired. A faithful Jew need not live within the entirety of the law as revealed in the scriptures and interpreted in rabbinic tradition but is permitted to make concessions to the contemporary setting.

3. Ask a Conservative Jew, and he will toe a line somewhere between the Reform and the Orthodox. Absolute adherence to past tradition is not required, but a strong sense of continuity and respect for the past still prevails.

For more on the different Jewish denominations, See Chapter 20, "When the Walls Came Tumbling Down: Germany," and Chapter 22, "America the Beautiful."

Yenta's Little Secrets

Orthodox and Conservative Jews believe it is the religion of the mother that defines the identify of the child, emphasizing the primary role of the woman as bearer and nurturer. In other words, if your mother is Jewish, you're Jewish. Reform Jews have in recent years accepted a patriarchal determinant as well—a child is considered Jewish if *either* parent is Jewish.

Sage Sayings

"There are only two kinds of Jews: religious Jews and not yet religious Jews."

—Rabbi Shneerson, Lubavitch rebbe

4. Ask a Reconstructionist, and he will stress the primacy of Jewish culture; it is the holiness of the people rather than of God that must be respected and preserved.

5. And just to round out the picture you must have heard of the Jewish atheist who is quick to tell you, "My grandfather was an atheist, my father was an atheist, I am an atheist, and please God, my children will be atheists." (It's not easy to get thousands of years of your past out of your system.)

Including Even Those Who Don't Agree With You

So who is right?

There you go again—wanting one, and only one, definitive answer to the exclusion of all others. There is something to be said about the apocryphal tale of two litigants who appeared before their rabbi. The rabbi listened carefully to one of them, shook his head in agreement, and said to him, "You're right." Then he heard the words of the second, nodded once more, and said to him, "You're right." A bystander could not contain himself and dared to ask, "But Rabbi, how could they both be right?" To which the Rabbi responded, "You know, you're also right." Judaism is broad enough to include under its wings, even the most wicked of sinners. "A Jew who has sinned is still a Jew" is the conclusion of the sages of the Talmud. An error of deed is not sufficient to cause you to be expelled from the fold. And so, too, an error of creed isn't enough to make you lose your status as a Jew.

Sage Sayings

"As God is One, though His name has seventy ramifications, so is Israel one, though dispersed among the seventy nations."

—Zohar

The Bottom Line

So we have come full circle. A Jew is…a Jew. Someone who chooses to identify himself as such and not as a member of another faith community. Someone who shares with other Jews a rich and glorious past—either biologically, as a descendant of Abraham, Issac and Jacob, or spiritually as a result of a voluntary act of conversion. Someone who chooses to share in the Jewish destiny—even if it means suffering the curses of anti-Semites. A Jew is a Jew because of a conscious decision to declare, as did Ruth many centuries ago, "Your people are my people, your God is my God."

Do you disagree strongly with what I've just said? Maybe that means you're also Jewish!

The Least You Need to Know

➤ It isn't easy to define the word Jew to everyone's satisfaction—they're still debating the issue even in Israel.

➤ It's easier to state unequivocally what Jews are not—not a race, not a nation, and not a chosen people as much as they are a choosing people.

➤ Jews believe in one God but have many different ways to approach Him.

➤ Despite spiritual failings or religious differences, Jews are still Jews.

➤ The choice of personal identification is probably the most powerful determinant for someone being a Jew.

Chapter 2

My Son the Doctor and Other Jewish Types

In This Chapter

➤ Why Jews are so smart and what made them get that way

➤ Why Jews are successful and what drives them so

➤ Why Jews flock to certain professions more than others—from medicine to comedy

➤ Why Jews have always been eternal optimists

Shaped by thousands of years of traditions, Jews have developed a certain ethnic and cultural view of the world that tends to unify them, no matter how far apart they may be scattered. Nursed from the Biblical bosom, reared in childhood by prophets and scholars, matured by a common history of suffering and tribulation, contemporary Jewry is marked by cultural characteristics transcending almost all geographical borders.

"The Jews are like other people," goes a famous proverb, "only more so." Small wonder. They have had so many years to learn from past mistakes, to absorb ever new teachings and insights, to question and to philosophize, to come to their own conclusions about the meaning of life and the goals we should strive for. Ralph Waldo Emerson put it well: "Life consists of what a man is thinking of all day." And it wasn't only comedian Jack Benny (who of course was Jewish) who said, "I'm thinking, I'm thinking." Jews have been thinking for generations, and the conclusions they've come to is what makes them the people we know today.

Are Jews Really Smarter?—The People of the Book

Do you think it's just a coincidence? Twenty-one percent of Nobel Prize winners have been Jews even though Jews comprise less than one-quarter of one percent of the world's population. Choose any field, and you will find that Jews have excelled in it. Think of the names of many modern-day figures most responsible for the intellectual turning points of history—Marx, Freud, Einstein—and you will find proof for the Biblical verdict: "Surely this is…a wise and understanding people." (Deut. 4:6)

There simply is no way to deny it. Jews really *are* smart. There must be a reason—and I can give you at least three of them.

Sage Sayings

Often when I found in China an artist of unusual talent or a mind more vivid than others among my students, the chances were good that he had Jewish blood in him. It is a creative strain.

—Pearl Buck, *My Several Worlds*

Heredity

Historians have pointed out a fascinating difference between Jews and Christians. In Christianity, as well as in many other religions, holiness was identified with asceticism, great spirituality with the practice of celibacy. For centuries the finest minds among Christians were urged to join the church and become priests. That effectively condemned their genetic pool of intelligence to an untimely end.

Jews, on the other hand, took quite seriously the first commandment to mankind—to be fruitful and multiply. Sex was never seen as sinful, but rather as one of those things created by God that he surely must have had in mind when he declared, in reviewing his work, that "Behold everything was very good." Among Jews, the most intelligent were encouraged to become religious leaders. As rabbis, they had to serve as role models for their congregants as procreators and "fathers of their countries." Brains got passed on from generation to generation, and Jews today are still reaping the benefits of the frequent sexual activities of their ancestors.

Environment

If challenge and response are the keys to creativity and achievement, it's no surprise that Jews are smart; they've been challenged more than anyone else on earth. The school of hard knocks is a wonderful teacher. Jews had no choice but to learn to be better than anyone else since the odds were always so very much stacked against them. When you're born with a silver spoon in your mouth, you tend to get fat and lazy. When you're born with the lash of a whip on your back, you quickly learn to become crafty, street smart, and knowledgeable in everything that will help you make it through life.

A Unique Value System

We still haven't touched on the most important reason of all. Jews are smart because they have been raised in a tradition that treasures education above everything else, that considers study the highest obligation of mankind, and that identifies the intellect as that part of us created in "the image of God." To be illiterate was unheard of in the Jewish world, not only because it was a sign of stupidity, but, more significantly, because it was a sin.

Jews are obligated by law to review the Bible in its entirety every year, dividing it into manageable weekly sections. The widespread custom when a child turned three years old was to write the letters of the Hebrew alphabet on a board in honey and have the child learn them as he licked them off, equating their meaning with the taste of sweetness. Jews studied the *Midrash*, and it taught them: The Sword and the Book came from Heaven together, and the Holy One said: "Keep what is written in this Book or be destroyed by the other." Jews studied the *Mishna* and it taught them, "Say not when I have leisure I will study; you may not have leisure." The Jews absorbed the teachings of the *Ethics of the Fathers*, and they understood its insight, "If you have acquired knowledge, what do you lack? If you lack knowledge, what have you acquired?"

Philosophical Tevye, that delightful creation of the Yiddish writer Sholem Aleichem and the star of *Fiddler On The Roof*, explained that Jews always wear hats because they never know when they will be forced to travel. What he didn't say, which is probably more important, is that they always made sure to have something under their hats and inside of their heads—because physical possessions could be taken from them, but what they accumulated in their minds would always remain the greatest "merchandise" a Jew possesses.

Are Jews Really Richer?—The People of the Buck

How rich are the Jews? According to the infamous anti-Semitic book *Protocols of the Elders of Zion,* Jews own the world: the banks, the press, the commercial markets, the governments of the world. Exposed as a forgery, many prominent people—including Henry Ford—believed it. Jews only wish it were really so!

Aha, That's It

Ethics of the Fathers is one of sixty-three sections of the *Mishna* that brings together the ethical and moral teachings and maxims of ancient sages. The orals laws, written in the *Mishna*, and the rabbinic discussions of these laws, written in the *Gemara*, together make up the *Talmud*, the great compilation of Jewish Oral Law.

Sage Sayings

The pursuit of knowledge for its own sake, an almost fanatical love of justice, and the desire for personal independence—these are the features of Jewish tradition that make me thank my stars that I belong to it.

—Albert Einstein, *The World As I See It*

Pulpit Story

Abie saw his friend Moishe reading the newspaper. Coming closer, he was astonished to see that he was engrossed in an article in one of the most vicious anti-Semitic papers written by Jew-hating Germans. "How could you possibly be reading that?" he asked.

"I read it because it gives me so much joy and pleasure."

"Joy and pleasure reading *that*? I don't understand you."

"What's not to understand? When I read the Jewish newspapers all I find are stories of Jews murdered, Jewish women raped, persecutions, and pogroms. But I read *their* paper, and I suddenly discover that we own the world. We own the banks. We have all the power. How can that not make me happy?"

The view of unlimited Jewish wealth is, of course, highly exaggerated, notwithstanding the "rich as Rothschild" proverb. But there is more than a grain of truth in the recognition that many Jews have succeeded financially, far in excess of what might have been expected, based on their numbers. Here too, we have to ask what explains Jewish mercantile ability? Is there really a Jewish gene for making money that is passed on from generation to generation?

Scholars offer three possibilities here as well to explain this anomaly.

Money Isn't Evil

For some people, spirituality demands suffering. Asceticism is an ideal. And chasing after money is just being too materialistic. In the New Testament, Christianity teaches that "it is easier for a camel to pass through the eye of a needle than for a rich man to pass through the portals of heaven." But that line of thinking has never found favor in Jewish tradition. Even matters of the flesh ought not to be renounced; rather their use should be sanctified.

Wealth, just like sex, is not ignoble, but instead presents man with a precious opportunity. God blessed Abraham with great wealth and many possessions and what was good enough for the first Jew is certainly good enough for all of his descendants. Philo had it right when he summed up the Jewish sentiment, "Money is the cause of good things to a good man, of evil things to a bad man." Jews acquired money because they never thought, as others may have, that there's anything wrong with it.

Yenta's Little Secrets

Good Catholics are encouraged to avoid sex on Sunday. It's God's holy day and inappropriate for the physical delights of sex. But for Jews, on Friday night, the inception of their sabbath, or "Shabbat," they are not only permitted but commanded to engage in sexual relations. As explained by the famous twelfth-century scholar sage, Nachmanides, "Let the holy act be performed on the holy day."

Money May Save Your Life

With constant edicts and decrees passed against Jews throughout generations, they had to find a way to save their lives to gain the good graces of their oppressors. Guess what they discovered? Money has a way of convincing people to change their minds. Bribes have a way of undoing the most baleful decisions. And one more thing. If you are suddenly ejected from the land where you have made your home for many years, it's really nice to be able to travel with a couple of diamonds in your knapsack so that you can start all over wherever you are forced to flee. Money talks, and Jews were forced to learn the language.

Money Can Acquire Mitzvahs

Jews have engraved in their psyches, from time immemorial, to make their lives worthwhile by doing good deeds—the *mitzvahs* that represent the 613 divine commandments of the Bible. And when Jews studied their codes of law, they realized quite readily that a great deal of the good they were required to perform on this earth could be fulfilled much more readily with adequate capital. Helping the poor, assisting the community in its needs, building synagogues and houses of study, and assisting friends, family, neighbors—all these mitzvahs mandated the financial means to perform

Aha, That's It

A *mitzvah* is a Jewish law, a commandment—more than simply a "good deed." There are 613 mitzvahs in the Torah, according to the count of the rabbis.

them. So that's why the lowliest, humblest water carrier would always fantasize, even when wrapped in prayer shawl and engrossed in the most sacred of devotions: "If I were a rich man…." No Jew ever said that money is the root of all evil. He knew far too well the amount of good he could do with it.

Are Jews Really Better?—The People of the Spirit

The Talmud says you can tell a Jew by three characteristics: modesty, mercy, and benevolence.

To say Jews are better than anybody else is to be guilty of a politically incorrect kind of chauvinism. But one thing is true: Throughout the ages scholars have taken note of this striking feature: "From the first moment we come upon the Hebrews, they have within them a tenderness and compassion from man to man that are essentially at one with Hosea and Isaiah." (Edith Hamilton, nineteenth-century American theologian)

It's probably true that you can tell a man by his enemies. That's why the villains of the world pick on the Jews to destroy them. Hitler made it clear that his hatred was based on the fact that the Jews gave the world a conscience: "The Jews have inflicted two wounds on mankind—circumcision on its body and conscience on its soul. They are Jewish inventions. The war for the domination of the world is waged only between these two camps alone, the Germans and the Jews." *(Mein Kampf)* To eradicate the traits of compassion and kindness, he had to eliminate their chief messengers.

Aha, That's It

Tzedakah, literally "righteousness," "justice," is the word used in Judaism for charity. Charity is seen not as a noble act, but a necessary one, the fulfillment of a divine commandment.

Sage Sayings

"Every Jew must either give or take charity for Passover."

—Sholom Aleichem

It would probably surprise you to know that there is no word in Hebrew for charity. The Hebrew word *tzedakah,* often used in connection with charitable giving, only means justice, righteousness. It is not a gift that you give to the poor, but rather the fulfillment of an obligation. God gives to you and you must give to others. You are the medium for the proper management of God's wealth here on earth. And if you won't do it right, the rabbis teach, God will find another "messenger" to help Him distribute His funds to the needy. That's why Sholom Aleichem said, Jewish beggars don't take; they demand alms as if they were collecting a debt. That's why when the pauper came to the rich man and was told he would receive nothing because "I had a bad year," the classic response was, "I don't understand—if you had a bad year, *I* should suffer?"

Why So Many Jewish Doctors"?—"Tikun Olam"

Of all the professions, perhaps solely with the exception of rabbis and teachers, Jews statistically seem to be overly represented in the field of medicine. Strangely enough, it isn't just Jews; even God himself wants to get into the act and identifies himself in the Book of Exodus, as "I am the Lord, your doctor." (15:26)

Why does every Jewish mother want to be able to introduce her child as "my son the doctor?" Why do they say in Yiddish that a rabbi is a Jewish boy who couldn't stand the sight of blood? It has to be more than coincidence. And the answer goes to the heart of a profound philosophic principle that is basic to Jewish religion and culture. In two words it is called *Tikun Olam*—the ideal constantly stressed by the rabbis and sages that means "fixing the world."

Judaism teaches "My Kingdom is of *this* world," not the next one. God only does so much for us and then expects us to complete the task of creation. That's why some scholars suggest the act of circumcision is the defining ritual for a Jew. Performed on the eighth day and completing upon the body of the child what was left undone by His creator, Jews acknowledge that God may have finished the world in seven days but he left tasks for human beings to continue perfecting on the eighth day and onward.

> **Aha, That's It**
>
> *Tikun Olam,* literally "repairing the world" is a major concept of Judaism—placing responsibility upon human beings for improving and perfecting the world in partnership with God.

And that's why circumcision is called "a sign of the covenant" in the Bible. Unlike what many people think, its purpose is never given as hygienic but rather symbolic. It's meant to remind Jews of a fundamental idea—you are to complete an unfinished world—not to make it healthier. (Don't you think Jews have noticed that uncircumcised gentiles are at least as healthy as they are?)

To perfect the world is in Jewish thought the obligation of every human being. And where better to start than by "fixing" the problems that befall our fellow man? Medicine is another way for the Jew, through his active involvement, to proclaim, "I'll do whatever *I* can."

Why Are There So Many Jewish Comedians?

Who is a comedian? Listen to Jackie Mason: "A normal person wouldn't become a comedian. The egomania, the neurosis, the need to overcompensate, the feeling that life is meaningless without stardom—it's too much suffering."

So who becomes a comedian? Groucho, Jack, Milton, Lenny, Jerry, the list goes on and on. There must be a reason here as well to explain not only why there are so many Jewish comedians today, but also why Jews throughout the ages have been known for their humor.

Maybe Mel Brooks understood it best: "I may be angry at God or at the world, and I'm sure that a lot of my comedy is based on anger and hostility… It comes from a feeling that as a Jew and as a person, I don't fit into the mainstream of American society." Feeling different, feeling alienated, feeling persecuted, feeling that the only way you can deal with the world is to laugh—because if you don't laugh you're going to cry and never stop crying—that's probably what's responsible for the Jews having developed such a great sense of humor. The people who had the greatest reason to weep learned more than anyone else how to laugh.

"With God's Help..."

And one last thing you have to know about Jews. Jews, at least most of them, have a special relationship with God. God is not a distant figure somewhere out in space. He's a Father as well as a Mother who cares about you personally, who knows everything you do, and who expects you to live up to your obligations. It's not easy to live your life when someone is always looking over your shoulder. It's not easy to live your life knowing deep in your heart and soul—because a culture and a tradition of thousands of years has implanted it within you—that you're *expected* to live up to certain ideals, that you're commanded to live up to certain commitments, that you have no choice. You have to be not only a Jew, but also a *mensch*, a truly good human being.

But the flip side of that is that a Jew knows that he is never totally forsaken. The Jew feels the presence of a higher Power. And a Jew has the assurance that eventually everything will turn out all right "with God's help."

Pulpit Story

An Italian, a Frenchman, and a Jew were condemned to be shot. Their captors offered them a final meal before the execution. They asked the Frenchman what he wanted. "Give me some good French wine and French bread." So they gave it to him, he ate it, and then they executed him. Next it was the Italian. "Give me a big plate of pasta." So they brought it to him, he ate it, and they executed him. Then it was the Jew: "I want a big bowl of strawberries," said the Jew. "Strawberries! They aren't even in season!" "Nu," replied the Jew, "so I'll wait."

Above all, Jews are optimists. If things are tough now, don't worry. After all, who is it that gave the world the notion of waiting—even if it means waiting until the end of time for the coming of a Messiah?

The Least You Need to Know

➤ Jews really are different; because of their past, because of their beliefs, because of their history.

➤ Jews worship knowledge, Jews work for wealth, and Jews strive for perfection.

➤ Jews want to help fix the world of its problems and complete the work of creation that God left undone.

➤ Jews have learned how to laugh, how to be patient, and how to wait for a better world even as they help bring it about.

Chapter 3

The Children of Israel Don't All Live in Israel

In This Chapter

➤ Why there are different names for Jews—and what they all mean

➤ The reasons for the special relationship between the Jews and the land of Israel

➤ How the Jews can be separated from their land and still survive

➤ Why Jews became the wandering people

➤ Where Jews make their homes today

If Israel is a Jewish state, does that make all Jews Israelis? Is everyone who lives in Israel automatically a Jew? If a Jew doesn't live in Israel, can he still be called a member of the children of Israel? And why am I asking so many questions? (The last one is easy—it's because I'm Jewish.)

Names can get confusing. Especially since they're so often used interchangeably when they really have very different meanings. Let's try to straighten out once and for all what we mean by the word Jew as opposed to Hebrew, Israelite, and Israeli.

Who's a Hebrew, a Jew, and an Israelite?

Let's start with the word Hebrew because that's really where it all begins. About 3800 years ago, a restless Semitic tribe of Assyrians began to challenge the might of the Babylonians and attacked them. In the City of Ur, a city-state of Mesopotamia, a man named Terah decided to flee, taking with him his son Abraham, Abraham's wife Sarah, and his grandson Lot. By the act of crossing the River Eber, Terah and his family became the first ones in the Bible identified as *Ivri*—Hebrew—the people who crossed over, those who came from the other side of the river.

Aha, That's It

A Hebrew is a descendant of Abraham who "crossed over" the river, in Hebrew, *"Ivri."* A Jew is a descendant of Judah, one of the 12 sons of Jacob. An Israelite is a descendent of any one of the 12 children of Jacob, whose name was changed to Israel. An Israeli is someone who resides in the land of Israel.

Sage Sayings

"It must be understood that Jews, who for two thousand years were dispersed among the nations of the world decided to return to the land of their ancestors. This is their right"

— Pope John Paul VI

Traveling six hundred miles northwest to the land of Haran, to what is now Turkey, they halted their journey. Terah died and Abraham had the experience that would change his life and the life of his descendants. It was at Haran that Abraham discovered God and established a covenant with him. This covenant gave much deeper meaning to his name "Ivri" —"from the other side" — because, as the Midrash puts it, it would place Abraham on one side of the world as opposed to all other peoples on earth. Abraham's descendants would be known as Hebrews—people who are different, strangers, revolutionaries for a divine cause that would always leave them on the other side of popular opinion and morality.

But not all of the children of Abraham followed in his ways. One son, Ishmael, became the father of the Arab nation. Isaac alone carried on his father Abraham's traditions. Of Isaac's two children, Esau rejected the covenant (he literally sold his birthright for a "mess of pottage"—his eternal blessing for the soupe de jour), but Jacob affirmed it. In doing so, God changed Jacob's name to Israel, "fighter for God." And it is Jacob's twelve children who became the twelve tribes and the children of Israel.

In the course of the years, ten tribes disappeared. Only two, the large tribe of Judah and the very small tribe of Benjamin, survived. Almost all of the descendants of Jacob/Israel today come from Judah—and that's why they are called Jews. If you're still following this, then you can see that Jews are therefore the small remnant of the children of Israel who survived.

Now here's where it gets a little tricky. After two thousand years of wandering in exile, these surviving Jews saw the fulfillment of the prediction of Isaiah, that the "ransomed of the Lord shall return with singing to Zion" (Isaiah 35:10). Just to complicate things a bit, they called this newly created state Israel, and that turned the Jews who reside there back once again into "Israelis."

> ### Yenta's Little Secrets
>
> Don't confuse Israelis with Jews around the world. Unlike Roman Catholics who commit themselves to the views of the Pope and the Vatican, Jews have no central "voice of authority." Ben-Gurion, the first Prime Minister of Israel, made clear: "The State of Israel represents and speaks only for its own citizens and in no way presumes to represent or speak in the name of the Jews who are citizens of any other country."

One more little problem: Israel was created not only as a Jewish state, but also as a democracy. Citizenship is open to all. You don't have to be Jewish to be an Israeli. Yitzak Rabin, the late Prime Minister of Israel, summed it up clearly:

> The non-Jewish citizens—the Palestinians, Moslems, Christians—should entertain all of a person's civil and political rights, because I believe that racism and Judaism by essence are in contradiction. The Palestinians in their schools, government-paid schools, are entitled—be they Moslems or Christians—to have their religion, to have their culture, their language, their heritage. I believe that they can be loyal Israeli citizens while maintaining their special identities.

So here you have it. Israelis who are Christians and Moslems, or Muslims as they are more often called today. Jews who aren't Israelis. Jews who are also Israelis. Israeli Jews who leave Israel and are still Jews. Leave it to Jews, as the Yiddish saying goes, to make such a *mishmash* (don't even try to find an English equivalent for the word!).

> ### Sage Sayings
>
> "Palestine is not primarily a place of refuge for the Jews of eastern Europe, but the embodiment of the reawakening of the spirit of the whole Jewish nation."
>
> —Albert Einstein

What's So Special About the Land of Milk and Honey?

If being a Jew and being an Israeli are two different things, then why is there such an emphasis on Israel by the Jewish people?

The Israeli Declaration of Independence (May 14, 1948) probably said it best:

> The land of Israel was the birthplace of the Jewish people. Here their spiritual, religious, and national identity was formed. Here they achieved independence and created a culture of national and universal significance. By virtue of this historic association, Jews strove throughout the centuries to go back to the land of their fathers and regain their Statehood.

Although Jews have always known that they could maintain their identity outside of Israel, "the land of milk and honey" (Exodus 3:8) always called out to them as a place with very special meaning for many reasons:

➤ Going to the land is the first commandment of the covenant God makes with Abraham: "Get thee out of thy country, and from thy kindred, and from thy father's house, unto the land that I will show thee." (Genesis 12:1)

➤ Inheritance of the land is the first promise God makes unto Abraham: "Unto thy seed will I give this land." (Genesis 12:7)

➤ Israel, in Jewish tradition, is the holiest place on earth.

> "Palestine is the center of the world, Jerusalem the center of Palestine, the Temple the center of Jerusalem. In the Holy of Holies there was a stone, which was the foundation of the world itself." (Midrash)

➤ To live in Israel is to fulfill a divine commandment, a mitzvah: "Residence in Israel is equivalent to the observance of all the Biblical commandments.... Who resides in Israel is assured of a place in the world to come...Better to reside in Israel, even among a majority of idolaters, rather than outside of Israel, even among a majority of Jews." (Talmud)

➤ After the Holocaust, Israel is both haven and homeland, the one place where, to paraphrase Robert Frost: "When you have to go there, they have to take you in."

That must be what the Bible meant with the metaphor "milk and honey." Milk is what sustains us from birth; it is our sustenance in infancy that assures our survival. Honey is sweetness, that which makes life worth living and joyous. The land of Israel—either as a longed-for dream or as a present-day reality—is an essential ingredient for Jewish survival.

Can a People Exist Without a Land?

What Jews have learned throughout their history, however, is that Israel may be crucial, but it is not critical. The stories of other nations ended with removal from their land. Jews lived on after exile. The reason is rooted in two major concepts shared by the Jewish people throughout the ages.

Judaism Transcends Geographical Boundaries

Jews have learned to take God with them wherever they go. Jews have discovered that with faith they can live anywhere. With God's law they can find fulfillment any place on earth.

Why, the rabbis asked, did God give the Ten Commandments in the desert of Sinai rather than in the holiest of all lands, Israel? So that, they explained, Jews would never be misled into thinking that the Torah is a constitution meant only for the State of Israel or that God's law is limited to a special place, no matter how holy and unique. The desert supersedes all national boundaries—and that is where Jews first heard the words of God. That is why exile did not destroy the Jewish people. That is why destruction of the Temple, not once but twice, did not bring the story of the Jews to an end. That is why thousands of years of wandering and homelessness could not destroy a people deprived of their land.

The Dream of Return

People are sustained more by hope than by reality. And never in all the years of their wanderings did Jews give up on the promise of the prophets. Rituals, such as fasting on the ninth day of Av, commemorated the tragedy of exile and kept alive the yearning for redemption. Prayers repeated three times a day expressed the dream and the reassurance of return. In the darkest of nights, Jews were sure the dawn would come. And so it did—probably because they believed it would.

Pulpit Stories

Napoléon, it is recorded, was riding through Paris one day when, peering through the open door of a synagogue, he was intrigued by what he saw. Seated on the floor, with ashes on their heads, was a large group of Jews shaking and sobbing.

Puzzled, he stopped to ask the cause of this wailing.

"They are weeping for the loss of their temple," his servant said.

"Go back and ask them when it happened. I have seen nothing of this in the newspapers."

The servant returned and said, "They told me close to two thousand years ago."

Amazed, Napoléon then said, "If a people still cries with such intensity for an event that took place so many years ago, you may rest assured they will eventually be restored to their land."

The Wandering Jew: Why Did He Go?

The Jew had left the Promised Land—but not because he didn't believe in the promise. History often decrees decisions that go against our will. Jews became wanderers over the centuries for many reasons:

➤ They simply didn't want to go. A conquered people has no choice. Assyria, Babylonia, Rome—major empires of the past—constantly sought to displace the Jews from their little parcel of land. Israel is a tiny country, consisting of but ten thousand square miles. Yet its position as a land corridor bridging three continents—Africa, Asia, and Europe—gives it even today a unique and strategic military importance.

In their quest for world power, the great nations of antiquity were obliged to deploy their armies through the narrow coastal plain of Palestine in order to invade other lands. The Holy Land for the Jews became the "must-have land" for the seekers of world power and dominion. And so—whether from a political perspective the Jews were weaker, or from a religious perspective the Jews broke their covenant with God—they were forced to flee by the ever-present invaders.

➤ The ongoing confrontation with Christianity throughout the ages. Christian theology turned the homeless state of the Jews into a religious statement: Those who rejected Jesus were condemned to wander over the face of the earth. And whenever Christian countries had the power to do so, they made sure the prediction came true.

➤ The need for survival. It is important to stress that in both Jewish religion and culture, the greatest mitzvah and moral imperative is to ensure your survival. "The saving of life—one's own or another's—supersedes everything else" is a Talmudic maxim. And so as important as it may be to live in Israel, if your children cry for food and your stomach growls for sustenance, Jewish law not only permits but demands that you go wherever you can make a living.

Aha, That's It

Diaspora is a term designating the aggregate of Jewish communities living outside the land of Israel. Since such communities often originated because of an expulsion from Israel, the term is *diaspora*, or "dispersion."

The Wandering Jew: Where Did He Go?

Having to choose a place to live that offered a greater chance for survival, where did the Jew go? That's easy. Wherever he was allowed to enter. The warmer the welcome, the greater number of Jews who would emigrate there. Sometimes it was one country that opened its doors, other times another. Rulers changed, national policy was altered, a friendly country at one time became a hotbed of anti-Semitism at another. But in all the great movements necessitated by these changes, in all the forced wanderings and diaspora years of existence, two great ironies surfaced:

1. The journeys from place to place drew the Jews out of a narrow tribal provincialism; it brought them into contact with other and sometimes more advanced cultures and gave them a world view; it allowed them to absorb the wheat and to discard the chaff of others among whom they were forced to live. It taught them to survive in every type of climate and in every kind of condition, and also to prosper. From the seed of their suffering bloomed the potential for great blessing.

2. The Jews were able to have a profound influence on many different countries. They were meant, according to the Bible, to be "a kingdom of priests" (Exodus 19:6). That means that the Jewish nation was to be to the rest of the world what the priest is to the Jewish people. The only way they could fulfill that would be by becoming a part of the larger world. Being forced to mix with others, they in turn served as a powerful moral force, social conscience, and teacher of all mankind. When historians look back at the places where Jews have been they discover a remarkable coincidence. Wherever Jews were welcomed, the countries prospered. When Jews were exiled, the lands that forced them to leave soon found themselves impoverished and declining in power. And that's one of the themes we'll be exploring in the course of this book.

Could it really be true that in all generations God's original promise to Abraham is being fulfilled: "And I will bless them that bless thee, and those that curse thee shall be cursed; and in thee shall be blessed all the families of the earth"?!

Estimated Jewish Population in the U.S., 1790–1990

Year	U.S. Population	U.S. Jews	% of Population
1790	3,929,000	1,400	0.04
1800	5,308,000	2,000	0.04
1820	9,638,000	2,700	0.03
1830	12,866,000	4,000	0.03
1840	17,069,000	15,000	0.09
1860	31,443,000	150,000	0.48
1880	50,156,000	230,000	0.46
1900	75,995,000	1,058,000	1.39
1920	105,711,000	3,389,000	3.20
1930	122,775,000	4,228,000	3.44
1940	131,669,000	4,870,000	3.69
1950	150,697,000	5,000,000	3.31
1960	179,323,000	5,531,000	3.08
1970	203,302,000	5,800,000	2.85
1980	226,546,000	5,921,000	2.61
1990	248,710,000	5,981,000	2.40

The Least You Need to Know

➤ Don't confuse the words Jew, Hebrew, Israeli, and Israelites. They all have their own special meanings.

➤ Jews have a special link with the land of Israel—even if they don't live there.

➤ Jews became wanderers for many reasons, but always prayed to be able to return to the "Promised Land," the land of "milk and honey."

➤ Jews are scattered around the world, but still continue to maintain a sense of communal identity.

Part 2
In the Beginning

Sex, murder, violence. Lust, romance, passion. War, conquest, rape. Think these themes have the makings for a great book? They do. It's called the Bible—the book of books. In it you'll find all of the above and more—the recorded history of the Jewish people, their law, and their lore.

To ask whether every word of the Bible is true is irrelevant. For fundamentalist Orthodox Jews it is; for Reform Jews it isn't. But for all Jews, the Bible stands above history. It has shaped the way Jews look at the world and at life. It represents the Jewish world view par excellence. And so it is to it that we must turn to understand the beginnings of the Jewish people.

Everything has to start somewhere. And so in this part of the book, we will learn about the beginning of the world according to the Bible and how Jews view creation; the beginning of the Jewish family with a man who dared to break with paganism and teach a belief in one God; the birth of a nation and how Jews gave the world the ideal of freedom; and the beginning of a relationship with a promised land predicated on spirituality and the idea of a covenant with the Creator.

Chapter 4

Happy Birthday to the World: From Adam to Abraham

In This Chapter

➤ The Bible begins with a story of someone who wasn't Jewish

➤ The reason for the difference between the Hebrew and the English calendar

➤ Why evolution is not in contradiction to the Bible

➤ What is unique about man and about woman

➤ The concept of responsibility according to the Bible

"In the beginning God created the heavens and the earth...."

So begins the Bible with a statement that became instrumental in shaping the history as well as the destiny of the Jewish people. It declared, unlike what many secular philosophers such as Plato and Aristotle believe, that the world *had* a beginning. Much later, in the twentieth century, science would eventually come to accept this view in its "Big Bang" theory of the origin of the universe. More significantly, the verse took a stand on a much more serious issue. "God created the heavens and the earth." The world didn't come into being on its own. Creation is not an accident of haphazard meetings and mutations. If there is a God, then the world must make sense. If there is a God, then coincidence is replaced with a sense of meaningful history. And because Jews took to heart this opening sentence, they would become the people bearing this message to the rest of the world.

Is God Jewish?

What is most amazing of all about the beginning of the Bible being the book of the Jews is that it doesn't even talk about Jews.

Wouldn't you have expected the Hebrew Bible to begin with the story of their origin? But think about it: The God of the Jews is the God who created the heavens and the earth, and that obviously makes Him the God of the whole world, not just one small group of people within it.

How important is this idea? It's important enough to be a major break with pagan philosophy and a turning point in the history of ideas. A God revered by the Jews who in reality is the creator of the whole world demands acceptance of these obvious consequences:

Yenta's Little Secrets

Why was one man created first rather than many? So that no person in the course of history would ever be able to say to anyone else, "My ancestry is greater than yours."

➤ God is a universal God who cares about all of His children.

➤ All people, not only Jews, are created in the image of God and hence all share in the sacredness of the divine.

➤ All of humankind are brothers and sisters because we share one Father.

➤ "All people are created equal with liberty and justice for all"—a consequence of this Biblical creed that would require thousands of years before being incorporated into the constitution of a civilized country.

➤ A Messianic ideal of world peace and universal harmony must be the will of one "Father" for his entire world "family."

And how long ago did all of this happen?

The Age of the World—A Jewish Calendar

Throughout the book we will be using dates, but we must warn you that there are two different "systems" to be aware of. Jews have a different calendar, and it's off by just a couple of thousand years from what you're used to. (Do you think that could explain why Jews are always a little bit late for appointments?)

Our western calendar, which is now approaching the close of the twentieth century, takes its starting point from an event that is of crucial significance to the Christian world. The letters sometimes added after the number, A.D., make this clear; they stand for *Anno Domini*, Latin for "in the year of our Lord." It is now close to two thousand years since the birth of Jesus, whom Christians consider Christ, literally the Messiah or the "anointed one." The years before his birth are appended with the letters B.C., Before Christ.

Yenta's Little Secrets

Did God create any worlds besides this one? Was there an "Earth," or planet like it, before us? According to Jewish mystics, surprisingly enough, the answer is "yes." The Bible itself gives us a clue for this amazing idea: the word Bible starts with the second letter of the Hebrew alphabet, bet, not the first, aleph, because someone was here before us.

Jews, as I indicated, have a far more universal vision. That's why their calendar starts with the time of the creation of Adam and Eve, the first human beings.

Note, I didn't say the creation of the world. Even according to fundamentalist followers of the Bible, the world could in fact be millions of years old, as current science believes. The first "week" of creation is clearly not measured by solar days as we know them because, as the Bible tells us, the sun was not created until the fourth "day." Obviously the first number of "days" were periods of time, which could have lasted millions of years. Recorded history starts with the first human ancestors who were no longer apelike, but created in God's image, Adam and Eve. From that time until today we have marked the passage of close to six thousand years.

Jews will happily compromise and refer to the secular date of the Christian world as long as they don't have to use the letters that acknowledge Jesus as Messiah or Lord. That's why you'll find that years before Jesus are appended with the letters B.C.E., for Before the Common Era, and years after Jesus with the letters C.E., for Common Era.

Now that you know that, I can tell you that according to Biblical reckoning, Adam and Eve first saw the light of day, met each other, and got married on the same day in the year 3760 B.C.E. (Probably because they could get away with just one present for both their birthday and anniversary, it was called Paradise!)

Adam and Eve chased from Paradise by the Archangel. (Courtesy of Corbis-Bettmann)

Evolution According to Darwin and God

In the nineteenth century, Charles Darwin shocked much of the world with his "theory of evolution." What bothered people so much was the idea that they were descended from the apes. (Why that should have come as a surprise to some people is beyond me.) For many, Darwin was the ultimate heretic. They claimed he replaced the divine image of man with that of a monkey.

Sage Sayings

"The idea that there is an evolutionary path upwards provides the world with a basis for optimism.... It is easy enough to see how the two (the theory of evolution and the Bible) can be reconciled. Everyone knows that these are topics that belong to life's mystery, are always dominated by metaphor, riddle, and hint."

—Abraham Isaac Kook,
Late Chief Rabbi of Israel

But they missed the main point. Evolution is a way of looking at the world that in fact goes back to the Bible. Rather than stressing what came before, its unique insight is one that parallels a major premise of the Creation story. Sequence and development follow an ascending spiral. What came before is less than what comes after it. Time brings with it development; man and woman are greater than what preceded them—and their potential is to become even more than they are today. Read the Biblical story and see that plants came before animals, fishes before fowl, fowl before animals, animals before man and woman. The order is in agreement with Darwin's theory. The only difference between the theory of evolution and the Biblical account is this: Both begin the story with "bricks" and simple "building materials" and work their way up to the completed mansion, but the Bible includes an Architect and Master Designer without whom none of it would have happened.

"...In the Image of God He Created Them"

Pulpit Stories

The Midrash tells us that when God was about to create woman from Adam, he considered which part he ought to make use of from which to fashion Eve. He said to Himself:

If I make her from his head, she will end up being haughty.

If I make her from his lips, she will be a tattler of tales.

If I make her from his heart, she will be guilty of envy.

If I make her from his feet, she will be stepped upon and feel inferior.

I know, he concluded, *I will use Adam's ribs, so that they will always stand side by side as equals.*

If apes came before men, that's because men were an improvement. The distance between them is not quantitative but qualitative. You will never understand the Jewish people unless you recognize this next leap of thought concerning the identity of mankind. Not only is there a God but God put a piece of Himself here on earth.

People were created "in God's image." What does that mean? Well, in good Jewish style, let me first tell you for sure what it doesn't mean. It's not that we look like God, because God has no physical form. That's one of the major beliefs in Judaism, so "in His image" can't refer to appearance. It has to mean something more suggestive of His essence.

Only Noah and his family are spared as God destroys the world with a flood and mankind is given a fresh start. (Courtesy of Alinari/ Art Resource, NY)

We share something of His that makes us godly. For centuries, scholars have debated what this characteristic is. Some say it's the soul and because that mysterious part of ourselves is like God, that makes us immortal. Others put the emphasis on our minds; what we share with the One who made us is His intelligence, the unique gift of our superior brain. More daring still is the view that man and woman, just like God, have free will. We can do whatever we choose—and *that* is the divine gift of being like our Creator.

Choose whichever interpretation you want. Or go ahead and be greedy and pick all three, but realize you've made the discovery that human beings are innately greater—and holier—than the beasts.

Yenta's Little Secrets

God made Adam from the dust of the earth, but from where did he get the dust? The Midrash says he took dust from all the four corners of the earth so that man could feel himself at home everywhere and so that he could consider himself a part of the whole world.

"—Male and Female He Created Them"

Aha, That's It

The name Adam comes from the Hebrew word Adamah—dust, earth. It reminds man of his origin and teaches him to be humble. The name Eve, Chavah in Hebrew, is related to life because Eve is told she will be the mother of all living beings. Man's name has him look to his past; woman to her future. Together they will be responsible for both history and destiny.

And don't forget that *cherchez la femme* was also part of God's original plan. Equal rights? God created both of them and in His own image to boot. Both are holy, both share divinity. Okay, granted, God did create Adam first. Maybe that's only because He knew, as we all do, you don't start with a woman. Or maybe it's because, as the evolutionary theory we talked about taught us, He kept getting better with practice. Whatever the reason, God gave man a woman—and then called it Paradise. From that day forward, celibacy had no place in Judaism and sex was considered one of those things about which God made the proclamation, "And behold He saw all that He created and He said it was very good."

Don't Eat That Apple—It's the Law

Once Adam and Eve were in the Garden of Eden, God made clear to them something that would become the key to the relationship between Him and the Jewish people: Blessings depend upon a Covenant. Human beings have to observe the law or else they are ejected from Paradise.

Anarchy is the ultimate evil. To be civilized means to honor some restrictions, and God didn't ask much: "From all the trees of the garden you may surely eat, but from the Tree of Knowledge of good and evil you shall not eat." It's like telling your kids you can play with all the toys you have except for one. You know of course which one the kid is immediately going to reach for. God wanted Adam and Eve to acknowledge that the ultimate definition of good and evil, right and wrong, is subject to a Higher Authority. In refusing to accept that restriction and in breaking the law, our first ancestors had to suffer the penalty for disobedience.

Crime and Punishment

The early stories of the Bible all pick up and develop this very theme. Along the way they add a few crucial points, as well:

➤ Cain kills Abel and discovers that you can commit crimes against man, not only against God, and be held equally liable.

➤ In response to the question Cain raises, "Am I my brother's keeper?" he learns in no uncertain terms that God expects everyone to be responsible for another.

➤ Sin can be tolerated for a while, but if the behavior of human beings knows no boundaries, no restraints, then the waters that are normally confined to their place will similarly break their boundaries, flooding the earth and destroying those who disregard God's moral requirements.

➤ God is personally involved with the world and even though there are a multitude of people on it, he will single out the good and righteous people like Noah and find a way to save them.

➤ God cares about the world, not just people (after all, you would expect the Creator to believe in Earth Day and ecology), and so he makes sure all the animals get saved on the ark as well.

➤ When technocracy and advanced scientific skills are used for evil purpose, like the builders of the Tower of Babel, they carry within themselves the seeds of their own destruction.

With these lessons learned over the span of twenty generations, the world is ready to move from Adam to Abraham.

The Least You Need to Know

➤ The Jewish God is far more than the God of the Jews; the Creation story endows him with universal significance.

➤ Jews and non-Jews have different calendars because they are based on different starting points.

➤ The theory of evolution is not in contradiction to the Bible.

➤ Men and women are equal, and both have a little bit of God in them.

➤ God relates to man and woman through the covenant of law, and crime must always be punished.

Chapter 5

At Last the Jews: From Abraham to Moses

> ### In This Chapter
>
> ➤ The contribution of Abraham that makes him Father of the Jews, Muslims, and Christians
>
> ➤ The belief system of monotheism and its implications
>
> ➤ How the Jewish tradition was passed down and led to the creation of twelve tribes and a people

Judaism doesn't begin with the birth of a nation, it starts with a family. That's why to this very day family is the most important unit to the Jewish people. And the home is where their heart is.

It wasn't until the family developed, learned from its mistakes, weeded out the bad from the good, developed its own identity, and grew in number that God finally—as we will see—brought them to the mountain of Sinai and said, "You will be my people."

And the family begins with one man who was a revolutionary in his day and who single-handedly changed the course of human history. His name was Abraham, and not only Jews but Christians and Muslims consider him their spiritual ancestor as well.

The Great Discovery: God Is One

In world history it was the height of the Bronze Age. In the city of Ur, the great center of Mesopotamian culture, pagan religion was widely practiced. Teraphim, statues of local deities, were found in every home.

Aha, That's It

Teraphim were household idols that offered protection and blessing. Many of them have been uncovered by archeologists and are a powerful reminder of the pervasive influence of paganism.

Interestingly enough, that was the business Abraham's father Terah was in. Terah, who traced his lineage back to Shem, son of Noah (that's why he and his descendants would be known as Shemites, or Semites), was the proud owner of a store that sold idols. Pity poor Terah when he tried to teach the business to his son Abraham. Perhaps it's just legend, but several stories have been passed down throughout the generations about the difficulties in managing this "father-son" shop.

In one story, Terah was out, and the little boy Abraham waited on a customer, an old man looking for "the perfect idol." Abraham turned to him and asked, "How old are you?" "Seventy years," the man answered. "What a fool you must be! How can you worship a god who is so much younger than you," little Abraham jeered at him. "You were born seventy years ago, but this idol was made only yesterday!" The old man threw down his idol in disgust and Abraham (happily) lost a sale. (So who says Jews are always good businessmen?)

In another version, Terah outlined Abraham's duties in the store. He told his son he would have to pour out libations in front of the idols, put food in bowls before them, and offer them incense to smell. Abraham did as he was told, but when the idols failed to respond, the boy ran to his father and exclaimed, "They have mouths but they speak not. They have ears but they hear not. Noses they have, but they smell not. They have hands, but they handle not. Feet have they, but they walk not!" These would be the very same words that King David would use in the Book of Psalms to describe the vanity and uselessness of idols.

In this story, the father is by law compelled to bring his son to the authorities as required in cases of heresy. "Don't you know," the ruler of Ur asked the boy, "that the king is Lord of all creation, of sun, moon, stars, and satellites, and that He must be obeyed in all things?" The boy Abraham pondered and then replied, "Since the world began and until this day, the sun rises in the east and sets in the west. Tomorrow, if it please His Majesty, let him command the sun to rise in the west and set in the east. I will then declare publicly that His Majesty is the Lord of the universe!"

No, not an easy little boy to handle—and just imagine what he became when he grew up. He personally chopped to pieces all the idols in his father's store, leaving only one of them, the largest, in whose hands he placed the axe. When confronted, he pleaded that the largest idol was the one who committed this deed. When his father claimed that was impossible—"Idols can't do anything" —he begged his father to hear with his own ears what he himself had just said.

The stories are all meant to express one and the same idea. Abraham was a revolutionary figure who broke—both literally and metaphorically—the idols of his generation. But Abraham's true greatness lay not only in what he rejected, but also in the idea with which he replaced it. His great discovery was monotheism. In a world of idolators, he came to the original conclusion that there is only one God, invisible and not physical, who created the heavens and the earth.

Yenta's Little Secrets

How's this for a coincidence: In modern times Jews came back to Israel and founded their nation in the year 1948. Abraham was born, according to the Jewish calendar, in the year 1948.

How Did Abraham Know?

It is a leap of unimaginable proportions. It is difficult from today's perspective to realize how mind-boggling and daring this new assumption was. What led Abraham to it is never clearly stated. Intelligence, spiritual sensitivity, profound insight—all assuredly played a great part. But according to the Midrash, the most convincing moment came one day when Abraham stared at a magnificent palace built to precise architectural specifications. He wondered to himself, who built this? When, for a moment he thought, perhaps no one, it just came to be there by itself, he dismissed this as an absurdity. And then he transferred this idea to the world and said, how utterly insane to believe that the entire universe, with its magnificent detail and design, could possibly have come into being on its own.

This in much more elaborate form would eventually become one of the major philosophic proofs of God, a proof known as the *proof by design*. The famous statistician George Gallup once said, "I could prove God statistically. Take the human body alone; the chance that all the functions of the individual would just happen is a statistical monstrosity." Abraham went George Gallup one step further. The chance that the world would just happen on its own is a statistical impossibility.

Sage Sayings

"A little science estranges men from God, much science leads them back to Him."

—Louis Pasteur

The Meaning of Monotheism

Monotheism, as opposed to paganism, brought with it a number of different ways of looking not just at God, but also at the world itself:

➤ Because there is only one God, there can be no mythological wars between gods—nor should there be wars between disciples of warring gods.

➤ Because there is only one God then evil in this world cannot be explained as the result of clashes between a God of good and a God of evil, as the ancient world believed. Evil itself must have a divine purpose or must be a good not yet clearly comprehended.

➤ One God who is invisible requires a ritual distinctly different from that of the surrounding pagans. A spiritual God is to be served spiritually and not physically, by walking in His ways and not by bringing Him food or drink to appease Him.

➤ One God who is immortal was, is, and will ever be.

➤ He never dies and never has to be resurrected. A spiritual God does not indulge in a sex life, which is why the Jews did away with all fertility rites.

➤ Finally, one God led to a vision of one world, living in peace and in universal brotherhood, as the prophets would later preach.

What Kind of God Is He?

One more crucial thing Abraham taught about the One God, the Creator: God is a god of goodness and justice.

Think about it for a moment. God, as king of the world, he could theoretically be an absolute monarch, a tyrant, or even a cruel dictator. Abraham not only taught that God is kind and compassionate, fair, and just, but, in what must be considered an ultimate act of *hutzpah*, even argued with God when Abraham felt that He wasn't living up to His character: "Will the judge of all the Earth not act justly?" Abraham dared to shout at God when he heard of the imminent destruction of Sodom and Gomorrah.

The God of Abraham might make seemingly harsh demands. But when He tests Abraham to see the depth of his commitment and asks him to offer his son Isaac as a sacrifice, the key to the story is that once the lad is bound on the altar, God demands that he stop. Unlike the views of pagan society, the Jewish God abhors and utterly condemns infant sacrifice.

Yenta's Little Secrets

When God stopped Abraham from sacrificing his son Isaac, He told Abraham to offer the ram caught in the nearby thicket instead. To remember the story and to emphasize that God detests human slaughter, Jews take a ram's horn on their New Years Day, Rosh Hashannah, and blow it, proclaiming the uniqueness of humankind and its superiority over beasts.

God is not only a good and just God, but also a personal God. He chooses to have a direct relationship with His creations based on a covenant of reciprocity. If people keep their side of the bargain, God will, too. The Jews have a choice of either being like the stars of the heavens or like the dust of the earth. They can be on top or on bottom. In simple English, God's deal with people boils down to five words, "It all depends on you."

Passing On the Tradition

Abraham had two children, Isaac and Ishmael. Ishmael went his own way to become the father of the Arabs. (Isn't it amazing that to this day when Jews and Arabs can't get along with each other it is in the truest sense of the word, brother against brother?) Isaac stayed and became the recipient of Abraham's blessings. Of Isaac's two children, Jacob and Esau, Jacob would be the one to walk in his father's footsteps and carry forward the new creed of his grandfather Abraham.

Notice something very unusual as we see which son in every case is "the good guy," the one carrying on the tradition? It's the younger one, not the older one. In ancient times, primogeniture was the rule. The firstborn had the birthright; everything was his due just because he came first. Here was another daring cultural revision built into the history of the Jewish people. *Worth* is more important than *birth*. You deserve what you get not because of your past but because of your present. Wow—this idea of covenant and carrying out of responsibility seems to surface everywhere in the story of the Jewish people.

When Jacob Became Israel

Jacob in his early years seemed, well, wimpy. He let everybody step all over him. Even when his prospective father-in-law switched brides on him and gave him Leah instead of his beloved Rachel, you hardly heard a whimper from him. But with maturity comes greater wisdom. In an encounter that shows a total personality change, Jacob fought back against an unnamed stranger and in doing so was worthy of a new name, one that would define all of his offspring and all of theirs.

God blessed him with the name Israel, which means "fighter for God," and in this name change there is also implicit an idea that was to guide him and his heirs in the future. Jews don't believe in the teaching of "turn the other cheek." Not to fight back is to invite the second slap. The new name carries with it a responsibility to fight for what you believe in. I'm not sure if the founders of the modern-day state of Israel had that in mind when they gave the new country its name, but it fits.

Yenta's Little Secrets

According to tradition, four couples are buried in the Cave of the Patriarchs in Hebron: Adam and Eve, Abraham and Sarah, Isaac and Rebekah, and Jacob and Leah. Because Rachel, Jacob's other wife, died on the way to Bethlehem while giving birth to Benjamin, she is not buried alongside her husband but in a special tomb of her own so she could pray for her children as they passed her on their way to exile.

The Cave of the Patriarchs, in Hebron, known as m'arat ha'mach-pelah— the "Cave of the Couples." (Courtesy of Corbis-Bettmann)

Oy—It's Not Easy With Children, Especially Twelve

You don't have to remember all of their names but at least once in this book they have to appear. After all, the twelve children of Jacob are the ones who became the twelve tribes of Israel.

Let's introduce you to them: Reuben, Simeon, Levi, Judah, Dan, Issachar, Zebulon, Naftali, Gad, Asher, Joseph, and Benjamin. Guess who was the most beloved? Of course, Benjamin, the youngest. Guess who was the most accomplished and successful? Of course, Joseph, the next to youngest. There's that same theme again—worth, not birth!

Two things you should know about these twelve. The first is that when they came to Canaan and divided the land among themselves, the descendants of Levi dedicated themselves to work and the Temple and took no portion of the land for themselves. As spiritual leaders, they were supported by the tithes and contributions of the people. The land was divided into twelve areas, however, with the tribe of Joseph being given a double portion and divided into parcels for both of his sons, Ephraim and Menassah.

The second interesting thing is the number of children in the family. Yes, there were twelve and each one was different. Twelve distinct types, twelve characteristics, just like there are twelve months in the year. Jewish mystics relate the twelve tribes to every single month, one for each tribe. Call it the Jewish signs of the zodiac!

And how did all these twelve kids get along? Don't ask. Just imagine taking a car trip with a dozen children, not in a van, but in a small sedan.

The jealousy between Joseph and his brothers is one of the most famous stories of all time. And what a plot it has! The brothers sold Joseph to a passing caravan and told their father that Joseph had died. With his extraordinary gift of being able to interpret dreams, Joseph ends up going from prisoner to prime minister. He saves the Egyptian economy (maybe he was the first really great Jewish businessman?) and is in charge of food distribution when his brothers are forced to come down to Egypt for bread to avoid starvation. The reconciliation scene between brothers and the theme of forgiveness serves as a fitting conclusion to the Book of Genesis, which began with the account of a brother killing his brother.

What's really important for Jewish history about this story though, is that it explains how the Jews got to Egypt. When they came, they came by invitation. One of their own occupied a seat of power next to the king himself. What would happen after that in the span of but a few hundred years would drastically alter their lives, as well as the lives of all of their descendants.

A Pyramid Scheme: Slavery in Egypt

We're not sure how it happened, but the Jewish story in Egypt is almost a precise model for most of the Jews' wanderings to come. They're welcomed "royally," they make a great contribution to society, and then "there arose a new king who knew not

Joseph." The guests became slaves, and the worshippers of One God were forced to build pyramids for their oppressors so that these oppressors might be buried in a suitable manner in which to meet their pagan gods.

Add another first for the Jews: They were the first victims of a pyramid scheme in history. How they would be saved deserves a chapter all to itself.

The Least You Need to Know

➤ Abraham was responsible for the great leap forward from paganism to monotheism.

➤ Monotheism means much more than believing in one God; its ramifications altered the way people understand God, the world, and the relationship between them.

➤ The Jewish God is one, invisible, immortal, just, and kind.

➤ The beliefs and the blessings of Abraham were passed on through Isaac to Jacob, whose name was eventually changed to Israel.

➤ Because of internal conflict within the family, the children of Israel end up in Egypt where at first they are welcomed, but in the course of time become enslaved.

Chapter 6

Let My People Go: The Birth of a Religion

In This Chapter

➤ The greatest man in Judaism, and why Jews so often ignore him

➤ The top ten reasons for Pharaoh to free the Jews, and why the Jews don't fully rejoice when they remember the ten plagues

➤ The real meaning and significance of the Ten Commandments as guides for the Jewish people

---

Historians have an interesting argument: Is history shaped by events or by people? Do major changes happen because of great movements or because of single individuals? It's hard to give a definitive answer, but surely for the Jewish people there is one man so much in a class by himself that we can say he is responsible for the birth of a religion.

Holy Moses

Moses is a major figure in Judaism, just as Jesus is in Christianity. But what a world of difference there is between them! There isn't a single Jewish holiday that revolves around events in the life of Moses as there are Christian holidays celebrating the life of Jesus. The Gospels are filled with the sayings of Jesus, but there isn't a single quotable "quote" in the entire Torah that can be attributed to Moses. Moses was the Jewish Abraham Lincoln who liberated the slaves and led the Jews out of Egypt. Yet in the *Haggadah*, a book used to describe these events, the name of Moses doesn't appear even once!

Page from a Hebrew Haggadah, the Passover service. (Courtesy of Corbis-Bettmann)

Aha, That's It

Passover is the holiday that commemorates the story of the exodus from Egypt.

Aha, That's It

Haggadah means "the telling," and it refers to the Passover night commandment to tell children the Passover story so that it is passed on from generation to generation.

Moses brought the Ten Commandments to the Jewish people from the top of Mount Sinai, yet the only visual image the Jews have of him to this day is a statue, not by a Jew, but by a Renaissance Christian, Michelangelo. Of course, Moses is important to the Christians also. (An interesting aside: Michelangelo gave Moses horns in his famous statue, giving rise to the misconception that "Jews have horns." Michelangelo made a mistake based on the Bible, which described Moses coming down from Mount Sinai and telling us that his face "shone." The word used in the Bible is "koran" from the word "keren" meaning to shine, or a ray of light, but it also means horn. The mistranslation was known to Michelangelo and that's what caused his error. No, really, Jews don't wear hats to cover their horns. You're welcome to visit me and I'll show you.) And when Moses finally dies before fulfilling his lifelong dream of going to the Promised Land, he is buried by God in an unmarked grave, precisely so that his burial spot will not become a shrine and a place of worship for future generations. All that happened to the greatest rabbi in history. So tell me, is being a rabbi really a job for a nice Jewish boy?

Statue of Moses by Michelangelo. (Courtesy of Corbis-Bettmann)

Actually there is a very good reason for all of these seeming slights. The very law that Moses brought to the Jewish people emphasizes the great sin of idolatry, the substitution of anything, be it sun, stars, or human, for the Almighty. What Judaism wanted to ensure was that as great as Moses was, he would never be mistaken for God himself. Jesus is called the "Son of God," Moses the "Servant of God." Moses may be holy, but he is far from being the Holy One.

Playing the Palace

Freud, in his book *Moses and Monotheism*, theorizes that Moses wasn't even Jewish. Actually, he's half right. Moses was born to Jewish parents but, when the decree was passed that every Jewish baby boy had to be cast into the Nile, his parents tried to hide him in an ark which, coincidence of coincidences, was found by the daughter of the Pharaoh. It was she who named him, and she who raised him. (I keep wondering if when she opened the ark and saw a baby inside she yelled out in surprise, "Holy Moses!")

She kept the child's identity secret from her father, and Moses grew up in the palace, safe from the persecution that befell the Hebrews. Yet he decided to share the pain of those he knew were his brothers. He took up their cause, and when he saw them beaten, he interceded on their behalf. Moses cared, and that's why God chose him to be the Jewish leader. Having grown up in the palace, he would also have the diplomatic skills he would so desperately need later in his role as spokesman for the Jews.

Yenta's Little Secrets

Moses means "drawn," and the daughter of Pharaoh named him that because she said, "From the water I have drawn him." His identity was the one drawn forth from the water, and later in life he would fulfill his mission by drawing forth the Jews from the waters of the Red Sea and bringing them to Sinai.

Moses' Weakness

Here's a little story about Moses that, while a bit of a departure, I just have to tell you. Would you believe that with all of his abilities, Moses had one very significant handicap? Moses had a speech defect. He had a lisp. When Moses was still a small child, Pharaoh became suspicious of the super-bright boy. Maybe he was the one Pharaoh's astrologers warned him about as the possible redeemer of the Hebrews. So he devised a test. He set before Moses a heap of gold on one side, burning coals on the other. If Moses had the wisdom to reach for the gold, Pharaoh planned to have him executed.

That's what Moses started to do, but an angel of the Lord interceded and forced Moses' hand to bring the hot coals to his lips instead of the gold. It saved his life but messed up his speech.

And that's why the greatest rabbi in history would never be able to get a job today with any congregation!

The Top Ten List #1—Ouch

In a remarkable scene in the desert, God appeared in a burning bush and delegated Moses to his leadership role. A stutterer (that's probably why he refused God twice, goes the old joke) and a truly modest, humble human being, Moses tried to turn God down, but it was literally an offer he couldn't refuse. And so Moses went back to Egypt with a request whose four words have resounded throughout the ages, "Let my people go."

Pharoah said "No" but God wasn't about to take no for an answer. He had a plan that would turn the request for freedom into an offer the Egyptian king couldn't refuse. Too bad Letterman wasn't on in those days. He would have had a ready-made top ten list for the plagues God sent against Egypt to convince them to free their slaves.

It probably is one of the most remarkable demonstrations of the character of a people that on Passover night when the Jews recall the ten plagues and recite them—blood, frogs, lice, wild animals, plague, boils, hail, locusts, darkness, and death of the firstborn—they dip a finger in their wine and spill out a drop. They do this as they mention every plague to indicate that their cup "is not full," and they cannot fully rejoice because their liberation had to come as the result of pain and suffering for others.

With the plagues upon him and his people, Pharaoh had to say yes to Moses, and the Jews were set free. Then, when the Egyptians chased after them after a change of heart, they were drowned in the Red Sea. A fitting end for those who had formerly drowned Jewish babies. Gilbert and Sullivan's line that "the punishment fits the crime" is really a rephrasing of the Biblical principle that wicked people get punished "measure for measure," in the very way in which they committed their crime.

The Top Ten List #2—Thanks

What happened next, though, is the key to the entire story. It was the real reason why this trip was necessary. The exodus from Egypt for the Jewish people is not mainly *freedom from,* but *freedom to.* Its historic importance lies in the fact that the Jews were thus able to come to a mountain and receive a body of law as revolutionary as the wheel, as influential as the plow, and as earth-shattering as any other major event in history.

The mountain was Sinai and to this day we do not know its exact location. Jewish sages say that its whereabouts were left a mystery so that the medium would not be confused with the message. If Sinai the place were known, there would be regular pilgrimages there. With the location a secret, the most fitting commemoration is study and commitment to the teachings handed down from there.

You must have heard Monty Python's great comedy routine. You know, the one where he has Moses coming down to the people and telling them, "I have good news and bad news. The good news is I got Him down to ten. The bad news is adultery is still in." The really good news, though, is that the ten that comprise the *Decalogue,* the Ten Commandments, helped reshape not only the Jews but all civilized peoples.

God gave them to Moses on two tablets of stone to impress everyone with their permanence. Unfortunately, for you my dear reader, paper will have to do. The list, as Jews number them, is as follows:

Aha, That's It

Decalogue comes from the Greek, meaning ten words. Ten Commandments equal the number of fingers on the hands so that you can always be reminded of God's laws whenever you look at what you're doing. And there are five fingers on each hand, just as there are five commandments on each tablet.

Yenta's Little Secrets

The Jews count "I am the Lord thy God" as the first commandment. It is a principle that requires confirmation. Christians feel that this is more of a statement than a commandment and therefore begin with, what for Jews, is commandment two. Christians make up for the missing commandment by either splitting the Jewish number two (Protestants) or number ten (Catholics) into two different commandments.

1. I am the Lord thy God, who brought thee out of the land of Egypt, out of the house of bondage.

2. Thou shalt have no other gods before me. Thou shalt not make unto thee a graven image, nor any manner of likeness of anything that is in heaven above, or that is in the earth beneath, or that is in the water under the earth; thou shalt not bow down to them or serve them: for I the Lord thy God am a jealous God, visiting the iniquity of the fathers unto the children, unto the third and fourth generation of those that hate Me; and showing mercy unto the thousandth generation of them that love Me and keep My commandments.

3. Thou shalt not take the name of the Lord thy God in vain, for the Lord will not hold him guiltless that taketh His name in vain.

4. Remember the Sabbath day to keep it holy. Six days shalt thy labor and do all thy work; but the seventh day is a Sabbath unto the Lord thy God; in it thou shalt not do any manner of work, thou, nor thy son, nor thy daughter, nor thy man-servant, nor thy maid servant, nor thy cattle, nor thy stranger that is within thy gates; for in six days the Lord made heaven and earth, the sea and all that in them, and rested on the seventh day, wherefore the Lord blessed the Sabbath day and hallowed it.

5. Honor thy father and mother in order that thy days may be long upon the land that the Lord thy God giveth thee.

6. Thou shalt not murder.

7. Thou shalt not commit adultery.

8. Thou shalt not steal.

9. Thou shalt not bear false witness against thy neighbor.

10. Thou shalt not covet thy neighbor's house; thou shalt not covet thy neighbor's wife, nor his man servant, nor his maid servant, nor his ox, nor his ass, nor anything that is thy neighbor's.

Two Kinds of Law

These Ten Commandments were given on not one, but two tablets with five on each. (Yes, I know. Since God called himself a doctor, he obviously was telling them to take two tablets and call Him in the morning.) Why in the world couldn't God list these ten laws on just one tablet? The answer represents one of the major breakthroughs implicit in this set of religious laws.

The first five define the relationship of a human being to God. (The fifth commandment, the honor due to parents, is on this tablet because they too are our creators and deserve respect comparable to that given to God Himself.) And the last five represent the category of law circumscribing the relationship of man to his fellow man.

In this way, God was teaching that religion is not just how you behave to God, but how you act in your everyday dealings with your friends, family, and neighbors. The first tablet, belief and respect for God, must be translated into human relationships if it is to have any meaning.

From 10 to 613

Ten laws wouldn't be so hard to handle, but the Torah, as a book of law, contains many, many more laws than that. The Ten Commandments are really ten categories or principles, just like the American Bill of Rights. It was the short form, that which would fit on the tablets and serve as a reminder of all the others. The total number of laws in the entire Bible is 613. The 613 deal with every area of life. They encompass business law, civil law, criminal law, and what we would normally call religious law. They share in common one ultimate Biblical ideal, "Justice, justice shalt thou pursue." (Deut. 16:20)

Yenta's Little Secrets

Six hundred thirteen is comprised of the numbers six, one, and three, which, when added up as individual digits, equal ten. The 613 are the derivatives of these ten master moral principles.

And the most important law of all from the entire code of 613? Perhaps it's too outrageous a question, but when a non-Jew once asked it of the famous sage Hillel, his response was, "Do not do unto others as you would not want them to do to you. This is the entire Torah. The rest is commentary. Now go and study it." And as the Talmud records, the non-Jew became so inspired that he did study, and eventually converted to Judaism.

Pulpit Stories

The Jewish sage Hillel was known for his compassion and intellect. His colleague Shammai was a man of vast erudition but of little patience. When a non-Jew came to Shammai and asked for a summary of Judaism while "he was standing on one foot," Shammai chased him away. (To expect a short *Idiot's Guide* to Judaism was, for him, disrespectful.) Hillel, however, did not hesitate to do as the non-Jew asked. And the codifiers of Judaism say, because Hillel was so patient and so insightful, the law is always in accord with his view.

Moving On: The Good, the Bad, and the Beautiful

With the Law, the Jews could now move forward to the Land. The two of them together would fashion a great nation. Of the two, the Jews could live without the land, but never without the law. With their newly given treasure, the Jews would spend forty years wandering in the wilderness. As a young people, they still acted like teenagers. They constantly rebelled and found fault with their elders, leaders, and God. They were more than a handful for Moses. Even God said he would prefer to see this entire generation die out so that a new one, uninfluenced by a slave mentality and uncorrupted by past experience, could enter Canaan and settle it. In the desert the Jews experienced the good and the bad. The beautiful was yet to come.

The Least You Need to Know

➤ Moses is the greatest Jew who ever lived but he still isn't God.

➤ Moses was sent on a dual mission: to get the Jews out of Egypt and to bring them to Sinai.

➤ The Ten Commandments represent the essence of Jewish law and their principles became codified in 613 specific requirements.

➤ The two tablets make clear the dual concern of Jewish law for the categories of person-to-God and person-to-person.

Chapter 7

Welcome to the Promised Land

In This Chapter

➤ The reasons for the long trip to Canaan

➤ The concept of shared responsibility for conquering the land

➤ The tragedy of the man with a dream who didn't make it

➤ The features of the land and their link with the Jews

➤ All about lotteries, luck, and God's will

Today we call it Israel. Before the Jews returned to it in modern times and created a state, it was known as Palestine, after the Philistines who lived there long ago. When the Jews left Egypt, the country was known as Canaan, after the Canaanites who were then in control.

The Jews, however, called it by another name. For them it was simply the Promised Land. They didn't think of it as a new place they had never been to before. In their minds, they were coming home. Home where their founding fathers had lived. Home where their patriarchs discovered God and established a relationship with Him. And most important of all, home to a land that God had promised to Abraham, Isaac, and Jacob as "an everlasting inheritance" to their children.

What Took You So Long?

What's really peculiar is why, if God saw this as the proper dwelling place for the Jewish people, He allowed or perhaps even stage-directed the period of exile in Egypt. Was this trip really necessary? Why did it have to take so long for the descendants of Abraham to return to the very spot where they had originally dwelled?

There are two important answers:

1. It was extremely important for the Jews to experience slavery in Egypt before they started their own narrative as a people, so that they would collectively know and remember from personal experience "that you were strangers in a land not yours," and therefore know how to feel compassion for the downtrodden and underprivileged. Egypt was the required school for training the Jews in sensitivity-awareness!

2. They were rebellious and were punished for it. The trip from Egypt to Canaan by camel, not by car, takes a maximum of about two weeks. Yet it took the Jews *forty years*. Why the big delay? Talk about being late for an appointment! The Bible makes clear it was sin that caused God to decree the lengthy stay in the desert. Even though God promised them they would succeed in their mission, the Jews were a bit skeptical and sent spies who spent forty days in Canaan "checking it out." They returned with a very pessimistic assessment—their chance of conquering Canaan was mighty slim indeed. As punishment, God—the Bible records—made them spend the next forty years wandering, a year for every day of their rebelliousness.

> ### Sage Sayings
>
> Abraham did not enter into a covenant with God till after he had entered the Holy Land.
>
> —Zohar

Tisha b'Av

The ninth day of the Hebrew month of Av, Tisha b'Av, has been marked by tragic occurrences throughout history. It was the day on which the first Temple was destroyed. Remarkably enough, it was also precisely on that day that the second Temple was destroyed. And stranger still, the Jews were exiled from Spain on that day, World War I broke out on that day, and many other tragic national events as well.

The rabbis link all of these tragedies with the first time in history that this date had special meaning. It was on Tisha b'Av that the spies who had gone to check out the land of Israel returned with a pessimistic report. They told the people, "We will never be able to conquer this land," and the people cried. To which God, according to Jewish tradition, responded, "You cry tonight for no reason; on this very night in the future I will give you cause to cry for good reason as punishment for your lack of faith."

Will Your Brothers Go to War?

As the time approached for the new generation to finally go into the Promised Land, a remarkable thing happened that would impact Jewish history and Jewish thought for all future generations. While they were still on the other side of the Jordan River, two and one-half tribes—Reuben, Gad, and half the tribe of Manasseh—decided they were pleased with the area they were in (it was particularly good for cattle), and they asked Moses for permission to remain where they were. They were the first Zionists who accepted the vision of Israel as the Promised Land—but weren't ready to make the promise relevant for them.

What they wanted was to free themselves from further responsibility of warfare and disassociate themselves from the travails of their fellow tribes. The response of Moses stirs a chord to this very day and has often been used to remind Jews of their communal responsibility to each other: "Shall your brethren go out to war, and shall ye sit here?"

At the very moment of entry into the land, the Jews were forcefully reminded that they were one people, with an equal responsibility to share their common burdens.

The Man Who Didn't Make It

There are many versions of the line, "I have good news, and I have bad news," but I can't imagine a more powerful illustration than this one between God and Moses. The good news: Moses' people would finally make it to Israel. And the bad: Moses himself would not live to be a part of this long-anticipated event. So Moses looked from the distance of Mount Nebo, and then God took the soul of the greatest Jew who ever lived.

Why Did Moses Die?

According to Jewish commentators, it was punishment for a sin. He was supposed to speak to a rock and bring forth water. Instead he struck the rock, ignoring his precise instructions. So what's the big deal, you ask? He still performed the miracle of bringing forth water from the rock. Why such awesome punishment for so small a sin?

It is here Jews see expressed the concept of *noblesse oblige*—nobility obligates. The greater the person, the higher the level of responsibility. For someone like Moses, there is no such thing as a small sin.

Yenta's Little Secrets

Martin Luther King spoke of reaching the Promised Land in his most moving address, "I have been to the top of the mountain...I have seen the Promised Land...I have a dream...." But like Moses, he wouldn't live to see his dream fulfilled either. Perhaps the very definition of greatness is to have dreams so large that whenever you die, you still stand on the threshold of greater achievement.

Listen to Your Bubbe

If you want to bless a Jew with a long life, lift a glass and toast him by saying, "May you live to 120." Why this number? Because Moses, the greatest Jew, lived to that age. You can pray that someone else live that long, but to ask for any more is to be disrespectful to the greatest Jew who ever lived.

Sage Sayings

"Palestine has the size of a county and the problems of a continent."

—Arthur Koestler, *Promise and Fulfillment*

Even Though You're Not My Son

A good leader makes sure that he does not leave a void with his passing. He ensures that there is continuity by designating a replacement. And so Joshua, one of only two spies who went to Canaan and returned with a positive, optimistic report of the place, was appointed by Moses before his death to carry on his work.

Joshua had a long relationship with Moses. He was his student, but remarkably was not his son—and yet Moses picked him. What happened to Moses' own children, Gershon and Eliezer? Wouldn't you expect heredity to be the most important consideration in transmitting leadership? Here again is a vivid example of the concept that worth is more important than birth. It must have pained Moses to pass over his own children. But a real leader does what is best for the nation, not for his own gratification or pride.

So This Is What You Look Like

What attracted the Jews to Canaan was a past and a promise. It was where their religion began, and it was the place where God said they were destined to flower as a people.

But what was it like? What was its uniqueness? Like the Jews themselves, the significance of the land was not size. A small people in the world, a small country on the earth. Yet it is a country that links three continents, just as the Jews were meant to link peoples around the world with their spiritual teachings.

Land of Extremes

When the Jews entered the land of Canaan, it was "a land of wheat and barley, and fig trees and pomegranates, a land of olive oil and honey." It was a narrow upland strip consisting of a stony plateau some one hundred fifty miles long, of low limestone hills barren and forbidding, broken in many places by broad deep valleys. To the west, the stony plateau sloped gently to the Mediterranean. In the east, the far end of the Jordan Valley set Canaan's boundary where the ancient lands of Gilead and Bashan began. Its northernmost borders touched what are today Lebanon and Syria. Its southernmost part is the Negev, "the barren land" where the patriarchs made their home.

The most defining description of the land is that it is a country of extremes—again, just like the Jewish people. In a comparatively small geographic area you can find the heat of southern California and the snowy slopes of Vermont. The land is barren and productive, dry and wet, pleasant and harsh. And that's why God told them it was the perfect place for His people; having every possible potential within it, the Jews would come to realize that whatever happened there would all depend on them.

Jewish Lotto

Under Joshua's able leadership, the Jews conquered first Jericho and then most of Canaan. At Jericho, it was the awesome sound of the shofar, the ram's horn, that frightened the inhabitants and, according to the Bible, made the walls of the city crumble. After that, it was the news of the initial victory and further successful battles that brought fear to the local inhabitants and allowed the Jews, in relatively short time, to conquer a major portion of the land.

To divide the land fairly among twelve different tribes, they used a remarkably modern system. They held a lottery. The only difference between their lottery and the ones we buy tickets for today is that in their case, everyone was a winner.

In relying on the results of a draw, they were giving expression to the feeling that nothing happens by coincidence; the decisions of a lottery are just God's way of expressing himself anonymously. And so the land was divided into twelve areas according to the size of the tribes, and the location

Listen to Your Bubbe

Should a Jew buy a lottery ticket or is that considered gambling, which isn't permitted? Here's an answer from a great Hasidic rabbi: Buy a ticket so that if God wants you to become rich, he has an easy opportunity to do so, but don't buy more than one ticket. Why waste your money? If God wants you to win, He'll do it with the one you have!

for each tribe depended not just on the luck of the draw, but the whispered message of God. (Guess what—they also didn't have to pick five lucky numbers exactly in order to win their allotted portion of land.)

The Least You Need to Know

➤ The period of slavery in Egypt was important to create a Jewish consciousness of empathy for strangers and slaves.

➤ Those who were not optimistic about their chances for conquering the land didn't make it.

➤ "All Jews are responsible one for another" was the message to the tribes who wanted to stay on the other side of the Jordan.

➤ Moses wasn't able to complete his mission but he passed on leadership based on worth, not birth.

➤ Israel is a land of extremes—just like the Jewish people.

Part 3
Judges, Kings, Prophets—Those Were the Days

Get ready for a real roller-coaster ride. Part 3 is going to take you first on a steep ascent, from anarchy to monarchy. Twelve tribes form one extended family, then take on seven nations that are occupying Canaan. Although comparatively small in number, the tribes' belief in one God gives them the moral strength to overcome their enemies. Led by heroes known as judges, and inspired by prophets, they create a world-recognized empire under the kingships of David and Solomon—the greatest days of Jewish glory.

But as steep as the climb, so dramatic is the fall. Internal strife, coupled with disregard of the covenant their ancestors made with God, leads to the Jews' defeat by their enemies and the destruction of their Temple. As they go into exile in the year 586 B.C.E., the Jews are left with memories of what once was and prophetic messages of what could be once again.

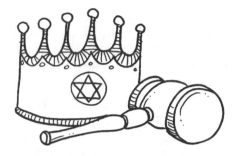

Chapter 8

From Judges to Kings

In This Chapter

➤ Heroic figures, known as judges, rise to lead the Jewish people

➤ Each in their own way, Deborah, Gideon, and Samson teach important lessons about leaders and leadership

➤ Monarchy finally comes to the Jews in spite of the warnings of Samuel

Joshua left the Jews with a land and a legacy. From 1271 B.C.E., when he led his people to the miraculous victory at Jericho, to the conquests that followed over a seven-year period, he gave them the confidence to believe that they would eventually become rulers over Canaan. But Joshua made this promise conditional on the fulfillment of an oath. The Jews would have to reject all forms of idolatry and alien cults if they were to receive God's blessings. With faith in Him, they would succeed; if they ever forgot their promise, they would no longer be worthy of the Promised Land.

The heroic figures who came after Moses and Joshua to continue these great men's mission were known as *judges*. In a time when, as the Bible tells us, "there was no king in Israel; every man did that which was right in his own eyes"—the judges were far more than judicial figures. They were military leaders, moral advisors, messengers of God, and inspirational figures all rolled up into one. Most amazing of all, these were leaders who were never elected to office. They were simply accepted without question by virtue of their unique talents and abilities.

The Jewish Joan of Arc: Deborah

If you are a male chauvinist pig, don't read the next section. Because, interestingly enough, one of the very first Jewish judges was a woman, Deborah the Prophetess, often referred to as the Jewish Joan of Arc. She had to have been very wise because people flocked to her for advice as she sat under her palm tree. (Imagine the first *Dear Abby* in history, from whom you could receive answers in-person instead of having to wait for the mail!) But greater even than her intellect was her bravery, which she attributed to divine inspiration.

God appeared to Deborah one day and told her she had a sacred duty to lead a revolt against the king of Canaan. She persuaded a tribal chieftain, Barak, to join her with ten thousand men against the Canaanite general Sisera. Barak agreed to go to battle only if Deborah accompanied him. Makes you think that women must have been held in extremely high regard if he wanted her along so badly, no? Yet probably closer to the truth about the attitude toward women in that society was Deborah's response: "Very well, I will go with you. However, there will be no glory for you in the course you are taking, for then the Lord will deliver Sisera into the hands of a woman" (Judges 4:8-9). What irony: A woman saved the day, but the victory was diminished because it was only due to a woman!

Deborah was successful against all odds. The Jews won a stunning victory at Mount Tabor. The enemy general, Sisera, was slain. Deborah's song of victory is a biblical highlight. But leave it to the Jews to recognize that the most significant aspect of this victory would manifest itself only centuries later: A descendant of Sisera would be the great Talmudic sage Rabbi Akiva. The Jew's enemy is finally vanquished not when he is physically destroyed but when his descendants learn the error of his ways and join in the spiritual destiny of the Jewish people.

Listen to Your Bubbe

Jews believe that a name, given at birth by parents, carries within it a person's mission in life and his or her character. The name Deborah means "bee." Deborah's greatness as leader was based on her ability to combine two traits: to sting—to be firm and ruthless with her enemies; and to be kind and sweet "as honey" with those whom she loved and cared for.

The Man Who Would Not Be King: Gideon

Canaanites, Amalekites, Moabites, Midianites—it seems like all the "ites" were out to get the Jews. Deborah's defeat of the Canaanites didn't put an end to the problems of the twelve tribes. For seven long years the Midianites attacked the Jews, stole their crops, and economically impoverished them. This time God called on Gideon to crush His people's oppressors.

Two themes stand out in Gideon's story:

1. Out of 32,000 volunteers for battle, Gideon selected only 300 based on the combination of their skill and their piety. If numbers had been the key to victory, the Jews would never have had a chance. But Gideon proved that, at least with regard to Jewish military victories, size doesn't matter—it is God's power, not man's strength, that brings success.

2. In the aftermath of a stunning victory, the people turned to Gideon and begged him to become their king. His reply was a remarkable expression of what for many years served as the Jewish view of leadership: "I will not rule over you, neither shall my son rule over you; the Lord shall rule over you." Other nations may desire kings. Jews believe in the King of Kings. Remember how the role of Moses was constantly diminished so that he would not be confused with the Almighty? Gideon reminded the people that having a king was too dangerous for a people whose Second Commandment is "Thou shalt have no other gods before Me."

Close Shave: Samson and Delilah

Judges came in all shapes and sizes. God probably gave the Jews the type of man or woman leader needed at the time. And to counter the Philistines, the strongest and most formidable of the Jews' enemies, the Jewish hero had to be the only superman in their history.

If your stereotype of a Jew is mild-mannered Clark Kent-Cohen, you should have met Samson! What a *shtarker* (Yiddish for a strong and brave person)! A lion roared against him, and Samson tore him apart. With the jawbone of an ass, he slew a thousand Philistines. (And, unlike Samson—with the jawbone of an ass, many politicians have proven incapable of accomplishing anything.) Wouldn't you like to know the secret of his strength?

It took Delilah a little while to coax it out of him, but I'll tell you his secret for nothing—not only what Samson foolishly confided to Delilah (who then used this information to destroy her lover as she handed him over to the Philistines)—but also the deeper secret behind what he shared with his betrayer. Samson was a *nazir*. He belonged to the most exclusive "nazir club" of all: He was a "nazir from birth," being dedicated by his mother for a lifetime of unique spiritual status during her pregnancy. He was divinely blessed because of the special commitment his mother made to God that he would never drink wine or cut his hair. If his locks were shorn, his vow would be voided and his special gift revoked.

Aha, That's It

Nazir, which comes from the root "to separate," refers to someone who chooses voluntarily to separate himself from wine and the cutting of hair—both of which express a willingness to remove oneself from society for greater intimacy with God.

Delilah remains the symbol of the unfaithful woman. Because of her, Samson's hair was cut while he slept, he was taken prisoner and was blinded by his jailers.

Yenta's Little Secrets

The Talmud finds very special significance in the punishment inflicted by the Philistines on Samson. Why was Samson blinded? Punishments must invariably follow the divine principles of "measure for measure." Samson sinned with his eyes by lusting after Philistine women. His eyes were the source of his sin so that's why he was blinded by his enemies.

To this day, Samson remains a powerful symbol: With all of his physical prowess, he could not withstand the temptations of the "weaker sex." Years later, no doubt with Samson in mind, the sages of the Talmud would declare, "Who is strong? He who can control his desire." And that's probably why brute strength was never so much a Jewish ideal as strength of character. Between might and bright, Jews invariably remember the story of Samson and choose the latter.

The "Samson Complex"

Samson died in a final act of revenge against his captors. When made to entertain the Philistines as a form of public humiliation, in a stadium filled with jeering thousands, Samson prayed for one last burst of strength. With the cry "let me die with the Philistines!" he pulled down the columns to which he was chained, causing his own death, as well as that of all his enemies around him. In Israel today the phrase "Samson complex" is used to describe the possibility that Israel, faced with the threat of annihilation, might conceivably unleash its atomic weaponry in a suicidal cry of "let me die with my enemies!"

Sage Sayings

"Oh Lord God, remember me, I pray Thee and strengthen me, I pray Thee, only this once, Oh God, that I may be this once avenged of the Philistines!"

—Samson's final plea to God for a return of his strength so that he might crush the Philistines.

Samson knocking down the Temple. (Courtesy of Corbis-Bettmann)

"Give Us a King"

Of all their leaders, the one who came closest to the spiritual greatness of Moses was Samuel. Small wonder, then, that his name in Hebrew was *Shmuel*, from the words *shoma E-l*—God has heard. His mother Hannah who had been barren, prayed with such fervor that "God heard" her pleas and granted her a very special son. She consecrated her son to God, and, as he grew older, he became recognized for his prophetic spirit. Somehow he accomplished what almost no other Jewish leader has been able to do to this very day: He was recognized and acclaimed by *all* of Israel.

But the Jews wanted more than a religious leader. Because of the constant attacks by the Philistines, they felt they needed the unifying strength that only a king could give them. And so the people turned to Samuel and begged him, "Give us a king!"

What an amazing reversal of the way things happened in other nations. Elsewhere, the religious leader is usually tolerated at the discretion of the king. For the Jews, the king comes into power at the discretion of their religious leader!

Samuel at first refused to grant the request with the same logic we heard from Gideon. Jews already have a king, and His name is God. And, anticipating Lord Acton by thousands of years, Samuel also knew that "power corrupts; absolute power corrupts absolutely." Samuel warned the people:

He will take your sons and appoint them to his chariots…and some to plough his ground and reap his harvest…he will take your daughters to be perfumers and cooks and bakers. He will take the best of your fields and vineyards…a tenth of your grain…the best of your cattle…a tenth of your flocks, and you shall be his slaves. (1 Samuel 8:10-18)

True, the Bible did allow for a king, but only if the Jews continued to insist that they "want a king to govern us like all the nations that are around us." It isn't a Jewish idea, but if you want to imitate others, then the Bible demands at the very least a constitutional monarchy, with a constitutional limit placed on the number of wives, wealth, and weapons the king may have.

Yenta's Little Secrets

How many wives are too many? According to the Bible, a king was restricted by law concerning the number of wives he was permitted to take. The text simply says, "He shall not increase overly much the number of wives." But how many is that? Jewish law, as clarified in the Talmud, teaches that the maximum permissible is 18. More than that probably means that with a greater number of mothers-in-law, a king could never really be a ruler!

But sometimes leaders have to give in to popular will. Facing near unanimous sentiment, Samuel chose for them the first King of Israel: Saul, a "mighty man of valor" from the tribe of Benjamin. And how did Samuel pick him from all the other contenders? By now you should be able to guess. He used a lottery—just as the Jews had divided the land among the tribes. Seems like the decision was therefore the will of God. But even the best planned schemes of God can be messed up by man. What might have been didn't turn out as planned because of a monarch who fell short of his mission and forfeited his crown.

The Melancholy Monarch: Saul

Saul had tremendous talents. With his able son Jonathan, he led the Jews to many victories over the Philistines. But Saul's tragic flaw was that he was given more power than he could handle. And then he began to suffer from supreme arrogance, an arrogance that led him to believe he didn't even have to obey the commandments of God. Shakespeare hadn't yet written King Lear but what a classic story of egomania leading to estrangement and ultimately emotional breakdown. The Bible calls it "an evil spirit that descended upon him." Unfortunately, the appropriate psychiatric diagnosis didn't exist at the time—and they didn't have Prozac. So the best they could do was to hire a harpist to try to soothe the king's mood with calming music. If you know your Bible, then you know that that was how David made it into the story. Talk about someone waiting in the wings to take over the main role!

Samuel knew that Saul, the first king of Israel, had failed. And so he secretly appointed another in his place. The "music man" from Bethlehem would soon become the greatest hero of the Jewish people. He is so important that he and his son Solomon deserve a chapter all to themselves.

The Least You Need to Know

➤ The leaders of the Jews, newly settled in Canaan, were known as *judges*.

➤ Deborah, one of the first of the judges, showed how a woman with wisdom and daring could serve as leader and military hero at least as well as a man.

➤ Gideon proved that military victory doesn't depend on numbers but rather on faith, and he reaffirmed the ideal that the ultimate king is God Himself.

➤ Samson proved the weakness of strength without self-discipline and the superiority of bright over might.

➤ Samuel cautioned the people about the possible misuse of ultimate power, but ultimately gave in to their request for a king and appointed Saul.

➤ A king who fails in his mission must be replaced. So the arrogant Saul is followed by humble David.

Chapter 9

Father and Son: David and Solomon

In This Chapter

➤ What made David so great and what is his lasting legacy

➤ What happens when king meets prophet in confrontation

➤ The problems of royalty and succession

➤ Where Solomon succeeded and where he failed

➤ A house for God—and its purpose

Who is greater: David or Solomon?

David gave the Jews Jerusalem; Solomon built for them the first Temple. David extended the kingdom considerably by war; Solomon preserved it by peace. David, with his spiritual sensitivity, composed the glorious book of Psalms; Solomon, with his incomparable brilliance, left us the legacy of the Book of Proverbs.

From a distance, these two stars shine equally bright, and we are incapable of comparing their luminescence. What we do know with certainty is that they stand high above us and that the rays they sent forth ages ago will continue to shine for generations yet to come.

From a Harp to a Slingshot

If our name is indeed our destiny, it's no wonder that the most beloved of all kings was David—for in Hebrew, David means "the loved one." And if ever a man deserved love, respect, adulation, and immortality, David was the man. The reasons for his greatness?

His Incredible Courage

A whole people stands paralyzed as the Philistines mock the Jews with a challenge: "Choose your man." Let's play one-on-one with our top physical specimen Goliath. If your man beats our man, we'll be your slaves. If our nine-foot giant pulverizes your representative, which we know is a foregone conclusion, you'll be our servants. Not a soul was willing to volunteer for this suicide mission (the health-care benefits didn't seem to be worth it), except for one little shepherd lad with a slingshot and five smooth stones.

To this very day, when we want to speak of an uneven match-up, we use the example of David and Goliath. But sometimes, one well-placed shot can beat the school bully; the courage of David against a superior force remains the inspiration for the underdogs of all times.

His Sensitivity and Moral Character

Just to prove that no good deed ever goes unpunished, David's great victory earned him King Saul's everlasting hatred. Sure, it couldn't have been easy for Saul to listen to the lyrics of the most popular song of his day, "Saul has slain his thousands / And David his ten thousands." What a put-down! But it didn't warrant throwing a spear at David while the young man was playing the harp for him. Nor did it justify Saul's other attempts to murder a national hero out of personal envy. Yet even after all this, David showed his greatness of character by holding back several times from slaying his pursuer when he easily could have done so—"Seeing he [Saul] is the Lord's anointed."

Imagine this: When David's sworn enemy, Saul, is finally killed in battle in an act of suicide to prevent public humiliation, David does not gloat but, filled with pity, weeps and utters a cry whose concluding line still has the power to move us: "How are the mighty fallen in the midst of the battle!"

Yenta's Little Secrets

In Jewish law, suicide is worse than homicide. To take your own life is to deprive yourself of a place in the World to Come. The Talmud teaches, "Surely your blood of your lives will I require" (Genesis 9:5) includes suicide, "except for a case like that of Saul." Saul's suicide was not a sin because it prevented the desecration of God's name. The enemy would have mocked a captured Jewish king and his God. This situation serves as the only legitimate case where suicide is justifiable.

His Poetic Power, Religious Passion, and Spiritual Fervor

Think of the paradox: A powerful warrior with the soul of a poet. A man who could master both the harp and the slingshot. A person who could conquer the Philistines and write the 23rd Psalm, indeed the entire Book of Psalms, the prayer book of the world. In every country, the language of this masterpiece has become part of the daily life of nations, passing into their proverbs, mingling with their conversation, and used at critical moments of their existence. The Book of Psalms, it has been said, is religion itself put into speech. And if the Bible is God speaking to humans, then the Book of Psalms is the daring—and successful—effort of people to properly speak to their Creator.

> **Sage Sayings**
>
> "I may truly name this book the anatomy of all parts of the soul. For no one can feel a movement of the spirit which is not reflected in this mirror. All the sorrows, troubles, fears, doubts, hopes, pains, perplexities, stormy outbreaks by which the souls of men are tossed, are depicted here to the very life."
>
> —John Calvin, speaking about The Book of Psalms

All This—and Jerusalem!

It was David who gave the holiest land on earth its holiest city. It was he who made it the political capital and then earmarked the Temple for it. It was he who brought the Ark containing the Ten Commandments to Jerusalem and dedicated a place for a national House of God. Like another shepherd, Moses, many years before him who led the people to the edge of the Promised Land but did not live to see it, David too dreamt the dream of a Temple—but it would have to be his son who would bring it to fruition only after his death.

Bathsheba in the Bath

David's achievements make him appear almost angelic. His faults helped keep him human. And so great a man was he that the people, and even God Himself, could eventually forgive him his one great, unspeakable sin.

Kings (just like presidents) seem to suffer from overheated sex drives. In a remarkable insight of the Talmud, preceding Freud by thousands of years, the rabbis intuited that "the greater the person, the stronger his libido." Greatness goes together with excessive energy, which can be sexually directed or sublimated.

Bathsheba wasn't a palace intern but she did live nearby. When David spotted her taking a bath, he immediately fell deeply in lust and arranged for an intimate get-together. The troublesome little detail, Bathsheba's husband, was soon taken care of by commanding general Joab to "send Uriah into the forefront of the hottest battle…that he may be smitten and die." You could probably call it a case of adultery and murder.

Yes, presidents could get impeached for less. But kings, from time immemorial, would have no trouble getting away with this and more. Yet, remarkably enough, not a Jewish king.

Even a King Can Be Wrong

Never before in history was there a scene such as the one that followed. The prophet Nathan appeared before King David, supposedly to ask advice about a minor crime:

> There were two men in the same city, one rich and one poor. The rich man had very large flocks and herds, but the poor man had only one little lamb that he had bought. He tended it and it grew up together with him and his children. It used to share his morsel of bread, drink from his cup, and nestle in his bosom.... One day a traveler came to the rich man but he was loath to take anything from his own flocks and herds...and prepare a meal for the guest...so he took the poor man's lamb and prepared it for the man who had come to him.

The prophet asked the king what should be done in such a case. In a rage David proclaimed, "The man who did this deserves to die." And Nathan, before the majesty of the monarch, proclaimed, "You are the man!"

Nathan and David: The Prophet rebukes the King. (Courtesy of Culver Pictures)

From where we sit, in the twentieth century, it is hard for us to grasp the significance and the awesome daring of this confrontation. It was the prophet against the state, the spirit against the sword, the mystic against the monarch. And the response of the king? "I have sinned—I stand guilty before the Lord."

Two master themes emerge from this story that have had powerful impact on the Jewish psyche:

1. The power of truth over might—no man, whatever his position, dare ignore the divine demands of morality.

2. The power of repentance—no matter how grave the crime, sincere remorse can effect forgiveness.

In spite of his faults, or perhaps *because* of them and his ability to surmount his failings, David is still revered 3,000 years after his death, and Jews continue to pray for "the restoration of the kingdom of David."

Hair Today, Gone Tomorrow—the Tragedy of Absalom

Did you ever hear the story of the three old ladies in Miami, sitting and rocking? The first gives out with a long, hard sigh. The second follows that with an immense and loud groan. The third, with obvious displeasure, says "I thought we weren't going to talk about the children."

Admit it: It makes some of us feel better to know that nobody has it all and even a king can have severe problems with his family. It might even be, as many moralists have pointed out, that when your kids grow up in a palace with all the advantages, the one thing they lack is not lacking anything. And so David had one son, Amnon, who was a rapist; another son, Absalom, so spoilt and power-hungry that he would do anything, even get rid of his father in order to gain the kingdom.

Absalom was movie-star gorgeous before there were movies—a hunk before anyone even knew what the word meant. "No-one in all Israel was so admired for his beauty as Absalom, from the sole of his foot to the crown of his head he was without blemish" (II Samuel 14:25). But in his soul he was deeply blemished with an outsized ego that made him anoint himself king and rebel against his own father. In a father-son military battle in which David had given strict orders that Absalom was not to be killed by his men, a divine irony caused the death of the rebellious son. Absalom's vanity made him most proud of his magnificent long hair—hair that became entangled in the branches of a tree and caused his own death.

The death of Absalom, from the Koelner. (Courtesy of Corbis-Bettmann)

Only a parent can truly understand David's remorse at the death of the son who fought to replace him: "My son Absalom! Oh my son, my son Absalom! If only I had died instead of you! Oh Absalom, my son! my son!"

"If I Could Have Only One Wish..."

We will never know if the pain caused him by Absalom and Amnon hastened the death of David in his seventieth year, but we can say with certainty that the glory brought to him by one of his children allows his legacy to live on to this day. Solomon was the answer to his father's prayers. And the reason Solomon was so great and so blessed was because of a prayer of his own.

Sage Sayings

"Solomon wrote first the Song of Songs, then Proverbs, then Ecclesiastes, and this is the way of the world. When young, we compose love songs; when older we write profound insights; and when old we speak of the vanity of all things."

—from the Midrash

Unsure of himself at the start of his reign, Solomon had a dream in which he could make one wish of God. Instead of selfishly requesting riches, long life, or the fulfillment of other personal pleasures, he prayed only for "an understanding heart to judge Thy people, that I may discern between good and evil." So God, according to tradition, granted him his wish, and Solomon became the epitome of a ruler with a wise and understanding heart, manifesting brilliance and compassion in the performance of his royal duties.

It isn't easy to earn the reputation of "the wisest of all men" from a people known for their wisdom. Yet that's what Solomon was known as by Jews, and subsequently around the world of his time. His wisdom and insights endure in the books he authored: Song of Songs, Proverbs, and Ecclesiastes.

But he too had a little problem with his libido. Seven hundred wives and three hundred concubines is really a bit much—and I don't see how he could have had too much time for any meaningful relationships. Smart people very often outsmart even themselves. And that, say the rabbis, is exactly what happened to Solomon. The Bible had warned about a king taking too many wives and gave a reason for the commandment, "Lest they turn his heart astray." I will allow myself many wives, he thought, because I am wise enough not to let that happen to me. And sure enough he proved to be wrong. The most polygamous Jew in history was responsible for allowing the foreign influences of many of his paramours to adversely impact upon his kingdom.

Pulpit Stories

One of the rabbis had a strange vision. On the day Solomon married Pharoah Necho's daughter, the archangel Michael descended from heaven. He looked around the world and then stuck a great pole in the sea. This spot gathered mud about it and the place eventually became like a thicket of leaves. It grew and spread even more and then formed the site of ancient Rome. What did the vision mean? It was only because of Solomon's improper marriages that the might of other empires would eventually arise and conquer the Jews.

Yet Solomon, too, in retrospect, is forgiven because of the two great gifts he brought to the Jewish people:

1. He lived up to his name Shlomo/Solomon, from the Hebrew word *shalom*, or "peace." His was a reign of unequaled and uninterrupted peace in the land, an age to which we still aspire as part of the messianic vision.

2. He created the supreme symbol of Jewish unity and submission to God, to be known, in recognition of his achievement, as Solomon's Temple, the first Temple in Jerusalem.

Solomon's Temple

His father, David, had willed it but was not permitted to build it. God had said to David, "You will not build a house for My Name, for you are a man of battles and have shed blood" (1 Chronicles 28:3). It was left for a man of peace to erect the House of God dedicated to a vision of universal peace.

Why does an invisible and noncorporeal God need a house? Of course *He* doesn't, but we, human beings, need it to constantly remind ourselves of His presence in our midst. The very architecture of the Temple would demonstrate this truth. The Temple's windows were narrow inside and widening outward in order to send forth light into the outside world, rather than bring light from the outside in. When, many years later, enemies would come to destroy the Temple, they would search in vain for statues of the Jewish God and be perplexed in failing to find any physical symbol of a deity. They could not understand that the Temple housed an idea, not a person. It was meant not as a home for a God, but rather as a message for His people.

A seventeenth-century reconstruction of the Temple. (Courtesy of the Library of the Jewish Theological Seminary of America)

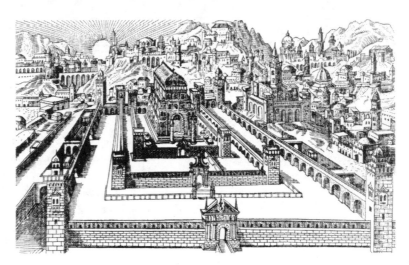

The Site of the Temple

How did Solomon know where to build the Temple? The Midrash provides the answer with a beautiful story.

Two brothers lived near each other. One was married and had a large family. The other lived alone. At harvest time, the single brother thought to himself: I am but one person. I hardly need anything. My brother has many mouths to feed. I know he will never accept charity from me, but if I bring him some bundles of wheat in the night and drop them off without saying a word, he will assume that they're his and enjoy them.

Meanwhile, the other brother was making his own calculations: My poor brother does not know the joys of family life. He has no pleasure from wife or children. Let him at least savor the benefits of wealth and abundance. I know he'll never take anything from me but if I just bring him some bundles of wheat in the middle of the night and drop them off…

And so from the two sides of the field, two brothers walked toward each other. Neither knew what the other had in mind. And then, in the darkness of night, they unexpectedly collided. They saw, they dropped their bundles, they quickly understood, and with tears flowing, they embraced in the knowledge of the love that they shared for each other.

On that very spot, the place that so profoundly demonstrated the highest level of brotherhood, compassion and affection, Solomon decided to build God's Temple.

And Inside the Temple...

In the Temple—120 feet long, 40 feet wide, and 60 feet high—were a number of holy objects:

➤ A menorah, a seven-branched candlestick symbolic of the light of wisdom

➤ An altar, for sacrificial offerings demonstrating man's dependence on God and gratitude for the many gifts he enjoys

➤ A table with 12 loaves of freshly baked bread, symbolizing God as the provider of daily sustenance for all of the 12 tribes

➤ A laver, a washbasin demonstrating the need for hygienic and spiritual purity

➤ Holiest of all, the Ark containing the tablets of the law received by Moses at Sinai (the Ten Commandments)

Listen to Your Bubbe

Don't ever make a menorah of seven branches. You can make one of eight—that's the menorah used for Hanukkah. But the one in the Temple had seven branches, and Jews are not permitted to replicate that which was so holy it belonged only in the House of God.

Before the Raiders of the Lost Ark

Even the holiness of the Temple itself had degrees. One section was holier than all the others. It was called the Holy of Holies. Only one man, the High Priest, was ever allowed to enter that area, and even he could only come into its precincts on one day of the year, Yom Kippur. There and on that day the High Priest would be allowed to recite the holiest, all-powerful 72-letter name of God with which he would pray for the safety and the security of the Jewish people throughout the coming year.

Only one item stood in this special section of the Temple. In the holiest part rested the holiest item. The Ark, symbol of the entire Torah, had this

Aha, That's It

Yom Kippur, literally Day of Atonement, is the holiest day of the year on the Jewish calendar. Jews fast, pray, confess their sins of the previous year, and hope that their repentance will secure for them forgiveness.

unique distinction. Because for the Jew, the Law of God stood supreme. It was his very definition of the essence of God.

The Raiders of the Lost Ark may never have found it, but that doesn't really matter to the Jews because the Ark's sanctity was based on the Torah, and the Jews always knew that their Book of Law could never be lost.

The Least You Need to Know

➤ David lived up to his name, "beloved," by virtue of his many achievements.

➤ As a warrior, David is most remembered for his inspirational victory over Goliath, as well as his all-important conquest of the city of Jerusalem, which he turned into the capital of his kingdom.

➤ As a religious figure, David remains unparalleled in his ability to give expression to the spiritual leanings of mankind in his Book of Psalms.

➤ Though his sin with Bathsheba was severe beyond words, his total repentance allowed him to be forgiven, and it serves as a profound lesson of the power of sincere atonement.

➤ The confrontation between Nathan and David epitomizes the power of the prophet over the king.

➤ "Vanity goes before a fall" may well be the biblical summary of the life of Absalom.

➤ Solomon will always be remembered for his wisdom, his bringing of peace to the land, and his building of the first Temple.

➤ Of all the holy items in the Temple, the Ark, which contained the tablets of the Law, was the holiest.

The Prophets: Hello...This Is God Calling

What makes a great nation lose its power? What is the real cause for the decline of an empire?

The history books always talk about attacks from foreign enemies. Defeat comes from an *outside* force. When you probe a little deeper, however, you see that invariably the root of decline is rotting from *within*. A nation first destroys itself—ethically, spiritually, socially—and then strangers come and pick up the pieces. That's exactly what happened to the Jewish people after the glory days of David and Solomon. And that's what the prophets kept preaching to the people, to no avail, until the ten tribes were lost and the remaining two were eventually exiled.

The Jewish Civil War

The two saddest words in the English language, it's been said, are "if only." If only Solomon had had an equally wise son to succeed him. If only Rehoboam, Solomon's heir, had shown a little understanding and compassion when the people begged him to diminish their taxes. If only the leaders of the ten tribes, angry at the total rejection of their request, didn't set up a new king for themselves and secede from the Davidic kingdom, leaving it only with the tribe of Judah in the south, together with its neighbor, the little tribe of Benjamin. Oh, what might have been, if there were unity among brothers and differences resolved!

That's the story in a nutshell. But the Jewish civil war, unlike its American counterpart many, many years later, didn't end with a United States of Israel. Instead it resulted in a kingdom in the north, Israel, with its capital in Shechem, and the smaller kingdom of Judah in the south, comprised only of the two tribes remaining loyal to the house of David, Judah and Benjamin, with Jerusalem as its capital.

A graphic illustration of the Jewish "civil war" and the fall of independence.

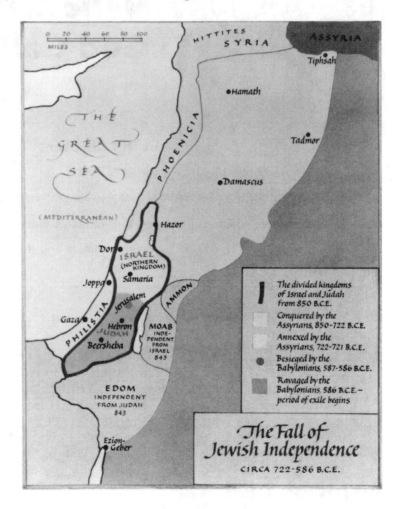

The secession took place in the year 930 B.C.E. About 200 years later, in 722 B.C.E., the kingdom of Israel was defeated by Assyria, and its occupants—according to the strategy of their conquerors who always removed the native population from its land—dispersed over the globe with no record of their destination. So that's how ten tribes, the major portion of the Jewish people, were lost forever as recognizable descendants of Abraham, Isaac, and Jacob.

Some super-optimists still believe that remnants will yet be found. Others explain fascinating words, rituals, and customs that appear to be Judaic in origin in some of the most exotic and faraway places on earth as vestiges of those ancient Jewish deportees. But when all is said and done—if only there hadn't been internal strife and divisiveness, if only the Jews didn't have their version of a civil war—their survivors today would be increased by a margin of close to 90 percent!

Yenta's Little Secrets

Lost is usually lost, but maybe some of the ten lost tribes were found. There is an old belief among some that members of the tribe of Dan ended up in Ethiopia and are the dark-skinned Falasha Jews. But their different color didn't estrange them from their ancient traditions and the rule of the Torah in their lives. In the 1970s, the State of Israel, in a daring rescue mission, helped bring these surviving Jews back to their ancient homeland.

Pulpit Story

No one knows where this story originated. Some people claimed to have seen it with their own eyes. There is a river called the Sambatyon. It separates the land of the ten lost tribes from the rest of civilization. It casts up stones from its riverbed so that no one can cross it and get to see the surviving Israelites. Only on Shabbat, on Saturday, the Jewish day of rest, does the river rest from its work of obstructing passersby from crossing. Some day, in Messianic times, when the world will be like an eternal Sabbath, Jews will be able to cross in both directions and once more be reunited.

Elijah, the Still, Small Voice

The northern kingdom of Israel, although far greater in number, lacked one thing that the southern kingdom of Judah retained—the city of Jerusalem and the Temple. To strengthen their own identity, the northern kings felt it in their best interest to sever connections with the Temple, as well as with its God.

One of the strongest voices pushing worship of local deities in place of the God of Sinai was that of King Ahab (876–855 B.C.E.). To be more accurate, Ahab was just a mouthpiece for his domineering wife Jezebel who was, how shall we put it, a real *jezebel*, worthy of the word she gave to the English language. Jezebel was a daughter of the King of Tyre, who brought to the marriage her Phoenician culture, religion, and forms of worship. The worship of Baal, represented by countless idols, quickly spread throughout the land.

Aha, That's It

Baal means master, lord, warrior. But most of all, it refers to a pagan god, with a variety of different names. There are at least as many Baals as Baskin & Robbins' flavors, each one promising a wondrously different blessing. Take my advice and stick with the ice cream—you'll get more for your money.

The times demanded a prophet—someone totally unafraid to stand up to even the king and the queen, someone who could become "the Thunderer of the Lord." Someone with charisma, courage, and total conviction. That man was Elijah of Tishbi. Remarkably enough, so powerful was his personality that Jewish tradition maintains he, of all prophets, is the one selected by God to reappear some day and announce the imminent arrival of Messiah.

Perhaps what gives Elijah such uniqueness is an experience he had while fleeing for his life from Jezebel's hatred. Hiding in caves, he longingly searched for God in the grandeur of a whirlwind, in the majesty of thunder and lightning, in the awesome manifestations of nature, only to discover that God was willing to be found only in the still, small voice within him. Perhaps that small voice, instead of thunderous multimedia, technicolored circuses, is the only proper prelude to a time when God's presence will finally make itself manifest on Earth.

Yenta's Little Secrets

There is an invisible guest at every Jewish circumcision and Passover meal—Elijah. Why him? He is the only prophet, according to tradition, who ascended to heaven in mortal form. He didn't die and therefore can come back when needed. Because he feared for the destruction of the Jewish people, he is permitted to be witness to two of the most important rituals demonstrating the ongoing vitality of the Jewish religion.

"Seek Justice...Relieve the Oppressed" (Isaiah)

The kingdom of Judah in the south was far from perfect either. During the reign of King Ahaz (735–720 B.C.E.) and King Hezekiah (720–692 B.C.E.), a prophet appeared in Jerusalem to point out those sins which, not too many generations later, would cause the destruction of the Temple.

Sage Sayings

"The prophet is appointed to oppose the king, and, even more, history."

—Martin Buber

Isaiah, like all great prophets, was blessed not only with deep spiritual fervor, but also with keen political insight and a profound vision of an ideal society. Many of his messages have as much relevance for us today as they did for his listeners way back when. Here are some examples:

➤ "Nation shall not lift up sword against nation, neither shall they learn the art of war anymore." If we would only believe it, the Messianic vision could become a reality. So far the nations of the world took this conviction and placed it on the wall across the street from the United Nations in New York. (Of course, so as not to offend many of the anti-Semitic delegations, the quote was posted without attribution, demonstrating how far we still have to go in removing hatred, even as the ideal is set up as slogan.)

➤ "The wolf shall dwell with the lamb, and the leopard lie down with the kid" (to which Woody Allen added the comment "but the lamb won't get much sleep"). Eventually, the absence of war will go hand in hand with the removal of bestial behavior and the elimination of the slightest tendency toward violence and warfare. Isaiah taught us that we don't have to be embarrassed to dream the impossible dream.

➤ "Cease to do evil, learn to do good. Devote yourselves to justice. Aid the wronged. Uphold the rights of the orphan. Defend the cause of the widow." By starting with little things like the way we treat our friends and our neighbors—this is how the Messianic Age will come about. If every single person were to live by these ideals, then the deeds of every individual could transform the world because society is nothing more than the sum of its parts.

➤ Isaiah took that idea a step further and turned individual responsibility into a divine demand for an entire people. He exhorted the Jews to fulfill their historic destiny by becoming an *or la Goyim*, a "light unto the nations." The Messianic ideal needs a messenger, and it is left to the Jews to play that role.

➤ And one more thing Isaiah taught, which was the most daring of all. To a people who had become accustomed to worshipping God in the Temple with sacrifices and libations, with the offerings of priests and the songs of the Levites (the descendants of Levi, son of Jacob, who were appointed to help the priests in the Temple services), Isaiah spoke out against the perversion of priorities he saw in his society. His emphasis on the obligations of man toward fellow man above even those of man to God was so powerful and so relevant that Jews have chosen this portion to be read from year to year on Yom Kippur, the holiest day of the year, as the focal point of their prayers. The message read in every synagogue has Isaiah explain in God's name why fasting doesn't suffice to secure God's forgiveness:

Cry aloud, spare not, lift up thy voice like the shofar, and show my people their transgression, and the house of Yaakov their sins. Yet they seek me daily, and desire to know my ways. As a nation that did righteousness, and forsook not the ordinance of their gods they ask of me judgments of justice; they desire that God should be near. Why have we fasted, they say, and thou seest not? Why have we afflicted our soul, and thou takest no knowledge? Behold, in the day of your fast you pursue your business and exact all your payments. Behold, you fast for strife and debate, and to smite with the fist of wickedness: you fast not this day to make your voice to be heard on high. Is such the fast that I have chosen? A day for a man to afflict his soul? Is it to bow down his head like a bulrush, and to spread sackcloth and ashes under him? Will you call this a fast, and an acceptable day to the Lord? Is not this rather the fast that I have chosen? To loose the chains of wickedness, to undo the bands of the yoke, and to let the oppressed go free and to break every yoke? Is it not to share thy bread with the hungry, and that you bring the poor that are cast out to your house? When you see the naked that you cover him; and that you do not hide yourself from your own flesh? Then shall your light break forth like the morning, and your health shall spring forth speedily: and your righteousness shall go before you; the glory of the Lord shall be your rearguard. Then you shall call, and the Lord shall answer; you shall cry and He shall say, here I am. If you take away from your midst the yoke, the pointing of the finger, and speaking iniquity; and if you draw out your soul to the hungry, and satisfy the afflicted soul; then shall your light arise in darkness, and your gloom be as the noonday (Isaiah 58:1–10).

Isaiah may have condemned the sins of his time, but he was basically a messenger of hope. It was left to another to deliver the prophecy of gloom and despair.

"I Hate to Tell You This, but..."—Jeremiah

The English word *jeremiad* means sad complaints and lamentations. One guess where the word came from. Pity poor Jeremiah, who had to spend most of his life telling his people, "I have bad news...and bad news." You would think that after the fall of the kingdom of Israel, the message Jeremiah had to teach about dealing with the consequences of one's actions would have been more readily accepted.

Isaiah and other prophets before him had already made the connection between religion and politics, between failure to observe the word of God and defeat at the hands of one's enemies. It had been preached that military disaster is in reality not due to physical weakness, but rather to spiritual sin. And other nations such as Assyria could even be, as Isaiah indicated, nothing less than a divine messenger bearing "the rod of Mine anger, the staff in whose hand is My indignation."

Sage Sayings

"Religion, it seems to me, functions in an ivory tower ...when it fails to have impact on people and state. As you well know, the prophets were in the thick of it; their voices rose above the people and they were eagerly heeded. And what was their message if not chiefly an ethical interpretation of the law?"

—Arthur J. Goldberg, Former U.S. Supreme Court Justice

Foretelling Their Worst Nightmare

What made Jeremiah's mission so much more difficult was that living around 600 B.C.E., in the last days of the first Temple, he had to foretell the national catastrophe that the people most feared: The fall of Jerusalem and the destruction of the House of God.

Jeremiah weeps for Jerusalem. (Courtesy of Culver Pictures)

Yenta's Little Secrets

A Jewish prophet doesn't have to predict the future. The English word *prophet* means "to see beforehand." In Hebrew a prophet is a *navi* which literally means "spokesman." A navi speaks for God, bringing His message to the people—warning, exhorting, criticizing, speaking out against corruption and injustice and pleading for righteousness. At times, he may even predict by telling the people the consequences of their actions if they do not repent. But a Jewish prophet is not a fortune teller. He is more of a rabbi—with a direct line to God.

Not that it had to be. A prophet doesn't so much predict as warn of dire consequences if his words aren't heeded. Here again, "if only" —if only the Jews would change their evil ways and cease their idolatrous behavior.

From Doom to Hope

A true prophet has to tell it the way it is and suffer the consequences of scorn and hatred when people don't like the message. So Jeremiah was flogged, called a traitor, left in a pit to die, and had the even greater misfortune of having to say, "I told you so," after all his predictions came true. And remarkably enough, it was only then, after the Babylonians conquered the Jews and destroyed the Temple, that Jeremiah changed his tune. For it was then that he turned into a prophet of hope, predicting a Jewish return to the homeland from which they seemed to be in permanent exile.

Go to any religious Jewish wedding today and you will undoubtedly hear the song with his lyrics, "Od yishoma—again there shall be heard in this place…in the desolate towns of Judah and the deserted streets of Jerusalem the sounds of mirth and gladness, the voice of bridegroom and bride." Never was anyone sadder than Jeremiah on seeing his prophecy of destruction come true. Never was anyone more visionary than Jeremiah in his conviction that the Jews, unlike any other people on Earth, would eventually return to the land from which they were forcibly expelled by their enemies.

Even God's Temple Can Be Destroyed

The Jews didn't want to believe Jeremiah, not only because they, like all people, have a natural aversion to bad news. No, it was almost as if they couldn't accept the words of the man of God for religious reasons! How could anyone dare tell them that the House of God would be destroyed? That the holiest spot on earth would be razed to the ground! God would surely never allow that to happen. God, the one God, could certainly not be defeated by the devotees of other false gods!

What they failed to understand from Jeremiah and the other prophets was that God considered His honor less important than teaching the Jews the need to live by the Law. And even the Temple can be destroyed—and later destroyed again after it was rebuilt—if the Jews didn't *deserve* to have God live in their midst.

Ironically enough, this idea would eventually save the Jewish people. Every other nation considered its own defeat the defeat of its God and proof that the one they worshipped was not as powerful as the god of their conquerors. But the Jews came to understand what the prophets taught: They were defeated not by the gods of their enemies, but by their failure to properly serve their own God who remained *melech haolam*, king of the universe. Babylonia did indeed destroy the Temple, as Jeremiah predicted, but they didn't succeed in defeating God—or His people.

The Least You Need to Know

➤ Ten tribes secede from the kingdom of David, known as Judah, and form a separate country, the kingdom of Israel.

➤ Although greater in number, the tribes' breaking away from their brothers eventually resulted in their disappearance; they became "the ten lost tribes of Israel."

➤ Prophets such as Elijah tried to warn the people that straying from God and sinning against fellow man would have dire consequences and bring about God's punishment.

➤ Isaiah reminded the people of Judah that ethics, justice, and righteousness are the supreme ways in which to serve God and that they have a mission to be a light unto the nations of the world.

➤ Jeremiah's jeremiads were ignored and the unthinkable happened: God's Temple was destroyed and His city of Jerusalem laid waste.

➤ The Jews finally understood that the cause of their downfall is a powerful message from God to mend their ways.

Part 4

Confronting Empires: Babylonia, Persia, Greece, and Rome

It's roller-coaster time once again. It will be a bumpy ride but one toward the top this time, as the Jews come home and rebuild their Temple. They face threats of destruction from the most formidable empires of the day—Babylonia, Persia, Greece, and Rome—and live not only to tell the tale, but to survive spiritually. They will even come away with two new holidays, Purim and Hanukkah, to remind them of their miraculous victories.

Things will begin to change, though, when the Romans arrive on the scene, intent on replacing the Jews' God with the Roman eagle. The roller coaster begins its downward descent, and a time of imminent annihilation brings desperate hope for a divine redeemer. One of these, a Jew named Jesus, was the founder of a new religion. Jews don't accept him in that role, marking the beginning of the rift between Jews and Christians.

When the Temple burns for the second time, the Jews realize the only thing that will save them now is a book they can carry with them wherever they go in place of the House of God that has just been destroyed. The Age of the Temple gives way to the Age of the Talmud. As we bring this part of the book to a close, the Jews weep for what they have lost, but treasure all the more its replacement.

Surviving the Destruction of the Temple

In 586 B.C.E., when Babylonia conquered Judah and destroyed the first Temple, Babylonia was the greatest power in the world. Its capital Babylon was "the city of merchants," and its prosperity and luxury were unparalleled.

The Babylonians were also brilliant. To make sure they had no trouble from the people they conquered, they removed them from their native surroundings and scattered them elsewhere. The best and the brightest they took home with them. That's why the Jews who ended up in Babylonia were the ones with superior education, skilled as artisans: knowledgeable, cultured, and sophisticated. Babylonia offered them freedom, opportunity, integration—at the cost of only one thing: assimilation. This was the deal: personal glory for national suicide. But strangely enough, most of the Jews refused to take it.

Life Without a Temple

With the tremendous changes brought on by their exile, the Jews reflected upon what once was, and some very peculiar things happened. Their national tragedy turned out in many ways to be a blessing in disguise.

Missing What They'd Lost

"Absence makes the heart grow fonder" may sound like a cliché but it also happens to be true. Kids who live at home never fully appreciate what they have—let them leave it for a while, and they really miss what they so long took for granted. So, too, for the Jews, who began to fully appreciate what they had once had. While in Babylonia, they developed a new fierce nationalism, turned toward Judah, and in the words of the psalmist, made a stirring vow:

If I forget thee O Jerusalem
Let my right hand forget her cunning.
Let my tongue cleave to the roof of my mouth,
If I remember thee not; if I set not Jerusalem above my
chiefest joy.

Sage Sayings

"Of all the places in the world, I love Jerusalem the most—when I am not there."

—Elie Wiesel

Exile Brought Insight

Previously, warnings of the prophets had fallen on deaf ears. The Jews rejected the calls to righteousness and the possibility that God would punish them for their sins. But now with the reality of their tragedy upon them, they came to the conclusion that what happened to them might very well be "a result of our own sins." There began an intense spiritual and religious awakening, a desire to return to the study of their ancient writings, and a commitment to the way of life of their ancestors.

Aha, That's It

The word *synagogue* is derived from the Greek *synagoge* and means "congregation." For a synagogue to be a congregation, it requires a minimum of ten people—a *minyan*. Worshipping God as part of a group experience is deemed holier than remaining isolated and alone. A synagogue expresses the notion of collective responsibility and unity in the service of God.

Replacing the Temple with the Synagogue

If there was no longer a central House of God, the Jews would have to create mini-temples. After all, if "God's glory fills the whole world," then his address does not have to be restricted to one location in Jerusalem. And with that epic epoch-making decision, Jews created the form of religious service that would later be imitated both by the church and the mosque. It was revolutionary because it universalized God's presence and truly made Him accessible to anyone anywhere on earth.

Synagogues were not the place for sacrifices, so prayer became the recognized substitute for the offering of animals. Priests were no longer crucial for the recitation of prayers, and so synagogues didn't need intermediaries to approach God. The synagogue turned every Jew into a priest, every person who could speak to God with prayers on his lips into a religious functionary. The Babylonians had unwittingly destroyed a national religious center and paved the way for a far more democratic and universal way of worshipping God.

Sage Sayings

"In all their long history, the Jewish people have done scarcely anything more wonderful than to create the synagogue. No human institution has a longer continuous history, and none has done more for the uplifting of the human race."

—Robert Travers Herford

Yenta's Little Secrets

There are three Hebrew names for a synagogue, and each describes one of its major functions: *Bet Tefillah*, a house of prayer; *Bet Knesset*, a house of assembly; and *Bet Midrash*, a house of study. The most common word today for a synagogue is the Yiddish *shul*, from the German word for school, suggesting that the third function, the house of study, is the most important.

Rabbis Become More Important Than Priests

With the diminishing role of the priests in a society without a temple, rabbis and scholars became far more significant. A *cohen*, or priest, did it for you. A rabbi taught you how to do it yourself. Judaism by proxy was being replaced by personal encounter. All you needed was knowledge, and you could do it *on your own*. This was the final breakthrough that would allow the teachers of the oral law and the Talmud to later play such a significant role in the life of the Jewish people.

Aha, That's It

Cohen is the Hebrew word for priest. It refers to a descendant of Aaron, who was chosen to serve in the Temple. The purity of this lineage is still recognized to this day and every Cohen, as a mark of respect, is called first to the weekly reading of the Torah.

"Them Bones Shall Rise Again"

Guess what? You don't have to live in Israel to be a prophet. Just like men and women can speak to God in synagogues of the Diaspora, so too can God speak to men and women in countries other than the Holy Land. Ezekiel, the first prophet outside Israel, proved this true. And he had a perfect record, two for two, in predicting the future.

Together with a few thousand other prominent Jews, Ezekiel was exiled from Jerusalem to Babylonia even before the destruction of the first Temple. From Babylonia, years before the event, Ezekiel prophesied that Jerusalem would be destroyed.

But his second prediction was much more powerful. Given in the form of a metaphor, it spoke to the Jews in his time, just as it spoke to the Jews of the twentieth century after the Holocaust.

Ezekiel had a vision of a valley with lifeless, dry and dead bones. It seemed impossible that they would ever come back to life again. But God told Ezekiel, "Say to the breath, thus said the Lord God: Come, O breath, from the four winds, and breathe into these slain, that they may live again."

Aha, That's It

Based on a poem by Naftali Herz Imber, the national anthem of Israel *HaTikvah* reflects the belief that "our cherished hope is not yet lost, the ancient hope not dampened, to regain our Fatherland, where David once encamped."

The corpses stood on their feet, the dead lived once more. And God explained it to Ezekiel: "O mortal, these bones are the whole house of Israel. They say our bones are dried up, our hope is gone; we are doomed." Thus said the Lord God, "I am going to open your graves and lift you out of the graves o my people and bring you to the land of Israel...I will put my breath into you, and you shall live again...I will set you upon your own soil."

Ezekiel, what a vision! You were right for the Jews of Babylonia. You were right for the Jews of the Holocaust. Your prophecy is the most enduring of all. It gave the Jews hope throughout the centuries. And hope—*HaTikvah*—became the national anthem of the modern-day State of Israel.

Who Can Read That Handwriting on the Wall?

The bad news is that God is strict and punishes. The good news is that He gives you a warning. The bad news is that you have to be able to read His handwriting on the wall (and I already told you that among all the other things He is, God is also a doctor).

According to the Bible, the Babylonian king Belshazaar, son of Nebuchadnezar who had destroyed the first Temple, made a great feast to demonstrate his power. To show off to the Joneses, and even more to the Goldbergs, he conspicuously used the gold and silver vessels that his father stole from the Temple.

But then a giant hand, shades of Godzilla without the "zilla," began to write letters in an unknown alphabet on the wall. Terrified, they called in the wise Jew Daniel, who was able to decipher the strange words, "Mene mene tekel upharsin." The message read: "God numbered your kingdom, you have been weighed and judged, and your kingdom will be divided between the Medes and the Persians." That night, Belshazaar was slain.

From that time on, the best advice for anyone is to see the handwriting on the wall—even as Bob Dylan (nee Zimmerman) much later would tell us, "The answer, my friend, is blowin' in the wind."

"Hey, Man, Haman...Hang up"

Thanks to the Persian empire that followed the Babylonian one, the Jews got a great gift: the holiday of Purim.

Do you know the quick summary of a Jewish holiday? They wanted to kill us, we survived, let's eat.

The longer version of the story of this particular holiday, Purim, is a whole book of the Bible, Megillat Esther. Its unique distinction from all the other books of the Bible is that God's name does not appear in it even once. Jews see in this strange fact the deeper meaning of the entire story of attempted genocide by the villain Haman, advisor to King Ahasuerus. Even when God is not openly revealed, He can stand behind the scenes and perform miracles under the guise of what we might call amazing coincidence.

Color illustration of a Megillah manuscript, any of five biblical books (Esther, Ruth, Lamentations, Ecclesiastes, Song of Songs) recited liturgically from a scroll, 16th century. (Courtesy of Corbis-Bettmann)

Yenta's Little Secrets

Haman was very happy when his casting of lots told him to pick the month of Adar to destroy the Jews. He knew that was the month in which Moses died. Surely that meant it was an unlucky time for the Jewish people. What he didn't realize was that Moses was also born in that very month. As a matter of fact, Moses died on his birthday, as most really righteous people do, to demonstrate that their lives were complete and full to the very end. To this day, Jews have a saying, "When Adar comes, let there be an increase of joy."

Listen to Your Bubbe

To celebrate Purim properly, you need a "gragger." That's a noise-maker that's rapidly turned and makes a whirring roar. Use it whenever Haman's name is recited in the Megillah and show that you understand it is dangerous to remain silent in the face of someone who seeks to destroy you. And if the noise gives you a headache, well it's Purim, so have a drink and forget about it.

But let's get back to the Purim story. Esther was always in the right place at the right time. She won a beauty contest and became the first Jewish Persian queen. (Unlike a Jewish American princess, a Jewish queen was not politically incorrect at the time.) Haman did not know the queen's real identity. Out of hatred for Mordechai, Esther's uncle, who refused to bow to him, Haman got the king to approve his "final solution" for the entire Jewish people—wipe them out. But Haman got hoisted by his own petard; he ended up hanging on the very tree he prepared for the Jew Mordechai. That's why every Jew-hater in history who is especially vicious, including Hitler in the twentieth century, is called a latter-day Haman, in the hope that he will meet the same divine retribution.

Purim Is "Lots" of Fun

Haman was superstitious. He picked the day for his plan of genocide to go into effect by "lots." In Persian "lots" is *purim*, and lotteries, as we have already learned, are determined by God. So the Jews read the book—the whole Megillah—boo Haman's name with graggers, and allow themselves to get drunk once a year to recall the miracle that all started at a feast with excessive drinking of wine. (That's when Ahasuerus got rid of his first queen and replaced her with Esther.)

A Purim wall decoration highlighting scenes from the story. (Courtesy of Jewish Museum/Art Resource, NY)

Is the Bible Finished Yet?

The Persian king Cyrus took some time before he allowed the Babylonian exiles to return to their land. In a stunning proclamation decreed in 538 B.C.E., Cyrus said (as the book of Ezra records), "Who is there among all you people whose God be with him and let him go to Jerusalem which is in Judah and build the house of the Lord God of Israel which is in Jerusalem." Truthfully, not everyone went back. But those who did—over 40,000 of them—rebuilt the Temple and dedicated it just a little over 70 years after the first Temple was destroyed.

Aha, That's It

Megillah means scroll. When you hear someone saying just the word *megillah*, she probably means the scroll of Esther. There are, however, four other scrolls in the Bible: Song of Songs, Ruth, Lamentations, and Ecclesiastes.

101

Half a century later, another dedication took place which, from the perspective of history, would prove to be even more important. Ezra, a brilliant leader and a profound religious thinker, joined the returnees from Babylon. He realized that what the Jews needed most to preserve themselves as a people was a fixed body of scriptural writings to which they could turn for religious guidance, instruction, and inspiration. He gathered together a group of learned priests, scholars, and scribes known as the "Men of the Great Assembly." Together, and according to Jewish tradition by divine inspiration, they closed the Book of the Law, the Torah, and gave it the final form it has to this day.

What Does Torah Mean?

Literally *Torah* means "doctrine" or "teaching," but specifically it can refer to one of three different things:

1. The Pentateuch (also called in Hebrew the *Chumash*). This is comprised of the five books of Moses, or the first five books of the Bible—Genesis, Exodus, Leviticus, Numbers, and Deuteronomy. These books stand in a class by themselves. From creation to the death of Moses, they represent not only the will but also the very word of God—for fundamentalists, literally, and for others, by divine inspiration.

2. The Bible. Ezra included two other categories of books into the Sacred Writings, which then made up the totality of Torah known as T'nach. *T'nach* is an acronym for **T**orah, the 5 books of Moses; **N**eviim, the 21 books of the prophets; and **K**etubim, the "writings" of the final books of the Bible, including Ezra and Nehemiah, Psalms, Job, and the five scrolls.

3. The Oral Law, as later codified in the Mishnah and Talmud together with all further discussions, debates, and commentaries that would follow throughout the centuries to this day. "Tell me a nice piece of Torah," a Jew will say to his friend, and he will probably mean this last category of personal interpretation or a new way of looking at an ancient text. It deserves the descriptive "Torah" for the best of reasons—because it weds modern insight with ancient truth, proving the immortality of God's words.

It Never Ends

The complete Bible is a combination of God speaking to man and man offering his reply. The first part was closed by Ezra and the Men of the Great Assembly. The second, leaving room for man's intellectual growth and spiritual maturation, goes on to this day. Some people might even say right to this very moment, because you are studying this book, you are "learning Torah."

The Least You Need to Know

➤ The tragedy of the destruction of the Temple brought with it some unexpected blessings.

➤ The creation of the synagogue was another revolutionary turning point, for it helped to universalize and democratize the Jewish religion.

➤ The vision of Ezekiel's dry bones coming back to life helped to sustain the Jews in every time of despair.

➤ There are always signs of warning for impending disasters, and we have to learn to be sensitive to "the writing on the wall."

➤ From Haman to Hitler, plans for "final solutions" to the Jews fail as a result of God's miraculous interventions—even if they appear merely as coincidences.

➤ Seventy years after the destruction of the first Temple, the Jews were permitted to return and to rebuild it by edict of Cyrus, king of Persia.

➤ The word *Torah* has different meanings, but in its broadest sense, it includes all spiritual and religious teachings.

Chapter 12

Hellenists and Hanukkah

In This Chapter

➤ The battle of Hellenism against Hebraism

➤ Hellenists, Hasidim, and Apikorsim

➤ The Maccabees and the miracle of oil in the menorah

➤ Hanukkah is not the Jewish Christmas

So far, the Jews were able to survive, no matter how severe the attempts to destroy them. From Egypt to Persia, the efforts of their enemies were unsuccessful. But with the coming of the Golden Age of Greece and the glories of Hellenic culture, the Jews faced their greatest challenge. This was a challenge not from someone who came to destroy them but rather to embrace them. The danger wasn't a dagger. It was a kiss—but a kiss, which if successful could have spelled the kiss of death for Jewish survival. With the meteoric rise in the fourth century B.C.E. of Alexander the Great, pupil of the philosopher Aristotle, Hebraism confronted Hellenism in what would prove to be a friendly fight to the finish.

It's Greek to Me

Did you know that to this very day Alexander is a popular Jewish name? Ask how it's possible for a conqueror to be so admired that people named their children after him, and you get some sense of the great influence Hellenic culture had on the Jews. Alexander didn't come to enslave the new members of his Grecian empire. What he wanted more than anything else was for everyone in the world to speak Greek, act Greek, and be Greek—the original "Grecian Formula" to make the world look better.

Sage Sayings

"The governing idea of Hellenism is spontaneity of consciousness; that of Hebraism, strictness of conscience."

—Matthew Arnold

Sage Sayings

"Let not the wisdom of the Greeks beguile thee/Which hath no fruit but only flowers."

—Yehuda HaLevi

To be honest, the attraction was considerable. Hellenism offered brilliant philosophy, magnificent art, a highly developed sense of beauty, respect and worship of the body and all of its possibilities for perfection, a reverence for a sound mind in a sound body—in short, those things that to this day have most influenced civilization.

So for the first time many Jews succumbed in large numbers to the seductive lure of their enemies' embrace. The conflict was between two ideals: Hellenism worshipped the holiness of beauty; Hebraism worshipped the beauty of holiness. The conflict raged not on the battlefield but in the gymnasiums, theaters, cabarets, and circuses.

Later, much later, there would be those daring enough to suggest that the ideal would have been a synthesis between the visions of these two great civilizations. In the twelfth century, the Jewish sage Maimonides would come to merge Greek philosophy with the Law of Moses. Others would seek to introduce Greek ideals of beauty into their efforts to glorify the worship of God. But the struggle for Jewish hearts and minds had just begun, and the soul of a people hung in the balance.

Today the saying on Madison Avenue goes, "If you want to be a success, dress British, think Yiddish." In the days of the Greeks it became fashionable, even for Jews, to dress in the style of the Greeks, assume Greek names, speak Greek, and even participate in Greek sports such as nude wrestling. (And you know how much of a big change that last one must have been for Jews if comedian Jackie Mason is right, and the favorite Jewish sport has always been watching other people exercise!)

Yenta's Little Secrets

If you think the shortest book on record is *The Guide to Jewish Gladiators,* think again. So pervasive was Greek influence that there were even gladiatorial contests between Jews. Resh Lakish, for example, was a big-name draw in these fights until he gave it all up to become one of the prominent sages of the Talmud. As a matter of record, he said that the intellectual disputes of his later years were far more difficult than the physical encounters of his youth!

The Septuagint

You get some idea of how far Hellenization went if the Hebrew Bible had to be translated for the first time into another language. It is the Septuagint, the Translation of the Seventy, and it made the Bible accessible to all. But the rabbis proclaimed a fast day to commemorate its completion in order to stress how sad it was that the holiest text for the Jews needed another language for it to be understood.

Pulpit Story

Tradition has it that in order to ensure an accurate Greek translation of the Hebrew Bible, the Greeks took 70 rabbinic scholars and placed them on 70 separate islands. They then demanded a translation from every one of them—and lo and behold a miracle occurred: their translated texts proved to be identical.

The modern version of the story has it that a far greater miracle would have occurred had the 70 Jews been placed all together in one room and *then* agreed upon one translation!

More Greek Than the Greeks

Greek lifestyle was guided primarily by the philosophy of the Epicureans, who taught that pleasure was the chief goal of life: "Eat, drink, and be merry for tomorrow you may die." Morality is foolish and immortality nonexistent. The views of Epicurius were totally antithetical to those of the Torah. And that's why to this very day a Jew who renounces the Law—or is a heretic of any kind—is called an *apikorus*, a Yiddish variant of an Epicurean.

Some Jews became so enamored of Hellenic culture that, as new converts to any cause invariably tend to do, they became more Greek than the Greeks. For the price of being accepted, they tried not only to ape their conquerors, but to outdo them in anything that smacked of the Greek way of life. They became known as Hellenists. Jews who felt they had a greater obligation to their own traditions and to preserve their prophetic past called themselves Hasidim (not to be confused with the much later disciples of the Hasidic movement), from the Hebrew word *hassid,* meaning pious. (For more about the Hasidim of our times, see Chapter 18, "Saving Our Souls: Spiritual Responses to Persecution.")

Had assimilation remained simply a matter of personal choice, who knows which of these groups would have proved to be the dominant voice of the Jewish people. Maybe we ought to be thankful for the change that turned force rather than friendship into official policy so that the Hasidim could muster sufficient support to fight against the disappearance of the Jewish people.

"If I Had a Hammer"—the Maccabees

Where Alexander had used tolerance, Antiochus Epiphanes decided on terror. Ruler of the Seleucid Empire, remnant of Alexander the Great's world kingdom, Antiochus decided he could hellenize his subjects by edict and get all the Jews to worship Jupiter simply by placing a statue of this god in the Temple.

Yenta's Little Secrets

People back in those days didn't have last names, but Antiochus gave himself the title Epiphanes, which is Greek for "god manifest." He would definitely not win the award for most humble man of the year. The great irony is that the only people who today remember this man who considered himself god are the Jews, who mention him by way of recording his inglorious defeat at their hands.

Aha, That's It

The word *Maccabee* in Hebrew means hammer. The word alludes to the strength of the members of the family of Mattathias and his sons, and in particular of Judah, their leader. Another more intriguing explanation is that *Maccabee* is a contraction of the first letters of their battle cry, "Mi camocha baeilim," or "Who is like unto Thee, O Lord?"

What a fool not to realize a strange quirk of human nature. Welcome Jews to play in the Olympics and they'll be embarrassed by their obvious circumcision and attempt with most painful surgery to undo it. Tell them that they are forbidden to circumcise themselves and they will fight to the death to protect their right to preserve religious practice.

Antiochus outlawed not only circumcision, but also the observance of the Sabbath and even possession of the Bible. He had his officers sacrifice pigs at the Temple, the ultimate symbol of the unclean in the place of the Holy of Holies. And that still wasn't enough. He sent his soldiers from town to town to order the local Jewish leaders to offer sacrifices of swine to the pagan gods. Even for many Hellenists that was too much.

In the town of Modi'in, an elderly priest Mattathius refused to carry out this order. With a daring that seems incredible in retrospect he, together with his five sons, instigated a rebellion against the might of the empire. No one in his right mind would have given this group of rebels, known as the Maccabees, the slightest chance for victory. That's why, when they won, the Jews called it a miracle, and to this day they celebrate the holiday of Hanukkah to commemorate it.

The First Oil Shortage

Judah the Maccabee "hammered" away at the Syrian Greeks until they sued for peace. In December of 164 B.C.E.—according to the Hebrew calendar, the 25th day of Kislev—the Jews returned to the Temple, removed all forms of foreign worship, and rededicated the Sanctuary once more to their God. The only problem they faced seems so minor it's remarkable they even took note of it. But it, rather than the military victory, became the focus of the way in which Jews celebrate Hanukkah.

As part of the ritual, the Maccabees had to light the *menorah*, the candelabra in the Temple. They only had kosher (pure) oil sufficient for one day's supply, and it would take them eight days to obtain a fresh, usable batch. They lit what they had and, to their amazement, found that the little cruse of oil that should have been enough only for one day lasted for eight. The first oil shortage in recorded history was solved by divine intervention!

It was a fitting conclusion to the story of their unbelievable military victory. It proved that God was really behind the scenes all along, allowing them and the Jewish people, just like the oil, to survive much longer than possible by the principles of natural law.

Yenta's Little Secrets

To celebrate Hanukkah, Jews must not only light a menorah of eight candles to remember the miraculous burning of the oil for eight days, they also must place this menorah by the window or door for public display. The law demands that they "publicize the miracle." It isn't enough to not assimilate and to remain a Jew. Jews must be ready to proclaim their identity to the world and show they aren't ashamed of being Jewish.

A collection of Hanukkah lamps, menorot, used to celebrate the "Festival of Light."
(Courtesy of Jewish Museum/Art Resource, NY)

One more thing about oil, the rabbis noted. All other liquids easily mix, blend, assimilate with other liquids. Oil is unique. Try to mix it with water and it separates, and rises to the top. The encounter with Hellenism in which Judaism almost perished via assimilation, is appropriately brought to conclusion with a miracle that involves oil, symbol of that which refuses to assimilate.

Hanukkah Isn't a Jewish Christmas

Hanukkah was lucky in one way, very unlucky in another. Occurring in December, it invariably is next-door neighbor to Christmas. And that's how it got to be the most popular and the most observed of all Jewish holidays. Don't worry, says the anxious Jewish parent, you too have a Santa Claus and will get your presents just like your friends. Maybe there's even what people call a "Hanukkah bush" so that the Jewish kids don't have to feel different. All to celebrate a holiday proclaiming that Jews are different and were miraculously able to stop the process of assimilation!

How's this for an irony: The two ways in which the word *Maccabee* still finds expression today are as the name of a popular beer in Israel, Maccabi, and the title of the Jewish Olympic games held in Israel, the Maccabiah, a modern-day reminder of the ancient Greek Olympic games, played in Tel Aviv since 1923!

For those who still think that Hanukkah is the Jewish Christmas, it's only fair to point out that the story of Hanukkah preceded the birth of Jesus by 164 years. More significantly, the Jews at that time were *the only monotheists in the world*. If Judaism had been destroyed, Christianity and Islam probably would never have come into being. Who knows—instead of Jews celebrating Christmas, maybe Christians should begin celebrating Hanukkah as recognition to the Jews for helping to make Christianity possible.

The Least You Need to Know

➤ The Greeks were a threat to Jewish survival not because of their persecution, but because of their pervasive culture.

➤ Many Jews came under the sway of Epicureanism and the ideal of "the holiness of beauty," as opposed to the Jewish tradition of "the beauty of holiness."

➤ For the first time the Bible was translated into another language, Greek, in the Septuagint.

➤ When Hellenism began to impose itself by force, the Jews responded with the rebellion of the Maccabees.

➤ The rededication of the Temple was accompanied by a miracle of oil lasting far longer than naturally possible, a fitting symbol for the unnatural survival of the Jewish people.

➤ The story of Hanukkah precedes the story of Christmas by over a century, and it's a commemoration of the victory of monotheism over paganism.

Romans and the (Jewish) Christian Messiah

For the Jews, the Greeks were seductive; the Romans, sadistic. The Greeks came with culture; the Romans with crosses. Greece wanted Jews to pay homage to their way of life; Rome wanted the Jews to pay heavy taxes to their emperor. Greece brought to Judah the ideal of the mind. Rome brought to Judah veneration of the sword.

The major fear Jews faced when they first encountered Hellenism was assimilation. With the coming of Pompeii and Julius Caesar, they were far more worried about annihilation. Rome renamed Judah "Judea," turned it into a Roman milk cow for taxes, and made corruption, cruelty, and terror the norm. Jews had to take refuge in their only antidote for total despair: Belief that surely, this, the worst of all possible times, must be the moment for the arrival of the Messiah.

Where Is the Messiah?

The English word *messiah* comes from the Hebrew *mashiach*, meaning "the anointed." Its Greek counterpart is *christos*. It refers to a savior sent by God to redeem His people and bring about the divinely destined time for universal peace and acknowledgment of the one God by all of mankind.

The prophets Ezekiel and Enoch had long before spoken of the eventual Last Judgment and of the Resurrection. The prophet Zechariah had promised that the day would come when "the Lord will be one and His name will be one." Isaiah predicted a supernatural redeemer who would bring the enemies of Israel to justice and who would usher in an era of the Kingdom of God on earth.

All of these great men could not have been mistaken. Messiah is a belief so ingrained in the Jewish psyche that it would eventually come to be formulated by the great Jewish sage Maimonides as one of the thirteen major beliefs of the Jewish religion.

Yenta's Little Secrets

"Just before the Messiah's advent, insolence will increase and honor dwindle...the government will turn to heresy...scholarship will degenerate, piety will be scorned...youths will be impudent...and a man's enemies will be the members of his own household."

This is from a mystic tradition in the Talmud. Now open today's newspapers. What do you think? Are we close to the Messianic Age?

No date was ever specified for his arrival. But there was one clue clearly known as the condition for his coming: In a time when all hope seems lost, God will step in—at the very last moment—and send His Deliverer. With thousands breathing their last painful breaths on crosses, with Jews being transported to Rome to serve as entertainment while being devoured by lions, with children torn from their mothers' breasts to be sold into slavery as payment for exorbitant taxes, a mood of consensus swept the land that the end of days was near, because "if not now, when?"

"My Kingdom Is Not of This World"—The Essenes

One group in particular committed itself to preparing for the imminent arrival of the Messiah. They were known as the Essenes, and they were so certain that redemption was just around the corner that they renounced normal life and formed communes to wait for the miraculous coming. They gave up property and wealth in the belief that their "kingdom is not of this world." They preached celibacy, a practice they knew would have doomed them if they had to think ahead to future generations. But they were certain that they would very shortly be transported into a nonphysical world. With regard to the Romans, they taught pacifism—turn the other cheek to your enemies—because there is no need for man to do anything when God Himself will very shortly carry out His will.

The Dead Sea Scrolls Are Alive

The reason we know so much about the Essenes is because of an incredible find in 1947, a find regarded as one of the most important archeological discoveries in all of history.

It was a Bedouin looking for a stray goat who ended up unlocking the secret of the birth of one of the world's major religions. In ancient pottery, hidden in a cave by the Dead Sea, he found scrolls of parchment with what turned out to be ancient Hebrew writing on them. They were Essene religious manuscripts dating back to about 200 B.C.E. The cave was an Essene *genizah,* and the scrolls revealed a religious doctrine that clearly served as inspiration and guide to the most famous Essene of all, the man Jesus—accepted by many (but not by Jews) as Christ, the longed-for Messiah.

Aha, That's It

Genizah, from the Hebrew for "hidden away," refers to a storage house for religious manuscripts. Jewish law forbids destroying holy texts. Old, used, or even unfit scrolls of Torah or writings with the name of God upon them can't simply be trashed. They must be given the same respect due to a human being who has passed away; they must be buried.

A close-up of pieces of the Dead Sea scroll called "The Manual of Discipline." (Courtesy of Corbis-Bettmann)

Aha, That's It

Pharisees, from the Hebrew *perushim*, literally means "separatists." This was the group who couldn't go along with the Essenes in their extreme views of withdrawal from life and instead stressed the ongoing interpretation of the written law by the Oral Law that subsequently became the basis for the Talmud.

Sage Sayings

"Each time he hears Jews groan, he tries to break his chains—but God has vowed not to release him (the Messiah) till the Jews tear the chains from his hands."

—Shalom Asch

Fight Or Flight?

While the Essenes preached pacifism—wait and God will take care of everything—others opted for what would become identified with a far more Jewish, Talmudically sanctioned approach. God helps those who help themselves, and Jews would always be reminded that one is not permitted to rely upon a miracle. Man must begin the task and only then will God complete it. Waiting for God, like waiting for Godot, is a pointless exercise in futility. Even Messiah himself doesn't come unless we pave the way for him.

And so if the Essenes chose flight, moving out of cities to patiently await redemption while they sat on their hands, the Zealots, drawn from the ranks of the Pharisees, preached patriotism, open opposition to Rome, and the use of arms to fight against their oppressors. The Zealots also prayed to God, but they took along their swords to help make their prayers come true.

The Jews now had two major groups intent on removing their Roman shackles. The activist Zealots hoped they would someday win the war. Jesus, the pacifist, came and said the war was already won with his coming.

Jesus the Jew

To talk about Jesus historically requires tremendous sensitivity—sensitivity to those who regard him as God and sensitivity to those who are unjustly accused of his death. Jews need to speak with respect about someone whom so many revere as the Son of God and Messiah. And Christians need to grasp why Jews can never agree with them about Jesus. The starting point for any rational conversation has to be the recognition (which strangely enough still comes as a shock to many Christians) that Jesus was born a Jew, lived a Jew, and died a Jew.

As Pere Hyacinthe, the founder of the Christian Catholic Church of Switzerland, pointed out, "It is an historic fact that he [Jesus] instituted no rite, no sacrament, no Church. Born a Jew, he wished to live and to die as a Jew, and from the swaddling clothes of circumcision to the embalmed shroud of sepulcher, he followed only the rites of his religion." Yes, Jesus was circumcised. Yes, he studied Torah. Yes, he observed the mitzvot—the Commandments.

Pilate washing his Hands

Jesus before Pilate (who washes his hands), high priests, and Roman soldiers. Mosaic. (Courtesy of Culver Pictures)

Someone who hated the Jews as much as Voltaire did nevertheless came to this conclusion: "If it were permitted to reason consistently in religious matters, it is clear that we all ought to become Jews because Jesus was born a Jew, lived a Jew, died a Jew, and he said expressly that he was fulfilling the Jewish religion."

That's why Jesus can be accepted, even by Jews, as a great teacher of morality and ethics. One of the greatest rabbis of the eighteenth century, Jacob Emden, didn't hesitate to say, "The Nazarene brought a double kindness on the world: He supported the Torah of Moses with full strength, and he sought to perfect gentiles with ethical qualities." Where Jews differ with Christians is not so much about Jesus; it's far more about Christ.

Sage Sayings

"If Christians were Christians, there would be no anti-Semitism. Jesus was a Jew. There is nothing that the ordinary Christian so dislikes to remember as this awkward historical fact. But it happens, nonetheless, to be true."

—John Haynes Holmes, Protestant theologian and minister (1879–1964)

117

Jesus the Messiah

Jews more than anyone else wanted Jesus' claim that he was the Messiah to be true. Perhaps during his lifetime there were even many Jews ready to become his disciples. But with his death, Jews were forced to reject the claim of Jesus (or, perhaps more correctly, that of his followers) for two powerful reasons:

Sage Sayings

"The Jew believes in the religion of Jesus; he cannot bring himself to accept the religion about Jesus."

—Charles Fagnani,
American clergyman

1. Jesus did not fulfill the messianic requirement to restore the national sovereignty of the Jewish people in the land of Israel and to gather in all the exiles.

2. Jesus did not fulfill the messianic criteria to bring about God's universal kingdom of justice and peace on earth.

Christians say, true, he didn't do those things, but he will when he returns once more. Jews say, if he didn't do them then, he wasn't the one. And if he does come back and performs what a messiah must do, we'll be happy to call him, or anyone else who then accomplishes the job, the real Messiah.

Jesus as God

The greatest divide of all between Judaism and Christianity—the concept that ensured the two would never be able to meet in compromise—is the doctrine that this Messiah was not only God's messenger, but God Himself in human form. For the Jew, the very meaning of monotheism is negated when a spiritual, invisible God is replaced by, or put in partnership with, mortal form. And most significantly of all, death denies divinity, for doesn't saying God died on the cross prove he wasn't really God at all?

The Cruci-fiction

Jews have a lot of problems with the way Christians deal with the death of their God aside from the theological ones—that as God he certainly could have stopped what was happening if he didn't want it to happen, and as an immortal God, he surely didn't stop "living," no matter what happened on the cross. But what bothers them most are two questions about the role Christians have assigned to the Jews with regard to the crucifixion.

Blaming the Jews for Jesus' Death

The first is why Jews have been blamed for centuries for something they didn't do. It was the Romans who put Jesus to death. It was the Romans who crucified him, a penalty never practiced by the Jewish people. It was the Romans who held a "trial" at a time on the eve of the festival of Passover when it is forbidden by Jewish law to hold court proceedings. It was the Romans who were afraid of the political ramifications caused by a man who called himself "King of the Jews." How strange indeed to accuse the very people who had given the world a God and whose whole life was inspired by devotion to God with the crime of deicide!

Blaming Future Jewish Generations

More even than that, what the Jews could also never grasp was why generation after generation was held liable for something that occurred long ago in the past. The Bible itself, the Bible that the Christians also hold sacred as the word of God, teaches: "Children shall not be put to death for the sins of parents, nor parents for the sins of children." What crime could the Jews of the *shtetl* in Poland, centuries later, be personally guilty of to warrant pogroms in retribution for the death of Jesus?

It took close to two thousand years for the Church, with the voice of Pope John Paul II, to set Jewish minds at ease with his long-awaited declaration:

> No ancestral or collective blame can be imputed to the Jews as a people for what happened in Christ's passion. Not indiscriminately to the Jews of that time, nor to those who came afterward, nor to those of today. So any alleged theological justification for discriminatory measures or, worse still, for acts of persecution, is unfounded. The Lord will judge each one "according to his works," Jews and Christians alike. (From a speech delivered on April 13, 1986 in Rome's Central Synagogue as he addressed the Jewish community of Rome.)

Thank God. After all, Jews aren't really guilty. But just imagine how many Jewish lives could have been saved if the papal verdict of acquittal would have come in just a little bit sooner!

The Least You Need to Know

➤ The terrible times of Roman persecution stirred an intense desire for Godly intervention with the coming of the Messiah.

➤ The Essenes, a sect whose religious teachings were revealed through the remarkable discovery of the Dead Sea Scrolls, preached pacifism, celibacy, and the imminent arrival of the Savior.

➤ The Zealots represented the opposing view to that of the Essenes, teaching the need for human initiative and military action in conjunction with faith in God.

➤ Jesus was a Jew who preached the ethical ideas of the Bible, together with the interpretations he learned from his association with the Essenes or that he introduced on his own initiative.

➤ Jesus is rejected as Messiah by the Jews because he did not accomplish what a messiah is expected to accomplish.

➤ Jesus was put to death by the Romans, not the Jews, and after 2,000 years, the Vatican at last officially acknowledged that the Jews are not to be blamed for the death of their Lord.

The Talmud Instead of the Temple

In ancient Rome, at the beginning of the Common Era (which, you'll recall, is the way the Jews refer to the time after the birth of Jesus), the lunatics took charge of the asylum. More often than not, the emperors were not only drunk, but literally insane with power. Caligula was crazy as a loon. The Caesars called themselves gods, divine and immortal, and then died unnatural deaths with surprising frequency. To live as their subjects meant you could be sure of only two things: death and taxes.

The Jews remembered only too well how they had fallen under Roman rule. Two brothers, descendants of the Maccabean dynasty, fought over the throne of Judah. Unable to settle the matter between themselves, they turned to Rome for a decision. Stupid, stupid, stupid! Rome decided in favor of Rome, and the Jews lost their independence. When puppets of Rome, like King Herod (please don't call this mass murderer "the Great") and the procurators who followed him made life intolerable, the Jews finally rebelled. A small people took on the might of the Roman empire. The results were predictable and catastrophic.

Yenta's Little Secrets

King Herod was a descendant of people who were forced to convert to Judaism. It was the only time that Jews forcibly missionized, and the result was tragic. That may very well be why conversion is such a touchy topic for Jews. When done out of conviction, the convert is to be the most admired of Jews—he or she is a "Jew by choice," not merely "by birth." But to force anyone to accept a belief system they don't really feel in their hearts runs counter to the Jewish idea that the greatest gift God gave to man was free will, the ability to make one's own decisions.

The Ninth of Av—Again

What was amazing was how long it took Rome to put down the uprising. The Jews had only some 23,000 fighting men. Rome had 60,000 of the most superbly trained and equipped soldiers of the time. Consider this: Alexander the Great had 32,000 soldiers to create his vast empire; Caesar had less than 25,000 to conquer all of Gaul and Britain; but Nero had to dispatch Vespasian, his greatest general, and finally bring his force up to 80,000 before Vespasian's son Titus could finally vanquish the Jews in Jerusalem and torch their Temple!

Judaea Copta coin: Emperor Vespasian. Rome, 71 C.E. (Courtesy of Jewish Museum/Art Resource, NY)

It took four years from start to finish, but eventually it was over. And when the Jews looked at their calendars, they recoiled with horror at the realization that the Temple went up in flames on the ninth day of Av—in Hebrew *Tisha b'Av—exactly* the same day on which their first Temple had been destroyed.

What did this amazing coincidence mean? Clearly it proved that it was no coincidence! God must have been behind these two great tragedies. And when the rabbis and scholars thought about it, they came to a conclusion that is embedded in Jewish tradition as the real cause for this disaster. The Jews didn't lose because of Rome's superior might, but rather because of their own spiritual failings. And the sin they were guilty of? The Midrash says it clearly: "The second Temple was destroyed only because of the unwarranted, needless hatred between Jew and fellow Jew."

Sage Sayings

"The Temple was destroyed only because of needless, undeserved hatred between Jews. It will only be rebuilt because of needless, undeserved love—when Jews show their concern for others, even when they differ from them in their values, ideas, and levels of observance."

—Rabbi Abraham Isaac Kook, former chief rabbi of Israel

"Judea Capta"—Hip! Hip! Hurrah!

It really looked bad for the Roman empire that a small people could cause so much trouble. Afraid that the Jewish rebellion might set some sort of precedent, the Romans went out of their way to glorify their victory. To cover up their tremendous losses, they staged a huge, spectacular, triumphal parade back in Rome. They struck special coins to commemorate their victory. They built the magnificent Triumphal Arch of Titus—an honor usually reserved for remembering successful battles over the mightiest nations against incredible odds. And on the Arch of Titus they wrote the words *Judea Capta*, Judea is destroyed. They even created a cheer: "Hip! Hip!" Ever wonder what that means? It stands for the initial letters of *Hierosolyma Est Perdita*, Latin for "Jerusalem is destroyed."

Yenta's Little Secrets

Whenever German knights headed a Jew hunt in the Middle Ages, they ran, shouting "Hip! Hip!" as if to say "Jerusalem is destroyed." The final "hurrah" probably comes from the Sclovanic *hu-raj* (to paradise) so that the shout, "Hip! Hip! Hurrah," means "Jerusalem is lost to the infidels, and we are on the road to paradise." That's probably not what you have in mind when you cheer on your favorite team, but once you know the derivation, it makes sense not to repeat it.

The monument was meant to prove that once and for all the story of the Jewish people had finally come to a close. And oh yes, the Arch of Titus is a "must-see" tourist stop for every Jew who happens to visit Rome today.

The Messiah Who Wasn't: Simon bar Kochba

Over 600,000 Jews were killed or died from starvation and disease during the siege of Jerusalem in the year 70 C.E. Yet another 600,000 were taken away as captives and slaves, according to the Roman historian, Tacitus.

Surely you would think, as the Romans did, that they would never again be bothered by these strange people who believed in one God. But defeat was something the Jews just couldn't accept. It went not only against their deepest hopes, but seemingly also against the words of their prophets. And so, when in 132 C.E., a mighty military hero inspired the masses to yet another rebellion, the people believed that Simon bar Kochba was at last their long-awaited Messiah.

Yenta's Little Secrets

In Aramaic "*bar*" means son. The Hebrew equivalent is "*ben.*" Jews to this day are called for Torah honors by their Hebrew name, so-and-so, son of so-and-so (compare it to the Irish McDonald—son of Donald). Simon bar Kochba's name was really bar Kozeba, Simon the son of Kozeba. But because everyone thought that he would be their "shining star," they called him bar Kochba, "son of a star." Too bad it was only a shooting star.

Even Rabbi Akiva, the greatest scholar of his day, was misled. He encouraged the people to follow this "messiah"—and he paid for it with his life. Together with nine other of the most prominent sages, he was cruelly tortured to death. Bar Kochba held out a while longer, but in 135 C.E., he and his followers were brutally butchered at the final battle in Betar. The blood of the victims, murdered men, women, and children, flowed, it was said, for a mile into the nearby sea. And the date on which this happened at Betar to bring the rebellion to a close? The ninth of Av!

Yenta's Little Secrets

The story of the ten martyrs and the horrible deaths they endured is read in every Jewish synagogue throughout the world two times a year: on Tisha b'Av, the ninth of Av, and on Yom Kippur, the Day of Atonement. We connect their deaths with the destruction of the Temple; the death of holy individuals is as tragic as the disappearance of a holy house. And on the day that Jews ask for forgiveness of sins, we plead that God take into account the suffering of His pious servants and add their merits to His people.

Rabbi Akiva, Sage and Scholar

Rabbi Akiva began his life as a shepherd with no education. When at age 40 he fell in love and was told by his beloved Rachel that she would only marry him on condition that he studied Torah, it seemed an impossible task until one day, when he came across a stone that was hollowed out by falling drops of water. He said to himself, "If water, which is soft, can hollow out a stone, which is hard, drop by drop, how much more would the words of the Torah, which are hard, be able to cut through and make an impression on my heart, which is soft?" Starting literally from scratch, Akiva became not only the greatest of scholars, but also the symbol of how much can be accomplished even later in life with sincere application and effort.

The Death of Rabbi Akiva

As Rabbi Akiva was being tortured with incredible cruelty, his students observed him reciting the words of the Jewish prayer, *Shema Yisrael*—"Hear O Israel, the Lord our God, the Lord is one." Unable to imagine how anyone could reach that level of piety, they asked their master how he could say the Shema even as he maintained a smile on his lips.

His response was, "All my life, when I said the words, 'You shall love the Lord your God with all you heart, with all your soul, with all your might,' I was saddened for I thought when will I be able to fulfill this command? I have loved God with all my heart and with all my might, but I did not know if I would be able to love him with all my soul, until death. Now that I am giving my life, and the hour for reciting Shema has come, and my resolution remains firm, should I not smile?" And with the recitation of Shema Israel, his soul departed.

"We'd Rather Be Dead"—the Tragedy of Masada

No Jerusalem and no Temple. But with the end of the Great Revolt in the year 70 C.E., there was still one fighting force left in the fortress of Masada near the Dead Sea. They had fled Jerusalem and held out for three years on top of an enormous rock. But Rome couldn't allow these last 960 Jews to survive. An entire Roman legion went after them, fully expecting a prize of slaves and prostitutes. But when the Romans finally took Masada, all they found were corpses. Elazar ben Yair, leader of this group of Zealots, preceded Patrick Henry with the idea of, "Give me liberty or give me death." Rather than becoming servants to Rome, he convinced his colleagues to take their own lives and die as free men.

The Fortress of the Zealots, site of the ancient battle at Masada, which ended in mass suicide. (Courtesy of Priit Vesilind/ National Geographic)

Masada became a symbol. Unfortunately its real message can sometimes be confusing. Suicide is not an acceptable Jewish solution. What should remain as inspiration from that tragic event is the idea put in the form of an oath taken by Israeli soldiers today on that spot, "Masada shall not fall again."

The Letters That Flew to Heaven

Among the ten martyrs was Rabbi Hanina ben Teradion. His "crime" was that he had been found teaching Torah, strictly forbidden by the Romans. With fiendish ingenuity, they wrapped his body in a parchment scroll of the Torah, soaked him with wool and water to make him burn more slowly, and put him, together with the Torah, to the torch.

As life slowly ebbed from him, his students begged him to tell them his final vision. With magnificent imagery he said, "I see parchment burning—but letters flying to the heavens." The truth he shared with his dying words was that a physical text may be burnt, but its message is immortal; a scroll can be consumed, but its contents will continue to be recalled forever. And indeed Hanina's students, as well as the Jewish people, were to discover that he was right!

Give Me One Wish

A very great rabbi, Yochanan ben Zakai had come to the same conclusion years before and done something remarkable because of it. The story reads like an implausible B movie. It was in 68 C.E. when General Vespasian had captured Judea, but not yet Jerusalem. The city was totally under siege and no one could go in or out. Yochanan ben Zakai knew that militarily the Jews were lost; it was just a question of time. But he had a plan to save the Jewish people. He was crazy enough to believe that he could get the enemy commander to agree to it. And, guess what, he did!

He had his disciples spread the news that he died. His students mourned, tore their clothes in grief, and carried their "dead" rabbi to the gates of Jerusalem. They got permission to carry him through to be buried outside of the holy city. Then the rabbi, very much alive, went to personally meet with General Vespasian in order to share with him a prediction and a request.

The prediction? That Vespasian would shortly become emperor of Rome. Either a very lucky guess or divine intuition. The request? One little favor, "Give me Yavneh and its wise men." Allow me and a few disciples to establish a small school of Jewish learning. What a small wish for such a wondrous prediction. General Vespasian very soon did become emperor and granted it. And at the same time that he was making plans to finally annihilate the Jewish people, he was sowing seeds for their continued growth, survival, and eventual supremacy over the decaying Roman Empire!

The Mission and the Mishnah

The mission of the Jew, as the prophet Isaiah put it, was to be "a light unto the nations." In order to do that they had to live by the Law, study the Law, and always hold it dear as their chief treasure. The Law was no less than the Will of God. And for centuries, the text of the Torah was transmitted with an even larger body of commentary and interpretation known as the "Oral Law."

Aha, That's It

Mishnah means repetition. The Mishnah "repeats" the laws and the ideas of the Torah, but in far more elaborate form. Jewish mystics have noted a remarkable fact: the Hebrew letters of the word Mishnah, when rearranged, make the word *neshama*—soul. They claim it's not a coincidence because the Mishnah is the very soul, the essence of the body of written law.

Why Oral Law?

Just as the Jews worshipped a book, they observed a remarkable rule: some things were not permitted to be written down, but had to be transmitted orally from generation to generation. And there was true genius behind this law, for a number of reasons:

➤ The Bible as text was closed in 444 B.C.E. With Oral Law it could continue to be "open," constantly refreshed, revitalized, and reinterpreted. It would be as alive as its students and as responsive to contemporary needs as its ever-changing disciples.

➤ Books are cold and dead objects; teachers are warm and alive. If a text would suffice, you could just be sent to your room with it. But if you needed the additional explanation of Oral Law, you had to have a teacher. And a teacher would care about you, inspire you, and present you not only with rules, but also with a role model.

➤ A book could be misunderstood, misinterpreted, read in many different ways. That's why the expression goes, "reduced to writing." Oral Law meant there would always be someone alongside you to make sure you understood it the way in which it was intended.

➤ Oral Law was a way of clarifying biblical texts for their proper legal meaning. The Bible said, "an eye for an eye" to show how serious the crime was of blinding another. You really *deserve* to get your eye removed if you did that to another person. But that's not what the law will really decide. The Written Law tells you what *should* happen to you; the Oral Law clarifies what *will* happen to you. The strictness of the text, which is meant as severe warning, is modified by rabbinic commentary that adds legal compassion.

➤ And do you think a book will catch you beginning to nod off and doze and get you back to studying? The Oral Law ensured that Torah would be taught with teachers who could wake you when needed, even as they made sure you fully understood what they were trying to teach you. (Do you get what I'm saying? Hello...hello...are you there?)

For all of these reasons, the Oral Law was just what it implied, an oral tradition, never reduced to writing.

Putting Words on Paper

So why did Rabbi Yehuda HaNassi disregard all this and turn the teachings of the Oral Law into the text of the Mishnah, the book of Written Law? Why did that which was never supposed to be written down become the longest and largest book of religious teachings for the Jewish people? The answer will probably surprise you. It was a compromise with reality.

Rabbi Yehuda HaNassi, in the second century C.E., realized that the Jews, after the destruction of their Temple, were on their way to exile and dispersion. Teachers would no longer always be available. A text would have to do as a better-than-nothing replacement. Yehuda prayed that he would be forgiven for his deed, and penned the first portion of the most important book in Judaism after the Bible.

Yenta's Little Secrets

At the close of the Passover meal, the *Seder*, there is a nursery rhyme that asks who knows the meaning of a string of numbers. "Who knows one," goes the first question, to which the correct answer is, "I know one. One is our God in the heavens and on earth." For "Who knows two," the correct response is, "Two are the tablets...; three are the patriarchs, Abraham, Isaac and Jacob...; four are the matriarchs Sarah, Rebecca, Rachel and Leah...; five are the books of Moses...." And now you know six—six are the orders of the Mishnah.

The Six Orders

The Mishnah was the first logically arranged, clear, and systematic exposition of the Oral Law that existed to that time. The books of Moses on which it was based consisted of five volumes. Perhaps that's why Yehuda HaNassi divided the Mishnah into six orders, subject headings, or books, to show that this was an extension of the Torah text. The different titles give a small indication of the vast scope of the work:

1. *Zera'im* (seeds) deals with all the agricultural rules and laws for foods, as well as all blessings

2. *Nezikin* (damages) summarizes civil and criminal law

3. *Nashim* (women) examines all the issues between men and women, including marriage, divorce, and sexual relations

4. *Moed* (holiday) deals with all the rituals for Sabbath and all the Jewish holidays

5. *Kodashim* (holy things) concerns laws of sacrifices and ritual slaughter

6. *Taharot* summarizes the laws of ritual purity and impurity

The laws of the Mishnah deal with nothing less than life itself in every possible aspect—from the mundane to the sacred, from the normal to the perverse, from the daily to the most incredible, from the moral to the criminal, from the rituals that deal with people's relationships with God to the social behavior that prescribes their relationships with fellow humans.

It was the Mishnah that made clear the most fundamental teaching of Judaism: Judaism is not a religion that tells you how to worship God in a temple, but a religion that teaches you how to live your life with an awareness of God wherever you may be, and whatever you are doing.

The Finishing Touch: The Talmud

The Mishnah was written in Hebrew in the land of Israel. It was studied, discussed, commented upon, analyzed, and elaborated in schools of higher learning called *yeshivas* for the next 300 years. Somehow these discussions, discussions that at the time were another example of Oral Law, were remembered and recorded because of the fear that they might otherwise be forgotten. Finally they were compiled as one large major work, the Gemarrah, and joined together with the Mishnah to form the book of the Talmud. The authors, Rabina and Rav Ashi, completed their work in Babylonia about 500 C.E., and the result is the 63 tractates, or books, of the Babylonian Talmud.

Aha, That's It

Gemarrah means completion. It is the text of over 90 percent of the Talmud that records all of the later discussions on the Mishnah.

Imagine a book so vast that if you were to spend a minimum of an hour a day, every day, on a page—which is probably the least you would need to make sense of a work written in Aramaic without any punctuation whatsoever in extremely complex, succinct style—it would take you close to seven and a half years to finish. It would probably surprise you to learn that that's exactly what hundreds of thousands of Jews do on a regular basis, studying the same page, (called *Daf Yomi*, the page of the day) until they finish, so that they can then start all over again the next day with the next page.

It must be quite a book if it can hold the interest of scientists, doctors, merchants, schoolboys, and simple Jews of every profession and calling. Yet, that's what the Talmud has been able to do for all the centuries since it was first written. Jews have studied it religiously—and as a religious act, a *mitzvah*, the fulfillment of a divine commandment.

The Whole Ball of Wax

What's in the Talmud that could possibly be so interesting? Here again, the answer is: Everything.

Talk about blessings and you remember how in *Fiddler On The Roof* they wondered whether there was a blessing for a sewing machine and another for the Czar? Well, the Talmud tells you the proper blessing for hearing thunder, seeing lightning, eating any food, experiencing a miracle—and even a blessing for when you just finish going to the bathroom!

The Talmud tells you how much you need to pay back when you steal (double the amount so that you suffer for your criminal action) and how capital punishment was carried out. It tells you your level of guilt if your ox gores somebody, your dog bites another person, and, by extension, what happens if you didn't check the brakes on your car and it crashes into a building or another vehicle. There is just no limit to the life situations that are part of the Talmud's concerns.

Aha, That's It

Yeshiva, from the word sitting, is the name for a school of higher learning where the scholars and sages "sat" and talked at great length about all the issues in the Talmud. The Jews were the first people in history to make education compulsory for everyone, so no matter where Jews lived, a yeshiva was one of the very first institutions they established.

Sage Sayings

"I am interested in learning Talmud."

—Hillary Rodham Clinton

It isn't even so shocking to read in it the story of the rabbi who was about to perform marital relations with his wife when he discovered his student hiding under his bed. When the rabbi angrily demanded to know what the student was doing intruding on his privacy in such a disrespectful manner, the student, without a trace of embarrassment, justified himself with, "But this too is Torah, and I need to know the proper way." And you know what? If you've studied enough of the Talmud, you believe his answer!

Be Thankful for (Seemingly) Little Things

Don't ever make fun of a blessing. Years ago, I told a group of high school teenagers that there was even a blessing recited after going to the bathroom. They laughed uncontrollably. Several weeks later, one of these students nearly died because his kidney failed to function properly. It wasn't able to excrete the poisons in his body, and it almost killed him. So then we took another look at the prayer and discussed how grateful we ought to be every day of our lives for the magnificent God-given wisdom of our bodies that allows us to function in good health. The class came to be awed by the beauty and majesty of the words of this blessing:

"Blessed are You O Lord our God King of the universe, who fashioned man with wisdom, and created within him many openings and many cavities. It is obvious and known before Your throne of glory that if but one of them were to be ruptured, or if but one of them were to be blocked it would be impossible to survive and to stand before You. Blessed are You, O Lord, who heals all flesh and acts wondrously." And yes, religious Jews say the entire blessing every single time they come out of the bathroom!

Add to this other categories within the Talmud—*halacha,* the law, and *aggadah,* stories with beautiful messages, insights, historic incidents, and even humorous asides—and you begin to get a small feeling for why Jews were prepared to die to preserve the Talmud, and why those who wanted to destroy the Jewish people felt it necessary to burn it.

The Ethics of the Fathers

Okay, I know this is a long chapter, but I can't leave the Talmud without saying just a little bit more about one of its most beautiful portions. There is a small section, just six chapters, that captures probably more than any other work, the essence of the Jewish spirit, culture, religion, and ethic. Its sayings are short, to the point, and lend themselves to memorization and repetition. Most of them have become proverbs that often roll off the lips of Jews. Hopefully they also serve to guide their lives.

How many of these have you heard or wish you had heard?

Say little and do much.

Don't judge your fellow man until you are in his place.

Don't say I will study when I have time, lest you never find the time.

It is not your responsibility to finish the work, but you are not free to desist from it either.

The world rests on three things: on Torah study, on prayer, and on the doing of kind deeds.

If I am not for myself who will be for me, and if I am for myself, what am I? And if not now, when?

Do not separate yourself from the community.

Who is wise? He who learns from every person. Who is strong? He who subdues his personal inclinations. Who is rich? He who is happy with his lot. Who is honored? He who honors others.

Delve in it (the Torah) and continue to delve in it, for everything is in it; look deeply into it; grow old and gray over it and do not stir from it because you can have no better portion than it...and the reward is in proportion to the exertion.

To Study Is Divine

Studying Talmud and Torah became the prime focus of Jewish life. The Age of the Temple was replaced by the Age of the Talmud, and the heroic figure was no longer the priest, but the scholar who mastered its pages. Priesthood was hereditary; scholarship, however, was open to all. So what the Talmud did was to create an aristocracy that for the first time was totally democratic.

This shocking rule of the Talmud best captures its daring vision: "A bastard, child of an illegitimate union, who is a sage, takes precedence (in matters of giving honor) even to a High Priest who is an ignoramus."

The Least You Need to Know

➤ The Ninth day of Av was a day of national tragedy for the Jewish people many times over, suggesting its significance was not merely coincidence, but some divine message.

➤ Masada was a heroic expression of "Give me liberty or give me death," but ultimately was a solution not sanctified by a tradition deeply opposed to suicide.

➤ The Arch of Titus stands as monument to a great empire's misconception that the Jewish people could be forever destroyed.

➤ Even a sage like Rabbi Akiva could mistake a man for the Messiah—with tragic consequences.

➤ Neither suicide nor messiahs would be as successful in preserving Judaism as students in a small school in Yavneh, whose dedication to the Oral Law would lead to the writing of the Mishnah and the Talmud.

➤ The six orders of the Mishnah that became the 63 volumes of the Talmud represent the teachings of Judaism on every subject of life.

➤ The "Ethics of the Fathers" is probably the best short summary of Jewish values, ethics, and morality.

Part 5
The Crescent and the Cross

Get ready to travel. Part 5 picks up with the Jews exiled once more from their land, carrying only the baggage of Bible and Talmud to remind them of their glorious past and their responsibility to the future. Their journeys take them to two different kinds of worlds.

In the world of the crescent, they meet Mohammed and Islam. Strangely enough, there the Jews discover tolerance, culture, love of learning, and intellectual excitement—so much so that they are part of a Golden Age of Jewry.

Unfortunately, their encounter with the second world, the world of the cross, is far less pleasant. With the rise of Christianity in the West come dark ages of bitter religious persecution, unbounded hatred directed specifically to Jews as Christ-killers, Crusades and Inquisitions, blood libels and torture—all in the name of "the religion of love."

"Run for your life" becomes an ongoing mantra, and it is only three major movements—each one emphasizing a different approach to God—that allow the Jews to maintain their sanity. These movements, Mysticism, Messianism, and Hasidism, help to redefine Jewish values, Jewish culture, and the Jewish people to this very day.

Chapter 15

The Crescent of Brotherhood

In This Chapter

➤ How Arab and Jew originally lived as neighbors

➤ Mohammed, his disciples, and their attitude to Jews

➤ The renaissance of the East and how it eventually saved the West

➤ The new kinds of scholars who harmonized the secular and the sacred

➤ The only man ever to be compared with the original Moses

➤ The summary of Jewish belief

Can Jews and Arabs ever live together side by side in peace? The question that plagues present-day politicians in the Middle East doesn't need a prophet for an answer. All it requires is a knowledge of history to realize that not only is it possible, it was already accomplished, and this peace lasted for hundreds of years.

When the Arabs first ruled the world, after the disciples of Mohammed overshadowed the once-mighty Roman Empire, Jews enjoyed one of their most peaceful, creative, productive, and dazzling eras. Philosophers, poets, Biblical interpreters, doctors, astronomers, grammarians, and mathematicians shared the stage with successful merchants, craftsmen, and artisans, as well as diplomats and advisors to the kings. The blessings of tolerance were clearly visible to both Arabs and Jews and proved beyond a doubt that the reward for mutual acceptance is a Golden Age.

Mohammed, Son of Abraham

It all started, strangely enough, with a camel driver. Mohammed (571–632 C.E.), an illiterate orphan, was a remarkable figure. He founded a new religion, inspired thousands of disciples, and changed the world to such an extent that within less than a hundred years his empire embraced half of the then-known world.

Yenta's Little Secrets

Mohammed borrowed a great deal of his teachings from the Jews. He modeled the mosque on the synagogue. He took from the Talmud prayers, forbidden food, circumcision, hygiene, laws for marriage and divorce, and the requirement of studying sacred books. His confession of faith makes clear his inspiration: "We believe in God, and in what has been revealed to us, and what has been revealed to Abraham and Ishmael and Isaac and Jacob, the twelve tribes, and in what was given to Moses and Jesus, and what was given to the prophets by their Lord." So much in common and, ultimately, such a different path for his followers!

Mohammed obtained all of his knowledge of religion from the Torah—"The Book of the Jews." The Jewish patriarchs, Abraham, Isaac, and Jacob, were his heroes, whom he later glorified in the Koran, his self-composed Bible. He loved the stories of Moses and Pharaoh, of Noah and the flood, and the tower of Babel. And because he revered Abraham the most of all the biblical figures, he showed him the ultimate kindness: He made Abraham a Muslim rather than a Jew, and a devout servant of Allah instead of the Jewish God.

Mohammed was sure that the Jews would be thrilled to hear that their religion had taken a new turn and that their God had appointed him as spokesman in place of Moses. When it didn't work out that way, Mohammed turned against the Jews. Happily his hatred was not (at least for a long time) made central to the teachings of his newly established faith. Jews were "part of the family," and they were still respected as—a term the Mohammedans (now known as Muslims, followers of the religion Islam) gave to the Jews—"The People of the Book."

Islam—Friend of the Jews

Today we think of the Christian world as haven for the Jews and the Arab world as hostile. In the beginning of the rise of Islam, it was just the reverse. Christians couldn't stand the fact that the Jews rejected their claim of the divinity of Jesus. Jews, who were closest to Jesus and yet nonbelievers, were despised more than anyone else. But the Arab world at that time had a different standard for measuring people. They divided the world into the intellectual and the ignorant, those interested in science and philosophy, and those incapable of grasping higher truths. By this barometer, Jews for them were in, and Christians were out.

Thus began an incredible link between two people that might still show the way for a new Middle East in the twenty-first century. For as long as Mohammedan civilization encouraged a Jewish Golden Age, it too prospered. The lifespan of the Islamic empire corresponds precisely to the time it extended a warm hand to its Jewish residents. When the Mohammedan empire killed off its Jews, it committed suicide.

Renaissance in Mufti

Those who live in the western hemisphere believe that civilization finds its highest expression in the West. The East is backward, the West the birthplace of true culture and refinement. But such broad assumptions, including this one, are usually wrong. During the Dark Ages, it was Europe that saw the light of reason almost extinguished and the Arab civilization that preserved the lamp of learning.

It was in the ninth and tenth centuries, while the West was reeling from the onslaught of barbarians, that a veritable renaissance took place in Arab countries. It was here that Hellenism and the wisdom of the Greeks were rediscovered. It was here that many cultures intermingled and where Jews were asked to translate the best of Greek and Arab thought into Latin and European languages. The real irony is that culture came back to Europe later by way of the Middle East, and mainly via the hands of Jewish scholars.

Jewish Scholarship Soars

With the openness of their society, as well as the sophistication, scientific spirit, and secular impact of Hellenic culture that was now once again so admired, Jews branched out into many areas that previously had been off-limits to them.

For the first time, a *gaon*, the most prominent leader of Babylonian Jewry, Sadya (892-942), introduced Aristotelianism into Jewish thought. He authored a book of Jewish philosophy, *The Book of Beliefs and Opinions*, that harmonized faith and rationalism, belief, and the free spirit of inquiry. He also wrote a rational analysis of Torah text based on scientific philology.

Aha, That's It

Gaon today means genius. From the eighth century to the decline of Babylonian Jewry, the term was used to describe the spiritual head of all Jews in the land. The gaon answered religious questions from Jews around the world and was usually revered as the supreme religious figure.

Suddenly there were authors who could in all truth be called "Jewish-Hellenic-Arabic-Renaissance-Rabbinic intellectuals"—a mouthful of seeming contradictions that nevertheless blended into a magnificent synthesis of scholarship. It is during this time that we find someone like Abraham Ibn Ezra who wrote magnificent love poetry, a Hebrew grammar book, and a Bible commentary—all still studied by Jews to this day.

A poet-philosopher, Solomon Ibn Gabirol (1021–1070), composed deeply emotional liturgical poems, still chanted in synagogues around the world, as well as a work of philosophy, *Fountain of Life*, published under the pseudonym of Avicebron, which was studied by Thomas Aquinas and had a profound impact on leading Christian scholars.

Yehuda HaLevi (1085–1140) wrote poems, prayers, and a work of philosophy, *The Cuzari*, which dared to pose serious questions of faith—How do we know there is a God? How can we be sure he wrote the Torah? How can we be certain that Judaism is truer than other religions?—and powerfully demonstrated how God could be "proven" by Jewish history.

Spiritual and Intellectual Harmony

What impresses us so much about all of these personalities is their openness, the breadth of their knowledge, the scope of their scholarship, and the harmony they are able to achieve between their active, professional lives and their reverence for the ancient texts and teachings of their religion.

If you think that being a rabbi means closing your mind to the world, read this testament that Hai Gaon (998–1038), the most important Babylonian religious leader of his day, wrote to his son: "I have provided you, too, with books on all the sciences…I have also made exhausting journeys to distant lands and brought for you a teacher of the secular sciences, counting neither the expense nor the dangers of the journey." The cultured Jew in Arab lands studied science and Torah, secular knowledge and holy text, to become a well-rounded intellectual rooted in the teachings of his faith.

From Moses to Moses, None Like Moses

But of all of the scholars, sages, rabbis, philosophers, and great personalities, no one, not a single one, comes even close to the man who stands head and shoulders above every Jew, as the popular saying has it, since Moses himself: "From Moses to Moses, there was no one like Moses." Moses ben Maimon, the *Rambam* (1135–1204), known as Maimonides, seems in retrospect more like a movement than one individual. Is it really possible that one man could have accomplished so much in his lifetime?

Most Influential Sage of the Middle Ages

In 1985, to commemorate the 850th anniversary of his birth, a UNESCO conference was held in Paris, and the Maimonidean scholar Shlomo Pines confidently asserted that "Maimonides is the most influential Jewish thinker of the Middle Ages, and quite possibly of all times." A Soviet scholar, Vitali Naunkin, said at this same gathering, "Maimonides is perhaps the only philosopher in the Middle Ages, perhaps even now, who symbolizes a confluence of four cultures, Greco-Roman, Arab, Jewish, and Western."

140

Moses ben Maimon, Maimonides. The script is his signature, in his own hand. (Courtesy of Corbis–Bettmann)

His writings are a library unto themselves. And yet he lived by the creed of the Talmud, which said that one should not turn Torah into "a spade by which to dig," not to make a living out of religious calling or service to God. So Maimonides became a physician to the Sultan of Egypt and worked long hours every day caring for all the prominent people in the palace. The rest of the time he wrote the books that still serve as the core of the curriculum for every budding Jewish scholar.

Yenta's Little Secrets

What was his real name? Are you confused by the different ways in which we refer to Maimonides? Here's the explanation: "ides" was usually placed at the end of a name, meaning son of. Maimonides therefore means son of Maimon. Giving his first name Moses, he would be called Moses ben (son of) Maimon. But it was also very popular to give important figures a name made from an acronym of the first letters of their name, beginning with the title rabbi. *Rambam* is therefore short for **R**abbi **M**oses **b**en **M**aimon. A man of so many achievements deserves at least three different ways to be remembered, don't you agree?

Maimonides' Great Writings

Just to skim the surface, you should know at least something about Maimonides' major works:

➤ *The Mishnah Torah*. The first code to systematically arrange all the laws scattered throughout the Talmud into a readily available and clear summary of *halacha*, or proper practice.

Aha, That's It

Mishnah Torah literally means a second Torah. The book was meant as a sequel, not—God forbid—to replace, but rather to assist in understanding the Torah and more quickly be able to find the correct law for any situation.

➤ *The Guide to the Perplexed*. A brilliant philosophic work enabling the confused, "perplexed," but serious searcher for truth in understanding God, Torah, and the teaching of the sages in a way that does not contradict reason and the system of thought as taught by the ancient philosophers.

➤ Commentary on the Mishnah. Clarifying that portion of the text that is a springboard for the entire Talmud.

➤ Medical treatises. Many of which are still astounding doctors today with the relevance of their insights and the ingenuity of their approach.

➤ "The Thirteen Principles of Faith." The most concise summary of the basic belief system of Judaism (see below).

Maimonides' Principles of Belief

This list was eventually turned into one of the best-known prayers in the synagogue, the *Yigdal*, and its impact has been so profound that even in this short summary of the Rambam's writings it deserves to be recorded in full.

Ask what a Jew believes and the answer for Maimonides and all those who have repeated his words to this day is the following:

1. I believe with complete faith that the Creator, Blessed is His Name, creates and guides all creatures, and that He alone made, makes, and will make everything.

2. I believe with complete faith that the Creator, Blessed is His Name, is unique, and there is no uniqueness like His in any way, and that He alone is our God, Who was, Who is, and Who always will be.

3. I believe with complete faith that the Creator, Blessed is His Name, is not physical and is not affected by physical phenomena, and that there is no comparison whatsoever to Him.

4. I believe with complete faith that the Creator, Blessed is His Name, is the very first and the very last.

5. I believe with complete faith that the Creator, Blessed is His Name, to Him alone is it proper to pray and it is not proper to pray to any other.

6. I believe with complete faith that all the words of the prophets are true.

7. I believe with complete faith that the prophecy of Moses our teacher, peace upon him, was true, and that he was the father of the prophets—both those who preceded him and those who followed him.

8. I believe with complete faith that the entire Torah now in our hands is the same one that was given to Moses, our teacher, peace be upon him.

9. I believe with complete faith that this Torah will not be exchanged nor will there be another Torah from the Creator, Blessed is His Name.

10. I believe with complete faith that the Creator, Blessed is His Name, knows all the deeds of human beings and their thoughts, as it is said, "He fashions their hearts all together, He comprehends all their deeds."

11. I believe with complete faith that the Creator, Blessed is His Name, rewards with good those who observe His commandments and punishes those who violate His commandments.

12. I believe with complete faith in the coming of the Messiah, and even though he may delay, nevertheless I anticipate every day that he will come.

13. I believe with complete faith that there will be a resuscitation of the dead whenever the wish emanates from the Creator, Blessed is His Name and exalted is His mention, forever and for all eternity.

Yenta's Little Secrets

What gave the Jews faith during the darkest days of the Holocaust? For many it was a song that they sang even as they were led to their deaths. The words were those of the twelfth of Maimonides' "Thirteen Principles of Faith": "I believe in perfect faith in the coming of Messiah." Knowing that the coming of Messiah would be preceded by a time of unprecedented horror, they prayed that their pain would be the prelude to the long-awaited time of the redemption.

Maimonides' Laws of Charity

According to the Rambam, there are good ways to give—and better ways to give. And here they are, in his own words. There are eight degrees in the giving of charity. They are as follows, from the least to the most desirable:

Listen to Your Bubbe

Of the many holy graves, that of Maimonides in Tiberias has always been important for those with special needs who would like the soul of the Rambam to intercede for them in the heavens. Don't miss it on your next trip to Israel. And bring along a prayer book and some money for charity—that's how you ensure your prayers will be answered.

1. He who gives reluctantly or with regret.

2. He who gives less than he should, but gives graciously.

3. He who gives what he should, but only after he is asked.

4. He who gives before he is asked.

5. He who gives without knowing to whom he gives, although the recipient may know the identity of the donor.

6. He who gives without making his identity known.

7. He who gives without knowing to whom he gives, and the recipient not knowing from whom he receives.

8. He who helps a fellow man to support himself by a gift, or a loan, or by finding employment for him, thus helping him to become self-supporting.

Pulpit Stories

The trees, it is said, came before God to complain about the ways of His creation. "Why," they asked, "did you create us and at the very same time allow the creation of an ax that would be used to chop us down and destroy us?"

"You foolish trees," answered God. "Have you never noticed that the ax has a wooden handle? If you would not have first given of yourselves to the enemy, it would be incapable of ever doing you any harm!"

How Book Burning Got Started

There's one last tragic footnote to the life of this second great Moses. Invariably, when a man stands too tall above his contemporaries, there will be those who try to pull him down to their level. Call it envy, stupidity, or the inability to understand what is beyond their capacity. Maybe it can even come as some comfort to heroic figures of every age who have to suffer criticism from mental pygmies of their time to learn that even Maimonides had his detractors.

They couldn't call him ignorant. That would have been ludicrous. So instead they called him arrogant and claimed he dared too much by opening the doors of faith to the inquiring knock of questions. And if the Bible itself spoke of the "hand of God," how could Maimonides call that a metaphor and insist that God has no form of a body and is not corporeal?

Believe it or not there were even some rabbis who decided that the Rambam must be branded an *apikores*, a heretic, and his books were banned. Not content with their edict, which they felt probably wouldn't be followed, they denounced Maimonides' books to the leaders of the French Inquisition who then went ahead and staged a public burning. This was the first time religious books were put to the torch, and it happened because Jews themselves bad-mouthed a Jewish leader.

Just a few years later, the Church started burning the Talmud, a practice continued into the twentieth century by the Nazis. What a powerful illustration of the fact that so often Jews are their own worst enemies.

The Least You Need to Know

➤ Arab lands, unlike Christian countries, were tolerant havens for the Jews in the early centuries.

➤ Mohammed saw himself as a descendant of Abraham and his disciples respected Jews as "The People of the Book."

➤ Science and learning were kept alive during the Dark Ages of Europe by Arab and Jewish scholars who subsequently exported hellenic culture back to the West.

➤ A renaissance of science, scholarship and culture took place under Mohammedan rule, enabling a Jewish Golden Age to coincide with the dominance of Islam.

➤ Of all the great men of that age, the one who stands out above all was Moses ben Maimon, Maimonides, the Rambam.

➤ The most concise and most widely accepted summary of Jewish belief is contained in the 13 Principles of Faith, as recorded by Maimonides.

➤ The burning of holy books began as an expression of Jewish hatred toward a fellow Jew, and ironically later became a practice employed against them by their enemies.

Chapter 16

The Cross of Shame: Western Europe

In This Chapter

➤ The tragic record of Christian cruelty and anti-Semitism

➤ The libels and slanders used to justify persecution

➤ The reason for ghettoes and what they accomplished

➤ The truth about the Crusades, the Crusaders, and the Inquisition

➤ The Marranos and their attempt to save their souls

➤ The inglorious end of the Golden Age of Spanish Jewry and the glorious potential for a new beginning

The boundary that separated the Golden Age of the Jews in Arab lands from other countries was marked with a cross. From the time that Christianity was declared the state religion of the Byzantine Empire by Constantine the Great in the fourth century, Jew hatred became not only national policy in Christian lands, but almost an uncontrollable obsession. After all, what did it say about the Church's claim that Jesus was universally divine if his own people disclaimed him? Jews had to be "saved"—even if Christians had to kill them to do so.

Shortly before his death in 1963, Pope John XXIII composed this prayer: "We realize that our brows are branded with the mark of Cain. Centuries long has Abel lain in blood and tears because we have forgotten Thy love. Forgive us the curse which we unjustly laid on the name of the Jews. Forgive us, that with our curse, we crucified Thee a second time."

Perhaps God will forgive. But for all those who were tortured, burned at the stake, forced to renounce their own faith, and accept Jesus as Savior, we owe at least the kindness of remembering.

Christian Scapegoats

When they asked Willie Sutton, the famous bank robber, why he chose banks as his major focus for crime, he answered simply, "That's where the money is!" You don't have to be a disciple of Karl Marx to agree that capital always plays a significant part in the real story behind events. "Show me the money," and I'll show you the motive.

Follow the story of crimes committed against the Jews "in the name of the Lord" and lurking somewhere behind the scenes invariably is the economic factor. The Jews were convenient scapegoats for everything on religious grounds—after all they were the Christ killers—so the princes could redirect the misery of the masses against them and then claim their money to boot. Here was the perfect whipping boy who could always be used to explain why peasants were poor and the populace was suffering. And because the scapegoat was also very talented, he could be used like a sponge; let him accumulate a lot through hard work so that the rulers could then soak him dry for their own personal benefit.

Sage Sayings

"If it is a mark of a good Christian to hate the Jews, what excellent Christians all of us are."

—Martin Luther

What a deal! It's almost as if, had there been no Jews, the aristocracy of the time would have had to invent them.

Ritual Murders

Before you could blame the Jews for something, it was pretty important to have a crime. Best to be something that would enrage the people, inflame them so that they could work out some of their anger and blow off steam that might otherwise be used against those who really oppressed them. And, with brilliant ingenuity, add a touch of religious fervor to rationalize the violence and frenzy by claiming that Jews were guilty of a satanic rite against Christians. Whoever thought it up had to be an evil genius. The fact that it was so blatantly outrageous didn't seem to matter because, as Joseph Goebbels would later note for the Nazis, "The greater the lie, the more it is believed."

So the story that was spread was that Jews needed the blood of a Christian baby in order to bake their *matzos*, their flatbread, for Passover. To do that they had to kidnap a little child on the eve of their festival and then re-enact the crucifixion.

"Blood libel" was the utterly baseless charge that Jews murdered Christians in order to use their blood in making the Passover matzot. (Courtesy of the Library of the Jewish Theological Seminary of America)

And if you believe that, I'd like to sell you the Brooklyn Bridge. But I could have sold a lot of bridges in the early Middle Ages, because they believed it in many places. In fact, once when townspeople found the murdered body of a child in a well, they tortured a Jew and had him "confess" to the deed as an act of ritual murder. This led to the expulsion of the Jews from England in 1290. (Can you guess on what day, by coincidence, this act of expulsion was signed? Of course it was Tisha b'Av—the ninth day of the Hebrew month of Av.)

Diary

Yenta's Little Secrets

If you want to observe Jewish dietary laws, then make sure that before you eat any eggs, you carefully crack them open and examine them for the slightest appearance of a blood spot. By law, if an egg has a drop of blood, it must be discarded. And that's what Jews have done throughout the centuries, so much do they abhor the idea of consuming even the smallest amount of that which defines life itself. Do you understand now how ludicrous it was for the Jews to be told that an essential ingredient for their religious food on Passover, the matzo, was a quantity of Christian blood?

149

Oh yes, don't let me forget one other small detail. The accused child "killers" were invariably the richest Jews. And so to atone for their sins, their estates were confiscated by the rulers and the Church.

Slanders of the Host

See if you can believe this next one as a crime often blamed on the Jews. Try not to laugh because it was responsible for thousands of Jews being brutally slaughtered.

Jews were accused of "kidnapping" wafers—yes, you read it right, wafers—and piercing, burning and defiling them. You see, Pope Innocent III (talk about names that are inappropriate) officially recognized the doctrine of "trans-substantiation." That meant the Christian worshipper, by drinking the wine of the sacrament, was considered to be drinking the blood of Christ, and by eating the holy wafer, or Host, was partaking of the body of the Lord. It didn't take long for some devious minds to script Jews stealing wafers and piercing them, much like they were originally accused of piercing the body of Jesus and crucifying him.

So to avenge the honor of the wafers they murdered hundreds of Jews. Somehow they also didn't forget to exact payment of large fines from all the surviving Jews who must have played a role in the "wafer caper." And the ruling princes didn't forget to add the magnificent gesture of freeing all Christians from their obligations to pay their debts to Jews, a little bonus that continued to make religious persecution of Jews ever more profitable—and popular.

The Black Plague

If the Jews were guilty of things that never happened, imagine how much more they must have been to blame for catastrophes that really occurred. When the Black Plague killed off a great part of the population in Europe between 1348–49, it was obviously the fault of the Jews, those "wicked people."

It is a source of constant amazement to note the paradox of Christian feelings toward Jews in those days. On the one hand they claim Jews are worthless human beings who can't do anything right; and on the other, they say Jews have the power to control nature and carry out nefarious plots in palaces around the world. Perhaps the only somewhat valid reason they had for assuming Jews were the cause of the plague was because Jews were suffering somewhat less from its effects. Who could know then that Jewish religious laws of washing were hygienically sound as well and served to protect them from the spread of the disease? But their ritual, which saved them from germs, couldn't protect them from prejudice.

Ghettos

Hatred against the Jews usually had two major outlets: For the rich Jews, find a way to blame them for a terrible crime, torture them to confess, kill them, and then confiscate all their money; for the poor Jews, demean and debase them so that everyone sees the affliction of those who don't accept Jesus as savior. And also make sure that no good Christians come in contact with these deniers of the Lord, who might possibly influence them to similar heresy. A yellow badge was one method for achieving the latter, the brilliant idea of the Fourth Lateran council in 1215, under the guidance of Innocent III. Jews could be easily identified, humiliated, and become social pariahs. (If you know your modern history, then you know that just such a yellow badge was used again, many years later in Hitler's time to mark the Jews.)

The thirteenth century witnessed yet another improvement on this effort to isolate the Jews. It turned out to be a curse that became one of the greatest blessings in disguise. The ghetto was a closed-off section reserved only for Jews. It separated Jews from Christians, but it also made sure the Jews kept together. Its motive was to demean the Jews; its practical effect was to give them a sense of pride and collective identity that only living together could achieve.

Aha, That's It

The first *ghetto* in Italy was established in Venice in 1516 near a cannon foundry called Gheta, in Italian. That's probably how the area restricted to Jews got its name. Two other intriguing possibilities, however, are that the word comes from the Italian "*guitto*," meaning dirty or from the Hebrew "*get*," meaning divorce.

When you think of the word ghetto, you can conjure up two totally different models: the Warsaw Ghetto of cruelty, or the Polish self-created ghetto, known as the *shtetl*. As long as it's not arbitrarily imposed, the ghetto of choice remains one of the few positive legacies of the tragic era of Christian anti-Semitism.

The Great Debates Between Christians and Jews

It's impossible to tell whether faith or finances was more important in the ongoing conflict between Christian and Jew. As you've seen by now, money surely played a great role. But we should not ignore the religious component. The Church really couldn't stand the continued existence of this cursed people who just wouldn't see the light. Pagans might refuse Christ because they didn't know any better, but Jews were members of the family. Their stubbornness was a constant thorn; how could the very people of the Old Testament not accept the New?

So the Church decided on what can only be called, in retrospect, a theater of the absurd. There would be great debates scheduled, tournaments, so to speak, of the mind "for God and for faith." The rules would be simple. Priests would debate rabbis to prove whose faith is correct. The referees would be the Church, and if these referees

Sage Sayings

"Would you believe that while the flames were consuming these innocent victims, the inquisitors and the other savages were chanting *our* prayers? These pitiless monsters were invoking the God of Mercy while committing the most atrocious crime."

—Voltaire, "Sermon of Rabbi Akiva"

decided that the priests' argument was the stronger, then the Jews would have to convert to Christianity.

Get the feeling that the game was fixed from the start? That's why Jews didn't want to play. But they were given no choice. The "religious disputations" went on and the Jews always lost. Fortunately we have the written record of one of these debates in 1263 between Pablo Christiano, a Jew who converted to Christianity, and Nachmanides, the famous talmudist and philosopher. At the close even the king had to grudgingly declare that he never before heard "an unjust cause so nobly defended."

But the Church used their "victories" in the debates to inspire the masses, to slander the Jewish religion, and—in many cases—to justify burning the Talmud, censoring Jewish writing, and establishing inquisitions.

Soporific Sermons

For those still not convinced by the debates, in 1450, Pope Benedict issued a papal bull introducing a new way to persuade the Jews: The Conversion Sermon. He decreed the required subject matter. The theme was always to be that "the real Messiah has already come" and that "the heresies of the Talmud prevent the Jews from knowing the truth." The Jews were forced to sit through these lengthy sermons, usually lasting for hours. From this probably arose the noble tradition, still scrupulously carried out in synagogues to this day, of sleeping during the sermon!

Your Money AND Your Life

What was truly incredible throughout all the years of this Christian persecution of Jews is how steadfastly the Jews refused to do the one simple thing that could have spared them all their suffering—convert. It has to be remembered that hatred of the Jews was rooted in something for which the Jews *had a choice*. It required only a word to prevent the continuing wounds.

The Christians wanted the Jews to say they believed, just like in Shakespeare's *The Merchant of Venice*. The decree for the Jew Shylock was not death, but rather that he must become a Christian. That alone would have removed "all his bad qualities," all his terrible Jewish traits. But Shylock moves off the stage proudly, unbowed, without making that commitment. And so too did a remarkable number of Jews, even though it cost them their money *and* their lives.

The Crusades and the Inquisition

The Jews who lived in Mohammedan Spain enjoyed a Golden Age. Once the Christian kingdoms took over, however, their days were numbered. Spain, where Jews like Hasdai Ibn Shaprut had served as a vizier to two caliphs and assumed the highest ranks of royal service, was now also home to the Inquisition.

If debates and sermons didn't do the job, then the sword promised to be far more convincing. In 1095, Pope Urban II called for the Crusades in order to regain Palestine from the infidels. It was supposedly a religious pilgrimage. Instead it was a trail of slaughter for those unfortunate enough to be in their way, who were given only one choice: conversion or death.

It must have been comforting for the Crusaders to know that while they were murdering tens of thousands, they were saving their souls. And when they finally got to Jerusalem in 1099, they gathered all the city's Jews into a synagogue and burned them alive. They must have also congratulated themselves on doing God's will in such holy manner, by destroying the heretics.

The Crusaders capture Jerusalem. (Courtesy of Scala/Art Resource, NY)

For the Jews who chose to see the light at the point of the sword and renounce their God for the true "God of Love," there was another surprise down the road. If they thought they could temporarily become Christians, and then, when the danger receded, go back to what they truly believed, they were profoundly mistaken. In 1201, Pope Innocent III issued this remarkable bull: "He who is lead to Christianity by violence, by fear, and by torture, and who received the sacrament of baptism to avoid harm receives indeed the stamp of Christianity...and must be duly constrained to abide by the faith that he had accepted by force."

In simple English, if you became a Christian by torture, we'll torture you even worse if you ever try to go back to your former faith. Just in case any Jew was tempted to dare to return to his roots, the Church set up the powerful mechanism of the Inquisition to weed out all sinners. Pity the person who wore his best clothes on Saturday, the Jewish Sabbath, even if by accident. Pity someone who was observed not eating on Yom Kippur. Pity someone who was seen to be eating matzo on Passover. And pity someone who was even suspected of these horrible crimes because with just a few days on the rack to assist their memories, they would surely remember that they had gone back on their word to become good and loyal Christians.

The Inquisition was extremely efficient and would somehow, with the help of excruciating torture, find ever more people implicated as secretly practicing Jews.

Yenta's Little Secrets

The holiest day of the Jewish calendar year, Yom Kippur, the Day of Atonement, begins with a moving prayer known as the *Kol Nidre*. In it, Jews ask forgiveness for all vows and promises that they will not keep. What a strange way to start a holy day in which you supposedly make commitments to become a better person! Many believe that the historic basis of this prayer is the story of the Marranos who were forced to make promises to become Christians, which on the holiest day of the Jewish year, they vowed to their God that they would not honor.

"Jews as Pigs"

To tell the truth, there were indeed some Jews who had accepted Christianity on pain of death and secretly continued to practice their religion. They are known as Marranos, which strangely enough means swine or pigs. Does the name come from Jews who despised them for their unwillingness to become martyrs rather than to convert? Or was it an insult bestowed upon them by the Christians for betraying their new religious commitment? No one is sure. What we do know is that to this day there are some very pious Catholics in Spain who go into their cellars on Friday night to light candles and explain that although they don't know the reason for this ritual, they still practice it as an ancient tradition that they received from their ancestors and were commanded never to abandon.

The Few Rays of Light

In Arab lands, freedom inspired the Jews to write books of philosophy. In Christian countries, the constant attempts to convert them made the Jews turn ever more inward to study their ancient texts; scholarship was religiously oriented. Creativity came in the clothing of ancient prophets and sages. Two people stand out for their contributions that still affect the lives of Jews, one because of his decrees, and the other because of his commentaries.

Rabbi Gershom

In the tenth century, Rabbi Gershom of Germany, a scholar admired by the entire Jewish world, dared to issue a number of laws that would irrevocably alter the status of women in Judaism. Whereas the Bible permitted polygamy, he declared that from his time forward it would no longer be an acceptable option. God may have allowed it, but He surely did not encourage it. The ideal for marriage was the first one, between Adam and Eve, and it was a monogamous relationship that defined human existence in Paradise.

Aha, That's It

Ashkenazim refers to Jews who come from Germany, France or eastern Europe. They are to be distinguished from *Sephardim*—Jews whose origin is from Sephard, Spain, as well as Arab lands. Of all the many divisions between Jews, this remains as one of the strongest, defining deep-seated cultural divisions that still play a major role in the State of Israel today.

Yenta's Little Secrets

Are there any Jews with more than one wife? Yes, and it's legal, too, if you come from a Sephardic background. Rabbi Gershom, who issued the decree against having more than one wife, was not known to Sephardic Jews who lived at a great distance from him, and this decree, therefore, never became binding upon them. These Jewish "Mormons" are allowed by law to have as many wives as they want, but most of them have already discovered that even though it's legal, more than one mother-in-law is too much for anyone.

More daring still, although the Bible permitted a man to divorce his wife against her will, Rabbi Gershom taught that with the progress of mankind, this too was now unacceptable. What's strangest of all, for a people so accustomed to quarreling, is that all of Ashkenazic Jewry—European Jews —accepted his words, and these new laws defined common behavior.

Rabbi Shlomo ben Isaac

The second luminary who would forever change the way Jews study the Torah and Talmud was Rabbi Shlomo ben Isaac (1040–1105) of Troyes, who is always known by his acronym Rashi. A great source of wonderment to Jews is how this rabbi ever became so proficient in his studies without the benefit of his own texts! Today you simply can't find a book of the Bible or of the Talmud without Rashi's commentary printed alongside. Rashi earned his living from tending vineyards. He earns his immortality for enabling Jews of every generation to study and serve in the vineyards of the Lord.

Goodbye Spain, Hello America

With the rise of the Grand Inquisitor, Torquemada, seeds were sown for the final tragedy. Torquemada was the confessor to Queen Isabella and his hatred of Jews intrigues scholars to this day. (Could it have anything to do with the fact that his grandfather married a baptized Jew, and he had Jewish blood in him?)

It was he who convinced the queen and her husband Ferdinand that the Jews had to be expelled from the land "for the greater glory of the Church and the Christian religion." Even the pleadings of her Finance Minister, Isaac Abarbanel (a Jew himself), together with the promise of an exorbitant bribe, had no effect. The edict of expulsion was signed on March 31, 1492, and the Jews were given exactly four months to put their affairs in order and leave the country.

The Jews again looked at their calendars and realized the very day on which their Golden Age officially came to an end turned out to be Tisha b'Av, the ninth day of the month of Av. What they did not yet know was that the year was even far more significant. In 1492, one great door was slammed in their face, but another would open—a far more glorious door to an age even more blessed than the Golden Age of Spain.

Yenta's Little Secrets

Christopher Columbus's voyage required a great deal of capital and it was primarily Jews, such as Abraham Senior, who helped finance it. In his book *Columbus and His Discovery of America*, Herbert Baxter Adams claims: "Not jewels, but Jews, were the real financial basis of the first expedition of Columbus."

Could Christopher Columbus have any inkling of the connection between the two when he wrote these words in his diary? "In the same month in which Their Majesties issued the edict that all Jews should be driven out of the kingdom and its territories, in the same month they gave me the order to undertake with sufficient men my expedition of discovery to the Indies." Or, as some scholars suggest, did Columbus recognize the importance of his journey to later Jews—one who himself was a Marrano, a Jew forced with his first name to conceal his faith and his real identity?

The Least You Need to Know

➤ Jews were used as scapegoats for every ill of Christian society, both for religious and monetary motives.

➤ The "blood libel," the accusation that Jews used Christian blood for the baking of matzos, goes back to this time.

➤ Ghettos were meant to isolate and punish the Jews as outcasts, but many of them served to create group identity and became a blessing in disguise.

➤ Christians rationalized the persecution of Jews as attempts to "save their souls," and the Crusades as well as the Inquisition serve as fitting reminders of the terrible crimes that can be committed in the name of God and religion.

➤ Marranos sought to save their lives by publicly converting to Christianity while secretly still practicing their Jewish religion, but they were most probably lost to the Jewish people in the course of time.

➤ Spain brought the Golden Age to a close, both for the Jews and for itself, by expelling the Jews from its country, but inadvertently in the same year sent Christopher Columbus on a mission that would be the harbinger of a far more glorious future for these outcasts.

Chapter 17

An Offer Too Good to Refuse: Eastern Europe

In This Chapter

➤ How Jews coped with the Age of Expulsion

➤ Why Jews were money-lenders and how that determined their fate

➤ How a Jewish kingdom started in Russia and the hope it offered for Jews in nearby lands

➤ How the czars weren't "lucky czars" for the Jews

➤ The welcome mat of Poland and the opportunity for self-government

➤ Yiddish as a language and a culture

➤ The Cossacks and a preview of the Holocaust

"Get out and don't come back. Leave your baggage here. We'll keep all your possessions." That was the theme of the Age of Expulsion that defined so much of the Middle Ages for Western European Jews.

Being kicked out of Spain was the straw that broke the camel's back. It left a scar on the Jewish psyche that hasn't fully healed to this day. If it could happen in Spain, where the Jews reached a kind of prominence that could probably only be compared to the Golden Age of American Jewry (which you'll read more about in Chapter 22, "America the Beautiful"), then is it merely paranoia to believe that it could happen again anywhere, anytime?

Movers and Shakers

Mention the name of almost any Western European country, and you will find that the Jews were there for a while, that they contributed to the economy of the land, and then when they had acquired enough to gain the envy of their neighbors, were told they had to get out—and leave all their wealth behind. The Jews were the movers, forced to flee constantly from one place to another—and the shakers, terrified always of when they would receive their next eviction notice.

Pulpit Stories

Rabbi Kahana tells a story in the Talmud he claims he saw with his own eyes. It's obviously impossible, and yet it may well be the story of the Jewish people: A boatload of Jews was shipwrecked. Happily, they swam toward an island, found safety, and lived there for many years. They planted and harvested, and rejoiced in their new land. But one day the earth beneath them shook. What appeared to have been an island was really the back of a large whale. The whale gave a turn—and there they were, back in the waters again, struggling for their lives. A whale and not land? Yes, that was the Jewish experience!

No small reason for this constant cycle of settling and then moving again was the money-lending profession, which the Jews were forced into by the Church. A mercantile system was just beginning in Western Europe and capitalism was becoming a force in international relations and trade. But according to the medieval Canon Law of the Church, Christians were forbidden to lend money at "usury," for interest. Yet, society couldn't function without somebody lending money.

The Jews were locked out of the feudal system of clergy, nobles, and serfs. They weren't allowed in the guilds, the union for artisans and craftsmen. So the Jews took on the one occupation that the Christians wouldn't touch themselves and became masters at it. Money-lending proved to be a blessing and a curse. Many Jews amassed great wealth in the profession, but it proved to be an ideal way for the Church to condemn them. The Church labeled them "despicable money lenders" and used this as an excuse to get the government to cancel all debts owed to them and then to expel them from their country.

This scenario repeated itself over and over, and the Jews prayed that they could find someplace where they could settle peacefully, a safe haven where the power of the Church was not so strong, where they would be allowed to develop their talents freely without fear of perpetual persecution. And for a while, they thought Eastern Europe and what are today Russia and Poland was the answer.

The Kingdom of the Jews in Russia

Long before Jews came to Russia, Russia came to the Jews. The story is so amazing that, were it not fully documented, we would have trouble believing it. But there was a kingdom of Khazars, a group of tribes that sprung from Hun or Turkish stock and occupied a vast stretch of territory north of the Caucasus, including the entire Volga region, which converted to Judaism about the year 740 C.E.

Their King Bulan had listened to a disputation by a Muslim mullah, a Christian priest, and a rabbi on the relative merits of Islam, Christianity, and Judaism. Both the mullah and the priest agreed that Judaism was the original religion but that it had been superseded by their own. Bulan couldn't believe that what was clearly given by God to 600,000 people at Mount Sinai was rendered invalid by the claim of either the mullah or the priest, no matter how great the credentials of each.

So King Bulan converted to Judaism and was joined by most of his subjects. By the 900s, Jews from abroad, from the Muslim cities, and the lands of Byzantium came to settle in this remarkable place where the language was Hebrew, the king was a Jew, and their faith was not a problem.

Yenta's Little Secrets

When Judah Halevi wrote a book about the Khazars, *The Kuzari*, he imagined the dialogue between King Bulan and the rabbi who converted him. He had the king ask a profound question: "Why, in the First Commandment, does God identify Himself as the Lord `who took you out of the land of Egypt, the house of bondage' when he could have said something far greater, like `the Lord who created the heavens and earth?'" Halevi had the answer: "No one witnessed the creation. There would be no point in referring to it as proof. But the exodus was experienced by all to whom God spoke at Sinai. Religion is best proved by personal experience."

Unfortunately, in 1016 C.E., the Russians, with the help of Byzantium, crushed the Khazar kingdom and brought it to a close. What happened to all the Khazar Jews, both the descendants of the converts and the settlers, is shrouded in mystery. They were certainly dispersed in many of the neighboring lands. It is conceivable, according to some scholars, that some of them are the forebears of the Polish and Russian Jews of previous generations. Who knows? If your ancestors came from these lands, you may have the blood of kings in you—not David and Solomon, but kings who voluntarily chose to join the fate of a people whose religion they acknowledged as true.

The Czars and Gripes Forever

The Jews counted their lucky czars when the balance of power between Church and commerce was in their favor. The Church demanded that Jews be treated as seducers of Satan. The Muscovite Ambassador in Rome, convinced of this truth, declared in 1526, "The Muscovite people dread no one more than the Jews, and do not admit them into their borders."

But in Kiev and in Lithuania, the rulers knew that the Jews could help them, and so they invited them to their land for the express purpose of developing commerce and improving their finances.

For some czars, the benefits of having Jews around was stronger than the pressure they were getting from the Church to expel them. But for others, like Czar Ivan IV (Ivan the Terrible), the decision was, "It is not convenient to allow Jews to come to Russia…for they import poisonous herbs into the realm and lead Russians astray from Christianity." And for some, like Czar Peter the Great, the reaction was mixed when he was petitioned by Jews in Amsterdam in 1698 to let them settle in Russia: "Tell the Jews that I am obliged to them for their proposal, and that I realize how advantageous their services would be to me, but that I should have to pity them were they to live in the midst of the Russians."

It was Czar Peter's successor, the Czarina Katherine I, who decided in 1727 to solve the problem of the Jews by expelling them "immediately from Russia beyond the border." It took only a year for her to realize how much her kingdom lost from this expulsion and so she offered this remarkable compromise: "The Jews are permitted to visit temporarily the fairs of Little Russia for commercial purposes, but they are only allowed to sell their goods wholesale, and not retail." To protest this unjust ruling, Jews to this very day like to buy—but not, God forbid, sell—wholesale, whenever they possibly can!

Poland Says Welcome

When the Jews had been expelled from Spain, some of them made their way, not to Europe, but to Turkey. And there the Sultan Bajazet welcomed them, watched his kingdom become blessed by the talents of these new emigrants, and exclaimed, "How can you call Ferdinand of Aragon a wise king, the same Ferdinand who impoverished his own land and enriched ours?"

Kicking the Jews out, as the Church wanted, came at a price. And it was Poland, interestingly enough, because of its late acceptance of Christianity, that realized how much it had to gain by welcoming these talented outcasts from other lands. So while so much of the world was saying, "Get out," the early kings of Poland, troubled by the breakdown of their economy, literally imported German-Jewish traders and money lenders to help turn them into a strong empire. By strange coincidence, the Hebrew name for Poland, *Po'lin*, means "here rest." Jews took it as a sign that it was almost divinely ordained for them to find a resting place in the one country that actually put out a welcome mat for them.

Jews who fled there to avoid being slain by the Crusaders were pleasantly amazed to discover that in 1264 the Polish King Boleslaw the Pius had issued a charter, eventually known as the Statute of Kalisz, giving equal protection to Jews and to Christians. The king forbade desecration of synagogues, Jewish schools, and cemeteries. Full protection was to be given to all Jews and their possessions. They were free to travel anywhere without molestation and if attacked, it was the duty of every Christian to come to their aid. Most remarkable of all, it was forbidden to charge Jews with ritual murder, which the charter clearly stated to be false and slanderous. If such a charge were pressed by Christians, it would be necessary for them to produce at least six reliable witnesses to the alleged crime—and three of these witnesses were to be Jews!

Poland permitted Jews to rent not only estates, but even entire villages from the feudal landowners. Eventually Jews would be granted the greatest right of all, the right to rule themselves.

Jewish Self-Rule: The Kahal

Poland prospered when it accepted this tradeoff: Let the Jews freely lead their own lives as they choose, but force them to liberally support the Polish king with their taxes. Jews were no longer restricted by religious bias from forming their own guilds and they soon proved to be excellent artisans and craftsmen. They excelled in handicrafts, small businesses, and even as stewards on the estates of the land-owning gentry. In return for their money, the king allowed them to form their own *kahal*, a Jewish community, to govern themselves as they saw fit and to take care of their own social needs.

Aha, That's It

Another word for *kahal* (community) is *kehilla*. To this day synagogues that serve as mini-*kehillas* often use the word *kahal* before their specific name. So, for example, the congregation "Men of Peace" would be *kehilla anshe shalom*.

The kahal proved to be a remarkable illustration of the indigenous culture and value system the Jewish people had when they were unencumbered by external forces. It created a system of universal education; it provided for all the needs of its constituents; it took care of its poor and sick, the indigent widow, and the dowerless maidens; it made sure orphans were cared for and the elderly not forsaken; it dispensed justice through the *bet din*, the Jewish court system. It ensured that business was transacted fairly, in accordance with the rules of the Talmud. It made sure the dead had a proper

Aha, That's It

A *bet-din*, literally, house of justice, is the name given to a Jewish court. It is comprised of three rabbis for monetary matters, 23 for major crimes, and 71 for the Supreme Court. It always consists of an odd number of judges to ensure there be no tie vote without a decision.

Listen to Your Bubbe

To prevent Jews from spending exorbitant amounts on celebrations, the Council of Four Lands imposed a limit on how much could be spent for any affair and how many people could be invited. Several Hasidic groups today have reinstituted this decree for themselves. Invite them to the Waldorf Astoria for a Bar Mitzvah and they'll refuse to come, so as not to encourage waste and the possible embarrassment of other people who can't afford to do likewise.

burial, assured proper circumcision of the newly born, and arranged for the appropriate supervision of dietary laws and the proper ritual slaying of animals.

For the rulers it was the most efficient way to collect all of their taxes. And for the Jews it was an opportunity at last to live a full life, governed by their own religious leaders.

...The Council of the Four Lands

By the sixteenth century, the kahal system was fully established in many regions. When issues came up that affected the total Jewish community, it was customary for the leaders of many kahals to meet at the famous Lublin fair where thousands of Jews gathered for trade. (Was this the first example of what would later become annual rabbinic conventions?) In time they formed the Council of the Four Lands, representing Great Poland, Little Poland, Red Russia (Eastern Galicia), and Volhynia. The Council had great authority and didn't hesitate to use it in many areas that affected the financial, social, religious, and cultural lives of the Jews in their domain.

Yiddish Isn't Hebrew

While Jewish culture was being defined by the kahal and its autonomous rule, Jews were conversing among themselves in a language that expressed the richness of their own heritage and a desire to maintain their own uniqueness. The ghetto was a physical form of separation; Yiddish, as their chosen language, served as a social barrier between themselves and their neighbors.

Yiddish, contrary to what some assume, is not Hebrew; it is German with a Jewish accent. Polish Jews had come mainly from Germany and Bohemia, and their former tongue was German. To make the language their own, they added intonations (*nu*, so what's wrong with that?), Hebrew words (sure you need *sechel*, brains, to do that), culturally rooted expressions, and even curses (you should burn like a Hanukkah light, for eight days). Mix in some well-known quotes from Torah and Talmud, sprinkle with a little *hutzpah* and a dash of Jewish humor (What's a Jewish millionaire? Someone who has almost half a million rubles!), and you get some idea of its flavor.

Yiddish has everything except an equivalent for one English word:

Sam says to Irving, "I'll bet you there's no Yiddish word for 'disappointed.'" Irving says, "That's impossible. My mother speaks only Yiddish. I bet she knows a word for it, and I know how to get it from her." So Irving calls his mother. He asks her in Yiddish how she would feel if he and all the grandchildren were to come over and visit. Delighted, she tells him in Yiddish how overjoyed she would be and how she would prepare an entire meal, from gefilte fish to strudel. "And what if," Irving asks, "at the last minute I were to call and tell you that we wouldn't be able to make it. How would you feel then?" "*Zehr* (very), *zehr* disappointed!" she says in English. Irving lost his bet because "disappointed" is foreign to the Jewish mindset and there is no Yiddish word for it.

But all the other words Yiddish has makes speaking it a real *mechayeh*, a pleasure. Preserving it, through the writing of Sholem Alechim and Isaac Bashevis Singer, the theater of Molly Picon and Maurice Schwartz, the humor of Menasha Skulnick, as well as the brilliance of countless of its spokespeople, keeps alive those whose personalities and whose cultures shaped the Jews of our time.

The Cruel Cossacks

But the good times were doomed to end. And they closed not with a bang, but with a massacre, a massacre so horrendous that in its own way historians call it a preview of the Holocaust. It was in 1648 that Cossack nationalists from the Ukraine, led by an arch anti-Semite, Chmielnicki, rebelled against the Poles, and as their first act of destruction took out their hatred of the king by brutally slaying his stewards, the Jews. It's the old story: The really rich own the building, the Jew is sent to collect the rent, and when the poor tenant can't bear it anymore, he takes it out on the one who seemed to be his oppressor on a monthly basis.

Sage Sayings

"Yiddish, far more than Hebrew, was the living Jewish tongue. It was the language of the Jewish masses; it vibrates with their history, follows the mold of their life and thought, and colors itself with their moods. It is to Yiddish that we must look for the truest repository of specifically Jewish sociology. From Yiddish we can build up a picture of the life of the *Judengasse*—the Jewish street."

—Israel Zangwill

Sage Sayings

"If Yiddish was good enough for the *Baal Shem Tov*, for the Gaon of Vilna, for Rabbi Nachman of Bratslav, for millions of Jews who perished by the hands of the Nazis, then it is good enough for me."

—Isaac Bashevis Singer, explaining why he writes only in Yiddish

Sage Sayings

We are ashamed to write down all that the Cossacks and Tatars did unto the Jews, lest we disgrace the species man, who is created in the image of God.

—quoted from an old chronicle by Sholom Asch

The sadistic ingenuity of Chmielnicki was so great that you simply can't read about it without being physically sick. In a year and a half of Cossack terror, about one-half of the total Jewish population of the Ukraine and Galicia perished. And when the Cossacks were finished with the Jews, the Poles, in their need for a scapegoat, turned around and accused the Jews of plotting with their enemies so that they too could join in the Jew-bashing.

"Would it ever end?" the Jews asked themselves. In desperation, they turned to their faith to find new ways to respond to the bitter persecution they had to endure.

The Least You Need to Know

➤ Expulsion became a way of life for the Jews in the Middle Ages, as they went from acquiring wealth by money-lending to having it taken from them by envious neighbors who then evicted them from their lands.

➤ A kingdom of converts to Judaism, the Khazars, offered an unbelievable haven for a time, as Jews came to a Hebrew-speaking land of their new-found peers.

➤ The czars couldn't quite make up their minds whether they would be more influenced by the blessings of the Church or the blessings they could gain with the help of Jewish residents. But they invariably ended up siding with the Church.

➤ Poland recognized the Jews as a people who could help them become a world power and welcomed them.

➤ The *kahal* and the Council of Four Lands allowed the Jews self-government and an opportunity to create a life for themselves that was guided by their own cultural and religious values.

➤ Yiddish, mainly spoken by Polish residents who had come from Germanic lands, gave a distinctive flavor to Jewish culture and has lived on to this day.

➤ The Chmielnicki massacre shattered the optimistic hopes of Polish Jewry and forced them to rethink their dreams for the future.

Chapter 18

Saving Our Souls: Spiritual Responses to Persecution

In This Chapter

➤ What Kabalah, Jewish mysticism, had to teach the people and why it gained so many adherents in the seventeenth century

➤ The secret of gematriya and the first Bible Code

➤ The time of the new Messiahs—and the Great Frauds

➤ The revolution of the Ba'al Shem Tov and the Hasidic movement

➤ The great controversy between Hasidim and Mitnagdim

➤ The role of science and religion—and the relationship between them.

What do you do when the real world around you makes life unbearable? You create a new world in your own mind and make your feelings more important than the stark facts that surround you.

The worse things got, the more Jews needed some way to reassure themselves that there still was hope. What they would never allow themselves to do was to fall into a depression of existential angst, concluding that life has no meaning. No, they were sure life had to make sense. There *is* a God who directs human destiny. And if they didn't understand, they had to search more intensely, seek different answers, discover new approaches that would help them to better cope with the persecution they were experiencing. So precisely because it was the worst of times, it was also in a sense the best of times for discovering new spiritual responses to Jewish misfortunes.

Kabalah—The Response of the Mystics

Kabalah, from the Hebrew word that means "to receive," is the name given to the mystic tradition in Judaism. Unlike Torah and Talmud, which were meant to be accessible to all, Kabalah was to be taught only "one-on-one" from master to disciple worthy of receiving it. Ideally, it couldn't be left accessible to the masses because of its great potential for misinterpretation, its possible perversion into superstitious practice, and its esoteric aspects that might even lead immature followers to madness.

Sage Sayings

"Religion is to mysticism what popularization is to science."

—Henri Bergson

Sage Sayings

"The microscope, no less than the telescope, has revealed unknown galaxies moving in tune to the same music of the spheres—a clue to the most awesome mystery of all, which is the Divine Unity in Nature."

—David Sarnoff

Mysticism has always lent itself to misappropriation by charlatans, as well as the demented. Crystal ball gazers, palm readers, and those who confuse hallucinations with heavenly voices have all given a bad name to an approach that by definition is nonrational. It was the German poet Heinrich Heine (see Chapter 20, "When the Walls Came Tumbling Down: Germany") who quipped: "I myself am just at present a Mystic, following the advice of my physician to avoid stimulants to thought."

But to confuse the nonrational with the irrational isn't really fair. Mysticism has a long history that includes saints as well as imposters, profound truths as well as implausible absurdities, and incredible insights about worlds beyond the reality of the five senses that may carry a far more accurate awareness of truth than reason alone can ever discover.

The master work of Kabalah is the *Zohar,* compiled by the Spanish mystic Moses Shem-Tob de Leon (1230–1305)—a book he claimed he didn't write himself but discovered from the writings of the Talmudic sage Simeon bar Yochai. Written in Aramaic, it almost defies simple understanding, which was probably its purpose. But oh, the themes it touches upon! Small wonder that Jews whose daily lives were a hell found such solace in a book and a tradition that told you all about heaven. If you were a beggar or pauper, you could take comfort in knowing that you would be reincarnated—and perhaps next time you could come back as a rich man or maybe even Shirley MacLaine!

The Talmud only teaches you how to serve God. Kabalah shows you how you can actually become one with Him. And one more thing: Kabalah shares with you the ultimate secrets of the Bible so that you can not only know more about your faith but even be able to predict the future.

Gematriya and the Ultimate Bible Code

Kabalah is a way of looking beneath the surface of everything. The world isn't just what it seems. The real essence of things can't be seen because it is covered by layers and layers of physical clothing. (And how crazy is that when you realize that science has finally told us the very same thing but in different language: A microscope reveals what is hidden from the eye; atoms are at the core of every material object, and even the atoms we now know are really manifestations of energy—perhaps allied to the ultimate energy of the universe, God Himself.)

And just as objects are more than they appear to be, so too are the letters of the Hebrew alphabet, which also correspond to numbers. With words, the mystics taught, God created the world, and words have a mathematical exactitude that may even link mysticism with science. Combine the numerical value of the Hebrew word "*em*" (mother), 41, with the word "*av*" (father), 3, add 1 for God who is the One of the universe, and you get 45. That is the very *gematriya* of the word Adam, the first man, and the Hebrew word for a human being—always created by the union of mother, father, and God.

Aha, That's It!

Zohar means brilliance, like that emanating from the sun. And just like the rays of the sun, one dare not stare at it openly for any length of time, for fear that its power will cause spiritual blindness or even madness.

Sage Sayings

"The story of Jewish mysticism is not ended. It has not yet become history, and the secret life it holds can break out tomorrow in you or in me."

—Gershon Sholem

When words can be analyzed from this perspective, as numbers, they can convey not only deeper truths but even predictions about when specific events will occur. Kabalists did not hesitate to detect countless Bible Codes that spoke to them directly and predicted events for their times. With their new-found knowledge, they looked for hints in the Torah for better times. More significantly, they even tried to discover the date for the arrival of the Messiah.

Frankenstein and the Golem of Prague

When I was a kid, I remember devouring Captain Marvel comics. I loved the idea that just by saying, "SHAZAM!" an average Joe could miraculously be transformed into a superhero. No matter how long I repeated the word, though, I still remained a 97-pound weakling. It wasn't until I started dabbling a bit in Kabalah that I realized there was a better way. There is a word, the mystics taught, that can give someone real power. Say it, and you can stop Tyson dead in his tracks before he gets a chance to bite your ear off. If you dared, you could even use it to create a Frankenstein who will unquestioningly follow your every command.

The word is the 72-letter name of God, which was pronounced in the Temple only once a year, by the high priest on Yom Kippur in the Holy of Holies, the chamber where the Ark and the Commandments were housed. Unfortunately, the name is known to only a few select masters of Kabalah and forbidden to be recited. But one of the great mystics, Rabbi Judah Low of Prague (1525-1609), not only knew the secret but, according to Jewish folk legend, had the guts to use it. Unable to bear the abuse of his Christian neighbors any longer, the rabbi went to the attic of his synagogue, the famous Altneuschul, and with the help of his mystic lore, turned a mound of clay into a *golem*, a "living" robot who followed his master's every command.

Pulpit Stories

On the forehead of the clay golem that Rabbi Low of Prague created with his incantations, he wrote the Hebrew word for truth, "*emet.*" When the rabbi realized it was time for him to stop making use of this supernatural figure and turn him back to dust, he erased the first letter, the *aleph*, leaving the word, *met*, which in Hebrew means death. *Aleph* in gematriya stands for 1, the number corresponding to God—the ultimate One of the universe. The golem could "live" as long as he had a dimension of God in him, but once God was removed, his fate was sealed with death.

Two Jewish boys in the twentieth century, Jerry Seigal and Joe Schuster created the comic strip Superman. But a rabbi four centuries before them had already brought into being the greatest defender of "truth, justice, and the Jewish way." It was this very story of Rabbi Low's golem that would be used by Mary Shelley as the basis for her Frankenstein tale.

For Jews, the golem story symbolized how belief in Kabalah could empower them with deeper understanding, with ways to come closer to God, with predictions that could give them hope for the future, and even with (to be used only in cases of extreme emergency) possible ways to overcome their enemies by supernatural means. No surprise then that the seventeenth century, the age of the brutal Cossack Chmielnicki and unparalleled barbarism, was also the age of Kabalah's greatest flowering and influence.

New Messiahs—The Response of the Hopeful

The impact of mysticism made Messiah all the more relevant. Mystics longed for another world in which they could be closer to God. Messiah as an ideal was supposed to fulfill this very promise. The old Kabalists not only prayed for the Messianic Age, but kept emphasizing that the fulfillment of every *mitzvah*, every divine commandment, has cosmic significance that helps to hasten the day of ultimate redemption. That day, they promised, could not be far off, and some of their gematriya calculations even "proved" that this was so.

The power of Kabalah as a major movement of the times was the driving force behind the unfortunate Age of the False Messiahs.

If it's true in nature, it's true in history as well. Whenever there is a vacuum, something (or someone) will rush in to fill it. Kabalists had said Messiah was on his way. The people were suffering and desperately wanted it to be true. And so a number of frauds appeared on the scene, claiming that they were the one. In retrospect, we can never know if these people were charlatans or suitable candidates for the "cuckoo's nest." But one of them, Shabbatai Zevi (1626–1676), had so much charisma that he had more than half the Jewish world of his time accepting his self-coronation. English Jews, known for calculating odds even before Lloyds of London became famous for it, were giving ten to one on Zevi riding his donkey to a victorious finish. People sold their homes, gave up their worldly goods, and made final plans for a spiritual life in Jerusalem.

Listen to Your Bubbe

Be careful of the evil eye. Kabalah teaches there is power emanating from the eyes, which are a direct conduit to the soul. An evil stare can harm, which is why we have the Yiddish expression, "*kin-ayin-hora*," which means "no evil eye." Say *kin-ayin-hora* fast, and in English it sounds like "canary." And that's how the old Brooklyn expression started: "Don't give me a canary."

Yenta's Little Secrets

There is an ancient mystic tradition that says that the Messiah would be born on Tisha b'Av, turning the traditional Jewish day of mourning into one of final joy. Would you believe that's when Shabbatai Zevi was born? And of course he used that odd coincidence to help bolster his claim to be the Messiah.

This engraving produced by Thomas Coenen in 1669 is probably the only authentic portrait of Shabbetai Zevi, the false Messiah. (Courtesy of the Library of the Jewish Theological Seminary of America)

The unavoidable letdown was almost too much to bear. The Turkish sultan, hearing that Zevi promised to liberate Palestine from Turkish rule and restore it to an independent Jewish state, imprisoned him and gave him a simple choice: convert to Islam or be tortured to death. And before you could say "false Messiah," Shabbatai traded his *yarmulke* for a turban and took the Muslim name Mehemet Effendi, offending every Jew who had put his trust in him.

The remarkable postscript to this story of the Redeemer who chose to redeem himself is that even after he converted to Islam, there were still many Jews who couldn't get themselves to stop believing and who rationalized the conversion as a "temporary descent" in order to rise again to an even higher level! Just goes to show you that wishing too much for something to be true can sometimes make you blind to reality. Sadder still is the fact that many of Zevi's followers finally threw in the towel and converted to Christianity. Judaism, they felt, had failed them once too often even if the failure had nothing to do with their faith, but rather with a fraud.

Listen to Your Bubbe

Be very careful about following a Messiah who clearly isn't. Would you believe that even after Shabbatai Zevi converted to Islam there was still a Jewish group called the Doenmeh, which survived until after World War I and believed that Zevi was the real Messiah and would soon reappear on his donkey?

It was left to another man and another movement to bring the masses back to their people and to their God with an intensity and a fervor the Jews had never experienced before in their history.

The Hasidim

How a single person can transform an entire generation is always a mystery. How one man could appear in the eighteenth century and create an entirely new way of defining a faith that had been in existence for thousands of years is almost beyond belief. But that is what Israel ben Eliezer, known by his disciples as Ba'al Shem Tov ("Master of the Good Name," 1700–60) was somehow able to accomplish. A recluse at first, growing up in the wilderness, an orphan, a misfit who never "succeeded" at anything, a man who never wrote a book or proved himself as an outstanding scholar, was able nevertheless to transmit the spiritual discoveries of his soul to all the generations that followed.

What is the key to his legacy, and why were his teachings so eagerly devoured by his ever-expanding circle of disciples, even to this day? It's hard to do justice to the genius of the Ba'al Shem Tov and the revolutionary nature of his movement in a short summary, but let's try at least to focus on some of the highlights.

Hasidism Respected the Simple Jew

Hasidism brought the uneducated Jew back to a place of honor at the table of God.

A famous Hasidic tale: All the scholars are praying on Yom Kippur, but the gates of heaven remained closed. God did not choose to hear their pleadings until a poor, illiterate shepherd entered the synagogue. He felt a profound love for God and wanted more than anything else to express it in Hebrew, but he could not read. At first he wept because of his stupidity. Then he began to whistle, knowing that was the only thing that he could do well and hoping that God would accept this as his heartfelt prayer. The congregants were horrified by this act of seeming desecration. But the Ba'al Shem Tov saw that at that very moment God broke out in a smile and proclaimed, "Now I will accept the prayers of My people."

Hasidism Stressed the Heart Over the Head

Hasidism emphasized the feeling over the act, the fervor over the deed itself.

Another Hasidic tale: A student wanted to learn the craft of a smith, fashioning horse shoes from iron. He scrupulously recorded every part of the work that was required. He took copious notes from a master, and he was sure he hadn't left out a single thing. Yet, when he got home, he found that no matter how hard he tried, he was unable to accomplish anything. Because he had neglected to write down the very first step, the most obvious one, without which nothing else is possible. He was supposed to light the fire, and without fire, without heat, every other instruction was pointless.

The moral: For centuries Jews had been paying attention to all the details of *Halacha*, the scriptures of the law, which explain what to "bend," how to "bend," and what to do with their "hearts of iron." But the most obvious of all—the need for spiritual fervor and warmth—they didn't feel necessary to record and, in the course of generations, forgot to practice. For that reason, religious worship had become stultified, cold, unfeeling, and ineffective.

Another story: On a frigid winter day, the Ba'al Shem Tov passed near a stream on whose banks some people had carved idols out of ice. "How remarkable," he said to his followers. "Water has the ability to purify. We immerse ourselves and become holy. And yet, even water, when it is frozen, turns into an idol. So, too, Jews who allow their spirits and fervor to freeze, end up with Pagan worship."

Aha, That's It

Halacha is the traditional Jewish law, based on rabbinic interpretation of the Bible.

Hasidism Returned Joy to Judaism

To study God's words is one way to serve Him. To move one's entire body in song and dance, exulting in God's creations and expressing happiness for being born as one of His people, is even greater. To laugh is to acknowledge that all is well in a world run by divine calculation. To be mournful is to question God's management of the universe.

An Hasidic tale: A deaf man walks by a hall in which a wedding is being celebrated. He looks through the window and sees people jumping and prancing in what to him appears insane activity. Why they are smiling as they contort their bodies is beyond him because he doesn't hear the music. So too, those who are insensitive to the divine symphony see only madness. Those who "hear the music," not only have a song in their hearts but also an ever-present smile on their lips.

Hasidism Preached Pleasure Rather than Pain

Hasidism spoke of "*simchah*," or joy, instead of sorrow, as the correct way to fulfill the will of God.

An Hasidic tale: A Jew went to his rabbi to boast about his piety. "I love God so much," he said, "that every morning I wake up early, rush out in the freezing cold to roll in the snow, and have my servant administer lashes on my back." To which the rabbi replied, "How very remarkable. I have a horse. Every morning he is aroused early. He is taken out into the cold, and he rolls in the snow. He is often given lashes. And do you know what? He is still a horse!"

Asceticism is not a Jewish ideal. God created the world and every day, when he looked at his completed work, he said, "Behold, it is good." Men dare not replace the goodness of God with self-imposed evil.

Hasidism Raised Sincerity Above Scholarship

Hasidism dared to suggest that on a scale of ultimate values, an unlearned, sincere Jew may be holier even than a scholar.

One more Hasidic tale: Two Jews lived next door to each other. One was a scholar, the other a poor laborer. The scholar would rise everyday at the break of dawn, go to the synagogue, study a page of Talmud, and say the morning prayers quietly and slowly until almost midday. His neighbor, the poor laborer, also rose early and went to work in order to feed his family, having no time to go to the synagogue to pray with the congregation at the proper hour.

Precisely at midday, the scholar left the synagogue to return home, filled with a sense of satisfaction. He would invariably meet his neighbor, the poor laborer, hurrying to the house of worship with great anguish and regret for his tardiness. The laborer would utter a mournful groan, bemoaning his inability to have fulfilled his religious obligations properly. At the same time, the scholar would look with scorn at his simple, working neighbor, and a smirk would form on his lips as he considered his superiority.

For many years it was so, until both of them eventually passed on to be judged by the Heavenly Court. For the scholar, they brought forth the scales and on one side put all of his good deeds, all of his study of Torah, and all of his brilliance. On the other they placed the smirk of contempt he had for a fellow Jew. Behold, the weight of the smirk turned the scale to guilty! For the poor laborer, they put his few failings on one side: coming late to the synagogue, not studying enough Torah. But on the other, they put the groan that issued from the depths of his soul, a groan that showed how much more he wanted to do had his poverty not prevented him. And the weight of the groan of the poor worker turned the scale to innocent!

Are Hasidim Really Heretics?

It was this last idea that for some of the more traditional rabbis put the Hasidic movement over the edge. It may have been all right to show understanding for the common man, but to denigrate the scholar and scholarship in such a disrespectful manner? "No, it is wrong," said the revered Rabbi Elijah, known as the Gaon (genius) of Vilna (1720–1797). Judaism survived only because of its attachment to Torah and Torah study. The Gaon of Vilna, it was reliably reported, knew everything as a teenager and yet continued to study eighteen hours a day for the rest of his life. For him, the head was indeed what made man created in God's image; a "Jew at heart" could end up being satisfied with good intentions instead of living in accordance with the law, as codified in the *Shulchan Aruch,* the book of Jewish law.

Aha, That's It

Shulchan Aruch literally means "the prepared table," and this work by Joseph Caro (1488–1575) is the definitive compilation of Jewish Law. Its title suggests that the legal system is easily accessible and "delectable."

Aha, That's It

A "*cherem*" is a ban of excommunication, placing someone out of the pale of social contact. No one is allowed to conduct business, marry, or even engage in conversation with someone in "cherem." Although rarely used, it was the most powerful—and in most cases the only—means of ensuring compliance with the norms of acceptable Jewish behavior.

For the Gaon of Vilna, Hasidism represented no less than a defense of ignorance, a justification for a minimum of study, a dire threat to the Judaism that for centuries had emphasized deed over creed, the act over intention. He felt so strongly about this that he actually issued a *cherem*, a ban of excommunication, against the Hasidim. Those who agreed with his views would be called *Mitnagdim*, opponents. And so was created yet another major rift between Jews and a division that still exists to this day—though not with the same kind of intense animosity.

A beautiful postscript has it that an attempt was made for reconciliation between the Ba'al Shem Tov and the Gaon of Vilna. A meeting was set, yet, for reasons that remain a mystery, it never took place. And, as the people who tell the story often add, if the two would have met and been able to merge their two teachings into one, then surely Messiah would have come.

The Response of the Intellectuals

Mysticism, Messianism, and Hasidism were clearly spiritual movements. Together with these, strangely enough, must be added the great leaps of scientific discovery of the times that had a spiritual source.

Today we often talk in terms of science versus religion. It was not always so. The great Jewish sage Maimonides (see Chapter 15, "The Crescent of Brotherhood"), speaking for the greatest majority of ancient Jewish philosophers and sages, posited that science and religion are two equally valid doors for entering the province of knowledge of God: "We can only obtain a knowledge of God through His works; His works give evidence of his existence. To study His works is to learn more about Him." In the twentieth century, Albert Einstein explained the relationship between them this way: "Science without religion is lame; religion without science is blind."

The Rabbi-Scientists

That's why some of the earliest scientists were rabbis, combining their search for God with a deep desire to know more about the workings of His wondrous universe.

What interested these rabbi-scientists most? Obviously, the heavens and the earth—astronomy to comprehend God's ways in the heavens, and medicine to understand the mechanism of God's most wondrous creations, man and woman.

In the fourteenth century, Rabbi Immanuel Bonfils composed the astronomical tables that were extensively used by explorers from his time forward and also invented a decimal system 150 years before the first one known in Europe. Levi ben Gerson (1288–1344), rabbi and philosopher, influenced Copernicus with his brilliant writings on astronomy and mathematics and even invented the *camera oscura*, the first camera in history. (How's that for a Jewish Kodak moment?)

Navigators, including Columbus, Magellan, and Vasco de Gama, all couldn't have undertaken their journeys without using the "Jacob's staff," a quadrant that Gerson invented. Columbus also made extensive use of astronomical tables drawn up by Abraham Zacuto (1450–1510). Here again, it was Jewish ingenuity, rooted in a rabbinic desire to know more about the stars, that allowed man to set sail on the journeys of modern-day discovery.

And Of Course the Doctors

Healing is not just a profession; it's also a *mitzvah*, a religious act with divine compensation. To cure someone is to allow the person more years to serve God. It's an ultimate expression of Jewish reverence for life. And so most often the court physicians, the healers, and the great medical innovators of the Middle Ages were Jews.

One of the greatest, Isaac Israeli (850–950), had a profound impact on Christian scholars, including Thomas Aquinas, as well as medical practitioners around the world. He was wise enough even then to push diet over drugs and to emphasize preventive medicine. Rabbinic academies included the study of medicine as part of the regular curriculum about the year 1000.

Anatomy, at least that of animals, was required knowledge for determining the Kosher status of meat. Every rabbi, therefore, had to be at least somewhat familiar with the major organs of the body and their functions. Greatest of all, of course, was Maimonides, whom we already met as physician to Saladin the Great in Chapter 15, "The Crescent of Brotherhood." From him, Jews continue to be inspired to dedicate their lives to both Jewish study and medicine, to the scriptures and science.

Oath of Maimonides

Many doctors around the world have chosen to add to their Hippocratic Oath, for the proper practice of medicine, the Prayer for Physicians composed by Maimonides. It closes with this beautiful paragraph:

> *May I be moderate in everything except in the knowledge of this science; so far as it is concerned, may I be insatiable; grant me the strength and opportunity always to correct what I have acquired, always to extend its domain; for knowledge is boundless and the spirit of man can also extend indefinitely, daily to enrich itself with new acquirements. Today he can discover his errors of yesterday, and tomorrow he may obtain new light on what he thinks him so sure of today. Oh God, thou hast appointed me to watch over the life and death of thy creatures. Here am I ready for my vocation.*

It is physician-rabbis like Maimonides who not only demonstrated the great link between science and religion, but also pointed out yet another way to respond to persecution: To make yourself so invaluable to the world at large through your intellectual contributions that you gain the rewards of respect and acceptance.

The Least You Need to Know

➤ Kabalah is a way to find escape from the hardships of this world by thinking about another, finding comfort in mysterious teachings about heaven, reincarnation, and the coming of the Messiah.

➤ Gematriya, the secret of letters as numbers, is another way to find deeper meaning in the Bible and perhaps even to discover "Biblical Codes" and predictions.

➤ Kabalah gave the Jews a sense of empowerment, enabling them to understand divine wisdom, commune with God Himself, and even, when necessary, to use the power of God's secret name for their salvation.

➤ Messianism gave people hope for a while, but proved harmful when abused by false Messiahs such as Shabbatai Zevi.

➤ Hasidism revolutionized Judaism with its unique approaches to the holiness of the common man, the primacy of feeling and fervor, and the role of joy in the proper worship of God.

➤ Hasidism was perceived as a threat to traditional Judaism, with its emphasis on the Law and on Study, and its adherents were excommunicated by Rabbi Elijah, the Gaon of Vilna.

➤ Hasidim and Mitnagdim represent the two surviving groups of this controversy, although they no longer excommunicate or battle each other, but consider their differences as alternative ways of serving God.

➤ Science and religion were originally perceived not to be in conflict, but rather complementary ways of sensing God's management of the world.

➤ Rabbis of the Middle Ages often combined their Jewish scholarship with secular studies, primarily in the fields of astronomy and medicine, to which they made major contributions.

Part 6
Emancipation and Enlightenment

As we approach modern times, history seems to have switched into fast-forward mode. Suddenly, for countless reasons (some of which defy understanding), the world explodes with change. The Industrial Revolution, scientific advancement, urbanization and the growth of cities all alter the lifestyles of people in dramatic fashion. More significantly, there appear singular changes in the social fabric of society. The power of the Church is replaced by the power of the people; democratic principles of equality and brotherhood, of liberty and equality, gain legitimacy and popular approval. For the Jews, the world at long last begins to shed its hostility and extends a hand of friendship.

Part 6 explores the meaning of this phenomenon as the former Jew of the ghetto begins to mingle freely with his neighbors. France, Germany, and England each witness the birth of a new brand of Jew—a Jew who responds to the opportunities of freedom in different ways while making a profound impact on the cultural, political and social landscapes of his place of residence. America, in a class all by itself as the "land of opportunity," creates yet another Jew—and a new kind of Judaism. Around the entire globe, there seems to be not a place where Jews can't be found and where they are not deeply affected by this age of dramatic change.

Chapter 19

The French Revolution Frees the Jews

In This Chapter

➤ What the French Revolution meant for the Jewish people

➤ The new status of Jews as free and equal citizens

➤ Napoléon and the reinstitution of the ancient Sanhedrin

➤ How Jews rose to the top in countless fields when they were given the opportunity

➤ The trial of the century—and how justice finally triumphed

How does change happen? Is it a slow, tedious, drawn-out process of little steps forward? (Like a wit once said, Jews only change *yiddle* by *yiddle.*) Or does change come unexpectedly, in a lightning flash of new insight followed immediately by thunderous calls for new and different approaches?

The end of the eighteenth century seems to suggest the latter. What was considered sacrosanct for millennia was suddenly scrapped in the junkyard of useless dogma. Kings were toppled, the Church was disempowered, and the voice of the people demanded to be heard. And all this happened literally almost overnight in the one country of Europe most able to influence change everywhere. "When France sneezed, Europe caught a cold" is the way historians put it. France didn't just sneeze, it exploded with the fury of the French Revolution, and the result was *gesundheit*, heard all over the continent.

The Revolution of the Mind

People rebelled because of ideas and ideals. The slogan of *"liberté, egalité, fraternité"*—liberty, equality, fraternity—didn't come to the masses by prophetic inspiration. It was the product of the intellectual thought of three of the greatest eighteenth-century French philosophers:

➤ Voltaire, with his great caustic wit, for the first time allowed people to free themselves from the stranglehold of the clergy.

➤ Condorcet, with his philosophy of the "infinite perfectability of man," laid the foundation for the optimistic spirit required to fashion a new society.

➤ Most significant of all, though, was Rousseau's development of the idea of the "social contract" —a concept that was not only to fuel the French Revolution, but also kindle the spirit of nationalism in most of the countries of Europe during the nineteenth century.

Rousseau's main idea, which seems so obvious to us in retrospect that it's hard to believe it came as revelation, was that the state has to be a popular expression of the will of the people, not of the ruler. The people have a right to break their contract, to "fire the boss," if he doesn't live up to his end of the bargain. Rousseau preached people power at a time when nobles and kings thought that the masses were only there for their pleasure and lived only to do their bidding.

People had rights. All men were equal. Even rulers don't have unlimited power. Do these breakthrough ideas of the late eighteenth century sound at all familiar? How remarkable to consider that the novel ideas that would reshape the modern world and at long last free the Jews were the ancient Biblical ideals of the Torah and prophets garbed in the more fashionable dress of sophisticated French philosophy!

Off with Their Heads

So it was the people against Louis XVI in an unthinkable match-up, and it was the King who lost his head at the guillotine (which was undoubtedly not his favorite style of furniture). For the first time, the shout was, "The King is dead—long live the people," not "long live the King." France was declared a republic. The nobles were marched in a seemingly never-ending chain to be deprived of their positions as heads of state, together with their heads as well. With the storming of the Bastille on July 13, 1789, the French proudly proclaimed that the ideals of the Revolution would now become a reality.

Are Jews Human? The Great Debate

One small detail still had to be resolved. When the French Revolution spoke of human rights, was that supposed to include Jews as well? The National Assembly was called on to discuss this matter. A delegation of Jews came from Alsace Lorraine to plead their cause. They were joined by Mirabeau, Cleremont-Tonnerre, and Robespierre. The opposition had bishops and clerics and a goodly remnant of fanatical anti-Semites. But when the dust cleared, the Jacobin Deputy Duport concluded: "I believe that freedom of worship does not permit any distinction to be made in the political rights of citizens on account of their creed...I demand that...a decree be passed that the Jews in France enjoy the privileges of whole citizenship."

Yenta's Little Secrets

Although France was the first European country to grant Jews equal rights, it was preceded by one other nation in the world. Can you guess which one? Of course it was the United States of America. At the time, the U.S. had fewer than two thousand Jews, but it nevertheless felt a moral obligation to live by the principles of the Declaration of Independence.

Free at Last

It was September 28, 1791. For the first time since the destruction of the second Temple in the year 70 C.E., Jews were declared to be equal with all other people in France. For centuries, Jews had been praying for the Messiah so that they could return to their homeland, Israel. Now it was France, the land where they lived, that could finally be called home. That was a breakthrough, they felt, that bordered on the Messianic.

The One Condition

But it was made very clear to the Jews that their acceptance was not unconditional. They would be considered Frenchmen, but only if they themselves defined their identity by that title. Clermont-Tonnerre, who had ardently fought for Jewish rights, made clear that he did so only if the Jews would be Frenchmen first and Jews second. He summed up his position very clearly: "To Jews as human beings—everything; to Jews as a people—nothing!"

Allegiance to the land where they lived—this became the trade-off for Jews wherever they were offered their freedom. How to find the proper balance between their national identity and their religious definition would become the greatest challenge to Jewish survival in the following centuries.

Napoléon and the Jews

Napoléon's size was the only thing that was small about him. Leo Stein said it best: "Napoléon was a little fellow; so is the uranium atom." Psychologists are still so impressed with his ego that the Napoléonic Complex (compensating for one's small stature by lording it over other people) is named after him. And Napoléon had a dream: He wanted to rule the world. If only he didn't have the misfortune of meeting up with his own Waterloo, he just might have succeeded.

What, you ask, does this have to do with the Jews? With about 77,000 of them in France at the time, Napoléon was smart enough to realize that it would be to his advantage to have these people on his side. With brilliant planning, he called together an Assembly of Notables, gathering the most prominent Jewish dignitaries of the land to answer a list of questions he put before them. What he really wanted to ensure was that they would put their loyalty to France ahead of loyalty to their people. When he got the right answer, he told them he wanted to convoke a Grand Sanhedrin, just like the one that the Jews had in their ancient days of glory, in order to give the decisions of the Assembly of Notables religious authority.

Yenta's Little Secrets

The Jews of the new Sanhedrin had no problems with questions like: "Do Jews born in France consider France their country and would they be willing to defend it?" And "Are Jews permitted to have more than one wife?" They had trouble responding, though, when Napoléon asked them if Jews and Christians could intermarry. Intermarriage would not be a sign of friendship, but rather an act of suicide for the Jewish religion.

Napoléon had his own devious motives, but for a while the Jews thought that they were lucky enough to live to see another sign of the Messianic Era—the reinstitution of their own ancient supreme court. Typical of Jewish reaction was a letter in a French newspaper by a grateful Jew: "France is our Palestine, her mountains our Zion, her rivers our Jordan." Even in some Hasidic *shtetels* in Poland, famous rabbis joined their disciples in singing the *Marseillaise*. Although the rejoicing was more than a little excessive, it captured the spirit of Jews who felt they owed a very big thanks to an unusually little man. Napoléon had replaced the Jews' yellow badge of shame with an emblem of pride.

"Carriéres aux Talents"

To rule the world, Napoléon would need the help of his most gifted people. And so he made it his national policy to open up *Carriéres aux Talents,*" careers for all the people of talent, no matter what their religion. It was suddenly as if the floodgates were opened and the only requirement for success was ability. Jews could hardly believe their good fortune, and many rushed to France for this incredible opportunity. Deprived for centuries of using their talents to the fullest, Jews now exploded on the political, economic, cultural, and artistic scenes to make an impact that left their neighbors gasping. France would remain indebted for this policy to this very day.

Statesmen and Bankers

Adolphe Crémieux, Minister of Justice in the Provisional Revolutionary government of the mid-nineteenth century, was probably the greatest public figure French Jewry produced. His two great social reforms—abolition of Negro slavery from the French colonies, and the elimination of the death penalty for political dissenters—were intellectual turning points. Later French-Jewish statesmen are names every French school boy is required to memorize: David Raynal, Eduard Millaud, L. S. Klotz, Paul Straus, Maurice Bokanowski, Georges Mandel, Jules Moch, and most influential of all, Leon Bloom, Prime Minister of France several times over.

Allowed now to reach the top as bankers, France had Rothschilds as well as Lazard Fréres. But the most interesting, the most influential, and the ones with the most impact to this day, were the Pereire Brothers—Isaac and Emil—who developed the credit concept as the keystone of the modern banking system. Any time you get your MasterCard or Visa bill, try to think kindly of these brilliant Jews, who probably would have warned you that you would be better off buying wholesale. It was their cousin, by the way, Olinde Rodrigues, who built the first railway in France in 1835. And, some years later, a network of railways throughout France, Switzerland, Spain, and southern Russia.

Music, Theater, Arts, and Literature

In almost a frenzy of artistic expression, now that they were allowed to be active participants in society, Jews proved that the descendants of David could excel in music; the children of prophets could declaim from the stage like no one else; the descendants of the most creative people on earth could paint and write and philosophize on the very highest level of mankind. Let's thank Georges Bizet for *Carmen;* Offenbach for *Tales of Hoffman;* Halévi for *La Juive;* Saint-Saëns for *Samson and Delilah;* Paul Dukas for *The Sorcerer's Apprentice.* Let's applaud Rachel and Sarah Bernhardt, the two greatest actresses in the history of the French

Sage Sayings

"I think of music as Jewish because it's dramatic, it's intense, it has a certain passionate lyricism to it. I can't imagine it written by a goy."

—Aaron Copland

theater, who established new styles of acting emulated around the world. Let's be grateful for playwrights and directors: Tristan Bernard, Henri Bernstein, Porto-Riche, Alfred Savoir, and Benoit-Levy.

Yenta's Little Secrets

Why do Jews make great actors? Arthur Miller once explained why the Jew Paul Muni was such an enormous success both on Broadway and in Hollywood. He said, "Muni threw himself in each role with a sense of dedication that can only be explained one way: He was pursued by a fear of failure." So too, every Jew always strove for perfection because he didn't dare to fail and prove to the world that it was right about him.

Sage Sayings

"I think that in the future art may yet speak as great poetry itself, with a solemn and majestic ring in which the Hebrew prophets spoke to the Jews of old, demanding noble aspirations, condemning in the most trenchant manner private vices, and warning us in deep tones against lapses from morals and duties."

—M. W. Watts

The list of French-Jewish artists, writers, and philosophers is at least as impressive. Think of a world that might never have known the works of Camille Pissarro (what an impression he left!), Chaim Soutine, Marc Chagall, Monet Katz, Jacques Lipshitz, and Hannah Orloff. Imagine never being able to read books by Marcel Proust, Andre Maurois, Edmond Fleg, Joseph Kessel, and Jules Romains. Think of modern philosophy without Henri Bergson and his master work, *Creative Evolution*.

Oh, the talent that would have gone to waste if the world didn't at last come to realize that careers should be determined by talent rather than curtailed by prejudice.

The Trial of the Century: Dreyfus

For a while, though, good feelings toward the Jews took a back seat when France was rocked by a political scandal. A Jewish captain, Alfred Dreyfus, was accused of selling military secrets to the Germans and betraying his country. "See," said the anti-Semites, "we were right all along. Jews aren't really Frenchmen first. They have their own agenda, and they can be bought for money." A document written by Dreyfus himself incriminated him beyond question. He was court martialed, found guilty, and branded a traitor to France. Stripped of his epaulettes in a ceremony of degradation, he was shipped off to Devil's Island, shouting, *"Je suis innocent! Vive la France!"*

The public degradation of Alfred Dreyfus. (Courtesy of Leonard de Salva/ Corbis)

It took years of determined investigative work until they found out that Dreyfus was framed, his incriminating letter a forgery. It had been a vicious plot to undo all the progress Jews had made in the preceding few years. Emile Zola, the great novelist, shook

Sage Sayings

"I accuse. Truth is on the march and nothing can stop it."

—Emile Zola

not only France but the entire world, which was captivated by the story, when he wrote his famous open letter, *J'Accuse*. In it he named names and made clear the extent of the conspiracy. In politics, frame-ups don't usually come with happy endings, but this one did. The truth finally came out; in 1906 Dreyfus was fully acquitted and restored to his former position, and he was awarded the Legion of Honor. The French people not only freed the Jews; they proved that there was justice for them as well.

Yenta's Little Secrets

The Jewish State, amazingly enough, was born at the Dreyfus trial. One of the spectators was a newspaper correspondent who attended the proceedings of the military court until they were declared secret. His name was Theodore Herzl, founder of political Zionism and architect of the Jewish State. In his diary he wrote of the impact the trial had upon him: "I can still see the defendant coming into the hall in his dark artillery uniform trimmed with gray. I still hear him give his credentials...and also the howls of the mob in the street in front of the ...école Militaire, where he was degraded, still ring unforgettably in my ears: 'Death! Death to the Jews!' Death to Jews all because this one was a traitor?"

The Least You Need to Know

➤ The fall of the Bastille ushered in a new age of freedom and equality for the Jews that would break ground for similar movements in the rest of Europe.

➤ After great debate, Jews, for the first time since the fall of the second Temple, enjoyed full right of citizenship in a foreign land.

➤ Jews had, however, to acknowledge that their first allegiance was to the country in which they lived and the rights granted to them were as individuals, not as a people.

➤ Napoléon sought to gain favor with his Jewish citizens so that he could proceed with his plans to conquer the world.

➤ The establishment of the Grand Sanhedrin seemed like a momentous step forward for the Jews, although it had no lasting consequences.

➤ Napoléon's policy of "careers for the talented" opened up the way for Jews to excel in countless fields.

➤ The Dreyfus case and his eventual acquittal was a true test of the French people and their newly proclaimed tolerance of the Jews.

Chapter 20

When the Walls Came Tumbling Down: Germany

In This Chapter

➤ How Jews coped with the blessings and challenges of their new-found freedom in Germany

➤ What happens when Jews don't want to be Jews anymore

➤ How Judaism was "reformed"

➤ When being a German was more important than being a Jew

➤ How the new religion of communism was fathered by a baptized Jew

➤ Finding a way to "live modern" and still be a Jew

➤ An explosion of geniuses

In 1798, in the City of Bonn, where young Beethoven lived, a remarkable scene took place: Christians and Jews marched together to the ghetto walls, carpenters used their tools to break down the gates, and in a dramatic act proclaiming brotherhood and equality for all, the ghetto walls were finally shattered. It was a symbol of a new age of enlightenment and a signal that feudalism and fanaticism were on their way out in the Age of Reason.

True, it was only a beginning. Full legal equality would have to wait until 1871, and there was still a great deal of bigotry and anti-Semitism. But it was clear that the world had changed, and in Germany more than anywhere else, Jews reacted to this change and the challenges presented by their new-found freedom in different ways—ways that still serve to this day as models for Jewish responses to modern life.

"Let's Not Be Jewish Anymore"—Heine

Heinrich Heine (1797–1856) is considered by many the greatest lyric poet Germany ever produced. A champion of democracy, Heine soon realized that although he had made it out of the ghetto, he still didn't make it *into* the world he so admired and wanted to be a part of. A Jew might be tolerated but he could never become a true equal. And so Heine took the dramatic step that in an age of freedom became a personal matter of choice: He renounced his faith for his future.

Voluntary Baptism

With his gift for words and succinct epigrams, Heine explained his submission to baptism as "an entrance ticket to European society." It was a marvelous phrase that put his conversion into perfect perspective. What for centuries had been attempted by the Church at the point of a sword and in the main had proved unsuccessful was now achieved without force, simply by holding out the pot of gold at the end of the non-Jewish rainbow.

Voluntary baptism became a new fad. It's estimated that at least half of Berlin Jewry was baptized during the first decades of the nineteenth century. But this didn't mean that Jews suddenly realized that Jesus was really the Son of God or the Messiah. No, it meant that they understood clearly that if they were willing to play the game and say that they now saw the light, their days would be brightened by greater opportunities for advancement, for wealth, and for acceptance.

"Author Unknown"

But what if you sacrifice a great deal to buy the ticket and still can't get in? What happened to Heine has touches of a sad soap opera ending. Looking back, years later, he concluded: "I regret that I was baptized. Now I'm hated by the Christians *and* the Jews. And I don't see that it's helped me very much."

Spending his final days as an incurable invalid among non-Jews, he recalled with envy the great kindness and compassion of his former people, who might have made his suffering more bearable. In his "Confessions" he acknowledged: "The writer of these pages might well be proud that his ancestors belonged to the noble house of Israel, that he is a descendant of those martyrs who gave the world a God and an ethic, who struggled and suffered on all the battlefields of ideas."

And the final irony of all: One of his greatest poems, "Lorelei," a classic of German literature, was later listed in all modern German textbooks over the signature, "Author Unknown." It seems the baptism entrance ticket can still be voided even after you've paid the price!

Pulpit Stories

Poor Heinrich Heine. In addition to all of his other problems, he had a shrew for a wife. She made his life miserable. Yet, when Heine realized his end was near, he left his wife all of his money—on one condition: "I bequeath all my property to my wife on the condition that she remarry immediately. Then there will be at least one man who will sincerely regret my death."

"Jewish Germans, Not German Jews"—Mendelssohn

For Moses Mendelssohn (1729–1786), rejecting your religion clearly wasn't an acceptable option. You don't cure a headache by decapitation, and you don't solve the pain of being a Jew in a non-Jewish world by giving up your heart and your soul. There must be a better way, he thought, long before the phrase became a Madison Avenue slogan. So began the daring effort of a little hunchback philosopher trying to straighten out the Jewish people so that they could stand proud and erect among their neighbors.

The Hunchback Straightens Out the Ghetto Jews

You can tell the greatness of a person by how much he or she has to overcome. For Mendelssohn, the disabilities were monumental; he was a Jew, he spoke with a pronounced Jewish accent, and he had a severe curvature of the spine. Despite all this he made it to the top of the social ladder in a society where the literary *salon* was the meeting place for the most important people of his time.

Mendelssohn's literary reviews made him the leading German stylist; his critical essays on art made him the founder of modern aesthetic criticism. He was brilliant; the philosopher Immanuel Kant called him a genius "destined to create a new epic in metaphysics and to establish an altogether new norm of criticism." He was witty; his *bon mots* regaled royalty and intellectuals. They called him "this little Jew Moses with a Socratic soul," and as he hobnobbed with the rich and famous, they respected his wish to be served only Kosher food.

Gotthold Lessing, then Germany's foremost dramatist, wrote a play, *Nathan the Wise*, in which he based the main character on Mendelssohn. The play became a smash success all over Europe. With the impact that only theater can achieve, the play helped to change the popular image of the Jew from the backward ghetto dweller to a proud and cultured modern thinker who has a great deal to offer the contemporary world.

*Moses Mendelssohn, the
"Hunchback Philosopher."
(Courtesy of Culver
Pictures)*

Pulpit Stories

Moses Mendelsson fell in love with a beautiful, wealthy woman. The match seemed highly unlikely, especially in light of Mendelssohn's severe physical deformity. When the matter was brought up, he shared with his "intended" a dream he'd had: "Before we were born, my soul was informed that the one I was to marry would have a hunchback. I knew it would be more difficult for a woman to suffer from something that mars her beauty than for a man. And so I begged the heavenly courts to switch this divine decree from you to me. Ever since, I've considered it a privilege to be able to constantly show the world this great proof of my love for you." And the two of them lived happily as man and wife ever after.

"If I made it to the top," Mendelssohn thought to himself, "why couldn't other Jews do the same?" The real problem, as he saw it, was not to get the Jews out of the ghetto, but to get the ghetto out of the Jews. For so long his people had been sealed in a closed world that they lost the ability to use their minds for anything other than their limited religious literature. Through no fault of their own, they were foreigners to music, literature, and the arts. Even the language of the land in which they lived was hardly known to them as they spoke a bastardized German-Yiddish.

Mendelssohn was determined that he would change all this. He would give the Jews back the German language and the German culture, and help to turn them into real German Jews, with an emphasis on the first word and not the second. At the heart of Mendelssohn's philosophy was the idea that the more Jews would be *like* the Germans, the more they would be *liked by* the Germans.

Reformed Judaism: How Far?

Mendelssohn began with what has to be the most unusual translation of the Bible in history. He turned the Torah into magnificent lucid German *written in Hebrew letters* so that the people who already knew Hebrew and the original text would be better able to learn the German of the translation! With a knowledge of German, he felt, Jews would then read secular literature, become integrated into the outside world, and become involved in modern culture. And with these aspirations, Mendelssohn fathered Reform Judaism of the nineteenth century.

Mendelssohn had turned the Bible into a vehicle for making a Jew a better German, but his followers decided to go him one better and have the synagogue achieve the same purpose.

In 1815, Israel Jacobson introduced the recitation of prayers in German. To make the service even more like that of the neighbors, he brought in the musical accompaniment of an organ. Soon, more daring "reforms" were introduced: Sunday was substituted for Saturday as the day of rest; every mention of Messianic redemption was deleted from Jewish writings and preaching, and, for the first time in history, the name synagogue was changed to Temple to make clear that German Jews no longer looked forward to the rebuilding of a temple outside of Germany for *"hier ist unser heimland und das ist unser tempel"*—"here is our homeland, and *this* is our temple."

Aha, That's It

Siddur is the name of the prayer book used by Jews, both in the synagogue and at home. The Hebrew root is *seder*, or order, because the prayers follow a prescribed order based on Jewish law and tradition.

Aha, That's It

Kosher means to be "fit," or "permitted." The word is usually applied to food prepared to dietary regulations (the laws of *Kashrut*), but may also be used for other things as well (that is, a miniskirt is not really "kosher clothing for a synagogue").

Rites and rituals observed outside of the synagogue that served in any way to separate Jews from other Germans were also relegated to the religious trash bin. Eating only *kosher* food meant you couldn't socialize easily, so that law had to be removed as unnecessarily primitive. Circumcision branded you as a Jew for life, so at the Reform rabbinical conferences in Breslau and Frankfort, it was abolished as being too barbaric.

There was one common theme clearly running through all of these early manifestations of Reform Judaism: In their intense love of the German people, they wanted to renounce their own peoplehood, keeping only their attachment to God. "Keep the faith"—but forget about fellow Jews around the world, declared the intellectual founders of original Reform Judaism—men such as Leopold Zunz, Abraham Geiger, and Samuel Holdheim.

Contemporary Reform Judaism today has very little in common with the excesses of its founders. Today there is a strong sense of peoplehood and a recognition that claims of kinship and family are not to be disregarded. Patriotism for one's own country is seen as compatible with love and support for Israel as a homeland of choice for all those who desire to live there. Distinctive rituals, even those that set Jews apart, are seen as valid expressions of personal tradition that enrich the larger culture of which Jews are a part.

Reform Jews today may differ with the more traditional Orthodox and Conservative views on the relevance of ancient laws (see Chapter 22, "America The Beautiful"), but they are in firm agreement with the Talmudic principle that *"chaverim kol yisroel"* — "all Jews are joined in friendship."

The Haskala: The Jewish Age of Reason

Moses Mendelssohn, it's been said, fathered two movements. The first, early Reform, stressed God to the exclusion of Jewish peoplehood. The second, *haskala* (Jewish enlightenment), emphasized the culture of the Jewish people to the exclusion of God. The *maskilim* (enlightened ones) loved scholarship but couldn't stand Judaism, delighted in Jewish culture but disdained its religious trappings. The maskilim hated Yiddish because it smacked of the ghetto and Torah; they hoped to bring about a cultural renaissance in a Hebrew divorced from any references to a Divine Being.

Haskala would have had a far more powerful impact had it stressed its positive love of learning rather than its negative animosity toward those who didn't share their secular views. Even the subjects for study often became ingenious attempts for Jewish self-denigration. Julius Wellhausen became the spokesman for Biblical "higher criticism" (although he didn't make clear what it was higher than) in order to prove that the Bible had many authors, that the Hebrews didn't discover monotheism, and that the Torah isn't an original Jewish document.

Whenever the motive of Biblical critics was a sincere scientific approach to the study of the Bible, it was certainly to be applauded. But when it became confused with self-hatred and the need to tear down what others revered, it shed an unflattering light on its disciples.

A Final Sad Legacy

The original Moses of old never lived to see the Promised Land. Moses Mendelssohn, dreamt glorious dreams for his Jews of Germany who, if only freed from their ghetto ways, would see the Messianic dream fulfilled in their native homeland. Mendelssohn was sure he found a way to perpetuate Judaism in a world where the ghetto walls crumbled. But like the Moses of old, he, too, was doomed to disappointment.

Aha, That's It

Haskala, from the Hebrew word meaning "wisdom," refers to the movement of Jewish enlightenment. Although the Age of Enlightenment is usually applied to the eighteenth century, Jewish historians use the term for the era beginning with Mendelssohn through the nineteenth century.

When he died at the age of 57, the Berlin press published an obituary that caricatured him. His two daughters and his son Felix (the father of the composer named Felix Mendelssohn) became converts to Christianity. The Mendelssohn name is today most well known not for Moses, but for Felix who composed oratorios for the Church, not for the synagogue. Moses Mendelssohn had lived his life as an observant Jew, but he has no Jewish descendants.

"Let's Start a New Religion"—Marx

Karl isn't one of the funny Marx Brothers. But considering how much Jews have suffered as a result of his theories, they can't help but wish that he would have been the one who couldn't say a word. Karl Marx (1818–1883) would never have passed even Groucho Marx's lenient standard—requesting admission to the anti-Semitic country club that rejected his son from entry to the swimming pool: "Since my little girl is only half Jewish, would it be all right if she went into the pool only up to her waist?"

Karl Marx, with both grandfathers rabbis, definitely wouldn't have been able to even dunk his toes. Yet, the father of communism, in one of those classic reversals we'll leave to psychiatrists to figure out, was not only baptized by his father at an early age, but spent the rest of his life trying to "emancipate mankind from Judaism." Marx was a renegade German Jew who thought in Messianic terms. He believed in the Biblical ideal of paradise, but he chose to expel God from its precincts and allow the

Sage Sayings

"Marxism is contrary to the Torah, which protects private property."

—Isaac Jacob Rabinowitz, renowned Talmudic scholar (1854–1918)

workers inside to remain as lords. His master work, *Das Kapital*, became the secular Bible of world communism and has had a major impact on history.

Why Jewish Boys Rebel

It shouldn't really come as a shock that the seeds of a revolution were planted by a mind with Jewish genes. It was, after all, Marx's ancestors who rebelled against their Egyptian task masters. It was the prophets who preached the necessity for a change of the social order predicated on justice and fairness. It was the Jewish spirit that had for centuries envisioned a better world. Marx responded with a Jewish heart, but with a pagan mind. The Bible may have been father to the revolutionary spirit, but communism was clearly a bastard child. How very wrong its misplaced faith was would become apparent in the blood baths and sufferings of the centuries that followed.

Sage Sayings

"The Trotskys make the revolutions, and the Bronsteins pay the price."

—Rabbi Mazeh, Chief Rabbi of Moscow, after Trotsky, né Bronstein, turned him down in his plea to prevent anti-Semitic pogroms.

Aha, That's It

Pogroms were organized attacks against the Jews to which the authorities turned a blind eye as the populace plundered, raped, and murdered them. Pogroms were extremely popular in late-nineteenth-century Russia, and used as a tool by the czars to divert the anger of the masses to a convenient scapegoat.

Why Trotsky Didn't Make It

Unfortunately, Jews were for many years identified with communism. The fact that the ideological founder was born a Jew, although baptized, was enough for some people to call communism a "Jewish plot for world domination." When one of the key leaders of the 1917 Communist Revolution in Russia was Leon Trotsky (1880–1940), born Lev Bronstein, the Jewish connection was once again reaffirmed.

The irony is that both Marx and Trotsky dedicated their lives to proving the old Yiddish adage that "only a born Jew can be a real anti-Semite." Marx's first major essay, *On The Jewish Question*, is filled with such hatred of the Jews and of Judaism that Hitler later claimed some of his own feelings were shaped by reading it. Trotsky, for his part, gave the green light to *pogroms*, and when appealed to by the chief rabbi of Moscow to put a stop to the killings because Trotsky, too, was Jewish, responded: "You are mistaken, I am a Social Democrat, that's all."

In the long story of the rise and fall of the communist movement, Jews had the unique distinction of playing the roles of both villain and victim. They were accused of being communists even while they were hounded, persecuted, and pillaged by them.

The saga of Trotsky himself serves as the most vivid example. It is he who almost destroys Jewish life in Russia. Yet, when Lenin dies, Stalin, not Trotsky, is designated to succeed him. Winston Churchill described so very powerfully what Trotsky must have realized: "He was still a Jew. Nothing could get over that. Hard fortune when you have deserted your family, repudiated your race, spat upon the religion of your father…to be balked of so great a prize for so narrow-minded a reason."

Trotsky, who would from then on most often be referred to as "the Jew, Trotsky," was kicked out of Russia and exiled to Mexico, and then murdered by an assassin sent by Stalin. That was to be his "reward" for the glorious part he played in the Communist Revolution. Before his own death, Stalin had grand plans to murder tens of thousands of Jewish intellectuals and doctors—a plan only averted by Stalin's sudden death on Purim day in 1953. (And tell me it was just a coincidence that before his evil plan could be carried out he would die on the same day as Haman of old!)

> **Sage Sayings**
>
> "Who called into being the Liberal movement in Austria?…the Jews! By whom were the Jews betrayed and deserted? By the Liberals! Who created the Pan-German movement in Austria? The Jews! By whom were the Jews left in the lurch?…Nay, more, spat on like dogs?…By the Germans! And the same thing will happen to them at the hands of the socialists and communists?"
>
> —Arthur Schnitzler, Austrian novelist (1862–1931)

As you can now see, the dream of Karl Marx, far from emancipating the Jews, ended in despair and disillusionment, in a disastrous nightmare.

"Let's Be Jewish and Modern"—Hirsch

With the walls of the ghetto crumbling, most of the Jews, just like Humpty Dumpty, had a great fall—and trying to put themselves together again afterwards wasn't easy at all. The stories of Heine, Mendelsson, and Marx were sad ones for Jewish survival. Fortunately, there was one other movement in nineteenth-century Germany that dealt with emancipation in a way that allowed for continuity of its descendants with the Jewish people to this day.

What's Neo-Orthodox?

From the beginning of Jewish history, Judaism didn't need any adjectives. But with the birth of Reform Judaism, it suddenly became necessary to identify the "brand" of Judaism you belonged to. Orthodox Judaism meant that you rejected "reforming" your religion in any way and accepted the "orthodox" traditional interpretation of your faith. But when Reform Judaism gained in strength, it was clear that Orthodox Judaism needed a new adjective to counter it, so Neo-Orthodoxy was born.

Identified with Samson Raphael Hirsch (1808–1888), this "new" or more modern expression of traditional Judaism was actually in many ways a return to the more worldly approach of Maimonides (see Chapter 15, "The Crescent of Brotherhood").

Sage Sayings

"The words of Rabbi Soloveitchik... voice a principled ideal for the unity of all human knowledge. There is sacred learning and there is learning which is sacred and...while we recognize the distinction between the two, we also affirm their affinities and mutual enrichment. We have the conviction... that every enterprise of true learning has its part in religious experience and deserves honor and respect."

—Dr. Norman Lamm, President, Yeshiva University

Ghettos made the Jews of necessity turn inward, to be restricted solely to the knowledge found in their religious works. With freedom and the challenges of an open society, Hirsch taught that it was time again to open Jewish minds to the dual sources of wisdom. He called his approach *Torah im derekh eretz*—Torah joined with modern culture.

Hirsch's first priority was, without question, Torah. The law was to be scrupulously followed as divinely commanded. But, unlike the Eastern European Orthodox Rabbinate that declared it heresy, Hirsch encouraged study at universities and considered secular writings aids to an even stronger and more intense religious commitment. Even the synagogue service was modernized with sermons in German—a really daring innovation that went against "tradition" but helped to keep many Jews from drifting from their faith. Hirsch created the ideal of a *jissroel-mensch* (Israel man), a synthesis of an observant as well as an enlightened Jew, an ideal that still serves as a role model for the contemporary movement of modern Orthodoxy (see Chapter 22, "America the Beautiful").

Geniuses at Work

The most powerful result of Jews being granted equal rights in Germany was the opportunity, as in France, for talent to shine forth, for genius to have an opportunity to prove itself, for native ability to be unhindered by prejudice. And like champion thoroughbreds, Jews couldn't wait for the starting gun to charge out of the gate, prove their speed, and claim their proper prize in the winner's circle.

"Show Me the Money"

A Jew never wanted to be as rich as Rockefeller; he always aspired to be richer than Rothschild. The founder of this remarkable banking family was Meir Anschel Rothschild of Frankfurt and, when he died in 1812, he left five little "Frankfurters" to play major roles in the "games" of the empires of Europe for the next century.

Pulpit Stories

A Rothschild stops at an inn in his travels and orders two eggs for breakfast. He finishes and asks for the bill. The charge is twenty-five rubles, an astronomical sum. "I don't understand. This is absolutely insane. Is it possible that eggs are so rare here that you charge a fortune for them?" he asked. "No, eggs aren't rare," was the reply, "Rothschilds are."

Other financial geniuses made their marks as well, and their family names are still recognizable in banks and on Wall Street. Oppenheim, Dreyfus, Speyer, and Warburg all played a major role in the commercial development and industrial growth of Europe. And with money made available through these financiers, other Jews started up major industries: the coke industry; railroads; chemicals; shipping; and the A.E.G. (Allgemeine Elektrische Gesellschaft), a great network of electric companies that supplied power to all of Germany, founded by Emil Rathenau (father of the statesman, Walter Rathenau).

The Arts

Like the oratorio *Elijah*? How about the *Violin Concerto in E Minor*? Or *Songs Without Words for the Piano*? You have Felix Mendelssohn to thank for those. Like German opera? Lily Lehmann was probably the greatest of all German operatic singers. Enjoy *The Threepenny Opera*? What would the world of music be without Kurt Weill!?

The theater had Max Reinhardt, one of the greatest stage directors of his time. Acting had Rudolf Schildkraut and stage sets had Oskar Strnad. There were the playwrights Ernst Toller, Franz Wedekind, and George Kaiser. And the list goes on and on.

In philosophy it was Hermann Cohen, Eduard Husserl, and Ernst Cassirer. Among novelists were Nobel prize winner Paul Heyse, Jakob Wasserman, Lion Feuchtwanger, and Georg Hermann. Just imagine how much of their past Nazis had to erase when they wanted to deny Jewish contributions to their culture!

Medicine

Doctors, doctors, doctors. I won't even try to list names of Jewish leaders in their fields. Fathers of branches of medicine, innovators, and Nobel prize winners. Medicine just seems to be a Jewish specialty throughout the ages. I just can't resist telling you that the German word for religious is *"ehrlich"* —and Paul Ehrlich, Nobel prize winner for his cure for syphilis, was clearly in the healing tradition of his religious forebears. (And if Jews can cure it, they have to be the ones to discover how to diagnose it, thanks to the "Wasserman test" by August von Wasserman.)

Yenta's Little Secrets

Sure, you've heard of Louis Pasteur, but the real founder of bacteriology was the great botanist, Ferdinand Julius Cohn. I guess it's much easier to say that you're going to pasteurize milk than you're going to Cohnize it.

Science

Biochemistry, chemistry, physics, and mathematics all had their Jewish "superstars." Sometimes their contributions even became immortalized in the names given to their discoveries. Radio and television became possible only because of the discovery of electromagnetic waves of slow frequency, today called Hertzian Waves, after Heinrich Rudolf Hertz.

Sage Sayings

"...Today in Germany I am called a German man of science, and in England I am represented as a Swiss Jew. If I come to be regarded as bête noire the descriptions will be reversed, and I shall become a Swiss Jew for the Germans and a German man of science for the English!"

— Albert Einstein

I can't help feeling sorry, though, for an inventor who got cheated out of having his name identified with his creation. The dirigible airship, supposedly the creation of Count Zeppelin, was actually the brainchild of an obscure Jewish inventor, David Schwarz, in 1892. Before he could make his trial flight he died, and Count Zeppelin bought the patents from his widow. If life were fair, we would really point up to the sky whenever we say a Zeppelin and yell out, "There's a Schwarz!" And of course then the rock group would also have to be known as Led Schwarz! And then, of course, there is the most important and the most influential physicist of modern times, Albert Einstein—and that's not a relative statement. $E=MC^2$ is probably the most ground-breaking scientific discovery of all time. Perhaps the most appropriate way to end this chapter is to remember that this great genius would not, however, be safe in Germany, the land of his birth, but had to find haven in the United States.

The Least You Need To Know

➤ The Age of Enlightenment and the beginning of freedom for German Jewry fathered several different responses and movements that serve as models to this day.

➤ Voluntary baptism was practiced by Heinrich Heine and many other Jews, who exchanged their religious identity for personal gain and social advancement.

➤ Moses Mendelssohn wanted to get the ghetto out of the Jews as Jews got out of the ghettos by making them more German and by emphasizing a religion of faith without peoplehood.

➤ Early Reform Judaism removed expressions of national aspiration and distinctiveness.

➤ The Haskala, or Jewish Age of Reason, emphasized scholarship and Jewish culture and diminished the role of religion and God.

➤ Communism was an attempt to create a secular paradise that, although rooted in Jewish revolutionary ideas, proved to be a curse for the Jewish people.

➤ Torah, in conjunction with modern culture, was taught as an acceptable Orthodox approach by the Hirschian school.

➤ Jewish genius flowered in every field of German culture, bringing international recognition in commerce, the arts, medicine, science and, most significantly—with the achievements of Albert Einstein—in physics.

Chapter 21

The Yiddish British: From Shylock to Lord

> ### In This Chapter
>
> ➤ How the Jews were allowed to settle in England after centuries of exile
>
> ➤ The difficult struggle for emancipation
>
> ➤ Jewish talent in finance, in politics, and even in boxing
>
> ➤ The Jew that saved England and became president of Israel

Shylock is probably the most famous Jew in all of English literature. But, remarkably enough, Shakespeare, his creator, never even met a Jew—ever. (Of course, if it's true that Shakespeare was really Sir Francis Bacon writing under a pseudonym, as some scholars suggest, Jews would assuredly have had nothing to do with him for obvious reasons!) England, as we've already noted, expelled all of its Jews in 1290. It would take almost 400 years, until 1656, that the Jews would finally be allowed to return, during the time of Oliver Cromwell.

The people who were portrayed in the most unflattering manner on the Elizabethan stage would have to struggle to gain acceptance and fight mightily—sometimes even with their fists, as we will discover—in order to gain equal rights. English Jewry lagged behind French and German Jews as well as others who had an early "continental breakfast" of equality. But as a result of their great contributions to English society and the role they played in British culture, the Shylocks of Shakespeare eventually became the Rothschilds, the Disraelis, the Montefiores, and the Lords.

You *Can* Go Home Again

England proved that Thomas Wolfe was wrong: Sometimes you can go home again. In the thirteenth century, Jews were expelled from English shores and condemned as blood-sucking moneylenders and blood-drinking ritual murderers. But England changed its mind in the seventeenth century for the most incredible of reasons. The Jews had to come back so that Messiah could come!

The reasoning was the remarkable brainchild of a prominent rabbi in Amsterdam, Menasseh Ben Israel (1604–1657). The rabbi was such an impressive figure that Rembrandt's famous portrait of him makes him the only rabbi I know with a multimillion-dollar face. Obviously, his gift for persuasion was equally great because he convinced Oliver Cromwell that England, with its exclusionary policy toward Jews, was delaying the "final coming of Messiah," based on a verse in the Book of Daniel. The Biblical prophesy was that the Jews had to be scattered "from one end of the earth to the other before the redemption could be realized." As long as there were places where Jews were not allowed to live, the prophecy could not be fulfilled.

The Puritans were then in power and were persuaded. So, for one of the few times in history, a sermon brought about a change in national policy—and Jews were told they could return in order to hasten the "End of Days."

Yenta's Little Secrets

Rembrandt's famous portrait of Menasseh Ben Israel dates from 1636, by which time the 32-year-old scholar had already founded the first Hebrew printing press in Amsterdam and written an important Biblical commentary.

"On the True Faith of a Christian"

But being allowed to live in England wasn't the same as being granted equal rights. With extraordinary skill, some Jews acquired great wealth. There were financiers like Isaac Goldsmid, Nathan Rothschild, David Salomons, and Moses Montefiore, whose fortunes helped England become an empire, but whose faith prevented them from being given the power of a voice in Parliament.

When the bill "For the Repeal of the Civil Disabilities of the Jews" came up for a vote, Lord Macaulay fought for the bill's passage. He put it bluntly, saying, "How is it possible to deny a Rothschild a seat, on the grounds of his race, when his signature on the back of a piece of paper is worth more than the royal word of three kings!" But the House of Lords threw the bill out.

As late as the mid-nineteenth century, Jews knew that even if they were ever elected to any office they would not be able to serve because of the Oath of Allegiance they would be required to take "on the true faith of a Christian." Lionel Rothschild continued to run for office, be elected, and yet was unable to take his seat in the House of Commons for more than ten years because he refused to take the oath and deny his heritage. It wasn't until 1858 that a Rothschild could finally serve in Parliament "on the true faith of a believing Jew."

Yenta's Little Secrets

The family name Rothschild comes from a "roth schild," or red shield, that once hung in front of the house of Isaac Elderman Rothschild who, in the 1560s, acquired a house on the main Jewish street in Frankfurt.

"The Blank Page"—The Jewish Prime Minister

Religious bigotry, however, wasn't based on race—as it would be a century later in Nazi Germany. Jews could escape the restrictions placed on them if they were ready to sacrifice allegiance to their heritage. No better example of this was Benjamin Disraeli (1804–1881) who was baptized at age twelve into the Church of England by his novelist father in order to improve his chances for success. He became Chancellor of the Exchequer and then twice Prime Minister. Disraeli knew that as a Jew he would never have been able to say, as he did at the end of his life, "Yes, I have climbed to the top of the greasy pole."

But even though baptized, he never forgot his origins. When taunted by the Irish Roman Catholic leader Daniel O'Connell in the House of Commons, with insulting aspersions to his Jewish ancestry, Disraeli fired back a memorable response: "Yes, I am a Jew, and when the ancestors of the right honorable gentleman were brutal savages in an unknown island, mine were priests in the Temple of Solomon."

Sage Sayings

"We belong to a race that can do everything but fail."

—Benjamin Disraeli

Queen Victoria couldn't help being puzzled by her Prime Minister who, although converted into the Anglican faith, never cut his ties to the Jewish people. When she asked him to explain, he told her: "Your Majesty, you know that in most editions of the Holy Bible there is the Old Testament and then there is the New Testament, and in between the two there is an empty, blank page. I am that blank page."

Disraeli was the real founder and leader of the Conservative Party in Great Britain, and he was the brains behind the Imperialist successes of the British Empire. How sad that he could do almost anything—except be himself.

The Jewish Sheriff

Not everyone had to convert to at least get close to the top. How about this for a great scene in a movie? "Get the sheriff," someone yells, and out steps an Orthodox Jew whose name is…Moses! As improbable as it sounds, Moses Montefiore (1784–1885) was not only Sheriff of London, but also became the personal financial advisor to Queen Victoria. He led the way for the industrial development of Great Britain and was responsible for illuminating London's streets by his Imperial Continental Gas Association, bringing a new twist to the ideal of Isaiah that the Jews become "a light unto the nations." He founded the Provincial Bank of Ireland and a number of other leading banking institutions.

His greatest talent, however, was not in knowing how to make money, but how to spend it wisely. His philanthropy reached every corner of the world, and it's hard to find places that weren't bestowed with his charitable gifts. For his contributions, he was the first Jew ever to be knighted by the Queen. After over three thousand years, Moses had finally become a Lord!

Listen to Your Bubbe

In Jerusalem, visit the famous windmill, built by Montefiore, to introduce a source of energy to the holy city. It is located in the famous Yemin Moshe quarter, the artistic colony, named after Moses (Moshe) Montefiore.

Yenta's Little Secrets

The family seal of the Montefiore family had only two words: think and thank. This motto reflected his two greatest concerns: education and philanthropy.

Boxing with Brains: The Jewish Contribution

Not every Jew had the talent of Montefiore, the brilliance of Disraeli, or the riches of Rothschild. In an England where Jew-hatred had a long history, survival in the streets often meant having to prove yourself with your fists when attacked by anti-Semites. And if you still think that nice Jewish boys don't know how to fight, you'll be amazed to learn that the father of modern scientific boxing is Daniel Mendoza (1764–1836), an East End Jew who fought under the professional name of "Star of Israel."

Yenta's Little Secrets

Daniel Mendoza was not only great with his right hand, he was also good with his write hand. He authored The Art of Boxing (1789) and revealed the secrets of a shrewd Jewish fighter.

Mendoza was able to beat opponents who were much bigger and stronger because he invented a new style of defense, a technique called "side-stepping." Jews had been trying to avoid punches for centuries. Mendoza adapted this cultural trait and turned it into a boxing technique. Some purists who thought boxing was all punches and no tactics criticized Mendoza for this "cowardly" kind of fighting. But the "Star of Israel" knew that even in boxing, brains will beat brawn, and he became the champion—as well as hero of English plays and songs and creator of a new kind of respect for his people. In 1965, Daniel Mendoza was one of the inaugural groups chosen for the Boxing Hall of Fame in the United States as a "father of modern boxing." Of all the Jewish contributions to modern culture, that one must have been the most unlikely!

Other Heroes and Lords

While a boxer helped elevate the image of the Jew for the masses, other Jews of talent also made names for themselves, which reflected very positively on their people:

Sage Sayings

"Here was a lecturer in Manchester...who decided that if some of his friends would help him with train fare to London three times a week, he would get the British government...to adopt the Zionist program, and he would then go to get the rest of the family of nations to adopt [it]. I call that a typical Zionist attitude—ninety percent fantasy and ten percent reality. But three years later, these things happened."

—Abba Eban

➤ One of the greatest of all English actors was Edmund Kean.

➤ The astronomer William Herschel is considered by many on a par with Galileo.

➤ David Ricardo, who developed the theory of the Iron Law of Wages, is ranked on the top rung of political economists.

➤ Sir Rufus Isaacs was Lord Chief Justice of England and eventually Viceroy of all of India.

➤ Sir Herbert Samuel, leader of the Liberal Party, was an industrial magnate, an accomplished philosopher, and the first British High Commissioner for Palestine.

But one of the greatest English heroes acquired a dramatic Jewish distinction as well: The scientist who helped England win World War I would eventually become the first president of the State of Israel.

From British Subject to Israeli President

Chaim Weizmann (1874–1952) was a brilliant chemist. In 1915, England faced a critical shortage of acetone for explosives, and Weizmann figured out a way to produce it synthetically from ordinary chestnuts, which were plentiful in England. In gratitude, the English government wanted to make Weizmann a knight. Instead of this personal honor, he pleaded that the British government proclaim its willingness to support the idea of a Jewish homeland in Palestine.

Chaim Weizmann, first president of Israel. (Courtesy of Culver Pictures)

Pulpit Stories

Throughout his lifetime, Chaim Weizmann had many enemies. Fellow Jews envied him his positions of leadership. Anti-Semites felt that he was a Jew who had risen too high. Arabs opposed to the newly created State of Israel considered him an enemy. Yet, as a diplomat, Weizmann had to hold his anger in check and refrain from responding many times when he was verbally abused. On his death bed, Weizmann was coughing badly and the doctor told him to spit. His last words, "But there's no one to spit at."

It was an unbelievable request, but remarkably enough, in 1917, the British issued the Balfour Declaration, marking the first time a world power threw its weight behind the idea of a Jewish return to Palestine. It was an explosive document—a fitting payback to the man who saved England with his formula for explosives. And the man who turned down a knighthood so that he could help his people would later be granted the privilege of being elected, in May, 1948, the first president of Israel.

The Least You Need to Know

➤ Jews had to wait more than three centuries to be readmitted to England after they were expelled in 1290.

➤ The road to equality was slow and difficult, and negative stereotypes of Jews were not uncommon, as Shakespeare's Shylock could attest.

➤ The wealth of the Rothschilds and their contributions to England helped Jews to finally become political leaders without having to take an oath on "the true faith of a Christian."

➤ Although baptized, Benjamin Disraeli helped considerably to dispel the negative image of the Jew, even as the philanthropist Moses Montefiore served as a magnificent role model of an Orthodox Jew.

➤ Necessity as the mother of invention produced the first great Jewish boxer who turned pugilism into a science and for the first time gave English commoners a Jewish sporting hero.

➤ Among the contributors to British culture and science, Chaim Weizmann stands out as savior of both his land and his people, rewarded with England's passage of the Balfour Declaration and Israel's selection as first president of the new State.

Chapter 22

America the Beautiful

In This Chapter

➤ How a Jew becomes the first white man to set foot in the Americas

➤ The first Jews in New York and their struggle for equality

➤ The first American synagogue and the first American president

➤ The role of the Jews in the American Revolution

➤ The Biblical foundations of the United States of America

➤ Making the American dream come true

➤ Creating a religious Judaism with an American accent

Coincidence? I doubt it. It had to be a Jew, Irving Berlin, who was moved to write these words:

> *God bless America,*
>
> *Land that I love;*
>
> *Stand beside her and guide her*
>
> *Through the night with the light from above.*

And it had to be a Jewess, Emma Lazarus, whose insight into the uniqueness of the United States of America would be inscribed as the greeting on the pedestal of the Statue of Liberty for every immigrant coming into New York Harbor:

Give me your tired, your poor

Your huddled masses yearning to breathe free,

The wretched refuse of your teeming shore,

Send these, the homeless, tempest-toss't to me.

For the Jews, no matter where they lived, America was always the Golden Land. Here was a country that defined itself as "one nation under God, with liberty and justice for all." America proved to be the greatest haven for the Jewish people, from the moment the first white man—who just so happened to be a Jew—set foot on its soil.

The Nina, the Pinta... and the Jew

The first ships to come to the New Land carried a Marrano Jew on board. Luis de Torres was invited by Christopher Columbus to accompany him on his journey because he was fluent in Hebrew. As de Torres wrote in his diary, "[Columbus] thought that when he would reach China and the Far East, he would locate the exiled Jews from the Ten Lost Tribes, and he wanted me to be able to communicate with them." De Torres was the son of a *sofer*, a Torah scribe, and was proud that he "was also educated to be a scribe, always surrounded by Hebrew books, manuscripts and Torah commentaries."

Aha, That's It

Sofer is a scribe, required by law to be a pious and observant Jew, who writes religious texts: a *sefer Torah*, which is the Bible; *mezuzot*, literally "door post," containing parchment with Biblical texts traditionally placed on the door of one's home; and *tefillin*, philactories containing passages from the Torah affixed to the arm and head during prayers.

He explained in his diary why he was so anxious to go on this dangerous trip:

> The fateful day, the day of our expulsion from Spain, was Tisha b'Av on the Jewish calendar in the year 5252/1492. That day marked the tragedy of the destruction of both holy temples many centuries before, and now, one more tragic event was added to that mournful day. Three hundred thousand people, half the amount that were redeemed from Egyptian slavery, descended to the Mediterranean shore, searching for passage to a new land, to a land where they could openly practice Judaism. I was among them. However, I was not a refugee; I had been commissioned to join Christopher Columbus's voyage of discovery. I agreed to accompany him because I hoped that if we found Jewish brethren, I would be able to live my life in peace and in freedom. Don Rodriguez, his uncle Don Gabriel Sanchez, Alonso de Loquir, Rodrigo de Triana, Chon Kabrera, Doctor Briena and Doctor Marco, all agreed with my reasoning and joined, but except for Rodrigo, they sailed on the other ships. We were a large group of *conversos*, living in perpetual fear of the Inquisition, hoping that we would find a way out of the precarious situation we were in.

After sailing for seventy-two days, the sailors spotted land and began to sing and dance. First to disembark was de Torres, whose Hebrew proved to be of no help at all with the locals, who spoke in their Indian tongue and probably, after seeing their first Jew, said, "There goes the neighborhood." But even as the discoverers of this New World took possession from Spain and rejoiced with a song of thanksgiving, de Torres took note of the special meaning of this moment for himself and his compatriots in his final diary entry:

> And I, Yosef Ben Ha Levy Haivri—Joseph the son of Levy the Hebrew—sang with my friends a different song, a song of thanksgiving to God for leading us to place where we might publicly acknowledge our Judaism.

Aha, That's It

Conversos is the word Spaniards used to refer to the "converted ones," who are better known among Jews as *Marranos*.

A Willow Branch for Hoshana Rabba

The holiday of Hoshana Rabba, a day on which the world is judged, is observed with the waving of a willow branch to the four corners of the earth. It was on Hoshana Rabba that the crew of Columbus's ships first sighted land in the distance. When Luis de Torres looked down into the waters, he noticed, as he wrote in his diary:

> Slender branches with leaves that were narrow, oval-shaped, tapering to a point, floated in the water and washed up near our ship. I was able to reach a branch, and when I pulled it from the water, I realized that I was holding a willow branch. I was overcome with joy. In this new place, God had provided me with a willow branch so that I might fulfill the *mitzvah* of Hoshana Rabba.

America not only welcomed the first Jew, but even sent him a ritual item he needed before he set foot on shore!

Luis de Torres was so overwhelmed with the freedom he found in the New World that he chose to stay there when Columbus returned to Spain. He would add yet another first to his credits as the first white man to discover tobacco and introduce its use into the Old World as a tobacco grower and exporter. In that way, although the surgeon general hadn't yet let him know it, he was able to repay the Spaniards for shortening the lives of his people. His successful absorption into the Americas would prove to be a wonderful harbinger for all those who followed him in the generations to come.

Coming to the Big Apple

It would take a while, though, until Jews came to settle in North America. And just like in the original Garden of Eden where an apple tested Adam and Eve, the first Jews to come to what would eventually be a Jewish paradise had to face the challenge of the Big Apple—the City of New York, then known as New Amsterdam.

Twenty-three Jews who had lived peacefully in Recife, Brazil, former residents of Holland, had to flee when the Portuguese conquered the city from the Dutch and instituted the Inquisition. Peter Stuyvesant, governor of the colony, tried to ask them in a friendly way to leave the colony. Part of his "friendly approach" was to write to the board of directors of the Dutch West India Company, which owned the colony, and petition "...of your Worships, that the deceitful race, such hateful enemies and blasphemors of the name of Christ, be not allowed to infest and trouble this new colony." The only thing Peter Stuyvesant forgot to check on was the names of the major stockholders of the company, many of whom were Jews.

With the backing of the Jews of Amsterdam, the Jews in New Amsterdam were encouraged to seek equal rights. The first issue they took a stand on was the right to be permitted to do guard duty with other citizens rather than paying a tax so that others would fulfill this civic responsibility for them. At first, the Jews were told that if they weren't happy with their forced exclusion from guard duty, they could feel free "to depart whenever and whither it pleases them." But, once again, when the Jews appealed to the directors of the Dutch West India Company, the colonial lawmakers were overruled. The first right given to these Jewish settlers was to stand with their fellow citizens and man the stockades against Indian attacks all along Wall Street. Protecting Wall Street would remain a very prominent activity for Jews in the years to come!

The Shul with a Tunnel

Newport, Rhode Island was home to the second settlement of Jews in the American colonies. Newport's laws were set by the remarkable charter for the Colony of Rhode Island, drawn up in 1636 by Roger Williams. No one living there could be "in any way molested, punished, disquieted or called in question for any difference in opinion." In retrospect, it's almost incredible to realize that in the early part of the seventeenth century there was already enacted into law the ideal, which one hundred and fifty years later would serve as the fundamental American principle of the First Amendment to the U.S. Constitution, providing for the separation of Church and State.

In this climate of tolerance, the Jews built a small Georgian temple in Newport, now known as the Touro Synagogue, the oldest synagogue in the United States. In 1946 it was officially designated a national historic site. Named for the generous philanthropist, Judah Touro, a Newport native who left a large endowment for its upkeep, the synagogue was built with one striking architectural feature. Underneath the table from which the Torah was read there was an opening to an underground passageway that leads out toward the street. Tradition has it that the Jews of the New World, who enjoyed freedom of worship, still carried the scars and memories of Marrano persecution and built a tunnel in their temple as an insurance policy—a ready escape from their communal place of prayer, just in case they ever needed it.

Thankfully, their fears were unfounded. In fact, by the time George Washington became the first president of the United States, the president of the Jewish community, Moses Seixas, received a letter of support and good wishes from the American leader that gave historic expression to the unique position Jews enjoyed in the American colonies:

Touro Synagogue at Newport, Rhode Island. (Courtsey of G. E. Kidder Smith/© Corbis)

The interior of the Touro Synagogue. The reader's stand at right covers the "escape tunnel." (Courtesy of UPI/Corbis-Bettmann)

"For happily, the government of the United States, which gives to bigotry no sanction, to persecution no assistance, requires only that they who live under its protection should demean themselves as good citizens, in giving it on all occasions their effectual support… May the children of the Stock of Abraham dwell in this land, continue to merit and enjoy the good will of the other inhabitants, while everyone shall sit in safety under his own vine and fig tree, and there shall be none to make him afraid."

Yenta's Little Secrets

The Puritans were so enamoured of the Old Testament that in England they were viewed as "Jewish fellow travelers." When Harvard was founded, Hebrew was taught along with Latin and Greek. Most remarkable of all, a motion was made in the Continental Congress that Hebrew become the official language of the land. The motion lost—and that's why this book is written in English.

It's in the Bible

It wasn't only George Washington who liked to quote from the prophets. America was created from the ideals that its early settlers revered as the word of God from the holy Book of the Bible. The Quakers found the source for their humanitarian spirit in the Biblical text they inscribed on the Liberty Bell in Philadelphia in 1773, "Proclaim liberty throughout the land, and to all the inhabitants thereof."

Sage Sayings

"Hebraic mortar cemented the foundations of American Democracy."

—William Lecky, Irish historian

Benjamin Franklin strongly supported a proposal that the seal of the United States should show the Israelites crossing the Red Sea with Pharoah's chariots in vain pursuit. Although the suggestion didn't make it, the theological justification for the American Revolution was the Biblical story of the Jews freeing themselves from the tyranny of a cruel king. Thomas Jefferson even suggested that the moral of the story, "Rebellion against tyrants is obedience to God," should serve as the motto of the new nation.

It was people steeped in the Biblical story of mankind's creation "in the image of God" who could write the daring words of the Declaration of Independence:

We hold these truths to be self-evident, that all men are created equal, that they are endowed by their Creator with certain inalienable Rights, that among these are Life, Liberty and the pursuit of Happiness. That to secure these Rights, governments are instituted among men, deriving their just powers from the consent of the governed. That whenever any form of government becomes destructive of these ends, it is the right of the people to alter or to abolish it....

What to the world plagued with prejudice was still incomprehensible, to the framers of the U.S. Constitution was not only perfectly clear, but, more, even self-evident! And at long, long last, Jews would finally benefit from those who studied and read the Bible correctly.

Soldiers of the Revolution

At the time of the American Revolution there were less than 2,000 Jews in the thirteen colonies. Yet there were Jews among these who fought at Bunker Hill and Valley Forge. During the siege of Savannah, David Emmanuel would show such bravery that his admirers elected him Governor of Georgia in 1801, and in his honor named its largest county "Emmanuel."

Francis Salvador came from England to help Americans in their fight for independence, and at the young age of twenty-nine was elected to the Provincial Congress of South Carolina, making him the first Jew to hold public office in the colonies. Salvador was that rare politician who had the physical courage of his convictions and volunteered to lead a night attack of militiamen against hostile Cherokees which, unfortunately, led to his death by scalping. The Continental Army even had one entire unit known as "The Jew's Company."

Historians agree that one of the most important contributions of the Jews to the American Revolution was the financial support of Haym Salomon, one of the first Polish immigrants to settle in New York. It is quite conceivable that without his money, the colonies would have failed in their efforts to break away from England.

After being arrested as a spy by the British and confined for two years, Salomon escaped and in a short time became one of the country's leading financiers. He had a unique way of doing business that anti-Semites called "not Jewish," but which in the most profound way of all, proved the depth of his Jewish convictions and the love Jewish immigrants had for their new-found haven of freedom.

James Madison, the future President, wrote how readily he could borrow money from Salomon, "but I never resort to it without great mortification as he obstinately rejects all recompense. The price of money is so usurious that he thinks it ought to be extracted from none but those who aim at profitable speculations. To a necessitous delegate, he gratuitously spares a supply out of his private stock."

Salomon would become known as the "Broker to the Office of Finance" and with reckless unconcern for his own interests, he personally endorsed the almost valueless

Bills of Exchange issued by the Continental Congress. The huge loans Salomon extended to the government were never repaid, and Hyam Salomon died bankrupt. Several times motions were offered in Congress to acknowledge the patriotic efforts of this great American Jew but, unfortunately, no action has yet been taken. For now it must be enough for Jews to take comfort in the knowledge that even as America gave them new life, Jews gave to America Hyam (whose name, of course, is Hebrew for life).

From Peddlers to Millionaires

The rumor in Europe was that in America the streets were paved with gold. As we know, the truth was not quite so dazzling. But for Jews who had been unable to make a living in other countries because of the bigotry they encountered and the restrictive laws that excluded them from so many fields, the American dream was truly a dream come true. This young nation allowed them to become wealthy beyond their wildest hopes. Centuries of exile had taught Jews how to travel with a pack on their back. When they came to America, they filled the pack with diverse goods and traveled from town to town until they made enough to open a store of their own. The work was incredibly hard, but the rewards were staggering. Best of all, what mattered wasn't your religion—only your readiness to struggle and to succeed.

Lazarus Straus was a good example. He drove a horse and wagon through Georgia after he arrived in 1852 from Bavaria. He scrimped and saved his meager earnings until he could open a little shop in the town of Talbottom and then finally sent passage money back to his family. His three sons, Isidore, Oscar, and Nathan, all helped in the store. From that modest beginning were born two great department stores: R. H. Macy's in New York, and Abraham & Straus in Brooklyn. And as the result of a Jewish family's great success, the whole country watches Macy's Thanksgiving Day parade, expressing gratitude to God for the gifts of this great land.

Another teenager who came from Bavaria (it must have been the "Bavarian cream" of society that emigrated to the States) peddled dry goods along the Mississippi, opened his first store in Indiana, and then, with his sons, developed the Gimbel department store name. People often had trouble deciding between the great sales at Macy's and Gimbel's, but no matter where they made their final purchase, a nice Jewish boy from Bavaria prospered.

And when Americans were stricken with gold fever in 1849, Jews also joined the Gold Rush—not so much to do the panning and digging, but rather to shrewdly sell the pans and pick axes, blankets and boots to those who did. Because the diggers also needed good solid pants, another Bavarian-born Jew—can you believe this coincidence? —Levi Straus, came to peddle dry goods from a wagon in gold towns called Michigan Bluff, Chinese Camp, and Fiddle Town. His clients were so happy with their pants that "Levi's" became the first designer jeans in history.

Some Jews were even smart enough to discover a way not to have to travel to buyers or even to stand in a shop all day. Julius Rosenwald showed how successful mail order could be when he developed Sears Roebuck & Company. Then he proved how charitable and concerned a Jew can be with the welfare of others not equally blessed when he gave away most of his fortune, through the Julius Rosenwald Fund, to provide manual, agricultural, and educational aid to blacks in this country.

Pulpit Stories

Levi Straus had a problem. In peddling goods from town to town, he was stuck with a load of canvas tenting cloth for which he found absolutely no buyers. With a flash of inspiration, he asked a tailor to make a miner a pair of pants from this material. The prospector, who wore them and wore them and couldn't wear them out, went from tavern to tavern boasting, "Doggone it, I doubt a man ever had a pair of pants as strong as Levi's before." Talk about turning a lemon into lemonade!

And the Not-So-Rich Workers

The success of the super rich masks the hardships endured by most Jewish immigrants. Between 1840 and 1930, an astonishing 37 million immigrants arrived at American shores, and the Jewish population grew from approximately 50,000 to 4 1/2 million. The new immigrants had to learn the language, adapt to American ways, compete with each other for jobs in a marketplace that had an overabundance of cheap labor—all the while maintaining the traditions and religious values of their ancestors whom they had left behind in the Old Land.

The American experience may have started with the emotions expressed on the Statue of Liberty, but the joy and relief the immigrants felt was followed by the harrowing experience that awaited them at Ellis Island. Between 1892 and 1947, some 20 million newcomers were herded from line to line, from doctor to doctor, from interpreter to interpreter, from official to official, from bureaucrat to bureaucrat. When someone became so disoriented that he couldn't remember his own name when asked and replied *"fergessan"* (Yiddish for "forgotten"), he was simply named Ferguson by the examiner—and that's why some Ferguson families are Jewish.

Those who didn't have people to vouch for them were sent back, and a few of them committed suicide rather than return. If they were lucky enough to be accepted, they moved to Jewish neighborhoods like New York's Lower East Side and struggled to find either "piecework" or a regular job in the notorious sweat shops where it was not unusual for workers to toil from dawn to midnight. Those who wanted to remain faithful to Jewish law and observe the Sabbath often found themselves fired every week when they didn't show up for work on Saturday and then out on the streets again Monday morning, looking for a new job.

"All Jews Are Responsible for Each Other"

What saved the Jews from despair and permitted immigrants to rise from poverty to professional life and success was the Jewish concept of communal responsibility that created the infrastructure of their daily life. From the minute Jews got off the boat, volunteers from the Hebrew Immigrant Aid Society (HIAS) greeted them, helped them find an apartment and work, and gave them practical advice and sufficient funds to start a new life. There were fraternal lodges, mutual aid societies, benevolent groups, benefit organizations, burial, and free loan societies. (Not only did these organizations help the immigrants, but every one of them had a president, vice-president, and lengthy list of officers that made their members feel important, gave them a sense of identity, and allowed them to claim that their organization was much better than any of the others run by *shleppers* and *paskudnyaks*.) Then there were *shuls* and *shtieblechs*, Hebrew schools and places for adult study.

Perhaps most popular of all were the *landsmanschaften*—societies made up of people from the same hometown or local area and who felt that their close ties of origin gave them a special kinship, not only for friendship but for mutual assistance and support. By 1935 there were over three thousand of these societies, each one bearing the name of a little town or village somewhere in Eastern Europe with, in all probability, a nonexistent Jewish population living on only in the memories of Jews in America.

Life was hard, but it was rich and it was exciting, and people were involved with each other. They stimulated one another intellectually, they helped one another emotionally, and they cared for each other as if they were one large extended family—including the infighting and sibling rivalry, of course.

Somehow the Lower East Side and other self-contained Jewish communities like it did something right because the percentage of successful Jews from them—in almost every field and profession—is staggering beyond belief. One of its "graduates," a billionaire living in Beverly Hills today, bewailing the aggravation he gets from his do-nothing kids who are still searching to "find themselves," looks back longingly at his youth and sadly notes, "I gave my kids everything—the only thing I deprived them of was the poverty that gave me so much when I grew up on the Lower East Side."

Aha, That's It

Shtieblech (singular, *shtiebl*) are little synagogues often confined to one room for intimate prayer. *Shtieblech* are usually associated with Hasidic groups, comprising the disciples of a particular *rebbe* (rabbi) whom they devotedly follow.

Sage Sayings

"The extraordinary European Jews who emigrated to New York were enriching the city's intellectual life with an intensity that has probably never been equaled anywhere during a comparable period of time. I was raised largely by these Jews... They were my teachers; they were my employers; they were my friends. They introduced me to a world of books and ideas that I didn't know existed."

—Marlon Brando

Look for the Union Label

Do you know why Jews can be hard on waiters in restaurants? Because if they don't like the food, they'll tell you, "You call this a steak? Take it back." Jewish religion teaches man not to accept the world as it is, but to play a role in improving it. Jewish culture, refined over thousands of years, pushes Jews to avoid acceptance of the status quo, to project that the possible can be made real and the intolerable need not be tolerated.

That's why it was Jews who responded to the horrendous working conditions of the late nineteenth century by creating labor unions. If Mafia connections today make us somewhat leery of organized efforts by workers for just compensation and livable working conditions, we must understand the reality of what starving workers without recourse had to face from unconscionable and cruel bosses. That makes us realize the tremendous contribution and courage of Jews like Samuel Gompers who founded the American Federation of Labor. Gompers was the most powerful and influential figure in the history of the American labor movement and paved the way for workers in many other industries.

The evils of the sweat shop were cruelly exposed in the infamous Triangle fire in New York City where 146 workers, mainly Jewish women, died because the exit door was locked by the factory owners to ensure that everyone could be properly checked at the end of the day for possible pilferage. The exploitation of the impoverished became a public scandal, and the International Ladies Garment Workers Union led a strike of New York City cloakmakers that brought the first labor settlement in the garment industry.

Sage Sayings

"The Lower East Side of New York is a great place—to come from."

—Anonymous

Sage Sayings

"Trade unionism helped very materially to obtain acceptance for the immigrant Jewish worker in the United States, for it was trade unionism, along with the public school, that constituted for the mass of immigrant Jews their first real initiation into American institutional life. As a trade unionist, the immigrant Jew began to speak a 'language' that Americans could understand."

—Will Herberg,
U.S. theologian, social critic

Three Jewish leaders were involved in the settlement that provided for a maximum work week of 54 hours and the payment of overtime: Jacob Schiff (1847–1920), a major financier and philanthropist; Louis Marshall (1856–1929), who would play a major role in the fight against anti-Semitism in the 1920s; and Louis Dembitz Brandeis (1856–1941), later to become the first Jewish Justice of the United States Supreme Court. It was Brandeis (yes, he is the one after whom Brandeis University is named) who laid the basis for a significant new approach to labor conflicts that, for the first time in American labor history, set up a process for negotiation, for presenting grievances, and for arbitrating disputes.

Thanks to Jews, workers were able to unite to save the capitalistic system!

Religion, American Style

Sage Sayings

"We are a nation of immigrants. It is immigrants who brought to this land the skills of their hands and brains to make of it a beacon of opportunity and of hope for all men."

—Senator Herbert H. Lehman

The difference between the Old Country and America, the common saying went in Europe, is that in the *shtetl* it's hard for a Jew to be a *goy* (a non-Jew), and in America it's hard for a Jew to be a Jew. Some Polish and Russian Jews felt so strongly that living in the freedom of the United States would bring an end to the piety of their children that they refused to allow members of their family to emigrate, in spite of pogroms and persecutions. "Better," they said, "that we die here as Jews than that we flee to live freely as gentiles." In European eyes, America was considered a *treif medinah*—a non-Kosher land of unavoidable and insurmountable temptations.

To some extent, of course, they were right. For many American success stories meant that Cohen became Kane, the synagogue was replaced with the country club, and religious identification went from Jew to Episcopalian. But, like Mark Twain, who read an obituary about himself in his newspaper, Judaism was prematurely buried and eulogized many times over. A famous 1964 *Look* magazine cover story wrote about "The Vanishing American Jew." And that magazine itself vanished some years ago, leaving living American Jews free to read other, more optimistic periodicals!

Judaism, although suffering many casualties on the battlefield against secularism, nevertheless continued to play a major role in the lives of millions of American Jews. It did this by adopting the American secret of success, so ably popularized by General Motors: Give the customer choices and let him pick what best serves his personal needs and preferences.

American Judaism comes in a fairly wide array of popular models:

Reform Judaism

Its United States version was introduced by a German-speaking immigrant from Bohemia, Rabbi Isaac Mayer Wise, founder of the First Reform Congregation in the United States, in Cincinnati in 1854. Wise opted for the radical version of Reform—topless mandatory (no head covering allowed), dietary laws abolished (at the Hebrew Union College Seminary's first graduation of Reform rabbis, the rabbinical school he founded, shrimp was served as the first course—a Biblical no-no), and services were switched from Saturday to Sunday. Rituals were replaced by an emphasis on ethics, and Jewish peoplehood and Zionism were rejected. (For an explanation of Zionism, the worldwide movement for a Jewish homeland in Israel, turn to Chapter 26, "The Final Return.")

Rabbi Wise's extreme views were eventually replaced by far milder changes. Reform Judaism eventually returned to the practice of many rituals, the belief in ties of kinship and mutual responsibility of Jews for one another around the world, as well as support for Israel. Reform Judaism retains for itself the right to change Jewish law, even those laws with a Biblical basis, to make Judaism more attuned to contemporary life and more in keeping with the world views of modern culture.

The Central Conference of American Rabbis is today the official body of reform rabbis. Hebrew Union College, headquartered in Cincinnati, remains its rabbinical school, and approximately 800 synagogues and one million members today identify with its movement.

Conservative Judaism

This is a uniquely American approach to an ancient religion challenged by modern alternatives. Conservative Judaism seeks the middle ground between maintaining the authority of Jewish law and accepting the need for growth and change. Founded by Solomon Schechter (1850–1915), its rabbinical school, the Jewish Theological Seminary, was established in New York City in 1887. The Conservative movement and its rabbinic arm, the Rabbinical Assembly of America, continue to play a middle role between Orthodoxy and Reform Judaism. Numerically speaking, Conservative Judaism is the major American Jewish denomination today, with an affiliation of more than one million Jews.

Orthodox Judaism

Orthodoxy proclaims total commitment to both the written and oral law, the Bible and Talmud, as well as its legal commentaries. It is an attempt to maintain traditional Jewry as it has been practiced throughout the centuries, in totally different countries and cultures. Its premise is that religion dare not be changed by the times, but has instead the role of changing the times. Orthodoxy's adherents like to say that unlike Reform and Conservative Judaism, which were founded in the nineteenth century, their denomination goes back thousands of years and was founded at Sinai by God Himself.

Yenta's Little Secrets

Rabbi Doctor Bernard Revel, the founding president of Yeshiva University, was honored in the 1980s with an American postage stamp showing him wearing a yarmulke—probably the only postage stamp ever issued outside of Israel picturing a Jew with this religious head covering.

Yet, even within orthodoxy, there are various shadings and levels of accommodation to modern life. Modern orthodoxy, institutionally represented by Yeshiva University in New York City, stresses the synthesis of *Torah u Mada*—the study of Torah in conjunction with secular studies. Its rabbinical arm is the Rabbinical Council of America, made up of 1,100 rabbis serving 800 Orthodox congregations throughout the United States. Further to the right are literally hundreds of smaller schools, many granting rabbinic ordination and devoted solely to the study of Jewish texts, avoiding secular subject of any kind.

Hasidic Orthodoxy and Lubavitch

Included among them are many Hasidic groups, followers of different charismatic leaders who identify themselves by their distinctive mode of appearance and dress; little details like the shape of their hats serve to differentiate them from the followers of other rabbis.

Aha, That's It

Ba'al T'Shuva, literally a returnee or a "master of repentance," is often referred to in the Jewish world as a B.T., as opposed to an F.F.B., or *frum*, meaning (religious) from birth.

The most famous of these Hasidic Orthodox Jews are the members of the Lubavitch movement, followers of Rabbi Menachem Mendel Schneersohn (1902–1994), who was so revered that his disciples believed that he was in fact the as-yet-unrevealed Messiah—until his death disproved that possibility. Lubavitch followers (also known as Chabad) are particularly known for their outreach programs and ability to bring back to Judaism many of those who lost their way to drugs, existential despair, or loss of spirituality. (These "returnees" have become so common that there is even a name for them—they are members of the *Ba'al T'Shuva* movement.)

Reconstructionism

This, the youngest of Jewish denominations, is the brainchild of Mordecai Kaplan (1881–1983). Born and raised as an Orthodox Jew, Kaplan loved Judaism but couldn't believe in a personal God. Removing the legitimacy of the first commandment, Kaplan was left with a culture more than a religion, a civilization rather than a faith predicated on observing the dictates of a divine law-giver.

Gefilte fish without God does have an appeal to many, but Kaplan's premise, as developed in his classic work, *Judaism as a Civilization*, was enough to get him labeled heretic by his opponents. Nevertheless, his emphasis on an "evolving religious civilization" led him to create the idea of Jewish community centers instead of simple synagogues for prayer, an idea subsequently taken over by almost all of the other denominations that has become a creative new contribution to American Jewish life.

And the Jews Gave to America...

America gave the Jews more than any other country in the world had ever given before. And in giving, it in turn was blessed as no other nation on earth with the talents of a people waiting only for the freedom and the opportunity to express themselves. Name a field and there Jews were in the forefront: medicine and law, entertainment and literature, science and the arts, politics and law, physics and philosophy, sports and humor—the list goes on and on, and the books detailing the contributions of Jewish legendary figures of American life run into the tens of thousands.

To do some justice to the incredible achievements of less than three percent of the population of the United States to its culture and intellectual vitality, we'll devote a later section to a Jewish Hall of Fame. For now let's content ourselves by taking note of the fact that by welcoming the Jews to its shores, the United States of America embraced a people that would contribute greatly to its becoming the most blessed and most powerful nation on earth.

The Least You Need to Know

➤ The first European white man to set foot on the American continent was a Marrano, a Spanish Jew, whose ardent wish to find a haven of freedom for his people would become amply fulfilled in the years to come.

➤ The first Jews to immigrate to the United States fled from persecution in Brazil and settled in New York, where they slowly gained equal rights.

➤ The first synagogue in the colonies, the Touro Synagogue, today a national historic site, marked the beginning of religious freedom of worship for Jews in the U.S.

➤ The founders of the United States were greatly motivated by the Bible and its ideals as they composed the Declaration of Independence and the U.S. Constitution.

➤ Jews played a significant role in the American Revolution, and Jewish financial support played no small part in the victory of the Revolutionary Army over England.

➤ With hard work and business acumen, some Jews became millionaires, while others struggled to achieve the American dream, helping each other and fighting for the rights of all workers in the labor movements.

➤ Different denominations within Judaism allowed a wide range of religious and spiritual expression, running the gamut from extreme orthodoxy to reconstructionism.

Chapter 23

East Side, West Side, All Around the Globe

In This Chapter

➤ How Jews coped with the prejudice, the persecution, and the pogroms of Russia

➤ The life of the *shtetel* and the Jew of *Fiddler on the Roof*

➤ The search for more tolerant homes as Russia becomes ever more ruthless

➤ The alternatives for Jews in major cities around the world, including Western Europe, Canada, and South America

It's a law of nature: the sun rises in the East and sets in the West. Strangely enough, the nineteenth century witnessed a reversal of this scientific fact, as far as Jewish history was concerned; a new dawn of liberty and equality was rising in the West while the major lands of Eastern Europe turned ever darker.

In the middle of the nineteenth century, there were approximately 4 3/4 million Jews alive in the world. Only 14 percent of them lived in Western Europe, 1.5 percent had found their way to America, and 72 percent of them were still under the oppressive regimes of the czars. For them, life was punishment without crime, and the only salvation would be to heed the advice of Horace Greeley and "Go West, young man"— to the worlds of freedom where the sun was at last rising.

The "Pale Jews of Russia"

While America "gave to bigotry no sanction," France proclaimed "liberté, egalité, fraternité," and England was slowly removing its restrictions on Jews, Russia found ever greater ways to maintain its legacy of anti-Semitism. The czars may have changed, but the *tsorus*—Yiddish word for suffering—always remained. Try some of the following for examples of Russian hatred of the Jews.

The Pale of Settlement

Enacted in 1772 and in effect as late as 1910, this was a giant ghetto that restricted Jews to very limited areas. Jews could only live, travel, and do business in confined areas. Not only was their freedom of movement severely limited, but so were their opportunities for securing a livelihood. Out of this intentional economic paralysis, there arose a new figure known as *luftmensch*, a "man of air," who had to make a living out of nothing.

The "grandfather" of modern Yiddish literature, Mendele Mocher Sforim (Mendel the bookseller), drew the classic portrait of these sad but optimistic figures who aspired to nothing more than make enough money to reach the glorified level of a pauper.

The Cantonists

Under the rule of Czar Nicholas I, Jewish children were drafted between the ages of 12 and 18 and sent to barracks (cantonments) far from their families—and any possible Jewish influences—to serve "their country" for *25 years* in the regular army. During that time they were exposed to taunts, torture, and constant pressure for conversion. Most of those taken away were never again seen by their loved ones. The entire Jewish community was threatened with great punishment if anyone did not comply with this order. So started the horrible saga of "chappers," Jews forced to *chap* (grab) little children away from mothers and fathers to be turned over to the government for military service.

Sage Sayings

"This blood libel accusation... is based on an absolute lie. Every Jew who has been brought up among Jews knows that throughout the length and breadth of Jewry there is not a single individual who drinks human blood for religious purposes... 'But,' you ask, 'is it possible that everybody can be wrong and the Jews right?' Yes, it is possible: Blood accusation proves it possible."

—Ahad Ha-am, essayist, philosopher

The Triple Play Plan

Czar Alexander III's Procurator of the Holy Synod, Pobiedonostsev (one of his tortures was to force people to spell his name correctly!), created a "mathematical formula" to deal with the Jewish problem. One-third of the Jews, he decreed, must be eliminated by conversion; one-third by expulsion; and one-third by starvation. It was as close to the twentieth-century Nazis' "Final Solution" as anyone would come during the nineteenth century.

Pogroms

These were spontaneous eruptions of the masses against Jews, planned, produced, and directed by the government. Descriptions of pogroms by those who witnessed them are heartrending. Police stood by as mobs raped, mutilated, tortured, burned, and pillaged. Pogroms were for Russia what the circuses had been for ancient Rome—an outlet for the frustration of the peasants and a scapegoat for massive violence that otherwise might have been directed at the rulers. It didn't hurt that every pogrom also allowed legal robbery of possessions from the "accursed Jews."

Blood Libel

Even the ancient "blood libel" was resurrected in Russia *in the twentieth century*. In 1911, a 12-year-old Christian boy was found brutally murdered in a cave on the outskirts of Kiev. Blood had been drained from the victim's veins and so, of course, it had to be a Jew who needed his "drink" for the Passover ritual. The false accusation of Mendel Beilis drew protests from around the world, but Beilis would have been put to death nonetheless if it weren't for the astounding last-minute confession of the real murderer. The judge and jury had to acquit, but still brought in the amazing verdict that "some unknown Jews" had committed a ritual murder.

Yenta's Little Secrets

How ingrained is the blood libel accusation in Western civilization? Thomas Masaryk (1850–1937), first president of Czechoslovakia, writes in his memoirs, "The superstition of Christian blood used for Passover cakes had become so much part and parcel of my existence that whenever I chanced to come near a Jew—I wouldn't do it on purpose—I would look at his fingers to see if blood were there. I for a long time continued this practice.... Would that I unmake all that anti-Semitism caused me to do in my childhood days."

Russia's Curse, America's Blessing

Here's a great way to know exactly when the worst pogroms and oppression took place in Russia: Note the huge waves of immigration coming from Eastern Europe to the United States. The horrors of the 1880s brought almost half a million Jews to America. During the four pogrom years, beginning with 1903, the time of the Kishinev massacres, another 410,000 Jews fled the land of the czars for the home of the free. To know what these Jews might have meant to the land of their birth that so cruelly abused them, we have but to realize what they achieved in the country wise enough to open its doors to the "huddled masses yearning to breathe free."

Aha, That's It

Aliyah, literally "going up," is used to describe emigrating to Israel as an indication that going to reside in the Holy Land is "uplifting," moving a step higher in one's spiritual pilgrimage.

And for those who weren't able to book passage to the New Land, another dream began to take form—the idea of *aliyah,* emigration to Israel by Jews looking for a better life. Ironically, we might well say that the czars of the nineteenth century were thus responsible for encouraging the establishment of the two greatest centers of Jewish life in the twentieth century—America and the State of Israel.

The Fiddler on the Roof

Anatevka is the *shtetl,* the little Jewish village, where Tevye the dairyman lived. *Fiddler on the Roof,* one of the most successful musicals in history, vividly re-created much of the reality of the life of the Jew in those days. Sholom Rabinowitz, far better known by his pen name, Sholom Aleichem (1859–1916), was able to capture the remarkable mixture of joy and of sorrow, of despair and yet of a closeness to God that allowed for an on-going conversation with the Almighty as a dear friend, always standing at one's side.

Yenta's Little Secrets

Sholom Aleichem, the pen name of Sholem Rabinowitz, literally means "peace be upon you" and is the greeting used by Jews around the world whenever they meet each other. It is the greatest symbol of the strong bond that links Jews everywhere, no matter their station in life, and a fitting description for the man whose last will and testament was, "Bury me among the poor, so my grave may shine on theirs and their graves on mine."

Yes, there was poverty. If a Jew ate a chicken, went the saying, it had to be that either the chicken was sick or the Jew was sick. But there was the comfort of a close-knit community, of people sharing and caring, of a social life that welded the community together through synagogue prayer and study. There was the commandment preached by the countless heads of Hasidic groups to be joyful, that the one sin that God would not forgive man for was the lack of cheerfulness in His creation. There were the *klezmer,* musicians always ready to turn occasions of celebration into memorable moments of unforgettable bliss—Jewish musicians whose skills would be genetically transmitted to the Yehudi Menuhins and the Vladimir Horowitzes of the future.

Tevye would pray, "If I was a rich man." But some people of great wealth might well exchange all their great fortune for the meaningful relationship Tevye had with God and for his spirit for life. Listen to the words of Sholom Aleichem, "I tell you, it is an ugly and mean world and only to spite it one must not weep—only to laugh out of spite, only to laugh." And so the Jews in the *shtetl* did just that, they hid their tears and they proclaimed in their prayers, "Let us give thanks unto the Lord, for He is good."

Aha, That's It

Klezmer, from the Hebrew *k'ley zemer*, musical instruments, were the bands of professionals who played Jewish folk tunes in Russia. Their stirring music, artfully blending emotion, sorrow, and laughter, is presently enjoying a major revival.

All Over Europe

In one of Tevye's unforgettable lines, as he is forced to flee, he ruminates on how Jews always have to be on the run and then concludes, "I guess that's why we Jews always wear a hat." To be a Jew is to be a citizen of the world. And Jews were to be found—and made major contributions in—all the countries of Europe.

➤ **Austria.** In Vienna, Max Reinhardt established the modern realistic theater. Austria was influenced by the literary genius of Stefan Zweig, Ferenc Molnar, Franz Kafka, and Franz Werfel. The greatest actor of the German stage during the nineteenth century, Adolf Sonnenthal, received a title of nobility from the Emperor Franz Josef for his services to the Austrian theater. Rudolf Schildkraut, originally a star of the Yiddish theater, became internationally famous through his work in cinema. Gustav Mahler and his pupil, Arnold Schoenberg, are considered the most powerful musical influences in Austria after Brahms. Nobel prizes recognized the ground-breaking medical contributions of Robert Barany and Karl Landsteiner.

➤ **Hungary.** This country had several hundred thousand Jews by 1850; in 1910, there were 1,000,000, with 200,000 of them in Budapest. They made enormous contributions to Hungarian commerce, industry, arts, and sciences. The Dohany Synagogue, built in Budapest in the nineteenth century, is the largest in all of Europe.

➤ **The Netherlands.** Amsterdam in the seventeenth century had so great and powerful a Jewish community that it acquired the name "New Jerusalem" among Jews of Europe. Here the great philosopher and religious dissenter Baruch Spinoza lived and was excommunicated for heresy. Amsterdam, one of the most important centers for Jewish diamond dealers today, was also the home of the Holocaust diarist Anne Frank.

Yenta's Little Secrets

A number of Hebrew words have entered the Dutch language. In The Netherlands, as in Israel, it is not unusual for one friend to describe another friend as "chaver"—the same word used so movingly by President Clinton in his farewell eulogy to Prime Minister Rabin when he bade him farewell, "Shalom chaver." Similarly, if one needs to pay a price of 100 guilders, it is common to be asked for a "meier."

Listen to Your Bubbe

Don't miss the magnificent boatlike monument erected in Jerusalem on the 25th anniversary of the rescue of Danish Jewry. Many cities and towns in Israel also have a street or square commemorating the heroism of the Danes. Moreover, one of the prominent items on display in the town of Yad Vashem is a small boat that was used to ferry Jews to safety in Sweden.

➤ **Denmark.** This was the first Scandinavian country to permit Jewish settlement, in 1622. From earliest times until the days of the Holocaust, when the Danes stood up to the Germans and refused to persecute their Jews, Denmark exhibited great tolerance and friendship for its Jewish citizens. Jews blessed the Danes in turn with distinguished novelists, painters, sculptors, composers, and scientists. Perhaps most famous of the latter is Niels Bohr, nuclear physicist and Nobel prize winner in 1922.

➤ **Sweden.** The first Jew to settle in Sweden, Aron Isak, so pleased King Gustaf III that he made him his Court Jew and told him that he was free to worship God in any way he chose. "In that case," Isak replied, "I need nine more Jews to worship in accord with the Jewish rite." And that's how, for the first time in history, a non-Jewish king gathered together a *minyan*, a Jewish prayer group. Although there are only 18,000 Jews today in a total Swedish population of 9 million, three of the "Big 18," the committee of the Royal Academy of Sweden that awards the Nobel prizes, are Jews.

➤ **Italy.** Judah Macabee, in the second century B.C.E., after his victorious uprising against Greek dominance in Israel, sent a diplomatic representative to Rome. This marked the first Jewish presence in Italy. With the rise of the Church, however, hostility to Jews was endemic and, as you may remember from Chapter 16, "The Cross of Shame: Western Europe," the first ghetto was created in Venice in 1516. It was well into the middle of the nineteenth century that the Papal State still required Jews to attend proselytizing sermons. Only when Rome was liberated from Papal control in 1871 were Roman Jews finally emancipated. In subsequent decades, Italian Jews contributed to many fields of public life, and an Italian Jew, Luigi Luzzatti, became premier in 1910. Italy also enjoyed a full complement of famous Jewish writers, artists, musicians, scholars, and scientists. Enrico Fermi, the Italian physicist, was a Nobel prize laureate in 1938.

Aha, That's It

Minyan is the quorum of ten people necessary for communal Jewish prayer. Although personal prayer is permitted, some of the holiest portions of the service, including the reading of the Torah, may only be performed in conjunction with a *minyan*.

In Canada, Too

In 1807, Ezekial Hart, an extremely successful businessman whose family started the Indian Trading Post at Three Rivers, won a seat in the Quebec Assembly. Since he couldn't take the Oath of Allegiance "on the true faith of a Christian," he wasn't permitted to take office. He ran again and was re-elected. Once more, he refused to take the Oath and was rejected. He gave up and resigned himself to being a banker. In 1831, his son ran for office, was elected, and was permitted to take his seat "on the true faith of a Jew." That's what Jews call *naches* from children!

Aha, That's It

Naches is both the Hebrew and Yiddish word for the kind of joy that can only come from the accomplishments of one's children. It is said that the G.N.P. of the Jewish people is not their gross national product, but rather their children who are their Great *Naches* Producers.

Jews built shipping lines, started the first street railway in Montreal, pioneered Canada's telegraph system, and laid the first transatlantic cable line from Canada. They were into fishing, whaling, and farming, as well as the more traditional fields of shopkeeping and trading. The two largest Jewish communities are those in Toronto and Montreal, today boasting populations of 175,000 and 100,000, respectively.

Yenta's Little Secrets

The rivalry between Montreal and Toronto Jewry is sometimes played out in discussions about the quality of the bagels produced by each community. The consensus, however, is that Montreal is the leader—a fact borne out by the sale of "Montreal bagels" in certain Toronto stores. To date, there are no shops in Montreal that sell Toronto bagels!

And in South America

In the sixteenth and seventeenth centuries, there were more than 900 trials brought against Marranos for the "Judaizing heresy." Today, incredibly, there are approximately 3,000 Indians in Mexico who claim descent from these early Marranos. Over 40,000 Jews still live there today, supporting 23 synagogues and 10 Jewish newspapers and magazines, as well as the National School of Medicine—which formerly housed the Inquisition authorities.

Aha, That's It

Shiva, literally seven, refers to the Jewish seven-day period of mourning for the death of one's closest relatives. In some homes, parents sat *shiva* for their children if they "died" spiritually by baptism or conversion.

Sao Paulo, the largest city in Brazil and the third most populous city in the world, had as one of its principal founders a shipwrecked Marrano, Joao Rimalho, who then proceeded to marry the daughter of the local Indian chief. (I can't help but remind myself of the story of the very pious Jewish woman whose son announced to her that he was going to wed an Indian princess and be married out of the faith, to which his mother replied, "Nu, in her honor, I'll change my name to Sitting *Shiva*.")

The Marranos introduced the cultivation of sugar cane to Brazil, and Recife, as you may recall from Chapter 22, "America the Beautiful," was the source of the immigrants who first came to New Amsterdam. The Brazilian-Jewish community grew into what it is today with the arrival of Russian Jews over the past century, and today numbers 130,000. The Hebraica Club in Sao Paulo, with over 20,000 members, is probably the largest Jewish community center in the world.

Yenta's Little Secrets

Jewish architects are responsible for much of the modern architecture in Brazil. Russian-born Gregori Wrachavchik built the first modern house in the country, in Sao Paulo in 1930. The most prolific Brazilian architect, working in the American skyscraper style, was Rino Levi. Henrique Mindlin's work changed the skyline of Rio de Janeiro, and Elias Kaufman worked on the plans for the country's new capital city, Brasilia.

Argentina, with a Jewish population of 230,000, has the largest number of Jews in Latin America. Its open-door policy has attracted many Jews from Western Europe, especially those fleeing the pogroms in Russia. Argentina's first Jewish *gauchos* (cowboys) arrived from Russia in 1889. Aided by philanthropist Baron Maurice de Hirsch, they established Jewish agricultural colonies, which at their peak were populated by more than 20,000 Jews. Argentine Jewry plays a prominent role in the nation's industry, commerce, politics, the professions, and the arts.

Persecution may have caused the Jews a deal of suffering over the centuries, but it did one good thing for them: It got them to travel and see the world!

The Least You Need to Know

➤ Life under the czars was filled with hardship for the Jews, as they were restricted to a Pale of Settlement, persecuted by pogroms, and, even up to the twentieth century, falsely accused of ritual blood libel.

➤ In spite of the difficulties imposed upon them by the outside world, Jews created a *shtetl* existence, in which they found much joy in their deep faith, their communal solidarity, and their optimistic spirit.

➤ When they could no longer endure their suffering and had opportunity to emigrate, the fortunate ones left for other lands, most notably the United States and Israel.

➤ All the while, Jews were creating communities and bringing the blessings of their talents to major cities in Western Europe, as well as far-flung communities in Canada and South America.

Chapter 24

The Ten Lost Tribes?

> ### In This Chapter
>
> ➤ What may have happened to some of the ten lost tribes
>
> ➤ Jews in the most unlikely places
>
> ➤ Some fascinating insights into Jewish life and culture in exotic and unusual places

There are still some Jews so optimistic that they believe we will find remnants of the ten lost tribes. They're not lost, they explain, they've just been misplaced and probably ended up in some of the most far-flung locations around the world.

The truth is probably far less romantic. Jews were exiled so often, homeless so many times, that they were grateful for anyplace they could find that allowed them the freedom to settle, to struggle, and to make a living. Climate hardly mattered, nor did distance. When an official asked a Holocaust survivor where he wanted to go and was told Australia, he asked incredulously, "So far?" To which the Jew simply responded "So far from where?" And so, you see, Jews ended up in the most unlikely of places.

On Safari in South Africa

Years ago, a play on Broadway seemed to have the most unlikely of titles: *The Zulu and the Zeide.* But history loves the humor of precisely these kinds of connections.

In the nineteenth century, Nathaniel Isaacs (1808–1840) was such a spectacular businessman that the Zulu King Tchaka designated him as his principal chief in the territory of Natal. Another Jew, Benjamin Norden, did him one better. He got an agreement from the King of the Zulus that allowed him to open up all of the copper fields in Mamaqualand. A generation later, Jewish Albert Beit, together with Cecil Rhodes, carved out a colonial empire in South Africa, acquiring exclusive rights to all metals and minerals found in the country. They formed a syndicate, together with Sir Ernest Oppenheimer, which would lead to fabulous fortunes from minerals, gold, coal, and diamonds. Barney Barnato, who as a little lad in Whitechapel, England worked in the fish-and-chips business, became the fabulous "diamond king" of South Africa.

Jews from Russia and Poland smelled opportunity and quickly followed. The two largest centers of Judaism in South Africa today are Johannesburg (55,000 Jews) and Cape Town (15,000 Jews). Smaller communities include Durbin (5,000), Pretoria (3,000), and Port Elizabeth (1,200). The total Jewish population is 92,000, mainly affluent, well-educated, and with a tradition of vocal opposition to apartheid.

Yenta's Little Secrets

Among old-timers, the town of Oudtshoorn in the semi-arid little Karoo, is known as "the Jerusalem of Africa." Lithuanian Jews were pioneers in the ostrich feather trade and developed it into an important export business. These Jews knew how hard it was to make a living in other places in the world—and they obviously didn't hide their heads in the sand!

Down Under

In 1839, Melbourne, the second-largest city in Australia, couldn't even muster a *minyan* (10 Jews for a prayer group). Today it boasts 45,000 Jews, and Sydney is not far behind with 35,000. The land of the kangaroos is today jumping with an active Jewish life.

Australia is the one place in the world where Jews wouldn't want the distinction of being descended from its first and oldest residents. Australia was originally populated by convicts deported from the United Kingdom in the eighteenth century. (It is a fact that about 1/2 percent of all convicts transported to Australia were Jews, but we still don't want to boast about it!) Most of the early Jewish settlers came from England looking for gold; almost all of the later settlers were Holocaust survivors hoping to be able to freely serve their God.

Although much smaller in number during the early twentieth century, the Jewish community produced a remarkable range of great men and women who contributed considerably to the development of the Australian nation. The two most famous Australian Jews are General Sir John Monash (1865–1931) and Sir Isaac Isaacs (1855–1948). Monash, a successful civil engineer in private life, became Australia's greatest soldier and commander of the Australian Corps in France during the first World War. He was probably the first Jew to command an army since Roman times.

Isaac Isaacs was successively Victoria's attorney general, federal attorney general, justice and chief justice of the high court, and Australia's first native-born governor general. Today, one of Australia's largest universities, as well as a village in Israel, bear his name.

Other Australian Jewish notables include Isaac Nathan, Australia's first composer and "the father of Australian music;" Barnett Levey, "the father of Australian theater;" Sidney B. Myer, founder of Myer Emporium, Australia's greatest retail chain; and Roy Rene, known as "Moe," probably Australia's most famous comedian and entertainer during his lifetime. Helene Rubinstein, the founder of the world-famous cosmetics company, began her business career in Victoria before moving to the United States.

Australian Jewry must be doing something right because it enjoys the highest rate of enrollment in Jewish day schools and the lowest rate of intermarriage in the world; the two figures almost certainly are related to each other. And it boasts the largest Jewish day school in the world, Melbourne's Mount Scopus.

Yenta's Little Secrets

Melbourne Jews are primarily of Polish background and most are religiously conservative and Hasidic. The Sydney community, with more Hungarian and German Jews, is considered far more liberal. Australian Jews compare their two cities with cities in Israel: Melbourne is like Jerusalem, and Sydney, Tel Aviv.

With the Maori Warriors

Documents in the Jewish Museum record the first business trade between a Jew and a native Maori warrior—a trade that symbolizes so much of the story of Jewish wandering. Thomas, the young lad of the family that came from London to settle in Auckland in 1843, had on his head a silver-tassled yarmulke, the traditional head covering for a Jew. A Maori pointed longingly to it and indicated he would trade what he was holding in his hands for this little hat. The boy, to be friendly, agreed and took the proffered pig in place of his yarmulke. The mother screamed *chazir*—pig—as her son held this most unkosher of animals. But the scene vividly captured a sense of what the future held in store for these Jews: religious rites gave way, in this totally alien environment, to the forbidden and the profane.

Were it not so fundamentally sad, the story of the first synagogue in New Zealand would be very funny. In 1858, Auckland Jewry was finally successful in starting its first congregation. Just one year later the following advertisement appeared in the local newspapers:

[Advertisement]

We, the undersigned privileged members

professing the Jewish faith, hereby

acquaint our Coreligionists and Christian

friends that from this date we do not

RECOGNISE

Mr. Charles Davis as President,

Mr. P. A. Phillips as Treasurer,

Mr. P. S. Solomon as Officiating Minister,

on account of their recent

BEHAVIOUR

in our congregational matters.

FURTHER,

for the sake of ensuring that Love & Harmony

of feeling, so necessary in parties meeting for

RELIGIOUS WORSHIP,

we have determined to form a separate congregation,

under the jurisdiction of our

DR. CHIEF RABBI REV. N. M. ADLER,

and have accepted the

REV. J. E. MYERS,

of the Jews' College, London, to be our officiating minister & c.

Imagine, after only one year, they already needed two synagogues, although they didn't have enough people to support even one! Assimilation—and lack of unity between Jews—have always been the two main reasons why Jews haven't been even more successful than they are.

Yet with its inauspicious beginnings, New Zealand still has been able to grow to a community of 5,000 Jews with six synagogues, two in Auckland, two in Wellington, one in Donedin, and one—would you believe?—in Christchurch. (I wonder how Jews there feel about being a member of the Christchurch Synagogue?)

Yenta's Little Secrets

In spite of its small Jewish population of only 5,000 in a population of over 3 1/2 million, New Zealand once had a Jewish Prime Minister. Julius Vogel (1835–1899) moved to New Zealand from Australia, where his mining ventures failed and, by 1873, in what was certainly one of history's greatest immigrant success stories, was elected Prime Minister. In 1875, he was knighted. Contemporaries compared him to Benjamin Disraeli, but unlike the British leader, Vogel remained a Jew all his life. Anti-Semitic detractors called him "Jew-lius Caesar."

Who Are Ye Men of Yemen?

Tradition has it that Jews came to Yemen before the destruction of the first Temple. The first recorded reference to Yemenite Jews appears in the third century C.E., detailing settlements of traders and merchants. Yemen is one of the few countries that has been governed by Jewish monarchs. King Abu Karib Asad converted to Judaism in the fourth century, and Dhu Newas, who ruled a century later, also converted, as did many of his subjects.

In 1172, the great Jewish scholar Maimonides (see Chapter 15, "The Crescent of Brotherhood") responded to the Jewish community's request for information and inspiration with his famous *Epistle to Yemen*, in which he begged the Jews to remain faithful despite the persecution they were enduring. Although impoverished throughout the centuries, Yemenite Jews have always excelled as artisans, and their exquisite jewelry is renowned throughout the world. More than any other Arab-speaking Jews, they have preserved their own synagogue music and melodies, which, because of their very distinctive beauty, have made a great impact on the musical culture of Israel today.

Between 1919 and 1948, prior to the establishment of the State of Israel, one-third of the entire Jewish population of Yemen, or approximately 16,000 Jews, made *aliyah*, emigration to Israel. This was the largest percentage of Jews from any single country to emigrate before the creation of the Israeli state. From 1949 to 1950, Operation Magic Carpet, the model for the later airlift of Ethiopians and other Jews, transferred almost the rest of the Yemenite community to Israel. Today there are perhaps 500 Jews left in Yemen, while the rest of the Yemenites, very possibly remnants of the ten lost tribes, have all returned to their ancient homeland. (For more about the creation of the State of Israel, see Chapter 26, "The Final Return.")

Pulpit Stories

The Jews of Yemen were so primitive at the time of Operation Magic Carpet that most of them had never seen an airplane. They had no idea that human beings could fly and were stunned when they were told that these "birds of the air" had come to rescue them. The young turned to their elders for a possible explanation of this miracle. The elders looked to the Biblical texts and proclaimed that it was no miracle after all. It was merely the fulfillment of a Biblical verse. Had God not taken the Jews out of Egypt, as the Bible teaches, "on the wings of eagles?" These, they concluded, pointing to the planes, must be larger eagles that God had sent them to bring them back to their land. And who knows? They were probably right.

Black Is Beautiful

In the Bible we are told that Aaron and Miriam, brother and sister of Moses, were severely punished for disparaging the *Kushite* woman, "the Black one," that Moses took for a wife. God would not allow bigoted comments against people of color. In fact, King Solomon, the wisest of all men, noted in his Biblical work, the Song of Songs, that "Black is beautiful." Is it possible that Solomon believed it so much that *falasha* tradition is correct, and they are descendants of the royal issue of the Queen of Sheba's visit to King Solomon?

Aha, That's It

Falasha means stranger, or immigrant, in the G'ez tongue, the language of Ethiopia. No matter that Jews have been in the land since the second century; for their neighbors, they were still *falasha*.

Fascinating is the fact that although *falasha* observed all of the Jewish festivals before being reunited with other Jews, they had no knowledge whatsoever of Tisha b'Av, which commemorates the destruction of both the first and second Temples. Obviously, their separation from the rest of world Jewry goes back thousands of years.

How remarkable all the more, therefore, to be witness to their rescue and return to Israel in 1991, in a daring rescue mission appropriately named Operation Solomon. Since 1948, 50,700 Ethiopian Jews have emigrated to Israel.

An Ethiopian Absorption Center in Atlit, Israel. Eighty-year-old Itzhal Gonzan, a black Ethiopian Jewish priest of the Falasha sect, sits over a large prayer book, gesturing and speaking, in this close view taken inside his room. (Courtesy of James Stanfield/National Geographic)

Bene-Israel of Bombay

Five thousand people in India out of a population of 944 million know that they are different. Their neighbors in Bombay call them *Shanwar Teles,* "Saturday oil men," because most of them are employed as oil pressers, but they refuse to work on the Sabbath. They know they are Jews, and their oral tradition tells them they are descended from those who fled Judea during the cruel reign of Antiochus Epiphanes, right before the Maccabean Revolt in 175 B.C.E. (see Chapter 12, "Hellenists and Hanukkah").

Their oral history also includes the major misfortune of their past: On their sea journey to India, they were shipwrecked and lost the only copy of their Torah. For that reason, they remained ignorant of most of the laws. But they never forgot the most important line of Jewish liturgy. To this day it is the refrain for every important occasion, be it services, circumcisions, weddings, or funerals: *"Shema Y'israel*—hear O Israel, the Lord is God, the Lord is one!"

Listen to Your Bubbe

When in Israel, try *injira,* a flat pancake that is the staple of the Ethiopian diet. It's prepared from a mixture of flour and water that's fermented for several days, then cooked in a circular pan and baked over an open fire. *Injira* is eaten with a piquant stew called *wat,* made of lentils or meat and spices, and is generally washed down with a beer called *talla.* Afraid to try it? Look at the *falashas*—most of them are beautiful and hardly ever fat!

Proof that living in an alien culture invariably affects all its inhabitants, Jews in the caste-ridden society of India have also developed two distinct classes that do not intermingle. The *Gorah-Israel*, the White Jews, consider themselves the "real" Bene-Israel; the *Kala-Israel*, the Black Jews, probably descend from Indian proselytes. So in India at least, even though Jews acknowledge that God is one, they insist Jews are two.

T'angs for the Memory

On a stone tablet in an ancient synagogue in K'aifeng, capital of Honan Province, was an inscription in Chinese characters that read in part: "Adam was the first man, Abraham was the founder of our religion, then came Moses and gave us the Law and the Holy Scriptures." The magnificent synagogue was constructed in 1163 by Jewish merchants who made their home there and were welcomed by the Chinese Emperors. While the Crusaders were brutally butchering hundreds of Jewish communities in Europe, the T'ang Dynasty granted Jews full protection. A Chinese Emperor welcomed the Jews with these words: "You have come to our China; revere and preserve the customs of your ancestors."

Yet the cultural differences were too great for Jews to create any sizable community in China. During the rise of Nazism in the 1940s, over 25,000 Jewish refugees fled to Shanghai, but almost the entire Jewish population later migrated to the United States, Britain, Israel, and Australia. Today, in a population of 1,320,000,000 Chinese, there are approximately 50 Jews left.

Jewish Irishmen?

Jews came to Ireland in the mid–nineteenth century and played a great role in the struggle for Irish independence. Robert Briscoe (1894–1969) was a great Irish patriot who was a leader in the Irish struggle against the British. He was eventually elected Lord Mayor of Dublin, the first Jew to hold that honor. On being told of the election of a Jew as Mayor of Dublin, Yogi Berra, the king of malapropisms and the great catcher/manager of the New York Yankees, exclaimed in awe, "Only in America!"

Although there are few Jews in Ireland today (1,300), the country was homeland to two of the greatest chief rabbis: Rabbi Isaac Herzog, who later became the chief rabbi of Israel, and Rabbi Immanuel Jakobovits, who became the chief rabbi of the British Commonwealth. And that's no blarney.

Cave Dwellers, Too

To further make my point about Jews being almost everywhere, I have to tell you that there are even Jews in one of the most desolate areas of the world: the caves of the Atlas Mountains, south of Tripolitania and Tunisia. They are home to several hundred Jews. Three-and-a-half-hours journey by camel from there is Tigrena, home to an underground community of close to 5,000 who live by sheepherding. Passed on from generation to generation is a beautiful custom observed by all these Jewish cave dwellers: Cutting out little paper boats with which they then decorate their synagogues, they fervently pray, "May a boat soon come and carry us to Jerusalem!"

Camels resting in front of rhorfas in Medenine, Tuni (rhorfas are cavelike storehouses and dwellings). (Courtesy of Library of Congress/ Corbis)

The Prediction Came True

The prophets predicted that Jews would be scattered around the world and no land would be exempt from their presence. The later rabbis of the Talmud suggested a reason for this decree from God. The Jewish message of monotheism and the Jewish commitment to Law must be shared with all of mankind. Only then, they explained, could Messiah come to usher in a time of universal peace and blessing. Today Jews turn to God and declare that they have fulfilled their part of the bargain.

The Least You Need to Know

➤ Although there is no record of what happened to the ten lost tribes, it is conceivable that some remnants are in fact the precursors of small and distant communities scattered around the world.

➤ Exile and economic hardship propelled the Jews to live wherever they could find a haven, bringing them to such diverse communities as South Africa, Australia, New Zealand, Yemen, Ethiopia, India, China, Ireland, and even the caves of the Atlas Mountains.

➤ The diversity of settlements spanning almost the entire globe is fulfillment of a Biblical prophecy that the rabbis of the Talmud believe serves as a prerequisite for the Messianic Era.

Part 7

Death and Rebirth:
The Twentieth Century

Elie Wiesel, survivor of the Holocaust and Nobel Peace prize recipient, has said of our age that: "We are the most cursed of all generations, and we are the most blessed of all generations. We are the generation of Job, but we are also the generation of Jerusalem."

For the Jewish people, the twentieth century bore witness to the two most starkly different events of all their years. The Holocaust was an unparalleled horror that succeeded in murdering six million Jews even while plotting the total annihilation of its people. Incredibly enough, the Nazis' "Final Solution" was immediately followed by the "Final Return"—the fulfillment of a two-thousand-year-old dream of a people in exile to regain their promised land of Israel.

These two traumatic, history-altering events—crucial both for the world as well as for the Jew—will be the subject of Part 7. We will try to comprehend what happened when the world went mad, and we'll explore the remarkable aftermath of the Holocaust, as a decimated, despairing remnant miraculously managed to create a new state that today flowers and prospers. In light of both the horror and the hope, we will have an opportunity to evaluate the accomplishments of the past as well as to explore the possibilities for the future.

The Final Solution

Jews are no strangers to suffering. Throughout the ages, many others have also been victims of unspeakable cruelty, but the judgement of Winston Churchill is almost certainly the definitive description of the uniqueness of the Holocaust: "The Final Solution is probably the greatest and most horrible crime ever committed in the whole history of the world."

Holocaust scholar Deborah Lipstadt points out two reasons why the German program of genocide remains in a class by itself as an example of evil: "It was the only time in recorded history that a state tried to destroy an entire people, regardless of an individual's age, sex, location, profession, or belief. And it is the only instance in which the perpetrators conducted this genocide for no ostensible material, territorial, or political gain." In fact, the Holocaust remains incomprehensible. But that is all the more reason why it must at the very least be remembered.

How Many Is Six Million?

One of the first ways in which people try to convey the enormity of the horror of the Holocaust is to recite a number. They will tell you six million perished. But that is wrong—for a remarkable reason.

Aha, That's It

Holocaust, the most common name used to describe the Nazi massacre of the Jews, comes from a religious term referring to sacrifices totally burned on the altar and offered to God.

There is a law in the Jewish religion about counting people. If, for example, it has to be determined whether a sufficient number for a *minyan*, a quorum of ten needed for prayer, is present, Jews will recite a special verse of ten words, apportioning a word to a person, to determine whether the right number has been reached. Never ever are you allowed to point to a person and say, "You're one, you're two, you're three" because that would turn a person into a number and not a unique individual created in the image of God.

Interesting, isn't it, that the first thing the Nazis did when they turned Jews into concentration camp inmates was to replace their names with a tattooed number. They would no longer have a personal identity but just be a cold statistic suitable for extermination.

Six million is meaningless because we as men and women can't identify with a number. We can't empathize with a row of zeros. We can't picture the faces of mothers who had children torn from their breasts, to have their brains bashed in front of their eyes; we don't visualize little children tortured before they could ever enjoy their years of life and love. Six million is so incomprehensible that it is in fact beyond meaning.

That's why the world first began to understand the true dimension of the crime when the number became a name. We could understand the pain of Anne Frank, and it became not six million Jews, but Anne Frank with six million different names, dreams, and hopes never to be realized.

Yenta's Little Secrets

Since Jews can't be counted by number, the Biblical census was taken by having every Jew donate half a shekel, the monetary unit of the time, and counting the total. Why half a shekel and not a whole to be used for the count? To symbolically say to every Jew that no one is whole without his neighbor; every Jew is but half, needing to join with others.

The Diary of Anne Frank

Anne Frank was 16 years old when she died in the concentration camp of Bergen-Belsen in March 1945. All that remains of her incredible literary gifts, her sensitivity, and her insights is her diary—written while living in hiding in Amsterdam—which has become an international bestseller. For many people around the world, Anne Frank made the Holocaust real.

(translation)
"This is a photo as I would wish
myself to look all the time. Then
I would maybe have a chance to
come to Hollywood."
Anne Frank, 10 Oct. 1942

Anne Frank's favorite picture of herself, with inscription. (Courtesy of UPI/Corbis-Bettmann)

Yenta's Little Secrets

The famous photo of Anne Frank that adorns her diary has an inscription in her own writing (see photo): "This is a photo as I would wish myself to look all the time. Then I would maybe have a chance to come to Hollywood."

—Anne Frank, October 10, 1942. (Although she never made it, her words did come to Hollywood—and to every corner of the globe.)

With her we can feel the fear. We can get a small inkling of what it means not to leave the cramped quarters of a house for over two years and be deprived of your youth just because you are a Jew. Tears flow as we read her words of hope and know that in the end she will be betrayed, deported, and meet the same fate as her fellow Jews. We find it hard to agree with her conviction that "in spite of everything, I still believe that people are really good at heart." We cry with Anne Frank because we have come to know her. Yet her agony was miniscule compared to so many others. If we only knew *them* as well, we would begin to grasp the real meaning of six million victims.

Pulpit Story

When the Nazis broke into the house where Anne Frank was hiding, the S.S. man in charge picked up a portfolio and asked Otto Frank, Anne's father, whether there were any jewels in it. When he was told it contained only papers, he threw it to the floor, together with Anne's diary, and took only the silverware and the candlestick he found in the room. What an error of judgement. The diary proved far more valuable than all the silver and gold he possibly could have stolen.

The Hall of the Children

That's probably why the most moving of all the exhibits at Yad Vashen, Israel's Holocaust Museum in Jerusalem, is in the wing known as the Hall of the Children. The darkness is claustrophobic and frightening. The only light comes from blinking stars in the ceiling, symbolic reminders of the children who perished. The only sound that is heard is a recitation, not of prayers, but of names—an endless list of infants, children, and teenagers, whose only legacy is the name they were given at birth. To stand for a time and listen, to meditate and realize that every name was a person as precious to their loved ones as our children and grandchildren are to us is to recognize in yet another way that the phrase "six million" hardly begins to describe the loss of the Jewish people and the world.

Yenta's Little Secrets

Yad Vashem, the name of the Holocaust Museum in Israel, is Hebrew for "a hand and a name." It is part of Isaiah 56:5 where the prophet tells Jews who are childless that they won't be forgotten in future generations because God promises, "I will give them in My house and in My walls a monument [a hand] and a name better than sons and daughters; I will give them an everlasting name that shall never be effaced."

"Just a Crazy Man with a Funny Mustache"

Between 1933 and 1945, Nazi Germany (according to William L. Shirer in his classic *The Rise and Fall of the Third Reich)* "instituted a reign of terror over the conquered peoples which, in its calculated butchery of human life and the human spirit, outdid all the savage oppressions of the previous ages." And all of this was perpetrated under the dictatorial and fanatical leadership of a former house painter, a political crank, and a maniacally anti-Semitic Charlie Chaplin look-alike, first dismissed by his contemporaries as "just a crazy man with a funny mustache."

If history teaches us anything, it is never to dismiss anything as impossible. The truly evil men of the past owed their success not so much to wide-scale acceptance by the masses, but to indifference. It was silence and inaction that proved to be Adolf Hitler's principal allies.

Hitler started the Nazi party with a few dozen members. He never won an absolute majority of the vote in any democratic election, but by intimidation, strong-arm methods, and assassination, he managed to achieve unprecedented power. His story is the classic proof of the theory that for the wicked to succeed, all it takes is for the good people to do nothing.

Mein Kampf ("My Battle")

Hitler was at least frank enough to make clear, long before he came to power, his hatreds, his obsession with the Jews, and his political intentions. In his manifesto for the German people, *Mein Kampf*, Hitler outlined the ideas that would become national policy for the Third Reich. He didn't hide his world view or his plans for the future: "It is true we Germans are barbarians; that is an honored title to us. I free humanity from the shackles of the soul; from the degrading suffering caused by the false vision called conscience and ethics."

And Hitler spoke of his dream for the Jews as early as 1922: "I shall have gallows erected, in Munich for example…as many as traffic permits. Then the Jews will be hanged, one after another, and they will stay hanging until they stink. As soon as one is untied, the next will take his place, and that will go on until the last Jew in Munich is obliterated. Exactly the same thing will happen in the other cities until Germany is cleansed of its last Jew."

Perhaps the most terrible sin of all is not that Hitler said what he did, but that the world didn't listen. Maybe we've got to learn to hear even the things we don't want to hear. Had we done so, we could have responded before it was too late.

"Peace in our Time"

If only Neville Chamberlain would have understood that lesson!

When Hitler announced that he was planning to annex the Sudetenland, a part of Czechoslovakia, in 1938, Chamberlain went to Munich to negotiate with him. Hitler assured him that this was the last territorial demand Germany would make. Chamberlain, who obviously didn't read Hitler's book, came back to England proudly announcing that he brought back "peace in our time." Within a year, Hitler demanded Poland and then the rest of Europe. His peace plan was to conquer the world, piece-by-piece. The message, unfortunately, was understood just a little too late: Appeasing the wicked only makes the inevitable conflict all the more difficult.

Why Was this Night Different?

Every Passover, when Jews remember the time of their slavery in Egypt, children at the seder ask, "Why is this night different from all other nights?" They follow this with the traditional "four questions," meant to emphasize the special rituals at the seder: the *matzoh* (the unleavened bread), the bitter herbs, the special dippings, and the eating in a reclining position.

Some day perhaps there will be a commemorative ceremony for the *Shoa,* the Holocaust, and Jews will again ask, "Why was this night different?"—followed by six million questions. But until ritual catches up with recent history, we will have to write our own text to explain why the tragedy of the twentieth century occupies a place by itself in the lengthy archive of Jewish persecution.

Aha, That's It

Seder, literally *order,* is the Hebrew word for the festive meal on Passover night that follows a prescribed order for food, drink, and prayer.

Genocide

At the fiftieth anniversary ceremony of the liberation of Auschwitz, on January 27, 1995, Elie Wiesel pointedly clarified why the Holocaust is primarily a Jewish tragedy: "It is true that not all victims were Jews, but all Jews were victims." To describe Nazi hatred of the Jews, the word anti-Semitism would not suffice; a new word, "genocide," had to be coined by Raphael Lemkin, a Polish-Jewish international lawyer.

Never before was there a program to wipe out an entire people. Never before was the enemy every descendant of a despised group, no matter how minimal the geneological blood line. Never before were the youngest infants, as well as the oldest elders, considered mortal threats to the purity of a superior Aryan race.

Aha, That's It

Shoa is the Hebrew word for the Holocaust. Preceded by the word *yom*, Hebrew for day, *yom ha Shoa* is the name of the official day set aside for the remembrance of the Holocaust on the 27th day of Nissan on the Hebrew calendar (usually some time in the month of April).

Genocide was Hitler's obsession. Only if he murdered every single Jew in the world would he be able to "cleanse it" of the Jewish idea of one God and one moral standard. When Hitler had to choose between trains for his troops and trains to deliver the Jews to the death camps, he most often picked the latter.

The day before he committed suicide, Hitler left his people with his "last testament." He demanded that his followers continue the struggle and be faithful to the new government that would follow him. But what he wanted more than anything else was his final concern: "Above all I charge the leaders of the nation and those under them to scrupulous observance of the laws of race and to merciless opposition to the universal poisoner of all peoples, international Jewry."

No one has yet been able to explain the profound depth of his hatred. Nor has anyone been able to adequately solve the mystery of how he was able to transmit this irrational hatred to so many of his people. (Is it really possible, as Daniel Goldhagen claims, that the Germans were "willing executioners" because of a fatal flaw in their national character?) But this much we know: The scope of the "Final Solution" has no equal.

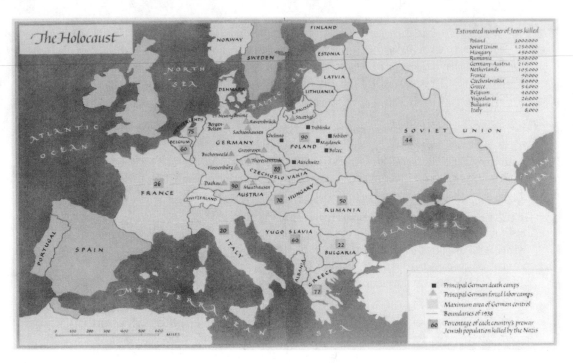

A breakdown of the concentration camps, their locations, and their number of victims.

"Sophie's Choice"

And the "night" of the Holocaust was different, too, because it was about much more than murder. How can one ever explain the sadism that became not only the norm but the ideal for German treatment of Jews? It was not just to work them to death; it was to beat them and to torture them all the while. It was not just to hang their rabbis, but to put the noose around their necks long enough to almost have them die and then revive them countless times so that they could literally die a thousand deaths. It was not just to send them to Auschwitz, Treblinka, Bergen-Belsen, and the other most gruesome concentration camps ever devised by man; it was to torture them for sport.

Jews were designated not only to labor and die; they also had to live in order to allow the Nazis to laugh, to gloat, and to rejoice at their suffering. Words simply do not exist to describe the full measure of sadism. What gave Nazis glee was the kind of pain they caused when they offered a mother "Sophie's choice." Choose which of your children will die, or we will slay them both.

We do not wonder that many of the Nazis' victims went mad. What is almost beyond belief is only that so many others retained their sanity and still wanted to survive.

Slave laborers in the Buchenwald Concentration Camp. Many had died of malnutrition when U.S. troops arrived and entered the camp. Elie Wiesel is the man whose face can be seen on the far right of the center bunk. (Courtesy of UPI/Corbis-Bettmann)

"Hell I Was in Already"

Years after World War II a survivor passed away in New York and left a most unusual request in his will. Religious Jews are by law required to be buried in *Tachrichim*, a ritual garment for the dead. The survivor, however, had carefully saved his Auschwitz "uniform" and begged that he be buried in it rather than the religiously required garb. "When I get to the other world and am required to stand for my final judgement, they will weigh all of my deeds to determine whether I am to be sent to Heaven or to Hell. I want to be able to point to the clothing I wore in my years in the German concentration camp and demand that I must be sent to Heaven because Hell I was in already when I was here on earth."

As a fascinating footnote to the story, the last request of the survivor was brought to Rabbi Moshe Feinstein (1895–1986), universally acknowledged as the greatest authority on Jewish law, for his decision. Rabbi Feinstein ruled that Jewish law in this instance would allow burial in the Auschwitz uniform. *Halachah* goes on record as declaring that the Holocaust was Hell.

Aha, That's It

Tachrichim is the special religious garb placed on the dead; its color, white, is a symbol of purity and meant to serve as witness to the purity of soul of the deceased.

"Civilized" Murderers

Perhaps the most inexplicable of all the aspects of the Holocaust—the question that forces us to come to grips with the very meaning of the word "civilized"—is the realization that it took place in the twentieth century and was the work of so-called "cultured," "civilized," highly educated Germans. "The death camps," as Franklin Littell pointed out, "were designed by professors and built by Ph.D.s." Nazis tortured by day and listened to Wagner and Bach by night. They put down the violin to batter a Jew to death. They used their advanced scientific knowledge to design crematoria and, most amazing of all, they had highly skilled doctors devise the most fiendish medical experiments to test levels of pain, how long someone could be immersed in freezing water before dying, and even, as the infamous Dr. Josef Mengele (chief "physician" at Auschwitz) was fond of doing, performed gruesome experiments on twins such as sewing two children together to create a "Siamese pair" and to measure their reactions.

Romain Gary, author of *The Dance of Genghis Cohn*, bitterly came to this shocking conclusion: "The ancient *Simbas*, a cruel, cannibalistic society, consumed their victims. The modern-day Germans, heirs to thousands of years of culture and civilization, turned their victims into soap. That desire for cleanliness, that is civilization."

The Holocaust was different because it came at the hands of those we would have been certain were incapable of committing atrocities. The Holocaust forces us to rethink the meaning of culture not rooted in a religious or ethical foundation.

The Silence of the Lamb?

The Jews were rounded up and herded like cattle to slaughter. For some, strangely enough, that makes the victims guilty of becoming accessories to their own murder!

Yes, it is true that the Jews didn't rise up *en masse* against their executioners. Like the rest of the world, which couldn't believe the horrors of the Holocaust even once they were over, the Jews couldn't imagine the extent of Nazi atrocities until it was too late to do anything about it. They believed they were going to be resettled and given an opportunity to be granted life in exchange for labor. They believed the sign at the entranceway to Auschwitz that proclaimed, "*Arbeit macht frei*—Work makes one free." They believed they were herded into synagogues to be addressed by the Nazis, not to be doused with gasoline and burned to death.

And when they finally suspected the worst, no one in the world would help them. They could get no guns; arms to defend themselves were unavailable. If one rose up to fight, a thousand would be cruelly punished and tortured. Jews were not led like lambs to slaughter. They were deluded, as was the world. They were isolated, and they were abandoned.

And yet these "lambs" managed an unparalleled demonstration of courage in the revolt of the Warsaw Ghetto. They were able to hold off the Nazis longer than it took these Germans to conquer all of Poland.

Mordecai Anielewicz, who died with his colleagues in the command bunker at 18 Mila Street, Warsaw, at age 24, wrote in the last entry of his diary: "The last wish of my life has been fulfilled. Jewish self-defense has become a fact. Jewish resistance and revenge have become actualities. I am happy to have been one of the first Jewish fighters in the ghetto. Where will rescue come from?"

Frightened Jewish families surrender to Nazi soldiers at the Warsaw Ghetto in 1943. (Courtesy of Hulton-Deutsch Collection/Corbis)

Rescue never came, but the Jews proved that given the slightest opportunity, they would fight to the death to protect and preserve their people.

No wonder then that the official day designated by the Israeli *Knesset,* its parliament, to commemorate the Holocaust is known as *Yom ha-Shoa ve-ha-Gevurah*—the Memorial Day for the Holocaust and for Acts of Courage. It is observed annually on the Hebrew date of the 27th of Nissan to coincide with the start of the Warsaw Ghetto uprising. In that way, the memory of persecution and death is linked with the recollection of Jewish valor and courage.

The Silence of the World

Hitler did have an all-powerful ally without whom he could never have succeeded. His ally was a world that chose to remain silent as Germany kept testing the limits of universal tolerance for its evil actions.

The Holocaust didn't begin with crematoria. Hitler moved slowly, cautiously escalating his anti-Jewish policies. In 1935, he passed the Nuremberg Laws, depriving all Jews of German citizenship. Jews were then barred from the professions, their stores were boycotted, they were singled out for special taxes, they were prohibited from "inter-marrying" with Germans. But on November 9, 1938, Hitler chanced a far more devastating step to test the waters of the world's reaction. "*Kristallnacht,*" the night of the broken glass, was a government-sponsored *pogrom* to break the windows of almost every German synagogue and to viciously beat any Jews who tried to protect their sanctuaries. With their genius for sadism, the Nazis then imposed a one billion Deutsche mark fine against the Jews to pay for the damages the Germans had inflicted.

But this was not enough to arouse the anger of the world. And so the progression that the great Protestant theologian Martin Niemöller described so powerfully was set into inexorable motion. Niemöller wrote: "When the Nazis went after the Jews, I was not a Jew, so I did not react. When they persecuted the Catholics, I was not a Catholic, so I did not move. When they went after the workers, I was not a worker, so I did not stand up. When they went after the Protestant clergy, I moved, I reacted, I stood up, but by then it was too late. By that time there was no one to speak up for anyone."

"Sharing the Guilt"

The opposite of love, it's been pointed out, is not hate. It is indifference. And if one can charitably say that the whole world didn't hate the Jews at the time of the Holocaust, most of the nations were, at the very least, strongly and strangely indifferent. Hitler gloated that while some spoke disapprovingly of his Jewish policies, no one was willing to take in the Jews that were fleeing Germany. The British imposed the White Paper, curtailing the promises of the Balfour Declaration and preventing emigration of Jews to Palestine. The United States refused to increase its limited quota for immigrants. When a Canadian official was asked how many Jews his country could accommodate, his answer was, "None is too many."

Although the allies had accurate maps of Auschwitz and their planes were able to find their way to the oil factory five miles away from the human slaughterhouse, they never bombed the crematoria or the gas chambers, which would have seriously hampered the German-programmed mass killings. Arthur Morse's groundbreaking book, *While Six Million Died*, makes tearful reading as we are forced to acknowledge the complicity of so much of the world in what is normally viewed as a crime of the Nazis.

Sage Sayings

"After the Holocaust, Jewish paranoia should not be dismissed as irrational delusion; even paranoiacs can have real enemies."

—Henry Kissinger

"The Voyage of the Damned"

The fate of the *S.S. St. Louis* is the most vivid example of the guilt shared by so many. Nine hundred thirty-seven Jews with visas for Cuba set sail from Germany in May 1939. They knew they could not remain in a land that had encouraged Kristallnacht. Cuba refused them entry, so the captain set sail for Florida. When the ship neared its territorial waters, the Coast Guard fired a warning shot, and the ship had to seek another port where it could land. The long journey in search of a haven eventually brought the *S.S. St. Louis* back to Germany and to death for most of its passengers. Once again, there was no room at the inn for the very people who gave the world Jesus.

"But There Were Some Exceptions"

At Yad Vashen, Israel's museum of the Holocaust, there is a special grove at the entrance called the "Avenue of the Righteous." Trees are planted in memory of those righteous gentiles who risked their lives to help Jews and who proved that some people are capable of rising above the cruelty of their neighbors.

Raoul Wallenberg is one of the most famous of these heroes. Descended from a very wealthy family in Sweden, Wallenberg saved the lives of tens of thousands of Jews. Eventually arrested and sent to a Siberian prison, his fate is unknown to this day, but his fame will live on forever by the grateful survivors he saved.

The film *Schindler's List* helped to immortalize another remarkable man who, although subject to many personal failings, nevertheless couldn't sit back and witness the killings without intervening to the best of his ability.

Best of all were the Danes, who proved that if an entire country stood up to the German plan of genocide, the Nazis would be unable to implement it. The Danes refused to round up the Jews. The king, Christian X himself, put on a yellow badge to turn the intended symbol of shame into a badge of pride—and all the Danes followed his example. The Jews consider all of Denmark a nation of righteous gentiles.

Sage Sayings

"I don't know what [Schindler's] motives were, even though I knew him very well. I asked him, and I never got a clear answer, and the film doesn't make it clear either, but I don't give a damn. What's important is that he saved our lives."

—Lewis Fagen, one of the Jews saved by Oskar Schindler

The Silence of God

On a wall in a cellar in Cologne, Germany, where Jews had hidden from the Nazis, there was found an inscription. The anonymous author who perished with his brethren left behind these words: "I believe in the sun even when it is not shining. I believe in love even when not feeling it. I believe in God even when He is silent."

Of all the difficulties Jews had to endure during the Holocaust, perhaps the hardest of all was the apparent absence of God. Jews cried, and their Creator did not seem to hear. Jews prayed and there was no response. Jews died *al kiddush ha-Shem*, sanctifying the name of the Lord with their last breath on earth, and the heavens responded only with silence. How could the Jews continue to believe? Is it conceivable for a compassionate God and the concentration camps to co-exist?

Aha, That's It

Kiddush ha-Shem, literally sanctification of the Name [of the Almighty], is the Hebrew term used for the act of martyrdom. To die *al kiddush ha-Shem* is to ensure oneself a place in the holiest portion of Heaven.

"Is There a God After Auschwitz?"

The wonder is not that there were Jews who lost their faith in Auschwitz. Far more remarkable is the fact that many Jews continued to cling to their faith and maintain their belief in their divine Ruler of the Universe. After the War, Richard Rubenstein pronounced God dead in his daring work, *After Auschwitz: Radical Theology and Contemporary Judaism*. He pointedly asked the question that would remain to this day the single greatest challenge to the monotheistic faith that the Jews had championed since the days of their father Abraham:

> I believe the greatest single challenge to modern Judaism arises out of the question of God and the death camps. How can Jews believe in an omnipotent, beneficent God after Auschwitz? Traditional Jewish theology maintains that God is the ultimate, omnipotent actor in the historical drama. It has interpreted every major catastrophe in Jewish history as God's punishment of a sinful Israel. I fail to see how this position can be maintained without regarding Hitler and the S.S. as instruments of God's will. The idea is simply too obscene for me to accept.

How, then, has God survived in the face of this rational onslaught? To believe that the Jews suffered as punishment for sin is indeed brutal insensitivity compounded by ignorance. It is, as Jewish theologians have suggested, destroying European Jewry yet one more time, besmirching these Jews' names after death even as they were degraded and murdered in life.

Sage Sayings

"If there is nothing after this life, then the Nazis and the Jewish children they threw alive into Auschwitz furnaces have identical fates. If I believed such a thing, I would either become an atheist or hate a God who had created such a cruelly absurd universe."

—Dennis Praeger

Jews have been able to maintain their faith because the Holocaust *affirmed* a fundamental belief of Judaism that makes religion all the more necessary. The Holocaust proved the failure *of man*, not the failure *of God*. In giving man free will, the option to do either good or evil, God effectively ties His own hands to prevent humankind from becoming merely puppets. What the world witnessed in the forties was how low it could sink when it forsakes ethics and law, and the moral conscience that has been the greatest gift of the Jews to mankind. Far from delegitimatizing God, the Holocaust made clear that without Him and His teachings, the earth could not survive.

"A Letter to God"

There is no more beautiful testament to the faith of a Jew than a document hidden in an empty bottle of petrol in one of the rooms of the Warsaw Ghetto amidst the rubble of stone and human remains. It was written by a Jew during the last hours of his life in the blazing ghetto. It deserves to be the last word on the theological problem of our generation:

Warsaw, April 28, 1943

I, Yossel Rakover of Tarnopol, a descendant of holy and righteous ancestors, am writing these lines at the time when the Warsaw Ghetto is ablaze. The house in which I am writing this is one of the last houses not yet touched by the fire. It has already been a number of hours since the terrible artillery fire was directed against us, and walls around me are collapsing like match-boxes. It will not be long before the house I am in will become like the other houses in the ghetto: a grave for its defenders and inhabitants.

I am forty years of age and when I look back on the years gone by, I can say with certainty, as far as a man is allowed to be sure of himself, that I led an upright life. I cannot say, after all I have endured, that my relationship with God has not changed; however, I am able to say with all certainty, I am proud that I am a Jew because it is very difficult to be a Jew. I believe that to be a Jew means to be a fighter, to swim eternally against the current of men's corruption and evil. The Jew is a tormented hero, a martyr.

You say, perhaps, that now the question is not reward and punishment, but rather, so to speak, the concealment of Your Presence, which explains that human beings are handed over into the power of evil men. But God, I ask You one question which is burning me up: What else has to happen to the children of Israel so that You should appear to us once again?

I feel that I have to speak to You openly. Now, more than at any other time in our history of endless suffering, humiliation and degradation, do we, who are now being trampled upon like vermin, buried alive and burned alive, degraded and humiliated, and being destroyed by the millions, have the right to know: How long can You be so patient?

I am telling You this because I believe in You more than ever. I know now that you are my God. You cannot possibly be their God because their dreadful deeds are the expression of vicious Godlessness. If those that hate and murder me are so dark and evil, then I must be the one who constantly carries something of Your light and goodness.

Death cannot wait anymore. I have to finish writing. The shooting is getting fainter. Our last heroic defenders are falling one by one. Warsaw the great, the beautiful, the city full of fear of God, Jewish Warsaw, is dying.

The sun is setting and I thank God that I will never see it again. I can see through a window that the sky is red like a pillar of blood. In a very short time I will be with my wife and children and millions who have perished, in the world which is all good, in which there are no doubts, in which God reigns supreme.

I die peacefully but not content, smitten but not in despair. I die believing in God. I followed Him even when He removed me from Him. I kept the Mitzvot even though I was punished. I loved Him even when He brought me to the lowest stage where we have become a mockery and laughing stock among the nations.

My Rebbe used to tell a story about a Jew who escaped from the Spanish Inquisition. In a little boat, he finally reached a rocky island. The sea was stormy and the weather was foul. Lightning struck and killed his wife. A terrible wave threw his child into the sea. Alone, naked and bare, frightened and scared, he reached the island. With his last ounce of strength he turned his eyes toward heaven and said: 'L-rd of the Universe, I have escaped here in order that I should be able to fulfill Your commandments and sanctify Your name. But You are doing a lot to make me leave my religion. If You think You will succeed in taking me away from the right path, I declare to You, my God and God of my Fathers, that it will never happen. You can depress me; You can take away the best from me. You can punish me to death. I shall always trust in You. I shall remain a Jew, and nothing in the world will make me change!'

These are also my last words. Nothing will change. You have done everything that I should deny You, I shouldn't trust You. But I die as I have lived—with a rock-like faith in You. *Shema Yisroel Adonay eloheinu adonay echod*—Hear O Israel, the Lord is My God, the Lord is one.

Sage Sayings

"The world rests on three things: justice, truth, and peace."

—quoted in the Talmudic tractate, *Ethics of the Fathers* [1:18].

"Justice, Justice, Shalt Thou Pursue"

The Bible commands the pursuit of justice. Punishment is not vengeance. It is making a statement of principle. To condone wickedness is to encourage it. And so the world that had sinned with both deed and with silence strove to redress its wrongs after the defeat of Nazi Germany. To its credit, the civilized world regained its voice in the post World War II era.

Nuremberg Trials

Hitler committed suicide on April 30, 1945, a week before Germany's surrender. The "heroic" leader of the German people chose not to face the consequences of defeat. But twenty-one other Nazi leaders mainly responsible for the criminal acts of the Germans survived.

It was at Nuremberg, in 1946, that an international tribunal was formed to bring these murderers to justice. No power on earth, of course, could bring the 11 million victims—six million Jews and five million others—back to life. But perhaps this act of the world going on record that it would not tolerate inhuman acts on this scale might serve to prevent similar horrors in the future.

Nuremberg represented a giant leap forward in the legal thinking of mankind. The defense of the Nazi officers, that they were "only acting under orders," was rejected; people must obey a "higher law" if the law of the land is clearly immoral. Murder can never be justified even when the government approves its practice.

Do you remember how the prophet Nathan had expressed this very same truth to King David, that even the most powerful ruler could not place himself above the law? (If you've forgotten already, peek back in Chapter 9, "Father and Son: David and Solomon," to refresh your memory.) It took many centuries but at long last, at the price of 11 million people, the world finally understood what the Bible had taught ages ago!

As Julius Streicher was led to the gallows, he inexplicably shouted out, *Purimfest*—Purim festival. Amazingly enough, Streicher had made a connection with an ancient story about the first attempt in Jewish history—the story of Haman—to destroy the entire Jewish people. That story ended with the ten sons of Haman hung and the Jews surviving. Is it simply bizarre coincidence that the judgement of Nuremberg, too, ended with exactly ten Nazi leaders condemned to pay for their crimes by hanging? And was Streicher's last word a "coincidence" that forces us to acknowledge this incredible linkage?

Eichmann Trial

The world felt a need for the trial at Nuremberg. But Israel knew it needed an even more important demonstration of justice in Jerusalem.

Adolf Eichmann was the man chosen by Hitler to carry out his infamous "Final Solution." It was he who boasted, "I will go to my grave happy that I murdered six million Jews." In spite of this, Eichmann managed to escape after the war and to find haven in Argentina. It was extremely painful for Jews to know that their archenemy had eluded justice and was now living a life of comfort while they were still hounded by nightmares. But more than knowing that evil in this case had gone unpunished, Jews were deeply plagued by the realization that a new kind of historic revisionism

Sage Sayings

"One Jew was put to death in Jerusalem two thousand years ago and the non-Jewish world has not ceased to speak of this death. Do we Jews not have the right, the duty, to keep alive the memory of the six million dead?"

—Elie Wiesel

began to doubt the inhuman details of the Holocaust. Because it was so unbelievable, there were people who refused to believe it ever happened.

And so Israel realized that there had to be at least one trial in which the Holocaust survivors would have an opportunity to tell their stories. Those who were still able to speak would serve as the mouths of the countless victims who prayed only that their deaths not be in vain. That their suffering be somehow remembered. That their memories be allowed to live on even if their corpses were not blessed with dignified burial, and their remains would forevermore remain unmarked.

In a dramatic story that became a movie, the famous Nazi hunter, Simon Wiesenthal, discovered Eichmann's whereabouts. Israeli agents kidnapped him in a fantastic cloak-and-dagger operation. And Eichmann was brought to trial so that the world might have a clear and indisputable record of the crime of the centuries. The transcript of the trial is available. The stories, which defy human understanding, can be read by anyone with a stomach for them. They confirm the profound depth of the tragedy. Eichmann, of course, was found guilty and was hanged on May 31, 1962. Among his last words was the remark that would show the extent of his self-delusion, "I am an idealist." Jews could only hope they executed not only Eichmann but the "ideals" he represented.

"Never Again"

Jews are a people of memory. In the Ten Commandments they are commanded to "remember the Sabbath day." In the Bible they are told to remember the exodus from Egypt, as well as the Amalekites who attacked them as they wandered in the desert. Memory is the key to survival. Indeed, as the philosopher and writer George Santayana so perceptively put it, "Those who cannot remember the past are condemned to repeat it."

That is why Jews feel a special obligation today to add yet another commandment of "remember" to their liturgy. Remember the Holocaust—so that it need never be repeated. Remember the Holocaust—so that its millions of victims be accorded at least the gift of living in our memories. Remember the Holocaust—so that, as the philosopher Emil Fackenheim has demanded, we do not give Hitler a posthumous victory by having us forget our past and our heritage. Remember the Holocaust—because, in the words of Elie Wiesel at the dedication of the United States Holocaust Memorial Museum in Washington in 1993, "To forget would mean to kill victims a second time. We could not prevent their first death; we must not allow them to be killed again."

Listen to Your Bubbe

The two must-see Holocaust memorial museums are Yad Vashem in Jerusalem and the United States Holocaust Memorial Museum in Washington, D.C. The quote from the *Ba'al Shem Tov* on a wall in *Yad Vashem* explains the urgency of visiting these commemorative sites: "In remembrance lies the secret of redemption."

The Least You Need to Know

➤ Jews do not count people by number because every person is a unique individual; that's why the victims of the Holocaust are not six million but one precious human being, like Anne Frank, six million times over.

➤ Adolf Hitler was obsessed with the Jews and made his intentions clear in his master work, *Mein Kampf.*

➤ Neville Chamberlain's acquiescence to Hitler's demands in order to avoid confrontation stands as a historic example of the danger of excessive compromise with cruel dictators of grandiose ambition.

➤ The Holocaust was unique in many ways from all other wars and persecutions in history.

➤ The world shares a measure of guilt with Nazi Germany for its silence, its passivity, and sometimes—as with the *S.S. St. Louis*—even its direct involvement.

➤ The silence of God during the Holocaust remains the primary theological problem of the post-Holocaust Jew.

➤ The end of World War II brought various attempts to bring evil-doers to justice, to express condemnation of the barbaric acts committed, and to verify as well as publicize the full extent of the crimes.

➤ Remembering the Holocaust is considered a sacred obligation, not just to recall the victims, but to ensure that there will never again occur anything like it.

Chapter 26

The Final Return

In This Chapter

➤ The Jewish dream of return to their homeland

➤ The founders of the Zionist movement

➤ Ways to reclaim a land and a language

➤ How Jews dealt with betrayal

➤ The birth of the State of Israel

The 1940s reversed the sequence of the lyrics of the *Fiddler on the Roof* song. Instead of "sunrise, sunset," Jews first experienced the sunset that almost marked their destruction. Then came the sunrise of miraculous redemption with the creation of the State of Israel. In three years, from 1945 to 1948, the Jews went from almost becoming an extinct species to bearing witness to the fulfillment of the Zionist dream that had eluded them for close to twenty centuries.

From the time of the Roman destruction of the Second Temple in the year 70 C.E., Jews had never entirely left the land nor renounced their claim to it. Zionism, based on the Biblical name for Jerusalem, Zion, sought a final return to a national homeland for the Jews. The Holocaust added an argument to the Zionist cause that made its realization irrefutable and inevitable: A people savagely persecuted and denied refuge in every corner of the globe needs at least one place of its own, one little spot to call home. Surely that spot to which it is entitled is the one from which it was exiled by force and to which it never gave up hope of returning in all the years of its existence.

To Dream the Impossible Dream

How strongly did the Jews yearn for their land? The words of the Psalmist capture the intensity of Jewish attachment to Jerusalem: "If I forget thee, O Jerusalem, let my right hand forget its cunning!" This theme of profound longing found its way into the daily prayers as well as the most important life cycle rituals of the Jews throughout the centuries:

➤ Three times a day, every Jew is commanded to pray. In the *Eighteen Blessings*, the central prayer of the Jewish service and the cardinal part of the liturgy, which lists the most important requests Jews require for survival, are the words, "And to Jerusalem, Your city, return us speedily in mercy."

➤ Every meal is concluded with a recitation of Grace, thanking God for the food just partaken and begging Him, "And rebuild Jerusalem, the Holy City, speedily in our days" so that Jews are not only physically sated but spiritually fulfilled as well.

➤ The holiest day of the year, *Yom Kippur*, is brought to a close with the resounding shout of the congregation, "Next year in Jerusalem." So, too, is the Passover *seder*.

➤ Every Jewish wedding ends with the groom breaking a glass underfoot. Some people say that's the very last time the groom will get a chance to put his foot down in the marriage, but it's meant to symbolize that as happy as the bride and groom are at this moment, their joy is incomplete. Their cup doesn't run over but is in fact broken because the Jewish people still live without land blessed with its spiritual essence, the Temple.

➤ Tisha b'Av remains the saddest day of the year, a day of 24-hour fasting, to recall the tragedy of the destruction of both temples and separation from the Holy Land.

Jews always remembered that the first thing God, obviously a good Zionist, told Abraham when he became a believer was, "Go forth from your land, from your birthplace, and from your father's house to the land which I will show you." The first Jew needed Israel in order to fulfill his spiritual strivings. His descendants could do no less. And a forced separation could only strengthen their love.

Waiting for God

But if the nations succeeded in driving them out of their land, reasoned many rabbis, then surely that must be God's will. Exile must be punishment for sin. Of course we want to return, but we dare not initiate that move. We have to wait for God to send the Messiah and lead us back with divine approval. Otherwise we would be going against the will of God, who is clearly responsible for our being in foreign lands.

It was an approach that seemed both reasonable and religious. It explains why to this very day there are still many Jews, considered extremely pious (they are called *Haredim*, literally those who tremble in fear of God), who are opposed to the creation of the State of Israel because it is the result of human effort rather than of divine intervention.

What this approach fails to acknowledge is that every human effort that succeeds is in fact the result of a partnership with God, requiring his approval. Judaism, unlike Christian Science, encourages the practice of medicine so that the doctor's skill may complement the divine will for healing the sick.

Yet, the striking paradox remains, as Connor Cruise O'Brien, the famous Irish author, so perceptively recognized: "The early Zionists were mostly secularists, but their enterprise derived most of its power and all of its territorial orientation from a religious book and the ancient longing it inspired." So the practical implementation of the religious dream of return was fathered not by a rabbi or an observant Jew, but by Theodore Herzl.

The Modern Day Prophet

Theodore Herzl (1860–1904) lived only 44 years, yet he managed to prove the validity of his personal motto: "If you will it, it is no dream."

Theodor Herzl leaning on railing, a famous pose for this man of prophetic vision. (Courtesy of Corbis-Bettmann)

273

Shaken to the core by the Dreyfus Trial (see Chapter 19, "The French Revolution Frees the Jews"), Herzl came to the conclusion that there was only one solution to the anti-Semitism that seemed to be thriving, even in civilized countries like France and Germany. A journalist and playwright by profession, Herzl became obsessed with Zionism. Only with their own state would the Jews find the security, the dignity, and the self-respect that is basic to every other nation.

With an attention to detail that seems almost ludicrous, Herzl penned his ideal vision of "the Jewish State," even describing its flag, the dress of its leaders, and its military uniforms. Many called him insane. Just think of what it means for one person to dream of creating a country. But Herzl burned himself out pleading with the Rothschilds and the de Hirschs, meeting with emperors, with kings, and even the Pope, all the while convincing the masses of the seriousness of his proposal and the possibility for its implementation.

With his charisma, his imposing prophetic appearance, and his political and diplomatic skills, he was able to successfully convene the First Zionist Congress in 1897, in Basel, Switzerland. (He couldn't call it in Germany, which was then the major center of Jewish life in Western Europe, because German Jews were fiercely opposed to the idea of Zionism, which would put into question their everlasting loyalty to Germany. Germany, they were certain, offered everlasting friendship for its Jewish citizens!)

Sage Sayings

"I would suggest a white flag [for the State] with seven gold stars: The white field symbolizing our pure life; the stars, the seven golden hours of our working day."

—Theodore Herzl

It was during this conference, on September 3, 1897, that Herzl wrote these remarkable words in his diary:

> "Were I to sum up the Basel Congress in a word—which I shall guard against pronouncing publicly—it would be this: At Basel I founded the Jewish State. If I said this out loud today, I would be answered by universal laughter. Perhaps in five years, and certainly in fifty, everyone will know it."

Poor Theodore Herzl. His prophecy didn't come true as he predicted. He was off by *one year*! It took until 1948.

When Herzl's heart gave out from the stress of his herculean efforts, he left behind a request in his will to be buried next to his father in Vienna "until such time as the Jewish people would bring his remains to Palestine for burial." Not *if* the Jews return, but *when*. And so in 1949, Herzl's remains were moved to the spot in Jerusalem today known as Mount Herzl. It is a mark of respect and of gratitude for tourists to visit the site.

Sage Sayings

"Zionism was the Sabbath of my life."

—Theodore Herzl

Redeeming the Land

Zionism was successful because it didn't stop with calling meetings or creating committees. (We all know that committees are places where people keep minutes and waste hours.) It was the genius of the early founders to turn ideas into practical policies and theories into programs. In three different ways, Jews discovered the secrets of redeeming the land.

With Money

When Moses took a census of the Jews in the Bible, he counted them according to God's instructions, by every person's donation of half a shekel. (Remember how we learned in Chapter 25 that Jews can't be counted by number—people can never be reduced to something that considers them less than unique beings in the image of God.) The First Zionist Congress understood that if the movement was to represent world Jewry, it must have a democratic and universal base. It wanted every Jew to be able to afford membership, not just the wealthy. So it made the annual purchase of a shekel (then about 25 cents) the nominal dues. For that sum a member received an exact replica of the shekel of "liberation" minted in Judea in the days of Bar-Kochba's last stand against the Romans.

In the days of old, this method was used to count the Jews. Now it would identify Jews who counted. For about a quarter, Jews became one with their brothers around the world and felt that with their contribution they were part of a movement that would liberate their people.

At the First Zionist Congress in 1897, Professor Hermann Schapira (1840–1898), a noted mathematician, drew up the plans for the Jewish National Fund (JNF) that would oversee use of the funds contributed by Jews worldwide for the purchase of land in Palestine. The land was redeemed acre by acre, *dunam* by *dunam* (quarter acre). Unlike the colonizers of, for example, Australia, South Africa, and North America, who came to a land not theirs and took it by conquest, *Jews returned to their own homeland from which they were forcibly expelled and redeemed it by purchase, most often at inflated prices.* American Indians should only have gotten as good a deal as the Palestinian Arabs!

The JNF also made it its mission to plant millions of trees in a barren, denuded country forsaken by its former occupants. To this day, Jews still commemorate special events by purchasing a tree in someone's honor. (Pity the poor honorees who, according to local Israeli legend, spend months looking for the particular tree with their name on it.)

Aha, That's It

Chalutzim, singular *chalutz*, means pioneers, specifically the early Israeli settlers who performed exceedingly hard physical labor to bring the land back to productivity.

Aha, That's It

A *kibbutz* is a collective settlement, socialistic in character, whose members share equally in land, work, and profits. A *moshav*, also a working and living community, is less socialistic than a *kibbutz*. Land and farm machinery are owned jointly, but settlers own their houses and can dispose of their income as they wish.

With Labor

A strong voice within the Zionist movement that would eventually shape much of its early philosophy was the call for "the Dignity of Labor." The soil had to be tilled, the swamps drained, a desolate land had to be brought back to life. The early pioneers, *chalutzim*, following the teachings of philosophers like Aaron David Gordon (1856–1922), made physical labor their religion, the sweat of their brow their prayers, and their back-breaking work their homage to God. Their idealism would be translated into the *kibbutzim* and *moshavim*, where personal gain would be made secondary to the good of the group.

When a tourist once observed the harsh lifestyle of one of these early pioneers, he couldn't help telling him, "I wouldn't do what you're doing for a million dollars." "Neither would I," replied the idealistic *chalutz*, "neither would I!"

Yenta's Little Secrets

The first kibbutz in Israel was established in 1910 and named Degania. The first child born in Degania was the future hero of the Six Day War, Moshe Dayan.

With Religious Fervor

And even among the "pious" who claimed that religion was opposed to Zionism because it interfered with "the will of God," there were a sizable number of Zionists. Rabbi Samuel Mohiliver (1824–1898) was one of the leading Orthodox rabbis of Eastern Europe. He was witness to the *pogroms* in Russia and Poland in the 1880s and came to the same conclusion as Herzl. For him, a return to the land was tantamount to the commandment to save one's life.

Mohiliver started the movement *Hovevei Zion* (lovers of Zion). With this group Rabbi Mohiliver became the founder of the religious Zionist party, today known as *Mizrachi*. The battlecry for the "lovers of Zion" became the famous motto of Hillel, the great Talmudic sage, "If I am not for myself, who is for me?" The first agricultural settlements of Eastern European Jews in Palestine were founded by these religiously motivated Zionists who served as an inspiration to their persecuted brothers in Russia, and were responsible for subsequent waves of immigration.

Palestine was slowly being bought back by Jews, reclaimed through the labor of Jews, and sanctified by those who revered its special spiritual status.

Reviving the Dead

It wasn't only the land that had to be brought back to life. A people returning to its ancient homeland would have to relearn its language, Hebrew. And that, the miracle of a "dead" language coming back to life after close to two millennia, is something that has never happened before in human history.

True, Hebrew had never been forgotten as the language of "the book." People read it but didn't speak it. And not being used in conversation for centuries, ancient Hebrew lacked words for all modern inventions, for everything that didn't exist in the days of the Bible. How do you suddenly create a modern language, begin to speak it, and have everyone else around you adopt it as the "official language of the land?"

How it happened is another example of one person crazy enough to dream an impossible dream and then create a new reality for an entire people. Eliezer Ben-Yehuda (1858–1922) had to be "insane" to think he could actually pull it off. He took a vow with his wife when they arrived in Palestine to speak only Hebrew in their home. For items that had no names in Hebrew he had to create new words. He couldn't look them up in the dictionary; there wasn't even a Hebrew word for "dictionary!" So Eliezer Ben-Yehuda dedicated his life to being the Noah Webster of Israel, with a special twist: He didn't define words that existed; he made up words based on linguistic principles that would allow them to be understood because of their roots. He then popularized them in his major work, a modern dictionary of the Hebrew language.

Today, the millions of Jews from all over the world who come together in Israel rapidly become unified by speaking a common tongue. Sometimes the words chosen for really modern innovations are very ingenious and amusing. The ancient Biblical word for sin in Hebrew is "*averah*." I'll never forget the first time I went to a basketball game in Israel and heard the referee shout at one of

Sage Sayings

"Anyone who is thoroughly familiar with the language and literature of a people cannot be wholly its enemy."

—Henri Bergson, French philosopher

Aha, That's It

Ulpan is the equivalent of a speedy Berlitz course in Hebrew for adults. It has successfully turned millions of immigrants into fluent Israelis who can converse, argue, and debate with each other in the same national language.

the players, *Averah!* I thought for a moment he had eaten a ham sandwich on court! It took me a moment to realize that that's the modern way Hebrew linguists have decided to describe a foul.

"Language," wrote the Hebrew poet Chaim Nachman Bialik (1873–1934), "is the key to a nation's heart." What Ben-Yehuda accomplished was to preserve the heart of the prophets in the daily lives of the people. The very first thing every immigrant is urged to do immediately after entering Israel is to attend an *Ulpan*, a Hebrew course, in order to become joined in the most powerful of ways with his neighbors—and with his ancestors. For that we can only say to Eliezer Ben-Yehuda, "*todah*" (Hebrew for thanks).

The Great Betrayal

The Jews who first came to Palestine in the early waves of immigration at the beginning of the twentieth century thought they would conquer it with the hoe. The hatred of the Arabs forced them, in an unfortunate reversal of the words of Isaiah, to beat their plow shares into swords and their pruning hooks into spears. Those who wanted nothing more than to be tillers of the soil and men of peace had to learn the art of war in order to survive the constant attacks from their Arab neighbors.

What became ever more clear was the real reason for the Arab incitements. The *effendis*, the privileged Arab land-owning class, had for centuries enjoyed the cheap labor of the oppressed Arab peasantry, the *felaheen*. With the coming of the Jews came higher wages and a higher standard of living for the Arabs. Effendis couldn't get cheap labor anymore. The feudal system was being infected with visions of democracy. So the effendis did what all privileged groups do to maintain their superiority: They spread slanders against the Jews so that the disadvantaged would turn against the only group able to help them find a better way of life!

All this time, Jews looked to the British Mandatory Government to give them the protection they were required to offer under the terms of the League of Nations' mandate. Unfortunately, history paints a grim picture of the British policy toward their Jewish subjects. In the Hebron Massacre of 1929, Jews were brutally murdered while Hebron officials turned a blind eye. So clear was their indifference to the plight of the Jews that the League of Nations formally reprimanded the British government for failure to protect the Jewish population. Yet, the terrorist attacks continued. And the Jews came to the only logical conclusion.

A Jewish Army

Vladimir Jabotinsky (1880–1940), a Russian-born Jew, together with his one-armed countryman, Josef Trumpeldor (1880–1920), convinced the British toward the close of World War I that a "Jewish Army could be of help to them." The British let the Jewish volunteers assist in the battles of Gaza and Beersheba against the Turks, but only as lowly mule-driver companies for the transport of ammunition. They were called the Zion Mule Corps; they carried a blue and white Zionist flag as their banner, and they proved their incredible courage in the Gallipoli campaign. Those who saw Jabotinsky and Trumpeldor in action said that even the legendary Lawrence of Arabia couldn't match their bravery.

These two brave men had every reason to believe that their efforts on behalf of England would be remembered. But both were to be bitterly disappointed. Trumpeldor was part of a group of Jewish settlers attacked at Tel-Hai, a settlement in northern Israel, in 1920. Fatally shot in the stomach, he uttered his last words, which became a slogan for Zionist settlers and Jews around the world: "It is good to die for our country."

When England did nothing to prevent similar killings, Jabotinsky concluded that Jews have no one to rely upon except themselves. Jabotinsky pushed for Jewish defense groups to be prepared to fight back when attacked. For this, the British arrested him "for carrying illegal arms."

Jabotinsky would eventually become a "hard-line" Zionist, founder of the *Irgun* (the Revisionists), whose extremist views alienated many of the more conservative Zionists. But Jabotinsky's rejection of moderation was surely fueled by his almost pro-phetic fear of impending doom for the Jews of Europe. In a speech on August 10, 1938, one year before the Nazis invaded Poland, he told the Jews in Warsaw:

Listen to Your Bubbe

The grave of Captain Josef Trumpeldor, who met a heroic death defending the frontier colony of Tel–Hai in Upper Galilee, has become a national shrine for pilgrims in Israel.

> For three years, I have been imploring you, Jews of Poland, the crown of world Jewry, appealing to you, warning you unceasingly that the catastro-phe is near. My hair has turned white and I have grown old over these years, for my heart is bleeding that you do not see the volcano which will soon begin to spew forth its fires of destruction…listen to my words at this, the twelfth hour. For God's sake, let everyone save himself, so long as there is time to do so, for time is running short.

Yenta's Little Secrets

Jabotinsky's Revisionist Party eventually coalesced into the Herut, later the Likud Party under the leadership of Menachem Begin.

Aha, That's It

TZAHAL is an acronym that stands for *Tzva Haganah Le-Yisrael*—Israel Defense Forces, or IDF. The name reinforces its purpose: to fight only in defense of the Jewish State and the Jewish people.

Jabotinsky preached the need for a Jewish Army way before there was even a State of Israel. The *Haganah*, founded in 1920 to protect Jewish lives, was the response of a people who would no longer be willing to sit back and watch their own destruction. By 1936, this defense force numbered 25,000. In 1948, with the birth of the State, the Haganah gave way to *TZAHAL*, the Israel Defense Forces, generally regarded as one of the best armies in the world.

The White Paper

The British betrayed their commitment to Jewish safety by closing their eyes to Arab terrorist attacks for decades. Worse still, the British betrayed the promise set forth in the Balfour Declaration, a promise that they "favor the establishment in Palestine of a national home for the Jewish people and would use their best endeavors to facilitate the achievement of this object"—with the passage of the White Paper on May 17, 1939.

The White Paper limited Jewish immigration to Palestine to only 75,000 people *over a five-year period,* and it stated that "His Majesty's government now declares unequivocally that it is not part of their policy that Palestine should become a Jewish State." The timing could hardly have been worse, for this was in 1939, when Jews clearly needed an alternative to Hitler's persecution. The British lack of concern for the Jews was taken by the Germans as open approval of their subsequent policy, the "Final Solution."

England, leader of the Allied Nations, was now making it abundantly clear that the fate of the Jews had the lowest priority. Chaim Weitzmann could observe with a great measure of truth that "There are now two sorts of countries in the world: those that want to expel the Jews and those that don't want to admit them." Jews were now faced with an almost impossible choice: How do you react to a country (England) that shows itself to be an enemy to Israel but is nevertheless your powerful ally in fighting against the Nazis, who seek the destruction of the Jewish people?

The answer was provided by the man who would some day become the first Prime Minister of Israel.

The Man Who Stood on His Head

David Ben-Gurion (1886–1973) was described by former Israeli Prime Minister Golda Meir as "the greatest Jew in our generation." That probably was a gross understatement. A man of his brilliance, charisma, diplomatic skill, and vision comes on the scene of world history very infrequently. Fortunately, he was the right man at the right time, when the Jews needed not just a leader but a veritable giant. For those who claim that the creation of the State of Israel wasn't a miracle of God, there must at least be admission that it was the product of a miraculous man.

Before yoga became popular in the western world, Ben-Gurion was already an avid disciple. He practiced standing on his head for many hours and that probably gave him the ability to view a world that had turned upside down from a proper perspective. Late in life, Ben-Gurion studied Greek so that he could read Plato and Aristotle in the original. His hobbies were full-time occupations for other people.

As a young man, Ben-Gurion worked in the orange groves of Petah Tikvah and in the wine cellars of Rishon Le-Zion. In 1918, he helped organize the Jewish Legion in which he served for the British during General Allenby's operations against the Turks. After World War I Ben-Gurion helped build up the Labor Party and found the *Histadrut*, the General Federation of Labor. In 1933, he was elected to the Jewish Agency Executive and then named Chairman of its Board. All this would serve him well as training for governing the new country as its first prime minister for 15 years.

Upon his death at age 77, Chaim Weitzmann, speaking for the entire nation, summed up Ben-Gurion's life: "He will be taking his place in the eternal history of the Jewish people alongside the great figures of the past—the Patriarchs and Kings, the Judges, Prophets, and spiritual leaders who have woven the fabric of our national life for four thousand years."

This was the man who found the right words to respond to England's betrayal of the Balfour Declaration with the White Paper: "We shall fight Hitler as though there were no White Paper, and we shall fight against the White Paper as though there were no Hitler."

Sage Sayings

"The State of Israel will prove itself not by material wealth, not by military might or technical achievement, but by its moral character and human values."

—David Ben-Gurion

Paul Newman, Israeli Hero

With the end of World War II, as the world first began to learn of the true horrors of the Holocaust, a wave of sympathy arose for the survivors of the most terrible genocide of all of history. Even hearts of stone couldn't fail to be moved by the stories of concentration camps and crematoria. All, that is, except for the stiff upper-lipped British who felt they still had to strictly enforce their tight restrictions on Jewish immigration to Palestine.

When the homeless tried to return to their ancient land, the British captured these human skeletons and shipped them off to D.P. (displaced persons) camps on the British-controlled island of Cyprus. Soon 26,000 Holocaust survivors were once more living in camps surrounded by fences, this time guarded by "friends" who just recently celebrated their victory over fascism for the "freedom and dignity of all mankind."

One story captured the full extent of the tragedy. It was so moving it was tailor-made for a movie. And so it became first a best-selling novel by Leon Uris and then a highly successful movie starring Paul Newman (yes, he *is* Jewish). Abba Eban, Israel's former Foreign Minister, once said that Paul Newman's portrayal of the Israeli hero in *Exodus* probably was the biggest P.R. boost to the country's image up until that time.

Exodus is the second of the Books of Moses in the Bible, but for the Holocaust survivors it was also the name of the ship meant to free them from their personal tale of slavery. The *Exodus*, packed with 4,500 displaced persons, set off with its human cargo to Palestine. Twelve miles from its destination, British destroyers closed in and opened fire. The crew surrendered, and the British Foreign Minister Ernest Bevin—later nicknamed Bergen-Bevin after the Nazi concentration camp Bergen-Belsen—decided these illegal immigrants didn't even deserve the internment camps in Cyprus. To set an example, the survivors were *shipped back to Germany*. With clubs, the British forced the Jews off the boat when it reached its German port, proving both their physical superiority and their moral insensitivity to the Jewish survivors. It was an act that would prove to turn world opinion against the British, at last.

Aha, That's It

Mazel tov, literally, "good constellation," is the Jewish way to express the hope for good luck in the future. The phrase is commonly used at every happy occasion.

This final act of betrayal helped seal the coffin of British rule over Palestine. One year later, the roles would be reversed: The British would leave Palestine and the Jews would at long, long last return home.

Mazel Tov—Israel Is Real

On November 29, 1947, the United Nations voted Israel into existence. Against the No's of all of the Arab states, the U.N. passed a vote for partition of Palestine into Jewish and Arab sections. Jews celebrated the right to a tiny portion of land. But the Arabs rejected the plan.

Pulpit Stories

President Harry S Truman had a close Jewish friend, Eddie Jacobson, who was once his business partner. When Truman was under tremendous political pressure not to recognize Israel, he refused to see Chaim Weizmann who had come to see him and plead with him for his support. It was then that Jacobson asked for a meeting with his old friend, the president. It was granted on condition that he not say anything about Weizmann's request to visit. Jacobson kept his word; he didn't say a thing about Israel. He just sat there crying. Truman understood and gave in. The tears were in no small measure responsible for the United States being the first country to recognize the new State of Israel.

On Friday, the eve of the Jewish Sabbath, May 14, 1948, the Union Jack was lowered in Jerusalem, and David Ben-Gurion announced the birth of the State of Israel. The Proclamation of Independence, 979 Hebrew words that took about twenty minutes to read, stressed the unbroken link between the Land and the Jewish people; referred to Herzl and the Balfour Declaration; declared that the State would be called Israel; that it would be "open to Jewish immigration and the in-gathering of exiles;" that it would "promote the development of the country for the benefit of all its inhabitants" and be based on liberty, justice, and peace "as envisaged by the prophets of Israel;" and that it would loyally uphold the principles of the U.N. Charter.

Members of the newly created state of Israel gathered to hear Prime Minister David Ben-Gurion read the Jewish "Declaration of Independence." (Courtesy of Corbis-Bettmann)

It called upon the United Nations to assist the Jewish people in the building of its State and appealed "in the very midst of the onslaught launched against us…to the Arab inhabitants of the State of Israel…to play their part in the development of the State on the basis of equal citizenship and due representation in all its bodies and institutions." To the Arab States and peoples, the Proclamation offered "peace and good neighborliness" and promised that the State of Israel would "make its contribution to the progress of the Middle East as a whole."

Only one major problem plagued the authors of this historic document. The religious insisted that the name of God appear in this momentous acknowledgement of national redemption. The secularists refused to sign if the credit for this great victory of human achievement was deflected to the Divine. The controversy would be a powerful preview of the ongoing debate in Israel about the proper place for God in a modern Jewish country.

Thankfully, the founders of the State found an acceptable compromise: Instead of mentioning God by name, they referred to the ambiguous Rock of Israel. That's how after almost six thousand years, the people who discovered monotheism ended up turning their God into a "Rock" star!

But at the very same time the Proclamation was being read, posters were hung by the *Haganah*, the Jewish army, on all the walls of public places in the city: "Shelters must be dug in all residential areas and the orders of Air Raid Precautions Officers must be obeyed." As the new country was born, the joy was tempered with the realization that war would soon break out.

The Least You Need to Know

➤ The dream of returning to the national homeland has always been a part of Jewish prayer, ritual, and custom.

➤ While some believed it was religiously necessary to wait for God to bring about the redemption, others—led by the visionary Theodore Herzl—founded the Zionist movement to hasten the time of Jewish independence.

➤ Jewish agricultural colonies were set up in Palestine by purchasing land from Arab owners and by diligent labor on the part of those who viewed toil as a religion of "service to God."

➤ Crucial to the reclamation of the land was the revival of its ancient language, a task almost miraculously achieved single-handedly by Eliezer Ben-Yehuda.

➤ England betrayed the mandate given to it by the League of Nations as well as its own Balfour Declaration when it issued the White Paper.

➤ The fate of the ship *Exodus,* in 1947, stirred the world's conscience and helped bring an end to British control over Palestine.

➤ David Ben-Gurion proclaimed the birth of the new State of Israel even as the Jews realized they would soon face attack by their combined Arab neighbors.

Chapter 27

Israel at Fifty

In This Chapter

➤ The on-going cycle of war and peace, violence and co-existence

➤ The battles of the past and the promise of the future

➤ The story of Israel's numbers; the incredible growth of a nation

➤ Biographies of Israel's major heroes

➤ Problems that remain and the status of a country that has reached the age of fifty

Imagine that a baby is born, and no sooner is it placed in the nursery than toughs in the neighborhood vow they're going to kill it. They gang up on the infant and try to murder him, but they don't succeed. As the child grows, the bullies continue to threaten his life. They attack him unexpectedly. They announce publicly they're going to throw him into the sea, they're going to rape his wife, and butcher his children. Somehow, no matter how hard they try, they can't accomplish their goal.

The name of the baby is Israel. From the moment he saw the light of day, six large neighborhood bullies—Egypt, Syria, Jordan, Lebanon, Iraq, and Saudi Arabia—ganged up on him for "a war of extermination." Amazingly enough, that little David of a country overcame all the Goliaths. In 1998, it reached the venerable age of 50. And it is stronger, more advanced, with a higher standard of living than all of those who still seek its destruction. If that isn't a miracle, it's surely about as close to one as you can ever get!

War and Peace—Not

The famous Czech author Milan Kundera once defined a small nation as "one whose very existence may be put in question at any moment. A small nation can disappear and knows it." Israel is a small nation. Four times in its brief history it has been forced to fight wars. It could not afford to lose any one of them. The alternative to victory, its enemies threatened, was total extermination.

The Jews were attacked by armies from the six Arab countries in the War of Independence, which began immediately after the State came into existence. The Arabs, rejecting the U.N. decision, declared their intentions clearly: Haj Amin al Husseini, spiritual leader of Palestine's Muslims, told his followers, "I declare a Holy War, my Muslim brothers. Murder the Jews! Murder them all!"

The Jews had only one secret weapon. It was a slogan that would so inspire them they would beat the incredible six-to-one odds and achieve a stunning victory: *Ein breira*, "we have no alternative," was motivation that could not be equaled. So after 15 months and 6,000 Israeli lives—a huge number for a small people—the Israel Defense Forces (IDF) succeeded in defeating Israel's invaders. In 1949, an armistice agreement was signed on the Greek island of Rhodes.

The Arab States, however, continued to refuse to recognize Israel. Following countless terrorist attacks, Israel finally retaliated with the successful Sinai Campaign in 1956. After much international pressure and assurances from world leaders that its boundaries would be protected, Israel withdrew from the Sinai Peninsula.

But terrorist raids increased. The Syrians bombarded settlements in the north, and a massive Arab military build-up took place on the Egyptian border. In 1967, Egypt's President Gamal Abdel Nasser unilaterally closed the Straits of Tiran as the first step in a planned program to "exterminate the Zionist entity and drown all the Jews in the sea."

The reaction of the world? Charles DeGaulle's strict advice to the Jews summed it up best: "Do not make war! In any event, do not be the first to fire." To which Rabbi Soloveitchik, leading Orthodox rabbi and scholar, commented: "Isn't it strange that only the Jews and not all Christian nations are expected to live by the Christian principle 'turn the other cheek' to which Judaism does not subscribe?"

When Syria and Jordan both joined in the war "to wipe Israel off the map," Jews around the world feared they would soon see another Holocaust. In what remains one of the most incredible and inexplicable military victories in history, Israel bested its combined enemies, captured the uncapturable Golan Heights, and, most stunning of all, reunified Jerusalem. Israel was suddenly acknowledged by the world as the greatest military power in the Middle East. It had won what would be known as "The Six-Day War"—a victory that miraculously took less than one week to accomplish.

And On the Seventh Day They Rested

In six days, according to the Bible, God created the world. In six days, in June of 1967, the Jews succeeded in changing their world. The Old City of Jerusalem and the area of the Temple itself were for the first time in the possession of the Jews. Even though the Jordanians had signed an armistice agreement in 1949 guaranteeing the Jews the right to visit the Western Wall, they never honored their commitment. The Jews came back to see that their holy places had been turned into latrines, their former synagogues used to stable pigs and horses, their cemeteries vandalized and desecrated. But still they rejoiced because the holiest spot on earth, according to the Jewish religion, was now once again in their hands.

Pulpit Stories

Why is the Western Wall the only portion of the Temple of Old to survive? The Midrash explains: "Everything else was built from the contributions of the rich. The poor pleaded for the right to contribute something from their meager funds to beautify the House of God. Their hard-earned monies went for the construction of the Western Wall. That Wall, built with the greatest demonstration of sacrificial giving, could never be destroyed."

"But Don't Let Me Catch You Praying"

There's an old joke about a young boy who had to give a message to his father who was seated in the synagogue on Yom Kippur night. He tried to go in but he had no ticket for a seat. (On the High Holy Days, seating is reserved for ticket holders who pay for the privilege—the only way synagogues can raise money in order to function since they don't take collections as churches do.) The boy explained he wouldn't be going in to stay; it was just for a moment that he needed to speak to his father. The usher grudgingly admitted the lad but then gave him a stern warning: "I'll let you in, but don't let me dare catch you praying."

That story has its counterpart in a remarkable ruling from the Israeli government. No sooner had the Six-Day War been won and the Israeli Army taken the Western Wall than Moshe Dayan, the conquering general, issued an order: The Israeli flag that had just been raised on the Muslim's *Al-Aqsa* mosque, built on the exact site of the ancient Temple, was to be taken down from its dome. Dayan went to the *waqf*, the charitable trust in charge of managing the Mount (the land where the Temple once stood and which now was the site of the Al-Aksa mosque) and made a momentous gesture. He told the *waqf* directors that, while all of Jerusalem now belonged to Israel, day-to-day control over the mosque area remained in their hands. Jews would be allowed to visit the Mount but would be forbidden to pray there. To this day, Jews and Christians can go on the Mount as tourists, but if they appear to be praying they are subject to removal or arrest.

Israeli soldiers standing at the Western Wall after its conquest in the 6-Day War, on June 7, 1967. The famous photo captures the emotion of the historic moment. (Courtesy of AP/ Wide World Photos)

Dayan hoped to create a bridge of understanding by this compromise. He wanted to show that Israeli conquest would not preclude respect for the rights of its present occupants. He wanted most of all to show that Jews were prepared to give up much for the sake of peace. But even this effort wasn't enough to change the climate of hatred.

The Yom Kippur War

It took only six years from the astonishing close of the Six Day War for the Arabs to try once again to destroy Israel. This time—in 1973—they picked the holiest day of the Jewish calendar on which to launch their surprise attack. And this time Egypt and Syria coordinated their version of Pearl Harbor with forces that equaled the combined strength of all of NATO in Europe.

Yenta's Little Secrets

Egypt picked Yom Kippur as the day on which to attack the Jewish State because it felt the Jews would be preoccupied with prayer and unable to quickly call up their reservists. In fact, since almost everyone was in synagogue, announcements could be quickly made to all, and then, with the roads cleared because of the holiday, soldiers were able to respond immediately and report to their posts. The choice of date was a blessing in disguise for the Jews.

This time, too, Israel managed to be victorious, but this time the Jews came perilously close to defeat. A phenomenally accurate gauge of the direction the war was taking was the intervention, or lack of intervention, by the United Nations. When the Arabs seemed to be winning, the U.N. was silent; as soon as the Israelis appeared to be on the threshold of victory, there were immediate calls for a cease-fire.

The Yom Kippur War cost the lives of 2,700 Israeli soldiers. There was hardly a neighborhood in all of Israel where the sounds of weeping could not be heard for seven days, the *shiva* period of mourning, after the war.

Peace For "Piece"

President Anwar Sadat of Egypt finally came to the conclusion that what war could not accomplish, a state of peace might be able to achieve. In a courageous visit to Jerusalem in November 1976, Sadat announced he was willing to abandon the doctrine of Israel's illegitimacy and give Israel peace in return for a piece of land. Give back the Sinai you took after we attacked you, and we will offer you the promise of nonbelligerence.

With the mediation of U.S. president Jimmy Carter, the former enemies went to Camp David in Maryland, the U.S. presidential retreat. The signing of an Israeli-Egyptian peace treaty seemed a great harbinger for the future, but the Arab reaction was anything but peaceful. The entire Arab world broke off diplomatic relations with Egypt. Sadat, for all of his efforts, was to pay an even greater price. Four years later, on October 6, 1981, he was assassinated by Muslim extremists who couldn't forgive his sin of recognizing Israel.

Egyptian President Anwar Sadat, U.S. President Jimmy Carter and Israeli Prime Minister Menachem Begin shake hands after signing the peace treaty between Israel and Egypt in the East Room of the White House, September 17, 1978. (Courtesy of Jimmy Carter Presidential Library/Corbis)

Scuds for Israel

The Gulf War of 1991 proved that when Arab nations go to war against each other, the only thing they can agree on is that Israel is the ultimate enemy. Sadam Hussein attacked Kuwait for its oil fields. The Allied Coalition wouldn't let him get away with it, and they declared war against Iraq. So what did Sadam Hussein do? He fired scud missiles against the civilian population of Israel, an innocent bystander in the neighborhood. The Jews couldn't help noticing that as the scuds honed in on their homes, Arabs stood on their roofs and cheered. This even though an errant missile might miss its mark and kill the cheering Arabs.

Will It Ever End?

The Madrid Peace Conference of 1991, following the end of the Gulf War, brought together Israel and all its Arab neighbors for multilateral talks. Years of the *intifada* frustrated both the Israelis and the P.L.O., the Palestinean Liberation Organization, headed by Yassir Arafat. It was clearly time to move forward and to take concrete steps for a final and lasting peace.

The breakthrough occurred in 1993 when, after lengthy secret talks in Oslo, Israel and the P.L.O. exchanged letters and signed agreements of peace and mutual recognition. The handshake on the White House lawn between Prime Minister Rabin and P.L.O. Chairman Arafat was a moment that would have been considered impossible just a few years before. That year Nobel Peace prizes were awarded to Prime Minister Yitzhak Rabin, Foreign Minister Shimon Peres, and P.L.O. Chairman Yassir Arafat.

Aha, That's It

Intifada is the "war of stones" led by children trained to throw rocks at Israeli soldiers on the assumption, proven correct, that Israelis will not respond with lethal bullets to rock-throwing by children.

What remains to be seen is whether the prizes were really well deserved or if they were won for merely hype and hope. When Arafat speaks to his people, he still uses the rhetoric of genocide. Three years *after* Oslo, he openly declared in Bethlehem, "We know only one word: *jihad, jihad, jihad.* We are in a conflict with the Zionist movement and the Balfour Declaration and all imperialist activities."

On the Israeli side, Prime Minister Rabin paid with his life for trying to make peace with the P.L.O. A Jewish extremist assassinated him at a peace rally in Tel Aviv on Nov. 4, 1995. Jews, too, unfortunately, have their share of crazies. This time the whole world joined in mourning the death of a leader whose only sin was that he was so deeply committed to peace.

Aha, That's It

Jihad is the Muslim word for holy war. Murdering Jews in a *jihad* is supposed to ensure eternal life in Paradise.

So where will it all end? Jews have been taught that to despair of the future is one of the gravest of all sins. On the other hand, the novelist and poet Don Marquis (1878–1937) was pretty wise when he noticed that "an optimist is a guy who has never had much experience." Experience makes the Jew fearful; faith makes him hope. The truth? Only God knows. And He doesn't seem willing to share the information.

The Book of Numbers

Numbers is the name of the fourth book of the Bible. Numbers are also a way for us to understand the meaning of the birth and the growth of modern-day Israel.

When Theodore Herzl convened the First Zionist Congress in Basel (1897), the total Jewish population in Palestine was fifty thousand. By the outbreak of World War I (1914), it had reached one hundred thousand.

During all the years of Jewish exile, there was a mystical rabbinic tradition that said that when the Jewish population in Palestine reached 600,000—the same number of Jews that were redeemed from Egypt, according to the Bible—the Jewish people would regain their independence and their land. In 1948, remarkably enough, the population of Jews in Palestine for the first time reached 600,000!

After the State was created, Israel's ushering in of hundreds of thousands of immigrants twice set world records. In its first two years of existence (1948–1950), the new Jewish state doubled its population by taking in 687,000 immigrants. From 1989 to 1995, Israel again admitted a similar number (700,000), primarily from the former Soviet Union, increasing the population by 15 percent.

The first great wave of *aliyah*, emigration to Israel, was almost evenly divided between Holocaust survivors and refugees from Arab lands. Subsequently, an additional 300,000 Jews came from the Arab world. This in-gathering of exiles from the four corners of the earth is known as *kibbutz galuyot*, the in-gathering of the Diaspora. It has brought 2.5

million Jews to Israel since the establishment of the State—59 percent of which came from Europe, 19 percent from Africa, 15 percent from Asia, and 7 percent from the Americas.

Aha, That's It

Kibbutz galuyot is Hebrew for "in-gathering of the exiles."

The up side of this tremendous influx of people from Algeria and Argentina, to Yemen and Zimbabwe, proved to be spectacular economic growth. Israel's per capita gross domestic product (GDP) is roughly equal to the United Kingdom's, despite the enormous burden of its military and the huge costs of immigrant integration. Israel shows the single strongest resource growth in the world. Thanks especially to its new Russian immigrants, Israel is, as *The Wall Street Journal* headlined on August 6, 1997, "a high technology paradise built on sacred ground." Israel is in the forefront of computer, communications, and biotech research, as well as a producer of high-end products for the most advanced engineering and scientific projects in the world. The gap between Israel and its neighbors has never been greater. Arab wealth is a product of what is hidden in the ground; Jewish success is the result of what is hidden in their people's heads.

Aha, That's It

Sabra, the word used to describe a native-born Israeli, is actually the name of a fruit that is tough on the outside and sweet on the inside. Its characteristics are meant to suggest the true nature of an Israeli.

The down side to this population explosion is the large and disparate mix of Jewish groups that now live in Israel and the difficulties of integrating them all into Jewish society. There are the serious ethnic divisions between Ashkenazim and Sephardim—Jews from western cultures and those from oriental, Arab lands. There are the religious tensions between Jews who believe the land is a gift of God whose Law must now be strictly observed and those who claim the country is the culmination of the efforts of its secular, Zionist pioneers. Add to that the cultural differences between *sabras*, or native-born Israelis, and newcomers with their own customs and traditions, and you get an idea of the potential for conflict and miscommunication.

Yenta's Little Secrets

The three largest cities in Israel are:

Jerusalem—603,000 (422,000 Jews) Tel Aviv—356,000 (341,000 Jews); and Haifa—252,000 (225,000 Jews).

Names You Should Know

"Great men," Friedrich Hebbel observed, "are the tables of contents of mankind." Israel couldn't have come into being without them. Any effort to understand the uniqueness of the Book of Israel demands at least some familiarity with the table of contents of its giants.

Menachem Begin (1913–1992)

Begin was a young boy of five when he sought shelter in a stack of straw as the Cossacks broke into an orgy of violence before his eyes. The episode, with its haunting message of powerlessness, was chiseled into his memory forever. Begin was an underground activist who helped expel the British from Palestine in the 1940s. After eight failed attempts at the premiership of Israel, he was successful, and led Israel from 1977 to 1983. He signed the 1979 Israel-Egypt Peace Treaty, for which he shared the Nobel Peace prize with President Sadat of Egypt.

Yenta's Little Secrets

After being universally condemned for his 1981 decision to bomb the nuclear reactor in Iraq, Begin asserted: "Better a condemnation and no reactor, than a reactor and no condemnation." When the Gulf War broke out in 1991, the world finally realized that Begin's daring strike against Iraq almost certainly saved It from a nuclear conflagration.

Moshe Dayan (1915–1981)

With his famous eye patch, Moshe Dayan proved that a hero with one eye is worth far more than a coward with two. As chief of staff of the Israel Defense Forces in the 1950s, he shaped the IDF into the most potent military force in the Middle East. He led Israel to victory in both the 1956 Sinai Campaign and the 1967 Six-Day War. Although blamed for Israel's lack of preparedness at the start of the 1973 Yom Kippur War, his reputation again soared when he helped shape the 1979 Israel-Egypt Camp David Peace Treaty.

Pulpit Stories

Although not personally religious, Dayan was deeply moved when he liberated the Western Wall and stood with his soldiers as they openly sobbed at this historic moment. He decided then to participate in the age-old ritual of inserting a prayer written on a piece of paper into a crevice between the great stones of the Wall, as Jews have done for centuries since the destruction of the Temple. His prayer, he later revealed, was, "May peace descend on the whole House of Israel."

Yitzhak Rabin (1922–1995)

Rabin was a soldier for 27 years, chief of staff of the IDF in the early 1960s, prime minister in the 70s, defense minister in the 80s, and prime minister for a second time in 1992. Rabin, born in Jerusalem, was the nation's first *sabra* prime minister. His most spectacular accomplishment was the successful Israeli rescue on July 4, 1976 of hostages aboard an Air France jet hijacked by Palestinean terrorists and taken to Entebbe, Uganda.

Yenta's Little Secrets

In the early 1960s, Israel had perhaps the single most successful program of peace-protecting volunteers and professionals in the world. How did the Israelis know so much about getting around the Entebbe Airport? They built it.

When on October 14, 1994 Yitzhak Rabin was named a co-recipient of the Nobel Peace prize, he responded with the words: "The work is not yet finished." Rabin would have no opportunity to conclude what he considered his mission on earth. His assassin carried out the deed, he said, in order to halt the peace process.

Natan Sharansky (b. 1948)

Born in the Ukraine, Natan Sharansky became an active Zionist after the 1967 Six-Day War. Seeking an exit visa from the Soviet Union to emigrate to Israel made him a criminal. He was accused of working for the CIA and convicted of treason, espionage, and anti-Soviet agitation. He spent 403 days in isolation cells with only a Hebrew prayer book to give him hope and comfort. He became the symbol of the Russian Refuseniks and was the object of an international campaign, led by his wife Avital, to win his release. And it was a campaign that brought immense sympathy to the Soviet-Jewish cause.

In 1986, after serving nine years in Russian prisons, Sharansky was released and flown to Israel. The former prisoner of conscience became Israeli Minister of Commerce and Industry in June 1996. When he arrived in Israel, he hugged his acquaintances, quipping: "I am very glad to have an opportunity to speak to an audience in which my criminal contacts are represented so widely."

Pulpit Stories

In October 1994, Natan Sharansky played to a surprise draw with world chess champion Gary Kasparov. "When I was in the darkness of solitary confinement," he said, "I used to play chess in my head to keep sane—and, of course, I always won all the games myself."

Shimon Peres (b. 1923)

Peres emigrated from his native Poland to Palestine in 1934. At 25, he became the first head of Israel's Navy and in 1959 was elected for the first time to the *Knesset*. In 1977, he became acting prime minister. From 1984 to 1986, he served as prime minister and brought inflation down from 800 to 20 percent per year. When Rabin became prime minister in 1992, he appointed Peres his foreign minister. For his role in securing the Oslo Peace Accord, Peres shared the 1994 Nobel Peace prize with Rabin.

Addressing American Jewish leaders in May 1994, he summed up his philosophy: "I don't think we should judge the peace process by the performance of Yassir Arafat. We're not negotiating with Yassir Arafat. We're negotiating with ourselves—about what sort of people we want to become. I do believe that while the dangers are great, the opportunities are greater."

Yenta's Little Secrets

When President Ronald Reagan decided, in May 1985, to visit the military cemetery in Bitburg, Germany where Nazi officers were buried, Peres commented: "When a friend makes a mistake, the friend remains a friend, and the mistake remains a mistake."

Golda Meir (1898–1978)

Golda Meir grew to adulthood in the United States but accomplished what no American woman was ever able to achieve: She became the leader of a country. Meir became prime minister of Israel. When, late in life, Pope Paul VI criticized Israel's "fierceness" at a private audience he had with her, she replied: "Your Holiness, do you know what my earliest memory is? A *pogrom* in Kiev. When we were merciful and when we had no homeland and when we were weak, we were led to the gas chambers."

First a school teacher in Milwaukee, she ended up becoming the Meir that made Milwaukee famous. She moved to Palestine and became, as Ben-Gurion said of her, "the only man in my cabinet." She served as Israel's first ambassador to the Soviet Union. In 1969, following the death of Levi Eshkol, she became prime minister, but she never stopped being a Jewish mother, a mother with a very special sensitivity. Her most famous comment on the Arab-Israel conflict was, "I can forgive the Arabs almost anything. I can even forgive them for killing our children. The one thing I cannot forgive them for is that they forced our sons to become killers."

Pulpit Stories

When Golda Meir was about to enter the quarters of Pope Paul VI for a private audience on January 19, 1973, she nervously said to her aides, "What's going on here? Me, the daughter of Moshe Mabovitch, the carpenter, going to meet the Pope of the Catholics?" To which one of her aides quickly replied, "Just a minute, Golda. Carpentry is a very respected profession around here."

Ezer Weizman (b. 1924)

Ezer Weizman is the nephew of Israel's first president, Chaim Weizmanh. During World War II, Weizman served in the Royal Air Force, stationed in Egypt and India. From 1958 to 1966, he headed the Israeli Air Force and shaped it into the unit that operated with such startling effectiveness in the open hours of the 1967 Six-Day War. As defense minister, he served for three years and played a major role in helping Israel finalize its peace treaty with Egypt. In 1993, he was elected president of the State of Israel, returning the position to the family that first occupied it.

Sage Sayings

"My Uncle Chaim, the first president, used to complain that he presided over a nation of 2 million presidents...Don't try and be a president in Israel."

—Ezer Weizman

Binyamin Netanyahu (b. 1949)

Netanyahu is almost never called anything other than by his nickname, "Bibi." (His last name may well end up being the name of the largest Internet company in the world if Netscape and Yahoo decide to merge and become "Net-an-Yahoo.") As one of the youngest Israeli political leaders in history, he first achieved renown indirectly, as the brother of Jonathan Netanyahu, the commander of the highly successful Entebbe rescue operation of July 1976, killed during that raid. Bibi was himself an officer in an elite unit in the IDF from 1967 to 1972.

Trained at the Massachusetts Institute of Technology (MIT), Bibi has the advantage of speaking a perfect, unaccented English, a skill that helped him considerably in his position as Israel's Ambassador to the United Nations and Deputy Chief of Missions to the United States. He became a highly popular spokesman for Israel, appearing frequently on American television. In an unprecedented jump to the top, he defeated Shimon Peres and became prime minister on June 18, 1996. As all Israeli politicians, he has ardent admirers and vicious critics. The campaign slogan that led him to victory was "Peace with Security." Whether his policies will achieve his goals remains to be judged by history.

Creating an Israeli Culture

Israel understands that the key to its achievements lies in its commitment to cultural growth. It spends fully a *fifth* of its national output on education, and although a small country, nevertheless has seven institutions of higher learning: the Technion in Haifa (founded in 1924), the Hebrew University of Jerusalem (1925), the Weizmann Institute of Science in Rehovot (1934), Bar-Ilan University in Ramat Gan (1955), Tel Aviv University (1956), Haifa University (1963), and Ben-Gurion University of the Negev in Be'er Sheva (1969). There is also an open university and more than 200 *Yeshivot*—rabbinical schools specializing in Judaic and Talmudic studies.

Israel has produced leading figures in all fields: literature, music, dance, theater, the arts, and even sports. One author, Shmuel Yosef Agnon, received the 1966 Nobel Prize for Literature for his work.

Visitors to Israel should not miss the Israel Museum (including the Dead Sea Scrolls housed in the Shrine of the Book); the Bible Land's Museum; the Rockefeller Museum; and the Tower of David—all in Jerusalem. In Tel Aviv, the Nahum Goldmann Museum of the Jewish Diaspora, known as *Bet Hatefutsot,* has a magnificent display chronicling the story of the Jewish people from ancient times until modern day. (After you finish reading this book, the museum will serve as a vivid pictorial guide to what you have learned so that you can make your new knowledge come alive.) The Tel Aviv Museum and the *Ha'aretz* Museum are also among the country's outstanding institutions.

To sit back and be entertained, you can then visit the *Habima,* Israel's national theater, the *Bat-Sheva Inbal* and *Bat-Dor* Dance Companies in Tel Aviv, and the Israel Philharmonic Orchestra with its home in Tel Aviv's Mann Auditorium, one of the world's most famous symphony orchestras.

Yenta's Little Secrets

When a tourist asked a guide at the Mann Auditorium who the auditorium was named for, he was told, "a famous writer." "What did this Mann write that made him worthy of this honor?" the tourist asked. "A check," explained the guide.

But the Glass Is Half Full

In 1998, Israel reached its 50-year milestone. In the Bible that number is very significant. It marks the Jubilee Year, a time commemorating freedom and rejoicing. Is this where contemporary Israel is at today? Has the time come to sing? Is Israel ready for unfettered celebration?

No, there are still too many problems to be dealt with, too many difficulties that haven't been blessed with solutions. The lack of real peace between Jew and Arab; the on-going disagreements between different Jews factions; the unresolved questions about "who is a Jew?"; and the unclear guidelines for the relationship between the Diaspora and Israel—all these touch on issues that have yet to be resolved satisfactorily.

The glass is clearly not full. But Jews of faith who have lived to see the miraculous become reality in their lifetime have certainly learned it is far wiser to emphasize that the glass is half full than to bemoan the fact that it is half empty. If the next fifty years achieve even half as much as the first fifty, Israel may well fulfill its prophetic mission of becoming a "light unto the nations," even as it serves as inspiration to Jews around the world.

The Least You Need to Know

➤ The first fifty years of Israel's existence were marred by repeated outbreaks of war, reflecting Arab refusal to accept the existence of Israel.

➤ The Oslo Peace Accord offers the possibility for an end to age-old hostilities, but its effectiveness has still to be judged by history.

➤ The numerous wars each took a heavy toll on the Israeli population and psyche, but the Six-Day War at least succeeded in returning and reunifying Jerusalem.

➤ Israel's cultural achievements are comparable to those of the most highly developed nations of the world.

➤ Although still burdened with many problems, Israel's accomplishments in the first half century of its existence augur well for its continued survival, growth, and success.

Well, there's bagels.. Bagels are nice...

There's a LOT more than that..

Chapter 28

What Have the Jewish People Accomplished?

In This Chapter

➤ What survival means for the Jewish people

➤ How a unique way of thinking about God changed the world

➤ The gifts of spirituality, a moral code, and the book of the Bible

➤ The concept of change as opposed to never-ending cycles

➤ The deeper reason for anti-Semitism

Okay, let's see if you can guess who made this observation about the Jews: "This extraordinary people continues to bear signs of its divine election. I said this to an Israeli politician once, and he readily agreed, but was quick to add: 'If only it could cost less! Israel has truly paid a high price for its election.'"

The speaker? Pope John Paul II, who readily acknowledged the uniqueness of the Jews. So special are their achievements that to many, including Pope John Paul II, they appear divinely ordained. Jews have paid a great price for the gifts they have, but they have left an unparalleled legacy to the world, to its culture, and to all of civilization.

Survival—For What?

In 1993, the Dalai Lama came to the United States to meet with Jewish leaders. He was concerned with the survival of his people and wanted to ask the Jews about their secret. "We Tibetans wonder if you can teach us to follow your example," he said. But the Jews themselves aren't sure of the answer. As the famous British historian Arnold Toynbee came to realize, the Jews simply don't obey any of the rules of history. Despite the express wishes of the major world powers over the centuries, despite repeated attempts to destroy them, the Jews live on almost as if they have a divine reason for being. And that is precisely what many Jews believe. Indeed, that may well be the source of their unique creativity.

Holocaust survivors, it's been discovered, often suffer from a psychological disorder known as "survivor syndrome." They have difficulty dealing with the fact that almost all of their loved ones perished, and yet *they* remained alive. To deal with it, they can only conclude that there must be some special purpose for their continued existence. They constantly seek ways to give meaning to their lives because they owe it to their past and to the gift of survival that they received.

Sage Sayings

"No people has ever insisted more firmly than the Jews that history has a purpose and humanity a destiny."

—Paul Johnson, contemporary U.S. historian

All Jews are survivors—survivors of history. That may well be why their lives must be endowed with purpose, their talents not be allowed to go unused. The Jews who represent the small remnant of a persecuted people so treasure the gift of life that they have always felt the need to share their gift with the rest of the world.

Yes, Virginia, There Is a God

The Catholic writer Thomas Cahill was so overwhelmed by his study of the Jewish contributions to world civilization that he authored what proved to become a national bestseller, *The Gifts of the Jews*.

The Jews, he concluded, literally transformed the world. Had a Jew written the book, its claims probably would have been dismissed as the exaggerations of a chauvinistic member of the clan. The fact that Cahill isn't Jewish makes his observations all the more credible.

Perhaps the first major gift of the Jews to the world was the new way of understanding God. The Jews not only discovered monotheism, they realized God was one, and they then explained why that made Him different from all the other pagan gods.

The Jewish God is above nature; a God whom even Albert Einstein acknowledged as "subtle but not malicious;" a God who, according to Maimonides' 13 Principles of Belief, "has no form of a body and is not corporeal in any way;" and unlike every other God who was revered before Him, he "cannot be manipulated."

Witchcraft and sorcery simply have no meaning for Jews. Such practices suggest that humans can manipulate gods. A god who can be manipulated is made in man's image; Jews believe the reverse, that man is created in God's image.

Cahill believes that the ultimate breakthrough in humanity's understanding of God came with the Jewish perception that God "is a real personality who has intervened in real history, changing its course and robbing it of predictability." God is more than the Force of Star Wars; he is the "I" of the First Commandment: "I am the Lord your God who took you out of the Land of Egypt, the house of bondage." God interacts with man and intercedes in history.

Yes, Virginia, there may not be a Santa Claus after all, but there is a Saintly Creator, and it was the Jews who taught the world to recognize and to worship him.

Sage Sayings

"The purpose of Jewish existence is to be a people in the image of God. The meaning of Jewish existence is to foster in ourselves as Jews and to awaken in the rest of the world a sense of moral responsibility in action."

—Mordecai Kaplan

The Greatest Book Ever Written

The Jews not only introduced the world to God but to His book as well. The Bible, transmitted from Moses to the Jewish people, has nurtured Christianity and Islam, Judaism's two daughter religions. Its teachings provided the soil for democratic ideals and the seeds of Western civilization.

From the Bible, the world learned the meaning of spirituality. Pagan Gods, being physical, wanted physical things from their worshippers. Not so the God of the Jews. As Cahill explains:

> God wanted something other than blood and smoke, buildings and citadels. He wanted justice, mercy, humility. He wanted what was invisible…There is no way of exaggerating how strange a thought this was…The word that falls so easily from our lips—*spiritual*—had no real counterpart in the ancient world.

Sage Sayings

"The Jewish religion…is a network of profound ideas and rich insights, which during its long history has generated the fundamental beliefs of all Western religion. It has contributed to the civilized world its crowning ideals and its most glorious convictions—among them the idea of one God, a system of jurisprudence, a structure of ethics and morals… and numerous ideas, ideals, and institutions."

—Maurice Lamm, contemporary rabbi and author

Because the Bible recognized man's spirituality, it could speak to his soul. And that is why the Bible, the book that came from the Jews, continues to be the world's biggest bestseller.

The Jew and the Canary

Dennis Praeger has pointed out a beautiful parallelism: The Jews are the world's canary:

> "Canaries are taken down to mines because they quickly die upon exposure to noxious fumes. When the miner sees the canary dead, he knows there are noxious fumes to be fought. So it is with the Jews. Noxious moral forces often focus first on the Jews. But their ultimate targets are the moral values that the Jews represent."

Sage Sayings

"The Jews are the yeast in the bread of civilization which causes it to grow."

—Ben Hecht (1884–1964)
U.S. author, playwright, screenwriter

Jews gave morality a transcendent source. If you say something is "bad," that's just an opinion. Someone else can disagree and claim it's "good." What makes your view more correct than his? You may think murder is wrong. But Hitler didn't. Ethical relativism, the belief that no moral choices are innately superior one to another, lets people kill without remorse, steal without feeling sinful, commit adultery without thinking they were involved in a crime.

The Jews gave the world these important words: "*right*" and "*wrong*." As Cahill puts it, "For the first time, human beings are offered a code without justification. Because this is God's code, no justification is required. . . . Who but God can speak . . . 'Thou shalt' and 'Thou shalt not'— with such authority that no further words are needed?"

Breaking the Wheel of Fortune

Cahill believes that the Jews' new world view was one of their greatest gifts. Until the Jews came on the scene, it was universally accepted that, as Cahill put it, "No event is unique, nothing is enacted but once...every event has been enacted, is enacted, and will be enacted perpetually; the same individuals have appeared, appear, and will appear at every turn of the circle." Only Judaism dared to reject this universal mode of thought.

Cahill writes:

> The Jews were the first people to break out of this circle...It may be said with some justice that theirs is the *only new idea that human beings had ever had*." And because of this idea came a host of new words that reflect this transformative way of understanding life: "Most of our best words, in fact— *new, adventure, surprise; unique individual, person, vocation, time, history, future; freedom, progress, spirit; faith, hope, justice*—are the gifts of the Jews.

Yenta's Little Secrets

What are the two most powerful words in advertising? Studies prove they are "new" and "improved." Now that you know these words are Jewish inventions, it's obvious that the Jews are also the originators of advertising.

Jews Made Science Possible

Because Jews taught the world that "we do not live in a fragmented universe controlled by fickle and warring gods," we can believe that the universe is controlled by laws. Science could not exist if we didn't assume there was universal order. The Jews brought to the world the concept of law, both natural and moral. And with that foundation scientists could recognize the law of gravity and other laws of physics, chemistry, biology. Again, it was perhaps the greatest scientific genius of all time, Albert Einstein, who confessed that "I shall never believe that God plays dice with the world." Because if he did, science couldn't be science; it would just be a crap shoot.

So Why Hate the Jews?

So, like the Russian asked when he was repeatedly told how wonderful communism is, "If everything is so good, why is everything so bad?" How can it be that the people who have given so much to the world have been so often and almost universally persecuted and despised?

One of the most insightful answers given by scholars is that *the Jews have been victims of their own success.* The best way to understand it is, interestingly enough, to compare the Jews to the United States. No country in the world has so many people who want so desperately to live in it. At the same time, no country, with the exception of Israel, is the object of so much criticism and hatred from the four corners of the earth.

The reason is simple: Success breeds envy. And Jews have been successful in a way that breeds jealousy. The Jews have the highest earnings of any ethnic group in the United States. They are significantly overly represented in the most prestigious and well-paying professions. As a group, their quality of life is recognizably better than their neighbors. And their children have higher IQs than other children.

Mark Twain understood it clearly: "Envy of Jewish talents and brains has moved the Gentiles to behave like wild beasts toward a people in some respects their superior."

So in a weird way, being hated by the world is really the biggest compliment, to which I'm sure Jews would respond, "If it's all the same to you, I really wish you didn't think so highly of me."

Fulfilling God's Promise

But their unique role in history shouldn't have come as a surprise to the Jews. They started their story with Abraham, the first man to discover God and the Father of the Jewish people. It was to him that God made a remarkable prediction recorded in the Bible: "And I will bless those who bless you, and those who curse you I will curse. And there shall be blessed through you all the families of the earth."

We have seen how these striking words have come true. The nations that treated the Jews well were in turn greatly blessed. Those who abused the Jews found themselves falling from history's grace. And wherever the Jews lived they made important contributions to every area of life. Anyone who studies the story of their wanderings throughout the centuries knows that through them all the families of the earth were indeed greatly blessed.

The Least You Need to Know

➤ Because the Jews survived against impossible odds, "survivors syndrome" drives them to find special meaning for their lives.

➤ One of the greatest gifts the Jews gave the world was their concept of one all-powerful, omniscient God, which was a radical and revolutionary departure from the pagan mindset.

➤ The Bible and its emphasis on spirituality, morality, and ethics is yet another major contribution of the Jewish people.

➤ In opposition to a cyclical view of world history that allows for no innovation or change, Jews brought a revolutionary world view that the new, the improved, the better are possible.

➤ The concept of Law, extended to the natural world, allowed for the discovery and recognition of rules that govern the workings of the universe—the key to all scientific progress.

➤ Jew hatred is in all probability profoundly related to Jew envy.

➤ Jews have fulfilled the Biblical prophecy of serving as a blessing to mankind.

Part 8

The Hall of Fame: A Jewish Who's Who

What would the world look like if there were no Jews?

The best way to begin to answer the question is to think about the names of those who would fill a Jewish Hall of Fame in the twentieth century. Putting together a "Who's Who" of Jews who had a crucial role in shaping modern culture and in creating, inventing and discovering so many things that have so significantly improved our quality of life is an amazing reminder of how a numerically insignificant people of the world have dramatically altered its existence.

Part 8 explores the Jewish contributions to Hollywood: the studios, the actors and actresses, the producers, directors and writers. It looks at the Jewish impact on the world of entertainment—comedy, radio, TV, theater, music, and sports; the healing arts of medicine and psychology; and the fields that changed the world and the way we perceive it—science, literature, and the arts, philosophy and religion.

If great people are those who leave their mark on the world and achieve immortality through their deeds, the Jews we single out in these last chapters deserve without a doubt to be included in our Hall of Fame.

Chapter 29

Welcome to Hollywood

In This Chapter

➤ The Hollywood Jews who created the American Dream

➤ How Jews were involved in every "movie first"

➤ The producers and directors who added the "Jewish touch"

➤ The Spielberg phenomenon that made Jewish values and ideas universal

➤ Unmasking the stars to tell you who's really Jewish

Most scholars agree that the movies have shaped American culture more than any other medium. Movies give us many of our heroes. Movies help identify our values. They help define for us love and life, the "good guys" and the "bad guys." They teach us to laugh and to cry. And most important of all, they imbue us with our dreams. Hollywood movies, probably more than anything else, created the American dream—and then exported it around the world.

And wonder of wonders, the founding fathers of cinema and many of the most important movers and shakers of this industry were none other than the descendants of Abraham. Progeny of the very people who in ancient days sought to influence the world by using holy wood to build a temple, would now create Hollywood to build an industry that would attract devout worshippers and insatiable devotees. The story of the birth of the movies is so fascinating, it ought to be made into a movie!

The Founding Fathers

How's this for an amazing coincidence about the first generation of movie moguls?

➤ Carl Laemmle was born in a small village in Germany, fled from the poverty of his background to come to America, and founded Universal Pictures.

➤ Adolph Zucker was born in Hungary, became orphaned as a small child, came to America lonely and unloved, and built Paramount Pictures.

➤ William Fox, also born in Hungary, came to the States as a poor immigrant selling soda and sandwiches and working as a chimney sweeper until he one day founded the Fox Film Corporation.

➤ Louis B. Mayer was born in Russia, fled his father's junkyard business, and eventually headed up the greatest studio of all, Metro-Goldwyn-Mayer.

➤ Benjamin Warner came from Poland to seek his fortune in America. Here he worked as a cobbler in Baltimore, peddled notions from a wagon, and tried to eke out a living so that he could feed his four sons, Harry, Sam, Albert, and Jack. Then he bought a broken movie projector and one thing led to another, until incredibly enough, Warner Brothers was born.

Yes, they were all Jews, but the connection goes deeper. They all came from a background of failure. They either had no father or their father was a *luftmensch* (remember the word from Chapter 23, "East Side, West Side, All Around the Globe?"—a man of the air) who could never find a permanent job. Maybe it's too Freudian (be patient—we'll get to Freud in Chapter 31, "The Doctor Is In"), but Neal Gabler, in his fascinating study of the Jewish influence on Hollywood, *An Empire of Their Own*, suggested:

> The evidence certainly supports the view that the sons, embittered by their father's failures, launched a war against their own pasts, a patricide one could say, against everything their fathers represented. To escape their father's fate meant escaping the past: The European roots, the language and accents, the customs and the religion. One had to erase it . . . and adopt a new style—a style for America. America was the baptism to cleanse and renew.

Yenta's Little Secrets

Louis B. Mayer claimed he forgot the day of his birthday. He preferred to pick a day of his own choosing—the fourth of July. He was able to reinvent himself as a "real" American and obliterate his past.

These were immigrants who not only wanted to assimilate in a new land, they wanted to re-create it in their own image. Movies gave them a power that was almost God-like: If they were too late to create the world, they could at least create America—its values and its myths, its traditions and its archetypes, its hopes and its dreams. And so it was the Jewish immigrants who came from the *shtetels* and the ghettos, who fled poverty and persecution, who thought up, produced, and then mass marketed nothing less than the American Dream.

The Movie "Firsts"

Even before the powerful movie studios ruled the industry, one-reeler shorts were made, forerunners of films as we know them. Probably the first one produced was *Cohen's Advertising Scheme*. The story line was pretty simple: A Jewish storekeeper tries unsuccessfully to make a sale. He finally gives up and gives the vagrant, who didn't buy it, a full-length coat as a gift. When the vagrant turns around, we see a sign advertising the store painted on the back. So the very first movie made clear that the Jews were great salesmen. It would become a fitting metaphor for the movie industry that would make its mark with brilliant advertising.

The first American feature film was *The Great Train Robbery* (1903), starring a Jew, Max Anderson, in the lead. Anderson went on to write, produce, and act in the very successful series of westerns—"Bronco Billy"—a theme Jewish producers would find irresistible, maybe, just maybe, because it portrayed the themes of heroism, conquering a new land, and overpowering the "strangers" (translate that to mean Indians or Cossacks) who wanted to kill you?

The first large Hollywood production, from Adolph Zucker's Paramount, was *Queen Elizabeth* (1912), starring the incomparable Sarah Bernhardt. Here was more than a Jewish American Princess; Sarah, in the first major film, actually made it to Queen. It was the success of this movie—the first film to be shown in legitimate theater halls—that allowed Zucker to claim film as a legitimate art form.

But the biggest "first" of all, the one that catapulted movies from a minor diversion to a major form of communication was the move into "talkies." And the Jewish connection wasn't only that it was Warner Brothers that made the picture. The first full-length talking film told the story of a young man who rejected the wish of his father, a cantor, who wanted him, too, to become a cantor. The cantor's son, instead of singing to God in the temple, chose to become a popular singer. The movie was really the story of Al Jolson's life. In a deeper sense, as the story of children breaking with their past for popular acclaim and fame, it was also the story of almost all the patriarchs of Hollywood.

Al Jolson starred in the first *"talkie"* motion picture, The Jazz Singer. *(Courtesy of Photofest)*

Yenta's Little Secrets

Louis B. Mayer may have changed his first name from the Jewish-sounding Lazar, but he couldn't change some very Jewish characteristics. It was part of the folklore at MGM that the studio commissary had to serve chicken soup with real pieces of chicken in it for lunch every day, at 35 cents a bowl, in honor of Mayer's long-deceased mother.

"Produced By..."

As the studios grew, so did the role of the Jews there. Barney Balaban became president of Paramount in 1936; Nicholas and Joseph Schenk became presidents of MGM; and Irving Thalberg, the *wunderkind* of the film industry and movie legend who was responsible for production at the age of 23, was manager of MGM from the end of the 1920s until his death in 1936.

When independent producers started to challenge the major studios, again the majority of them were Jews. Probably the most outstanding independent was Mike Todd, producer of *Around the World in 80 Days*. Todd was responsible for the Todd-AO new method of cinematography and, according to many, responsible for Elizabeth Taylor joining the *mishpachah* and converting to Judaism.

David O. Selznick, son of industry pioneer Lewis J. Selznick, produced *Gone With The Wind* (1939), one of the all-time movie classics. Hal Roach made us laugh with the Harold Lloyd series and the Laurel and Hardy films of the 20s and 30s. Sam Spiegel used his high artistic standards to produce such fine films such as *The African Queen, On The Waterfront, The Bridge On The River Quai,* and *Lawrence of Arabia*. Stanley Kramer, another independent producer, was responsible for some of the best films to come out of Hollywood after 1945: *Home Of The Brave, Champion, High Noon,* and *Death of a Salesman*. He would later direct *On The Beach, Judgement At Nuremberg,* and *Ship Of Fools*.

Aha, That's It

Mishpachah is the Hebrew as well as the Yiddish word for *family*. It has more than a biological reference, though; it also conveys a "warm and fuzzy" feeling of friendship.

"Directed By..."

To be a director has to be a Jew's dream job. Descended from people who throughout the ages have been told what to do by others, it must be the ultimate thrill to finally be able to tell others what to do. No wonder so many Jews made their mark as film directors! Ernst Lubitsch came to this country from Germany in 1923, after making a name for himself in his native country. He directed sophisticated comedies with such finesse that a new phrase was coined in Hollywood, "The Lubitsch touch." To him we owe *Ninotchka, To Be Or Not To Be,* and *Cluny Brown*.

Erich van Stroheim and Josef von Sternberg began the trend toward realism. To Sternberg we owe Marlene Deitrich's performance in *Blue Angel*—and from then on Deitrich considered him her permanent director.

Any movie buff will know and appreciate these other names in our Jewish Hall of Fame: William Wyler, Billy Wilder, Jules Dassin, Garson Canin, Fred Zinnemann, Joseph L. Mankiewicz, Sidney Lumet, John Frankenheimer, Roman Polanski, Michael Curtiz, Mervyn LeRoy, Otto Preminger, Richard Brooks, George Cukor, Daniel Mann, and Robert Rossen.

Yenta's Little Secrets

Otto Preminger's father was the first Jew to be appointed Chief Prosecutor of the Austrian Em-pire. Otto achieved fame very early in Austria as well and, as a young man, was offered the di-rectorship of Vienna's State Theater on one condition—conversion to Catholicism. He refused and instead accepted an offer from Joseph Schenck of Twentieth Century Fox. He was 29 years old.

The Director with Jewish Angst

As the Jacob-of-all-trades, one of the most famous of all in the movie industry is Allen Stewart Konigsberg. Oh, maybe you don't recognize him by the name his parents gave him when he was born in the Flatbush section of Brooklyn, New York. But of course you've heard of Woody Allen—director, screenwriter, playwright, actor, and self-described genius.

Like many other Jews, Allen had problems coming to terms with his past and his heritage. In his early stand-up routines, Allen would quip about his parents: "Their values are God and carpeting." He explained his problem about believing in God this way: "If only God would give me some clear sign! Like making a large deposit in my name in a Swiss bank." He obsessed about his mortality: "It's not that I'm afraid to die. I just don't want to be there when it happens." And, as a Jew, he was so depressed by the lessons of history that he told a 1980 college graduating class: "More than any other time in history, mankind faces a crossroads. One path leads to despair and utter hopelessness. The other, to total extinction. Let us pray we have the wisdom to choose correctly."

Sage Sayings

"I draw my ideas from everything I've done and everything that interests me...You can have 600 jokes in your film and if two gags are Jewish, the picture will be perceived as Jewish comedy. This is a false perception, I think."

—Woody Allen

Woody Allen may well be neurotic. For some he is a prototypical "self-hating Jew." And his private life has had its problems. But his incredible talent simply cannot be denied; his creative genius set the standard for comedy as an art form.

How many of these would you rank among the all-time great films ever produced, directed, and written? *What's New Pussycat?*, *Play It Again Sam*, *Take the Money and Run*, *Everything You Always Wanted to Know About Sex (But Were Afraid to Ask)*, *Annie Hall*, *Interiors*, *Manhattan*, *Stardust Memories*, *Zelig*, *Radio Days*, *Hannah and Her Sisters*, and *Crimes and Misdemeanors*. And that is only a sampling of Allen's films. Not bad for a college drop-out from NYU and City College.

And "The Spielberg Phenomenon"

Steven Spielberg says that his earliest memory is a brightly lit room with a red light at one end, filled with white-bearded old men wearing black hats—the Cincinnati synagogue into which he was carried by his parents when he was six months old. Since then he probably hasn't forgotten a thing. And he can describe everything with total recall.

Spielberg was a self-described "Jewish nerd" who felt like an alien in the gentile world around him. That may well make him the subconscious role model for *E.T.*—and reveal for the first time that E.T. was really Jewish!

Bar mitzvahed in an Orthodox synagogue, Spielberg's movies all have a profound link with his identity. They share his perception of the world as a member of a people who have been considered outsiders for countless centuries. *Close Encounters of the Third Kind* is really a religious conviction that "there's something else out there." *Raiders of the Lost Ark*, a movie about an American archaeologist vying with the Nazis to find a sacred relic with cosmic power, is a parable of good struggling with evil for control of the religious power that comes with the past. *E.T.* is the way a modern Jew would record an encounter with a Biblical angel. *Jurassic Park* tells the incredible tale of a dinosaur—an animal that surely should have been extinct by now—coming back to life.

Sage Sayings

"When we moved to Phoenix, I was one of only five Jewish kids in elementary and high school. There was a lot of anti-Semitism against me and my sisters. In study hall, kids used to pitch pennies at me, which would hit my desk and make a large clatter. It was called 'pitching pennies at the Jew,' and it was very hurtful."

—Steven Spielberg

Do you know Ezekiel's vision of the valley of dry bones from Ezekiel 37:1–14? Spielberg did the last editing cut on *Jurassic Park* while he was filming *Schindler's List* in Poland. The remarkable connection between the two couldn't have been lost on him: By all logic, the Jews should have disappeared during the Holocaust just as the dinosaurs did eons earlier. But a remnant survived. That remnant served as the remarkable conclusion to *Schindler's List* when those who were saved filed past the grave of Oskar Schindler to give thanks. The screen told us how the hundreds who didn't perish were blessed to become thousands and thousands in the next generation.

Whenever the Torah is carried back to the Ark after being read in synagogue services, the congregation recites the prayer, "Renew our days as of old." Sounds a lot to me like *Back to the Future*, a theme so important to Spielberg that he went ahead and made *Back to the Future II and III*.

Sage Sayings

"I couldn't find any Jews in Poland to be the Jews in the movie—because Hitler had murdered them all."

—Steven Spielberg, explaining why he had to import so many actors from outside Poland to appear in *Schindler's List*

By all accounts, as well as by its seven Oscars, *Schindler's List* is the most powerful, the most revealing, and the most sensitive movie ever made about the Holocaust. It has probably been able to make a greater impression on humankind than all the Holocaust museums combined. And, as Spielberg made clear on the screen, the aim of this masterpiece is to make the world understand a simple Talmudic teaching: "He who saves one's soul is as if he has saved an entire world."

The Oscars keep coming to Steven Spielberg, whose depiction of the Holocaust in the film Schindler's List *is probably the most powerful reminder of this horrible time in history. (Courtesy of Photofest)*

We might have thought that after this there was surely nothing Spielberg could do for an encore. Real genius, however, knows no limits. The greatest Jewish ideal of all is *shalom*—peace. Who else but Spielberg could have given us *Saving Private Ryan*—the movie that will assuredly go down in history as the ultimate depiction of the horrors of the war. It is the one movie that may perhaps turn the prophetic ideal of peace into reality.

"Starring..."

Let's play a game. You're welcome to try it with your friends. I call it "Name That Jew." I'll give you the birth names of some famous stars, and you see if you can tell me who they are:

1. Issuri Danielovitch-Demsky
2. Fanny Rose
3. Melvin Israel
4. Emanuel Goldenberg
5. Allen Stewart Konigsberg
6. Judith Tuvim
7. Julius Garkinkel
8. Simone Kaminker
9. Shirley Schrift
10. Ira Levi
11. Joseph Levitch
12. Theodoria Goodman
13. Pauline Marion Levee
14. Milton Berlinger
15. Benjamin Kubelsky
16. Asa Yoelson
17. Tula Ellice Finkler
18. Betty Jane Perski
19. Leslie Stainer
20. Joan Molinsky

21. Jill Oppenheim
22. Sophie Abruzza
23. Jerome Silberman
24. Robert Zimmerman
25. Laszlo Loewenstein
26. David Kominski
27. Eugene Orowitz
28. Erich Weiss

29. Bernie Schwartz
30. Howard Silverblatt
31. Michael Igor Peschowsky
32. Al, Jimmy, and Harry Joachim
33. Sophia Koscow
34. Avram Girsch Goldberger
35. Isaiah Leopold

And the answers are (match them by number):

1. Kirk Douglas

Issuri Danielovitch-Demsky became a big Hollywood star better known as Kirk Douglas, but he never forgot his Jewish origins. (Courtesy of Photofest)

2. Dinah Shore
3. Mel Allen
4. Edward G. Robinson
5. Woody Allen
6. Judy Holiday
7. John Garfield
8. Simone Signoret
9. Shelly Winters

10. Yves Montand
11. Jerry Lewis
12. Theda Bara
13. Paulette Goddard
14. Milton Berle
15. Jack Benny
16. Al Jolson
17. Cyd Charisse

18. Lauren Bacall

Betty Jane Perski, cousin of Israeli prime minister and Nobel Prize winner Shimon Peres, is better known as Lauren Bacall. (Courtesy of Photofest)

19. Leslie Howard
20. Joan Rivers
21. Jill St. John
22. Sophie Tucker
23. Gene Wilder
24. Bob Dylan
25. Peter Lorre
26. Danny Kaye
27. Michael Landon

28. Harry Houdini
29. Tony Curtis
30. Howard DaSilva
31. Mike Nichols
32. The Ritz Brothers
33. Sylvia Sidney
34. Mike Todd
35. Ed Wynn

Get the feeling that even though the studio heads were Jews, they didn't think it was a good idea to let the world know the real identity of their stars? Wendy Wasserstein is probably right. In an interview she claimed, "If I were twenty years older, my name probably wouldn't be Wendy Wasserstein because of those Jewish movie moguls in Hollywood who made people change their names. I'd probably be Wendy Waters because that's what it would have taken to get it done."

"But the times," as another famous Jew said, "they are a-changin'." Jews could surely say, "We've come a long way, baby," when someone who really didn't *have* to have a name like that, chose of her own free will to make her way as Whoopie Goldberg. And even with *two* strikes against her, her race and her name, she managed to become a superstar! (You didn't think that was actually her given name, did you? She was Caryn Johnson and one day, as a joke, she changed her name to Whoopi Cushion. "My mother said, 'No one gonna respect you with a name like that' So I switched it to Goldberg." So today Goldberg *gives* you respect—you don't have to get rid of it!)

A Jewish-sounding name doesn't seem to have hurt the career of Whoopi Goldberg—who isn't Jewish but chose the name anyway. (Courtesy of Photofest)

Pulpit Stories

A Jewish boy comes home to tell mom he's in love. His mother asks him the name of the girl and he tells her: "Mary McCarthy." "If you marry out of the faith," says the mother, "I'll kill myself." So the boy breaks it up. Then he meets another woman and tells mom her name is Cindy LaRue. "You may as well put a gun to my head," she tells him. Ten years later, he finally finds the girl of his dreams. He knows his mother won't like it, but this time he's determined. He tells his mother he's engaged, and when she asks the girl's name, he says, "Goldberg." "Whoopie," the mother yells with delight. "How'd you know her first name?" asks the incredulous son.

Now that you've read this chapter, you'll understand why it's often been said in Hollywood that of all the stars there, the most important is the Star of David.

The Least You Need to Know

➤ Jewish immigrants are the founding fathers of almost all the Hollywood studios, and they continue to bring their vision of the American Dream to the screen.

➤ All the movie firsts—first one-reeler, first feature film, first talkie—all have an important Jewish theme or dimension.

➤ Jews played and continue to play a major role as producers and directors of some of the most important films in cinema history.

➤ Woody Allen occupies a unique place in movie history for his multifaceted genius and his comic ingenuity.

➤ Steven Spielberg has managed to universalize Jewish values in a way like no one else and leaves an unparalleled legacy that includes the most powerful films ever made about war and the Holocaust.

➤ There were many famous Jewish actors and actresses who were compelled to change their names so that they'd appear more "American."

➤ It's much easier today in Hollywood for Jews to be successful without having to hide their background.

Let Me
Entertain You

For Jews, happiness isn't just a state of mind. It's also a way of being holy. The Bible teaches, "And you shall rejoice before the Lord your God." Joy is a way of acknowledging that you live in a world created by God.

The Midrash has a beautiful story: Elijah was sent back down to earth to perform missions for God. One day, he was recognized by a sage in Jerusalem. "I must know," asked the scholar, "who among all the people assembled here is assured of a place in the world to come?" Elijah pointed to the least likely of all the candidates, a clown in their midst, and replied: "He is the one. He entertains people and makes them happy. Through him, people appreciate being alive. He best fulfills the will of the Almighty on earth." So in a remarkable sense, entertainers are really Godly messengers who fulfill the great mission of spreading joy on earth. Small wonder that so many Jews have chosen this way to express their talents.

Ha, Ha, Ha…

You don't *have* to be Jewish to be a comedian, but obviously it helps. The number of Jewish comics is so disproportionate to their percentage of the population that it clearly proves the profound link between Jews and humor.

Can it be genetic? I doubt there's a gene that has jokes imprinted on it. In all probability, it has to do with Jewish experience. Freud—okay, I know, I know. I didn't get to him yet…just wait one more chapter. And I promise I'm not avoiding him for any subconscious reason—suggested that humor is really a form of verbal aggression. Those who can't fight back physically, for whatever reason, find a way to react to blows, not with fists, but with words. Jewish humor, Freud adds, may even serve as a double-edged defense mechanism—aggression disguised as masochism. What Freud meant is that the jokes say to the anti-Semite, "I can put myself down much better than anything you can say about me, and that makes me cleverer than you are."

But whatever the reasons, Jews are simply extraordinarily funny. And for many of them, it's not just that they're comics who happen to be Jewish, but they really are Jewish comics. There's something about their style that is part of their Jewish psyche and their culture. Let's look at some of them:

➤ Woody Allen is the intellectual observer.

➤ Jack Benny learned what every Jew must to survive—proper timing.

➤ Groucho Marx's wit could almost be called Talmudic.

➤ Milton Berle's memory of every joke he ever heard or stole could have made him a rabbinic scholar.

➤ Eddie Cantor, Jerry Lewis, Don Rickles, Red Buttons, Jack E. Leonard, the other Marx Brothers, Ed Wynn, Hennie Youngman, all come from a tradition of Purim players and *badchanim* who did their best, even if they made themselves look stupid, to bring joy to their fellow Jews in depressing times.

➤ Lenny Bruce and Mort Sahl, who were obsessed with *tikun olam*, "repairing the world" from its stupidities and injustices.

➤ Sam Levenson, who used the skills he learned as a school teacher in his stand-up routines, which were almost funny sermons.

➤ Jackie Mason, who not only has profound insights into Jewish character, but the national traits of other people as well. ("If an Englishman gets run down by a truck, he apologizes to the truck.")

➤ Mel Brooks, who had the *chutzpah* to put on the screen American Indians who spoke Yiddish. He used the ironic genius of his people to respond to an interviewer who asked if he hates Germans, "Me? Not like Germans? Why should I not like Germans? Just because they are arrogant and have fat necks and do anything they're told as long as it's cruel and killed millions of Jews in concentration camps and made soap out of their bodies and lampshades out of their skin? Is that any reason to hate them?" Yes, Mel Brooks almost sounds like an oral version of the Yiddish humorist Sholem Alecheim.

➤ And of course, there's George Burns, who not only almost took the blessing to live "till 120" literally, but who also took the Biblical statement that man was created in the image of God so seriously that, in the movie *Oh, God!* he had the nerve to play the role of the Almighty.

Here's an incredible statistic: Research has shown that among the most famous nationally known humorists in America, eighty percent are Jewish! And that's no joke.

Aha, That's It

Badchanim, singular *badchan*, were the entertainers who were a traditional part of every joyous Jewish occasion. They were jacks-of-all-trades who could sing, dance, make up brilliant verses on the spot that included the "stars" of the particular ceremony, and, of course, regale their audiences with tales from the Midrash or from their own creative, fertile minds.

George Burns didn't get to be 120—the Jewish ideal—but he did get to play God. (Courtesy of Photofest)

323

Yenta's Little Secrets

George Burns admitted that he got so carried away with the part he played in *Oh, God* that, "Yesterday, when I was on an elevator, a woman got on and said, 'Nice day.' I said, 'Thank you.'"

On the Radio

There was a time before television when people could be entertained at home only by radio. Yet the programs weren't good enough to make people want to sit and listen—until March 29, 1932. A comic named Jack Benny was invited as a guest on newspaper columnist Ed Sullivan's program, and he began his monologue this way, "Ladies and gentlemen, this is Jack Benny talking. There will be a slight pause while you say, 'Who cares?'" But care they did for the next 23 years.

Nobody can really explain what made Jack Benny funny. He didn't tell jokes, he didn't do slapstick, but his mannerisms, his deadpan looks, his slow burn, and the way he said, "Well!" or "Now cut that out!" followed by a perfectly timed pause had audiences in hysterics. Once, in 1948, when Benny played the London Palladium, a member of the audience asked a critic during one of Benny's prolonged pauses, when would the comedian actually do something. The critic later said, "I explained that Jack Benny never did anything, which was his particular genius."

Jack Benny was the master of timing, which he parlayed into a phenomonal 40-year career. (Courtesy of Photofest)

Jump from Jack Benny to the 90s and the most-watched TV program of all time, and you find a remarkable parallel. *Seinfeld* owned Thursday night, just as Benny had Sundays. When Jerry Seinfeld and friends finally went off the air after nine spectacular seasons, people wept and some claimed they didn't know how they would survive. And what was this terrifically popular show about? It was a show about nothing, they kept telling you. I guess the most deprived people of all know how to make something even out of nothing!

Radio, in its heyday, reached all of America in a way vaudeville entertainers, restricted to tiresome road tours, had never been able to accomplish. One of the true giants was Isidor Iskowitch, a product of the Lower East Side, whom you probably would recognize much more readily by his stage name, Eddie Cantor. (Amazingly, he changed his name to conceal his Jewishness and became a cantor in the bargain!)

With a show "about nothing" Jerry Seinfeld enthralled viewers with his comic depiction of a group of wacky New Yorkers. (Courtesy of Photofest)

The Tube

But if radio brought voices into the nation's homes, the miracle of television would go one better and bring in pictures. TV without a doubt changed the world. And TV caught on because of Milton Berlinger, aka Milton Berle. At age five, his stage-door mother entered him in a Charlie Chaplin look-alike contest and he won. From then on, aside from telling jokes, he loved to masquerade and, in 1948, he became the first variety show host on the new medium of television. People still

Sage Sayings

"It takes twenty years to make an overnight success."

—Eddie Cantor

didn't know how to watch television so they would set up chairs, formal style, in their living rooms and invite guests to sit and watch "Uncle Miltie" as if they were in a theater. For seven seasons, restaurants and night clubs around the country would close because they couldn't compete with TV's first superstar. His fans called him "Mister Television," and that will surely be part of his legacy.

Born Milton Berlinger, better known as Milton Berle or "Uncle Miltie," he became the first variety-show host in the early days of television. (Courtesy of Photofest)

Sage Sayings

"I have a lot of regrets about things I did and said, for the way I pushed and shoved and bullied during those hysterical years. My only defense, which is no defense, is the pressure. If a youth becomes a star too early, it will be a miracle if that kid doesn't grow up to be a man who believes he's Cassanova, Einstein, and Jesus Christ all rolled up into one."

—Milton Berle

Jews excel with words, so it's no surprise that some of the superstars of TV are Jewish interviewers and journalists. Barbara Walters became co-host on *Today* in 1974 and had a string of exclusive interviews with personalities of international status that were replayed around the world—including Fidel Castro and Anwar Sadat. The name of her book, *How to Talk with Practically Anybody About Practically Anything*, really sums up her very special talent.

Mike Wallace, born Myron Leon, helped make *60 Minutes* the most popular news magazine program on the air.

Paddy Chayefsky took television to new heights and showed how it could become a vehicle for serious drama. In a number of his works, Chayefsky drew on his first-hand knowledge of Jewish life and tradition. *Marty* (1953) was a television masterpiece that warmly portrayed a Bronx butcher's love for a teacher. It was later made into a successful motion picture that won an Academy Award in 1955. One of his most powerful plays, *The Tenth Man* (1959), re-created the legend of the *dybbuk*, a dead spirit taking over the body of a live person, with the story set in the modern-day Bronx. *Gideon* (1961), inspired by the Biblical account of the Hebrew Judges' victory over the Midianites (I hope you remember this story from Chapter 8, "From Judges to Kings"), dramatized man's dependence on and rebellion against God. In 1974, Chayefsky was awarded the Laurel Award, the most coveted prize of the Writers Guild of America.

And the man who can call presidents and kings to be interviewed is a King in his own right, probably the greatest interviewer of all times. Larry King was born in Brooklyn as Lawrence Harvey Zeiger, son of Russian-Jewish immigrants. He was raised in a kosher home and he celebrated his *bar mitzvah*. He started as a delivery boy and mail clerk, did other odd jobs, and then broke into radio in Miami—that is, if you can call sweeping floors at WAHR a job in radio. King worked his way up, and on January 30, 1978, he began hosting *The Larry King Show*, broadcast from Washington, D.C. It was the first national radio talk show, whose weekly listening audience grew to five million. In 1985, King switched to Cable CNN, and its international scope made him the most popular talk show host in the world.

Lawrence Harvey Zeiger became "King" of CNN and the most prestigious interview program on television, "Larry King Live." (Courtesy of Photofest)

Yenta's Little Secrets

Larry King attributes his great success to one personal trait: "I've been innately curious since my earliest memory. I was never the kind of kid who wanted an autograph. I'd run along the street asking the Brooklyn Dodgers questions like, 'Why did you bunt?'"

Curtain Going Up

All the world's a stage—and someone is always watching. Who better than Jews to feel that their lives are theater, observed and perhaps even directed by someone in the wings. Jews always loved the theater, and their role on the American scene is legendary.

Sam S. Lee, and J. Schubert managed and owned a great number of theaters all over the country and especially in New York. They also produced many successful plays and musical comedies. David Belasco was probably the most influential figure of his time in the American theater. Theater lovers will recognize the names of many of these great producers: Morris Gest, Sam H. Harris, Edgar Selwyn, Jed Harris, Herman Shumlin, Max Gordon, Oscar Serlin, Arthur Hammerstein, Richard Rodgers, and Oscar Hammerstein II, Alfred Bloomingdale, Kermit Bloomgarten, and Walter Fried. There also was Max Liebman, discoverer of Danny Kaye and Sid Caesar; Alexander H. Cohen, who became known as Broadway's "millionaire boy angel"; and Mike Nichols, one of the outstanding stage and film directors.

Jews not only produced the plays, they very often wrote them: S. N. Behrman, George S. Kaufman, Lillian Hellman, Arthur Miller, Moss Hart, Elmer Rice, Clifford Odets, Garson Kanin, Sidney Kingsley, Irwin Shaw—the names are legends of the theater world and their plays will probably continue to be performed as long as there will be performers and audiences.

The Great Musicals

Jews especially like music (see later in this chapter) and so the musical comedy, the musical revue, or in its earliest form, vaudeville, have all been dominated by Jews. Florenz Ziegfeld paved the way with his *Ziegfeld Follies* that, between 1907 and 1931, were the top rung to which entertainers aspired. Ziegfeld introduced Irving Berlin and Jerome Kern. The 1920s witnessed the rise of Richard Rodgers and George and Ira Gershwin. The team of Rodgers and Hart became one of the most successful in American musical history, producing 27 musicals. *Showboat* (1927), by Jerome Kern and Oscar Hammerstein II, based on a book by Edna Ferber, is considered the classic of the American musical theater.

In the 30s, America suffered terribly during the Depression, and musicals were a way to escape reality. *Of Thee I Sing* (1931), a satire on American politics, by Morrie Ryskind, George S. Kaufman, and George and Ira Gershwin, was the first musical to win the Pulitzer Prize for Drama. George Gershwin was able to empathize with another minority group and reached the heights of musical expression with *Porgy and Bess* (1936). *Pal Joey* (1940), a Rodgers and Hart hit, was one of the first "adult" musicals to deal with the seamy side of life. *Lady In The Dark* (1941), with libretto by Moss Hart, score by Kurt Weill, lyrics by Ira Gershwin, and produced by Sam Harris, was the first play to deal with the previously unexplored (in theater anyway) world of psychoanalysis.

In 1943, a world torn by war found some relief in Rodgers and Hammerstein II's ode to the simple life in *Oklahoma*. *Carousel* (1945), *South Pacific* (a 1949 Pulitzer Prize winner), both by Rodgers and Hammerstein; *Annie Get Your Gun* (1946), with music by Irving Berlin; and *Brigadoon* (1947), with book and lyrics by Alan J. Lerner, proved the power that music, in the context of a story, could have on stage.

Frank Loesser wrote the music and lyrics for *Guys and Dolls* (1950). *The Pajama Game* (1954) and *Damn Yankees* (1955) were the work of the songwriting team of Richard Adler and Jerry Ross. Frederick Lowe composed for Alan J. Lerner's *My Fair Lady* in 1956. And Leonard Bernstein introduced a whole new dimension to music in his masterful *West Side Story* (1957). In 1961, *How to Succeed in Business Without Really Trying*, with words and lyrics by Frank Loesser, earned the remarkable distinction of being the fourth musical play to win the Pulitzer Prize for Drama.

The play that nobody predicted could possibly be a hit, based on Yiddish stories of Sholom Alecheim, succeeded in breaking all-time records. *Fiddler On The Roof* (1964), with a score by Sheldon Harnick and Jerry Bach and choreography by Jerome Robbins, taught America all about the *shtetel* and Jewish life in Eastern Europe in a way that created not only sympathy, but also love and understanding for a way of life that was finally snuffed out by the Holocaust. Zero Mostel's role of Tevye is an unforgettable creation, and thousands of amateur groups have performed this play in theaters around the world.

Sage Sayings

"Comedy is rebellion against falsehood...against all evil masquerading as true and good and worthy of respect."

—Zero Mostel

Zero Mostel may have gotten his first name by flunking school, but he got his reputation from his memorable role as Tevye in Fiddler On the Roof. *(Courtesy of Archive Photos)*

It was the Broadway musical stage that was also responsible for skyrocketing the career of Barbra Streisand as the singing sensation in *I Can Get It for You Wholesale* (1962) and *Funny Girl* (1964).

Barbra Streisand grew up in Brooklyn but gives her listeners a taste of heaven whenever she sings. (Courtesy of Photofest)

Pulpit Stories

Arab censors were deeply upset that Egyptian movie star Omar Sharif kissed Barbra Streisand in *Funny Girl*. They decided to ban the film in 1968. When they told Barbra Streisand about the censors, she said, "You think Cairo is upset? You should have seen the letter I got from my Aunt Rose."

"Hamlet—Translated and Improved"

Yiddish theater is the only theater in the world that began with a holiday. Historians say that it was the festive day of Purim (go back to Chapter 11, "Surviving Destruction," if you don't remember) with its Purim Players, whose job it was to put people into the holiday spirit and who eventually developed into the Yiddish theater. The historian Israel Abraham notes, "Nothing marks the continuity of Jewish life more clearly than the survival of the Purim plays into modern times."

Plays helped make life bearable in *pogrom*-dominated Russia. With the Russian Edict of 1883 prohibiting Yiddish plays, Yiddish theater came to the United States. With them came Boris Thomashefsky, Jacob Adler, and David Kessler, who would become theatrical idols to the masses of Jews on the Lower East Side.

Yiddish Takes Center Stage

Jacob Adler scored his greatest success in 1893 at the New York Academy of Music where he played Shylock in Yiddish with a distinguished supporting cast of gentile Shakespearean actors who performed in English! Talk about a bilingual educational experience.

There was so much demand for good plots and "respectable" plays that Shakespeare somehow turned into a Yiddish writer. Second Avenue marquees in New York City proclaimed a showing of "*Hamlet*—translated and improved." There was even a Jewish *Hamlet* in which Hamlet was a Yeshiva student whose uncle, a rabbi, informed on his own brother and had him exiled in Siberia so he could seduce Hamlet's mother.

Yiddish theater had a star system unlike any other. Supporting roles were there only to give the star cues for his grand scenes. The stars were like the Hassidic rabbis in the *shtetel* who were devoutly worshipped. When the star was on stage, the lights were bright; when he exited, half the lights were turned off. The audience loved the performances so much that they often demanded that the star repeat a monologue, a song, or even a death scene. Talk about dying a few times on stage on the same night!

Sage Sayings

"No, my Shakespeare! For me, the Jew, your answer is not enough. My life has been no brief moment, no tale signifying nothing. When I measure it with the measure of my feelings, it has been an eternity, an ocean."

—Jacob Adler

The audience came not just for the plays, but for a social experience as well. The theaters were the secular synagogues—and more. They were also the gateways to American culture and to the realization of the American dream of the "great melting pot." To be an American meant to go to "de tea-ter." The sweatshop peddlers and workers came, bringing along their supper and talking with their friends during the show. It was customary for hawkers to walk down the aisles selling blintzes, knishes, and bottles of seltzer. Matchmakers had the great idea of giving one ticket to a young man and another for the adjacent seat to a young woman whom they thought might be a suitable match. If the man liked her, he bought her a bag of peanuts, and they were almost engaged.

Tragedy and Comedy

A good Yiddish play had to do two things, sometimes at the very same moment: Make you laugh and make you cry. That, after all, was the prototypical Jewish experience. And love on stage may have been in, but sex was definitely out. The summary of a typical play, as one critic noted, was: "In the first act, he wants and she doesn't; in the second act, she wants and he doesn't; in the third act, they both want and the curtain goes down."

But the quality of the acting of many of the stars was, by all accounts, on the highest level. Maurice Schwartz was much praised by the non-Jewish press. Others, like Rudolph Schildkraut, were lured away by Hollywood, as was Paul Muni. Several actresses found their way to the English-speaking stage, notably Bertha Kalich, Sophie Tucker, and Molly Picon. Sadly, with the decline of Yiddish came the death-knell of its theater. Some of the now-unemployed Yiddish actors traveled to the stages in the resort hotels of the Catskills, an hour's drive from New York City, during the summer season. When that, too, came to an end, an era was over.

"With a Song in My Heart"

Music, said the Talmud, is prayer. And who could be better at praying than Jews? When they were delivered from the pursuing Egyptians by a miracle at the Red Sea, they burst into song. From that day forward, Jews have sung in their temples, in their synagogues and their special moments of life, and in their daily efforts to find joy in a world created by God.

We've already seen how the Irving Berlins, the Gershwins, and the Leonard Bernsteins changed the face of musical theater. The list of Jews who made major contributions to the art of music would fills countless volumes. I could hardly do justice in this brief survey to their scope and their number, but I'll mention a few, to give you some idea:

➤ Serge Koussevitzky was the famous conductor of the Boston Symphony Orchestra; Bruno Walter led the New York Philharmonic; Fritz Reiner did the same for the Cleveland Symphony Orchestra.

➤ Among pianists, Vladimir Horowitz, Artur Rubinstein, and William Kappell come readily to mind.

➤ Isaac Stern, the internationally famous virtuoso violinist, has been called America's greatest musical ambassador. The violin tugs at the heart and seems to speak from the heart. So, like Isaac Stern, we have a number of other Jewish geniuses of the violin: Mischa Elman, Efrem Zimbalist, Jascha Heifetz, and Yehudi Menuhin.

➤ Benny Goodman, son of an immigrant tailor from Warsaw, is an icon of the big band era of the 1930s and 40s. Goodman was the first major white band leader with black and white musicians together on stage. At the age of nine, Goodman and his brothers borrowed musical instruments from the neighborhood synagogue. Benny, being small, got a clarinet. He would always wonder, later in life, what kind of career he would have had "if I had been twenty pounds heavier and two inches taller." Jews sway during prayer, so maybe it's not that strange that one of them would end up being "The King of Swing."

Yenta's Little Secrets

Jascha Heifetz was a child prodigy who began playing the violin at the age of three. He was so good that once, after a performance, George Bernard Shaw visited him backstage and scolded him for playing too perfectly: "Nothing may be perfect in the world or the gods become jeal-ous and destroy it. So would you mind playing one wrong note every night before you go to bed?" Heifetz simply couldn't comply with the request.

And then, of course, the voice. The gift of the angels who also sing to God. The voice is the human instrument that could probably move people more than any other. Oh, to listen to Jan Pearce, Richard Tucker, and Robert Merrill. They all began as cantors and trained in the holiest and toughest place of all, where you had to please the Highest Critic. Oh, to hear Beverly Sills. And those popular lyrics from Bette Midler and Barbra Streisand. Their notes have to come not just from their voiceboxes, but from the very depths of their souls!

"Take Me Out to the Ballgame"

Okay, Mark McGwire and Sammy Sosa aren't Jewish. But, contrary to popular opinion, that doesn't mean Jews aren't good at sports or that they can't play at least a passing game of the national pastime.

Try this for an all-time, all-star Jewish baseball team:

Pitchers: Sandy Koufax, Edward Reulbach

Catcher: Johnny Kling

First Base: Henry "Hank" Greenberg

Second Base: Charles "Buddy" Myers

Third Base: Al Rosen

Short Stop: Andy Cohen

Left Field: Sid Gordon

Center Field: Art Shamsky

Right Field: George Stone

Owner: Barney Dreyfus

Just so you won't argue about the selections, I'll tell you a little more about why each one of these deserves the honor of playing on the New York Yankels:

➤ Who's going to argue about Sandy Koufax? With four no-hitters, the youngest player ever admitted into the Baseball Hall of Fame, 40 shut-outs for the Los Angeles Dodgers, Cy Young Award winner three times in four seasons, *Sporting News* Pitcher of the Year every year from 1963 to 1966, lifetime struck-out 2,396 batters—Koufax is considered one of baseball's greatest pitchers ever.

Sandy Koufax, considered one of baseball's greatest pitchers, was the youngest player to be admitted to the Baseball Hall of Fame in Cooperstown, New York. (Courtesy Sporting News/ Archive Photos)

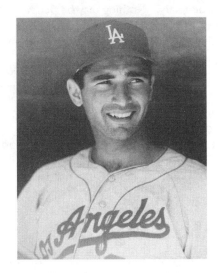

Pulpit Stories

In October 1965, when the Dodgers and Minnesota Twins were playing in the World Series, the opening game fell on Yom Kippur. Koufax did not show at the ballpark out of respect for his holiday. The next day the St. Paul Pioneer Press lambasted him for his unwillingness to pitch the opening game of the Series. Koufax had his revenge: He pitched the seventh and deciding game, which the Dodgers won to take the World Series title.

➤ Back-up pitcher Edward Reulbach was the only pitcher to pitch two shut-outs in a double-header during the 1908 season. His career record was 181-105. He once pitched four shut-outs in a row.

➤ Johnny Kling is considered by many to be one of the greatest catchers of all time. He was the first catcher to stand up close to the batter at all times and throw from a crouching stance. He played with the Chicago Cubs when they won four Pennants and two World Series in 1906, 1907, 1908, and 1910.

➤ First baseman Henry "Hank" Greenberg is considered the best "everyday" player of all the Jews in baseball. He led the American League in homeruns four times; in RBIs four times; he had a career batting average of .313; he was named the American League's Most Valuable Player in 1935; and he challenged Babe Ruth's record of 60 homers in 1938—then an almost incredible feat.

Sage Sayings

"After all, I was representing a couple of million Jews among a hundred million gentiles, and I was always in the spotlight...I felt a responsibility. I was there every day and if I had a bad day, every SOB was call-ing me names so that I had to make good. As time went by I came to feel that if I, as a Jew, hit a home-run, I was hitting one against Hitler."

—Hank Greenberg, commenting on the 1938 season, when he hit 58 home runs and was approaching Babe Ruth's record of 60

➤ Second baseman Charles "Buddy" Myers had a career batting average of .303; in 1935, he led the American League in hitting with a .349 average; in 1928, he led the American League in stolen bases with 30.

➤ At third base, Al Rosen was the unanimous choice for Most Valuable Player in the American League in 1953, won the home run championship in 1950 and 1953, was Rookie of the Year in 1950, and had a career batting average of .285.

➤ At short stop we have Andrew Cohen who wasn't the greatest ballplayer but was signed by the Giants because they wanted a drawing card to woo the Jewish fans. We need a short stop so we'll take him, too, with his .281 career batting average.

➤ In left field there's Sidney Gordon, with 13 years in the major leagues, 202 career homeruns, and a .283 career batting average.

➤ Art Shamsky's in center field; he once hit four homeruns in four times at bat, tying a major league record.

➤ In right field we play George "Silent George" Stone, American League batting champ in 1906, with a .358 average.

➤ And Barney Dreyfus owns the team. As the owner of the Pittsburgh Pirates from 1900 to 1932, he brought them Rube Waddell, Honus Wagner, and Fred Clarke, winning six National League Pennants and two World Series.

➤ And now for our team's secret weapon: manager Moe Berg. Moe was far and away the most intelligent player ever to play in the game. A Princeton graduate with an IQ close to 200, he studied for a law degree (which he easily got) in his spare time on the bench. He was a linguist who knew dozens of languages. He was prevailed upon by the United States govern-ment during World War II to become a spy and cull information from European scientists about the nuclear bomb.

Listen to Your Bubbe

For a fascinating read about an in-credible life, don't miss *The Catcher Was A Spy: The Mysterious Life Of Moe Berg*, by Nicholas Dawidoff.

With Moe Berg's brains and Koufax pitching, this Jew-ish team can't lose!

White Men *Can* Jump

As long as we're at it, let's try for an all-star Jewish basketball team as well. Although the team would probably do very well against anyone else, I wouldn't want to see them playing the Chicago Bulls. It's just too much to expect the Jews to perform the miracle of the Jordan more than once in their history!

➤ Neal Walk, center, was All-American in his senior year when he ranked in the Top 10 in scoring and rebounding. He signed with the Phoenix Suns and played from 1969–1974; moved to the New York Knicks in 1974 and played two seasons; averaged over 20 points per game in the 1972–1973 season; and later played in Israel.

➤ Dolph Shayes, forward, is definitely a candidate for the greatest Jewish athlete ever: Rookie of the Year in 1949; All-Star 12 times; scored almost 20,000 points, 6,979 of which were free throws; and is a member of the Basketball Hall of Fame.

➤ Arthur Heyman, forward, was a three-time All-American at Duke University and averaged over 25 points per game there. In 1964, he was named to the All-Rookie team of the National Basketball Association.

➤ Nat Holman, guard, was an original Celtic from 1921–1929—arguably one of the greatest basketball players of all time. With Holman the Celtic's record was absolutely mindblowing: In 1922–23, it was 193-11; in 1923–24, 204-11; and in 1924–25, 134-6. The team lost only 28 games and won 531 in three years. Then Holman became one of the great coaches of the game at City College, New York.

➤ Max Zaslowsky, guard, entered St. John's University in New York and became one of their top basketball stars. He led the league in scoring in 1948 with a 21-point average. He later played with the New York Knicks, and then with Baltimore and Milwaukee. At the time of his retirement, he was the third-highest scorer of all time in the National Basketball Association.

➤ Arnold "Red" Auerbach, coach. How could anyone else be the coach of the Jewish All-Star Team? Auerbach's achievements as a coach and general manager of the Boston Celtics made him a legend in his own time. His teams won nine National Basketball Association titles (eight in a row) during 1950–1956. Unbelievable! His coaching record is 1,037-548. Tops ever recorded.

Nine, Ten... You're Out!

We know that Jews can box. Remember Daniel Mendoza back in Chapter 21, "The Yiddish British: From Shylock to Lord"? But he wasn't the only one to show that the people of the book can also be the people of the "hook." Benny Leonard retired as undefeated lightweight champion of the world (1917–1924). He fought 210 bouts and, amazingly enough, lost only two. Many experts consider him the most skillful and scientific boxer in modern boxing history.

Would you believe a Jew, Joe Choynski, defeated Jack Johnson and fought Jim Jeffries to a draw in twenty rounds? Albert Rudolph, who fought under the name Al McCoy (making him, obviously, not the real McCoy), was world welterweight champion (1914–1917). And Barney Ross held three world titles in 1934: lightweight, junior welterweight, and welterweight.

Sage Sayings

"Benny Leonard has done more to conquer anti-Semitism than a thousand textbooks have done."

—Arthur Brisbane, U.S. journalist

Maxie Rosenblum held the light-heavyweight title from 1930–1934. Hal Singer was lightweight champion in 1930. And Max Baer was briefly heavyweight king in 1934.

"Better Than the Hulk"

Who said Jews can only wrestle with their conscience?

The reigning World Championship Wrestling heavyweight champion is a 6'4", 285-pound muscle mass known simply as Goldberg. You may well ask, "Why is this wrestling champ different from all other wrestling champs?" Well, for starters, when this 31-year-old son of a Harvard-educated doctor and a classical musician found his true calling, his father, Jed Goldberg, said, "He never wanted to be a doctor, anyway."

Goldberg, who for some unknown reason circumcised his first name Bill, removing it from his calling card, decided not to use a pseudonym. He said he wants "everyone who attended his *bar mitzvah* to remember who he is." When Goldberg appears live, either in the Deep South or the Midwest, adoring fans chant, "Gold-berg! Gold-berg!" In July of 1998, Goldberg jackhammered Hulk Hogan to win the W.C.W. title, putting him now at the top of the sport.

Rabbi Irwin Kula, President of the Center for Learning and Leadership, a New York-based think-tank that questions the meaning of Jewishness, is a loyal fan and believes that Goldberg "opened a new chapter in Jewish-American history." Before Goldberg, Kula explains, "Jews wrestled only with their identity. They wrestled with God. What this says is, "Look at us! We're not ververbalized! We're not weak or wimpy! We're the heavyweight champ!"

The Female Lion

And if Goldberg can do it, so can the "Zion Lion," her femininity notwithstanding. Jill Matthews, newly crowned Junior Flyweight Champion of the World, stands 5'3", 105 pounds, and with her ponytail shining a strawberry blonde color, she looks—well, gorgeous. But I wouldn't want to be in the ring with her if she heard me describe her that way. Most of all, this daughter-in-law of a Conservative Rabbi wants to be taken seriously as a fighter. She slugged her way to the top, and she plans to stay there. She won her 106-pound weight class in March 1998 and defended her title on June 30, defeating Lisa Houghton, 26, a former kick boxer from England. The Zion Lion celebrated her Atlantic City victory with a back flip in the ring. Jill wears a Star of David on her black silk boxing robe over hips so slim that the $3,000 championship belt hangs low, like it belongs to her daddy.

She feels she's really achieved something in life. "But," she said, "tell that to my in-laws. They say, big deal, so when am I getting pregnant?"

"Teach Him How To Swim"

It's a law in the Talmud that a father must teach his child how to swim. The reason? The child may need it some day for survival.

Mark Spitz's father may have had a better reason. Mark would go on to win seven gold medals and set a new world record in every event he competed in at the 1972 Munich Olympics. That makes him candidate, according to many, for the title of the "greatest Jewish athlete of all time."

In 1977, Mark told a reporter for an Israeli magazine: "I feel that being a Jewish athlete has helped our cause. We have shown that we are as good as the next guy. In mentality we have always been at the top of every field. I think the Jewish people have a more realistic way of looking at life. They make the most of what's happening at the present while preparing for the future."

There couldn't be a better way to say it—or a better way to end this chapter.

The Least You Need to Know

➤ Jews are funny for reasons that probably are related to their identity, and their different types of humor express a host of Jewish characteristics.

➤ Jews helped radio and television become the powerful mediums of entertainment that they are today.

➤ Jews played an especially important part in developing the American theater as we know it, with particular emphasis on musicals and musical comedies.

➤ The Yiddish theater enjoyed a glorious era, one that unfortunately came to an early close with the decrease in Yiddish-speaking audiences.

➤ Jews have always had a special talent for music, no doubt partly because music is so important in synagogue services.

➤ Baseball, basketball, boxing, and wrestling have all had their share of prominent Jewish athletes—and even a woman who won the Junior Flyweight Championship of the World.

➤ Swimming cannot only save your life but, if you're Mark Spitz, can let you win seven Olympic gold medals.

Chapter 31

The Doctor Is In

In This Chapter

➤ Why medicine and Judaism are so profoundly linked

➤ Jewish Nobel Prize winners and their great discoveries

➤ Freud and his followers have become the intellectual leaders of a field known by many as "the Jewish science"

Sam Levenson (U.S. comedian, 1914–1980) had a great response to an anti-Semite who wrote him a vicious letter attacking Jews. He wrote, "Dear Sir—It's a free world. You don't have to like Jews, but for those of you who don't like Jews, I suggest you boycott certain Jewish products: the Wasserman Test for syphilis; digitalis, discovered by Dr. Nuslin; insulin, discovered by Dr. Minokofsky; chlorohydrate for convulsions, discovered by Dr. Casamir Fink; streptomycin, discovered by Dr. Zalman Waksman; the polio pill by Dr. Albert Sabin; and the polio vaccine by Dr. Jonas Salk."

And those are just a few of the life-saving medicines brought to the world by Jews. We've said it many times in this book. Jews consider medicine as important as religion. A doctor heals the body, a rabbi heals the soul. We need both in order to live and to fulfill whatever our mission is here on earth. The list of contributions by Jews to the field of medicine requires a book rather than a chapter, but let's at the very least look at some of the major Jewish giants of medicine and their discoveries.

"The Little Rabbi"

Jonas Salk (1914–1995) was born to Orthodox Jewish parents in the Bronx. He was the eldest of three sons and the most observant. "My brothers call me the little rabbi," he used to say. He went to Hebrew school from the age of eight and on his way he remembered, "There was a school at the end of the street, and the kids would throw stones and make nasty remarks."

Much later in life, he attributes to these incidents some of the reasons for his life's direction: "I was impressed early in life by tragedies in life, to say nothing of what had happened to our forbears." For so many generations, he felt, his people had suffered. Jews knew better than anyone else about the meaning of pain. And Jonas Salk decided that in some small way he wanted to bring an end to this vicious cycle. He was going to do something positive for humanity as a whole.

At the University of Pittsburgh, where he became research professor of bacteriology, he began to investigate infantile paralysis, poliomyelitis, a disease that caused paralysis and death. At that time, yearly polio epidemics were common.

Salk had an idea. He was going to develop a polio vaccine from killed viruses. That challenged medical orthodoxy, which held that only vaccines made of living viruses can provide effective, enduring immunity. To proceed with his work, he had to persist in a belief that was strongly in the minority—something Jews had been doing with their faith for millennia.

On April 12, 1955, Salk was able to proclaim three words that would dramatically alter the fight against a disease that since the turn of the century had killed or disabled at least a million Americans, including a president of the United States (Franklin Delano Roosevelt): "The vaccine works!"

Salk became an international hero. He was awarded the Presidential Citation and the Congressional Medal for Distinguished Achievement.

Jonas Salk developed the first effective vaccine against polio and his Salk Institute is now working on a vaccine for AIDS. (Courtesy of Photofest)

Yenta's Little Secrets

New York City wanted to give Jonas Salk a tickertape parade to honor his achievement. A manufacturer wanted him to endorse a line of pajamas emblazoned with the words, "Thank you, Dr. Salk." Dr. Salk declined both honors.

When he started his career, he wanted to work on rheumatic diseases, but his application to work as a researcher was turned down because of his religion. Salk always believed that if one door is closed, then there is another that's open. He switched to research in influenza, and this led him to his great discovery. So you might well say that anti-Semitism contributed to finding the cure for polio!

Salk himself believed that his Jewish ancestry was responsible for his success in yet another way:

> The process of natural selection undoubtedly resulted in a stock that has been passed on to its successors. It gave me whatever qualities were necessary to survive and to evolve. So I've seen adversity as an advantage. Jews have developed an innate wisdom about how to manage to continue to thrive and strive. I could see that in the way my mother brought up her children. What she wanted more than anything else was for us to go beyond her status.

Not All Blood Is Alike

Karl Landsteiner (1868–1943) won the Nobel Prize "for his discovery of human blood groups" in 1930. Without him it would be impossible to get a blood transfusion and survive.

Landsteiner discovered that there were four types of human blood groups: A, B, AB, and O. Going all the way back to the Egyptians, medical practitioners had very often caused death by failing to realize that blood types are not necessarily compatible. You have to match suitable donors and recipients—so Landsteiner was really the first major medical matchmaker. (Is that, perhaps, what Tevya's daughters really had in mind when they prayed, "Matchmaker, matchmaker, make me a match?")

His discovery has saved millions of lives; blood transfusion today is a safe and simple procedure, and blood banks around the world are what make surgery possible. So if people who hate Jews spread the slander that Jews control the banks, there's just a germ of truth in that: Jews created the banks that help to save the lives of people around the world!

Yenta's Little Secrets

A very important benefit of blood typing was the ability to determine paternity with certainty. The Bible had created the institution of marriage so that mankind could be sure of "who is the father." Centuries later, a Jew made it possible to get this information even when the Biblical Law was ignored!

"C"—I Told You

Tadeus Reichstein (1897–1996), a Swiss endocrinologist, succeeded in synthesizing vitamin C (ascorbic acid) in 1933. This discovery is still used in the vitamin's industrial manufacture. If Nobel Prize winner Linus Pauling was right about the almost miraculous effects of this vitamin, then Reichstein should have also received a Nobel Prize for this discovery alone.

But Reichstein was far more interested in another medical problem. He was on the trail for a cure for Addison's disease, and he wanted to isolate the active principle of the adrenal cortex that seemed to prolong the lives of people who suffered from it. After years of laboratory work, he isolated a number of hormones, one of which he called "cortisone." In 1948, he injected the first dose of cortisone into the muscles of an arthritic woman. The results were so good that he then gave cortisone to 14 other crippled patients. Within a week all 14 were walking freely and painlessly—the miracle of cortisone had come to sufferers of rheumatoid arthritis. For that, Reichstein, together with his associates Edward Kendall and Philip Hench, was awarded the 1950 Nobel Prize in Physiology and Medicine.

A "Chain" Reaction

Ernst Boris Chain (1906–1979) came from a family in Berlin whose original name was *Kheyn*, which is the Hebrew word for "charm." If that isn't charming enough for you, let me tell you how this refugee from the Nazis ended up winning the Nobel Prize in 1945 "for the discovery of penicillin and its curative effect on various infectious diseases."

Chain immersed himself in a systematic investigation of antibacterial substances produced by microorganisms. He was sure that earth or air could produce a yeast, mold, or fungus that could in turn produce a therapeutic agent capable of saving the lives of war casualties. Those whom the Nazis—those barbarians who made him flee to England—would wound, Chain wanted to cure.

Yenta's Little Secrets

Cortisone is not only beneficial for the treatment of arthritis. Asthma, a variety of skin conditions, inflammatory diseases of the eye, intestinal diseases such as ulcerative colitis, as well as certain mental disorders have all been helped considerably by this hormone.

After an intensive search, Chain realized that the mold discovered by Sir Alexander Fleming (1928) could be the lifesaver they were looking for. Chain was able to isolate history's most effective bacteria killer. A way was eventually found to produce tons of penicillin in time to save thousands of allied lives. It was used in Normandy on D-day and every day thereafter. By the end of World War II, more than seven billion units of penicillin were being produced a year—enough to treat seven million patients.

Chain's achievement must surely stand as the highest form of revenge against a German regime that forced him out of their country for being part of a "people with no redeeming human qualities!"

Yenta's Little Secrets

Professor Chain was an ardent Zionist, and he became a governor of the famous Weizmann Institute in Rehovot, Israel.

The Wonder Drug

Selman Abraham Waksman (1888–1973) was sure that "there are probably more different kinds of tiny plants and animals in the soil than there are on top of it." As a Jew, I guess he realized what thousands of years of history have taught the Jewish people: There's more to life than what meets the eye.

He was also sure that there was a continuous "civil war" in the earth between the countless microorganisms that exist there, just as there are conflicts between those who live on its surface. What he wanted to do was isolate the "chemical weapons" for which he coined a name, "antibiotic," meaning "against life." If he could only harness them correctly, he could use them to destroy those microorganisms—and only those microorganisms—that cause injury to humans.

He worked for 28 years with innumerable disappointments. But at the end, in 1952, he won the Nobel Prize in Physiology and Medicine for his discovery of streptomycin, the "wonder drug" that became medicine's miracle worker after penicillin.

Pulpit Stories

In 1941, an official at Rutgers University argued that Waksman, who was earning $4,620 a year, be dismissed. "A university has to think about economics," he kept insisting. "Besides," he said, "there's no possible future to Waksman's research." Rutgers decided to take a chance on the less-than-$5,000-a-year salary. And thank God they did!

Listen to Your Bubbe

Waksman's autobiography, *My Life with the Microbes*, became a bestseller. Don't miss out on a great read that makes you understand the trials, the tribulations, and the tremendous joy that go with being a scientific researcher.

Waksman suggested streptomycin be tried on the most desperately ill patients suffering from tuberculosis at the Mayo Clinic. It immediately proved successful. For the first time, there was a potent weapon against the "white plague." Streptomycin was soon shown to be effective against a host of other diseases as well. It's estimated that it has saved many more lives since its discovery than were lost in all of the Napoléonic Wars.

That's why a Jewish doctor born in a little town in the Ukraine ended up not only with a Nobel Prize, but also with the Order of Merit of the Rising Sun from the Emperor of Japan and induction into the French Legion of Honor.

The Sex Life of Bacteria

Joshua Lederberg (b. 1925), son of an Orthodox rabbi, became one of the three recipients of the 1958 Nobel Prize in Physiology and Medicine as a result of work done at the age of 21 with Edward Tatum, a corecipient. At 33, he was considered one of the world's outstanding young geneticists.

He made the remarkable discovery that bacteria have a sort of sex life, which Lederberg termed "sexual recombination." He proved that cell-to-cell pairing allows genetic material to pass from one cell to another, and this proved that biochemical genetic principles apply to bacteria. That discovery opened the way to studies of a whole host of genetic and physiological processes in bacteria and helped to explain the characteristics of many virus forms, among other things.

It also led to the conclusion that viruses attacking bacteria can add something to their host's genetic make-up. This process, called "transduction," means that genetic fragments can be transferred from an invading virus to adjacent cells to produce a new virus strain. Without going into detail, this phenomenon holds tremendous promise for tackling the problem of cancer, which is essentially a transformation of normal cells into malignant ones. Transduction provides the missing link that may help science reconcile the virus and mutation theories of cancer.

And if Lederberg's work ever leads to a cure for cancer, the world will have to think of an award for him that outranks even the Nobel Prize!

And So Many Others

Don't expect to find every Jewish medical giant in this chapter because it's simply impossible to include all those who did so much to help improve the lives of human kind. But I can't leave this distinguished group without at least mentioning a few more names. There's Bela Schick, who devised a diagnostic skin test for diphtheria that bears her name. And William Dameshek, the pathfinder in the field of immuno-suppression. Metabolic processes became understood because of Max Meyerhof and Sir Hans Adolf Krebs, giants of biochemistry. And poor Burrill Crohn, who described a bowel disease that then ended up bearing his name!

Add to this list the thousands of Jewish physicians in the States (they comprise, for example, 20 percent of the internists in this country), and you can understand why Jews always toast each other with the word "*l'chaim*—to life." That's not just a prayer, it's also advice for a suitable profession.

"Lie Down on the Couch"

There's only one field that has a higher percentage of Jews practicing in it: psychiatry. Jews make up 30 percent of the world's psychiatrists. And it's not just because Jews gave the world the word *meshuggah,* the Yiddish word for crazy that's even crept into English. Jews always believed that a human being was more than a body. There is something special inside—religion names it "soul."

Id and Ego

It wasn't too great a step for Sigmund Freud eventually to come along and replace what had been known as the key to the "*yid*" with the "id." Freud (1856–1939) is usually ranked as one of the three or four people who did the most to change the thinking of the Western world in the 19th and 20th centuries. His ideas of the subconscious, of regression, of dream interpretation, of suppressed sexuality as the key to almost all behavior, of infantile Oedipal longings, of the deeper sources of hysteria and depression, and of the profound mind-body connection, have transformed the way we view human behavior. Freudian psychology, not just as practiced by professionals but also as used in everyday language and as part of the contemporary mindset, has literally infiltrated every area of life and culture.

Founder of psychoanalysis, Sigmund Freud has had an immense impact not only on medicine, but also on art, literature, and contemporary culture. (Courtesy of Archive Photos)

Throughout his life, Freud had one great fear: that psychoanalysis would become known as a "Jewish national affair." Freud was petrified that anti-Semites would dismiss psychoanalysis as "a Jewish science"—which of course is what the Nazis eventually did. But, truth be told, there must be serious reasons why Jews, of all people, were most attracted to this particular science of human behavior. And the reasons probably require a good psychiatrist—preferably a Freudian—to figure them out!

Beyond Freud

What didn't go unchallenged, though, was Freud's belief in the supremacy of sexual desire as motivator for all of people's actions. It remained for another great Jew, Alfred Adler, to develop the field of "individual psychology." He reduced the significance of childhood sexual factors to a minimum and developed the theory that neurosis stems from childhood experience of overprotection or neglect, or a mixture of both.

Sandor Ferenczi, although strangely enough not as well known, made a contribution to psychoanalysis that has been considered second only to that of Freud. He correlated biological and psychological phenomena in his scientific method known as bioanalysis.

Yenta's Little Secrets

Among Freud's inner circle was only one non-Jew, Ernest Jones. Jones psychoanalyzed the effect of Freud's Jewishness on the evolution of his ideas and work. He attributed the firmness with which Freud maintained his convictions in spite of great opposition to them as "part of the inherited capacity of Jews to stand their ground in the face of opposition and hostility."

Of the hundreds of Jews who made significant contributions to this field, a few must be mentioned for their very special insights:

➤ Theodor Reik, who specialized in greater understanding of the masochism syndrome: If you're Jewish, how can you not want to understand what it means to be a masochist?

➤ Melanie Klein and Anna Freud (daughter of Sigmund) were originators of the psychoanalytic treatment of children.

➤ Kurt Lewin gave us a profound understanding of personality.

➤ Erich Fromm made us appreciate how passions and behavior are determined by the creativity and frustrations of society.

➤ Victor Frankel, a survivor of the Holocaust, who witnessed first hand the potential for human beings to sink lower than beasts or to maintain commitment to their belief system even in the direst circumstances of the concentration camps. He came to the groundbreaking conclusion in his classic work, *Man's Search for Meaning*, that finding meaning for life rather than sex is the most essential prerequisite for mental health.

Sage Sayings

"It is basic to Jewish tradition that God reveals Himself anew in every generation, and some of the channels of this revelation in our day are in the healing principles and insights of psychology and psychiatry."

—Joshua Loth Liebman

What all of these professionals in the study of human behavior share is a conviction that goes back all the way to the great rabbi-doctor of the twelfth century, Moses Maimonides: The mind and the body are so intimately connected that one cannot be treated without the other; the sicknesses of both must be treated so that a "whole" human being can find a measure of joy on earth. For after all, as the Book of Proverbs teaches, "A merry heart doeth good like medicine."

The Least You Need to Know

➤ Jonas Salk, discoverer of the vaccine for polio, attributed his achievement in great measure to his Jewish identity—both the anti-Semitism he experienced and his inheritance of Jewish talent.

➤ Jews have received Nobel Prizes for a host of pioneering and groundbreaking achievements that gave the world blood transfusions, cortisone, penicillin, streptomycin, and the start, perhaps, of the cure for cancer.

➤ Jews have always been dedicated to the field of medicine because they consider it on a par with religious service.

➤ Jews not only founded the field of psychiatry but have remained its most fervent practitioners and greatest achievers, probably because of its emphasis on behavior and the inner essence of man, which in ages past was referred to as the soul.

Changing the World

Some people see the world as it is and complain. Others see the world as it could be and create. These latter are the scientists, the artists, the writers, the philosophers, and the theologians. All the progress of the world depends upon them.

The Bible tells us that God created the world in six days and rested on the seventh day. For Jews that implies that He didn't finish His work. He left the world incomplete. Why? So that people would have an opportunity to become copartners with God in the act of creation. There can't be a better way for us to finish this book than to meet some of the Jewish giants whose creativity has helped all of us to live in a better world.

The Power of a Little Atom

The Jews are a very small people but they have shown tremendous power to achieve. Here's another great coincidence: Jews were the ones to discover the power implicit in the atom. And the secrets of the tiniest particle of matter can, just like the Jews, change all of human history.

Albert Einstein (1879–1955) (who we already talked about in Chapter 20, "When the Walls Came Tumbling Down: Germany") was considered by George Bernard Shaw to be one of the very few "universe builders." His contributions stand out as the greatest of all modern conceptions. His revolutionary concepts of time and space, as explained in the "Theory of Relativity," are epochal. Einstein received the Nobel Prize in 1921 "for his contribution to mathematical physics and especially for his discovery of the law of the photoelectric effect." But no matter what the words, Albert Einstein changed the world we live in. And, for better or for worse—it will be up to humankind to decide—it was he who fathered the atomic age.

Albert Einstein revolutionized physics and is regarded by many as the greatest scientist of all time. (Cortesy of Archive Photos)

Matter is energy. There is an incredible amount of energy locked up in every form of matter, regardless of how small. There is an essential unity between all things in the universe. (And does the fact that the world is really one, a unified whole, suggest an ultimate One as its source?) Einstein's theory explained the entire relationship of mass, gravity, space, and time. It declared that every part of the universe is affected by every other. (And doesn't that sound a little like the fundamental Jewish teaching that all people are connected and responsible one for another?)

The Second "Father"

It's 1922 Nobel Prize winner, Niels Henrik David Bohr, who is called the "other Father of Atomic Energy." He revolutionized conceptions of the structure of the atom. He solved the seemingly insoluble problems of atomic theory and discovered U-235, a rare uranium isotope, as the source for splitting a uranium atom. Bohr was connected to "Tube Alloys," the code name for the Allied atomic bomb project. He was given the first Atoms-for-Peace Prize of the Ford Foundation in 1956 and was chairman of the Danish Atomic Energy Commission.

Yenta's Little Secrets

Bohr returned to Copenhagen soon after making the announcement that the atom had been split. He was working there when the war started, but the day the Nazis invaded Denmark he ordered all atomic research at his institution halted. This was his protest against Hitlerism.

Atom-Splitting Fermi

Enrico Fermi (1901–1957), winner of the Nobel Prize in 1938 "for his discovery of nuclear reactions brought about by slow neutrons," was the first person ever to split an atom. That was in Rome in 1934. Eight years later in Chicago, he built the world's first atomic pile, and with it produced the first atomic chain reaction in history. Fermi had to flee with his family from the fascist regime of Benito Mussolini's Italy in January 1939. He came to the United States, and with him came the secrets that helped the allies win the war against fascism.

Oppenheimer and the Power of the Bomb

Jay Robert Oppenheimer was the American physicist to direct the ultra-secret Manhattan Project, which created the first atomic bomb during World War II. On July 16, 1945, Oppen-heimer witnessed the first atomic bomb explosion in the New Mexican desert. Immediately, he wrote the following lines from the sacred Hindu poem, the *Bhagavad-Gita*:

Listen to Your Bubbe

Read *Atoms in the Family: My Life with Enrico Fermi*, written by his wife Laura. She describes how the first atomic pile "was erected by a small group of scientists in a squash court under the football stands. They worked in great secrecy... pressed by the urgency of their aim. ...They were the first men to see matter yield its inner energy, steadily, at their will. My husband was their leader."

> *If the radiance of a thousand suns*
>
> *Were to burst at once into the sky*
>
> *That would be the splendor of the Mighty One*
>
> *I am become death*
>
> *The destroyer of worlds.*

In 1946, Oppenheimer received the Presidential Medal of Merit in recognition of his contributions to science. *Life* magazine, in a special Fall 1970 edition, named him one of the top 100 Americans of the 20th Century. But Oppenheimer would always be plagued for the rest of his life with his misgivings about unleashing the power of such a tremendous force on earth. He hesitated to do further work on the hydrogen bomb for fear that it might be used to wipe out the human race. In the McCarthy Era, his patriotism was questioned, but he was eventually fully cleared.

In 1963, four years before his death, President Lyndon Johnson presented Oppenheimer with the Atomic Energy Commission's highest honor, the Fermi Award. Sort of like one Jew to another.

Yenta's Little Secrets

At the age of thirty, Oppenheimer taught himself his eighth language, Sanskrit, so that he could study Hindu scriptures in the original. He owned no telephone, never listened to a radio, read no newspapers. But of course, he was a scientific genius.

"A Rabi Is Not a Rabbi"

Isador Isaac Rabi was born into an Orthodox Jewish family in Austria. They moved to the Lower East Side of New York, where Isador attended school. Every day when he came home his mother would ask him, "Did you ask any good questions today?" Now that's a real Jewish mother! And she was more concerned with good questions than with good answers. It's knowing what to ask that really makes a person stand out from his peers.

Rabi went to the local branch of the Brooklyn Public Library and read the books there alphabetically, starting with a book on astronomy. The subject of his *bar mitzvah* speech was, "How the electric light bulb works." That must have been really enlightening!

In 1944, Rabi won the Nobel Prize "for his resonance method for recording the magnetic properties of atomic nuclei." He developed a method of measuring magnetic properties of atoms, molecules, and nuclei with a degree of precision that hardly seemed possible. As the president of the physics section of the Nobel committee said on the occasion of the award, "Rabi literally established radio relations with the most subtle particles of matter, with the world of the electron and of the atomic nucleus."

Rabi also was present when the first atomic bomb was tested in the New Mexico desert. Of this moment, he wrote, "The Atomic Age came at about 5:30 in the morning...it was a sight that I had attempted from time to time to describe. I never felt successful in doing it. One has to go back to the Bible, to witnesses of the ancient miracles, to get some impression of the tremendous emotional experience it produced."

He, too, was fearful of the misuse of atomic energy and tried very hard to use his influence to reduce its easy accessibility and potential for destruction. He concentrated on finding peaceful uses for it. His efforts made possible the precise measurements that were necessary to develop the laser, the atomic clock, and the diagnostic scanning of the human body through the use of nuclear magnetic resonance. He literally fulfilled, in the scientific sphere, the prophetic call to turn implements of war into items for peace. Perhaps, after all, Rabi really did turn into a "rabbi."

Sage Sayings

"Science is a great game. It is inspiring and refreshing. The playing field is the universe itself."

—Isador Isaac Rabi

"His Master's Voice"

Moses probably could have used the trademark, "His Master's Voice," for the books of the Bible. But David Sarnoff ended up taking it as his slogan for the Victor talking machine company that he acquired for RCA. Sarnoff, a Talmudic genius originally from Russia, acquired his fame on the night of April 14, 1912. Operating an experimental wireless station on the roof of Wanamaker's New York department store, he picked up the message, "*SS Titanic* ran into iceberg, sinking fast." For the next 72 hours, he was the messenger to the world, bringing news of the disaster. It wasn't long until he became the commercial manager for RCA, the Radio Corporation of America.

He founded the first broadcast network, NBC, in 1926. Later, as head of RCA, he was a pioneer in the development of radio, early television, and eventually color TV. With his acquisition of Victor, forming RCA Victor, he led the company to become the leader in electronics.

Yenta's Little Secrets

Sarnoff was proud of his heritage. In an interview to the *Jewish Journal* in 1960, he said, "The essential Jewish identity is worth preserving because it is an influence that conditions the for-mation of a better type of human being. Jewish ethics, morality, and wisdom are constructive influences."

In whatever he did, he realized he would be judged not only for himself, but as a member of his people. His cardinal rule, he said, was, "Every individual Jew must therefore assume responsibility for the honor of the entire Jewish people and realize clearly that improper conduct on his part may be damaging to all Jews by encouraging anti-Semitism."

"The Rabbi of Vitebsk"

Marc Chagall's father was a herring packer. His grandfather was a cantor and kosher butcher. A member of a large, poor, and pious Hasidic family, Chagall as a boy gave up swimming on Saturdays in order to study the Bible.

But God had other things in mind for him. Chagall began to paint: family scenes, friends, landscapes, skyscapes. His paintings had a dreamlike, fairytale quality. From Naturalism he moved to Fauvism and Cubism, but he went beyond any category. What is a Chagall painting? A Chagall!

He painted *The Rabbi of Vitebsk*. He did *I Am the Village*. And from somewhere deep in his imagination, he found the fantasies that included flying cows, dancing fiddlers, airborne violins, and soaring brides.

Marc Chagall, the quintessential 20th-century Jewish artist, created the Chagall windows for the Hadassah Hospital in Jerusalem. (Courtesy of Limot/Archive Photos)

Yenta's Little Secrets

Chagall left the Soviet Union in 1922 because he was considered a nonperson by the Soviets. He was a Jew and a painter whose work "did not celebrate the heroics of the Soviet people." Their loss, our gain.

One of the major tourist attractions in Jerusalem is the series of stained glass images, the Chagall *Windows* he created for the Hadassah Hospital in the city. These windows, each one dedicated to one of the twelve tribes of Israel, are perhaps the finest work ever done in this medium. Chagall also did the peace window for the United Nations Secretariat in New York, windows for the Vatican, and the Cathedral of Metz in France. His work can also be seen in the ceiling of the Paris Opera and in two large murals at New York's Lincoln Center.

Art critic Robert Hughes called Marc Chagall "the quintessential Jewish artist of the 20th century."

Descendant of Spinoza

Amadeo Modigliani traced his heritage to the Jewish philosopher Baruch Spinoza. His work, however, was not to be dominated by the mind, but rather by his feelings. In 1906, he left Italy and settled in the Montparnasse district in Paris with other Jewish immigrant artists such as Chagall, Lipschitz, Soutine, Zadkine, and Delaunay.

Pulpit Stories

Modigliani came to Paris the same year that Captain Dreyfus was acquitted of treason. Anti-Semitism was rampant in Paris at the time. Unintimidated, Modigliani went out of his way to show his fearlessness: When he sketched patrons in cafes to earn a few francs, he signed them "Modigliani—Jew."

Modigliani was so poor that he was often forced to paint on both sides of his canvases rather than buy a new one. For his sculpture, he scrounged for railroad ties at the building sites of the Paris subway. When construction in France stopped at the onset of World War I, Modigliani couldn't sculpt because there were no more building sites from which he could get his stones.

Sick, alcoholic, and mainly unappreciated in life, Modigliani was not fully recognized during his lifetime. Some say that he sang the *Mourner's Kaddish* for himself at a friend's house, when, at 36, he knew he was dying.

Aha, That's It

Kaddish is the Jewish prayer for the dead recited by mourners for eleven months after the death of a loved one. Its theme is not death, but rather praise of God and acceptance of His ways.

Soon after his death, museums began to acquire his sculptures and paintings. In 1989, Sotheby's auctioned off a Modigliani portrait for over eight million dollars.

Yenta's Little Secrets

When the Italian dictator Benito Mussolini asked art experts to name the greatest contemporary Italian artist, they all unanimously gave the nod to Modigliani. Yet, because he was Jewish, Modigliani and his works were officially ignored by Mussolini.

"And Behold, It Was Very Good"

The artist sees things we cannot. It is a divine trait to be able to look at a harsh and oftentimes cruel world and be able to declare, as the Bible does, "And the Lord saw all that which He had made and behold it was very good." And that is the artist's great gift; through his or her work, we can see the inner beauty of the world.

Visit the museums that have the works of some of these great Jewish figures: Ben Shahn (see his powerful 1944 painting *Concentration Camp*), Max Weber, Raphael Soyer, Moses Soyer, Chaim Soutine—and the incredibly imaginative and original works of Ya-akov Agam, Israeli painter and sculptor.

The Power of the Word

And God said—and it was. Mystics say that with words God created the world. Words to this day, in the hands of master craftsmen, are able to create new worlds, to change the way we think about things, and even to enable us to begin to change ourselves. Jews have always known the power of words. The people who gave the world *The Ten Words*, the Decalogue or the Ten Commandments, continue to give it the gift of meaningful words.

Novelist Saul Bellow (b.1915)

Saul Bellow's mother wanted him to become either a violinist or a rabbi. He decided instead to make beautiful music with words, as a novelist who would go on to win the Nobel Prize for Literature. The Swedish Academy cited his "exuberant ideas, flashing irony, hilarious comedy, and burning compassion." They praised Bellow's typical hero, who keeps trying to find a foothold during his wanderings in our tottering world, one who can never relinquish his faith, who believes that the value of life depends on its dignity, not its success. How's that for a rabbinic sermon? Who can ever forget *The Adventures of Augie March; Henderson The Rain King; Herzog; Mr. Sammler's Planet;* and the book that won him his Pulitzer Prize, *Humboldt's Gift.*

Yenta's Little Secrets

Saul Bellow's first nonfiction work, *To Jerusalem and Back: A Personal Account* (1976), was based on a visit he made to Israel the previous year. Of the Israeli people, he wrote, "These people are actively, individually involved in universal history. I don't see how they can bear it."

Bellow proudly identifies himself as a Jew: "Here and there some looney or other will now and then identify me as an assimilationist. I am no such thing."

Playwright Arthur Miller (b.1915)

Widely considered one of the leading American playwrights of the 20th century, Arthur Miller won the Pulitzer Prize in 1949 for *Death of a Salesman*—one of the most significant American dramas ever staged. Miller dealt with the McCarthy Era hysteria in *The Crucible*, by using the witch trials in Puritan New England as a metaphor for contemporary events. He credits his parents' reverence for family values, based on their Jewish tradition, for shaping his outlook on life.

The Israeli Wizard (b.1939)

Amos Oz is Israel's best-known and most successful writer. It wouldn't be an exaggeration to say that Oz is a wizard. When he was five years old, he learned the alphabet, and when his father taught him how to type, "The first thing I printed was my name and the subtitle: writer." Oz was born Klausner, but adopted the name *Oz*, Hebrew for "strength," when he was a teenager. His works, written in Hebrew and translated into English, are one of the finest ways to understand the true inner strength of Israelis.

The New York Times called Oz's best-known work, *My Michael* (Hebrew, 1968; English, 1972), "One of the most accomplished foreign novels to appear here." In 1989, Oz received France's top literary award, the Paris Prize, for the best foreign novel of the year, *Black Box*. Two of his other important works are the novel *Touch The Water, Touch The Wind*, and the nonfiction report on life in Israel, *In The Land of Israel.*

Roth and the Jewish Antihero

Philip Roth (b.1933) is—well, Philip Roth. Even he is still having trouble figuring himself out, which is why he plays such an important part in so many of his novels.

But to understand Jewish-American life, its problems, its torments, the struggle that American Jewish men face in the conflict between their heritage and their attraction to the Christian-oriented American culture, you've just got to read Roth. *Goodbye Columbus, Portnoy's Complaint, Patrimony, Our Gang, The Great American Novel, My Life As A Man, The Breast, The Professor of Desire, The Ghost Writer, Zuckerman Unbound, Anatomy Lesson, The Counter Life, The Facts, Deceptions, Operation Shylock: A Confession*, and *Sabbath's Theater* are funny, farcical, depressing, serious, profound, and deeply stirring. Some of his heroes may be obnoxious, but his writing is simply in a class by itself.

Jewish American novelist Philip Roth gave us the classic works on Jewish men in search of their identity and masculinity. (Courtesy of Photofest)

Best-Selling Wouks

Herman Wouk (b.1915) catapulted to fame with his bestselling novel, *The Caine Mutiny*, winner of the Pulitzer Prize in 1951. Since then, his books have consistently had Jewish themes. Two of the most popular ones, *The Winds of War*, and its sequel, *War and Remembrance*, are deeply moving stories that interweave the Holocaust and the major battles of World War II. When they were published in the People's Republic of China, Wouk became the most popular foreign novelist in that country.

Wouk gave us the stereotype of the Jewish-American Princess in *Marjorie Morningstar*. But, as an observant Jew who still studies the Talmud daily, Wouk also helped explain Judaism as a religion to the world in his nonfiction book, *This Is My God*, written soon after the death of his son. The book is credited with encouraging many Jews to return to their faith and their heritage.

Wouk firmly believes that the survival of the Jewish people "looks like the hand of Providence in history." His works try to share that conviction with his readers.

Wiesel, Helping Us Remember

Elie Wiesel (b.1928) won the 1986 Nobel Peace prize for his human rights work. His books speak in a language never heard before—the language of concentration camp survivors who experienced what words never truly express and who write not from the mind but from the soul. Elie Wiesel is known as the eloquent voice of the six million.

Seared into Wiesel's memory is the horror of watching his father die a slow death from disease and starvation. For years after World War II, he could hardly speak, never mind write. But once he published *Night*, the words poured out of him as if there were no stopping them.

In *Night*, Wiesel introduces himself as "Witness." It was the first full-length account of what really happened in the Holocaust, and it didn't appear until 1956. People had previously not been interested; the Holocaust wasn't spoken of in "polite society."

Wiesel has become one of the leading figures in American Jewry, playing the role almost of prophet. His lectures draw thousands. His series of books, *Dawn, The Accident, The Town Beyond the Wall, Twilight, A Beggar in Jerusalem, The Oath, The Fifth Son,*

Sage Sayings

"Words aren't only bombs and bullets—no, they're little gifts containing meanings."

—Philip Roth

Sage Sayings

"World War II was an Everest of human experience, and as always, you cannot see the mountains until you get some distance away. It started with a horse-drawn army into Poland and ended with the atom bomb. Its outcome was crucial to the human race, and it is important to realize how close an outcome it really was."

—Herman Wouk

and *The Jews of Silence* all attempt to deal with the event that cannot be explained—yet must be remembered.

During a visit to Israel in 1991, Wiesel remarked, "Whenever I write, I always have in front of me a picture of the house where I was born. We must always ask, 'Where do I come from?' and 'Where are we going?' There must be a sense of history. If I had to sum up my mission in one sentence, it would be: "'Not to make my past your future.'"

Singer, The Yiddish Wordsmith

Isaac Bashevis Singer (1904–1991) proves how even novels translated from Yiddish into English can be true masterpieces. Imagine, a Yiddish writer received the Nobel Prize for Literature in 1978! In his acceptance speech, Singer noted, "I am not ashamed to admit that I belong to those who fantasize that literature is capable of bringing new horizons and new perspectives… In the history of all Jewish literature, there was never any basic difference between the poet and the prophet. Our ancient poetry often became law and a way of life."

His major works are *The Magician of Lublin*, *Enemies: A Love Story*, and his memoirs, *In My Father's Court*. But his most famous story is *Yentl, The Yeshiva Bocher* [The Yeshiva Boy] because it ran on Broadway as *Yentl* and was made into a movie directed by and starring Barbra Streisand (1983).

Sage Sayings

"The belief in God is as necessary as sex."

—Isaac Bashevis Singer

And the List Goes On

You've got to read Abraham Cahan's *The Rise of David Levinsky* and Henry Roth's *Call It Sleep* is a classic. Leo Rosten's *Christopher K*A*P*L*A*N* is simply hilarious; Chaim Potok's *The Chosen* lets you peer into the Hasidic world; and Bernard Malamud is pure genius in *The Assistant*.

The "*Elan Vital*"

It's only fitting that we end this book with two philosophers. Philosophy, after all, comes from two words that mean "love of wisdom." And if you've come this far, then you, too, must be a bit of a philosopher.

Henri Bergson (1859–1941), born into a Hasidic family, was the most Jewish kind of philosopher possible. Bertrand Russell, in his *A History of Western Philosophy*, said that Bergson was the chief representative of what he called "practical philosophers." They consider action the supreme good, happiness an effect of action, and knowledge the instrument of successful activity. (Remember the breakthrough of the Hasidic movement and the *Ba'al Shem Tov* in Chapter 18, "Saving Our Souls: Spiritual Responses to Persecution"?)

At the foundation of Bergson's philosophy is a "life-drive," the *elan vital* of the universe, a power that permeates everything that is alive. It creates life's movement and energy. Bergson's interpretation was in stark contrast to the mechanistic world view that previously dominated the thinking of the nineteenth century. He never fully defined the source of this *elan vital*, but can there be any question that the idea was rooted in his Jewish heritage—one that stressed a Divine Force as key to the life of the universe?

Bergson's most famous work is *Creative Evolution.* Here he argued that evolution couldn't be explained by adaptation to environment. It is really a creative process, like the work of an artist. But his magnum opus is *Matter and Memory* (1911), and it is here that he put forth the idea that memory is independent of the body and only uses the body for its own ends. That, too, almost smacks of the Hasidic emphasis on a soul independent of the body.

Sage Sayings

"Action is what matters. We are present where we act."

—Henri Bergson

When the Nazis occupied France during World War II, Bergson had an opportunity to be exempted from the anti-Jewish laws. The Vichy government offered to treat him as a kind of honorary Aryan. Though in extremely poor health, Bergson insisted on standing in line along with every other Jew to be registered as being Jewish. This surely hastened his death in 1941.

Seeing the Unity Through Buber's Thou

Martin Buber (1878–1965) was one of the leading spiritual figures of his generation. He left his impact not only on Jewish thinking, but on Christian theology as well. In his masterwork, *I and Thou* (1937), Buber developed a philosophy of God, man, and society that emphasized dialogue. He argued that the world could be divided into two fundamental forms of relationships. The I-Thou is a relationship between one person and another that emphasizes mutuality, openness, directness and empathy. And the I-It relationship is distant, uncaring, and treats individuals as things.

Buber described the relationship between man and God as I-Thou. He became a great enthusiast of Hasidism and devoted himself to collecting stories that taught genuine religiosity and spirituality. Buber was infatuated with the Hasidic traits of cleaving to God, humility, enthusiasm, and joy. It can truthfully be said that he brought Hasidism to the attention of the Western world.

He expanded his concept of dialogue to the Jewish-Christian relationship as well. He thought it was possible to recognize somebody else's view of spirituality and encouraged Jews and Christians to recognize one another's religions. He looked forward to cooperation not only between Jews and Christians, but also between Jews and Arabs and, for that matter, between peoples of the entire world. For too long in history, the "other" had always been an "it." Buber taught the world the importance of "thou."

Isn't that, after all, the most important Jewish message of all? That's why every blessing always begins with the words, "Blessed art Thou." Once the world understands that everyone is a "thou," it will certainly be blessed!

The Least You Need to Know

➤ Creativity is an aspect of godliness, and creative geniuses in every field are copartners with the Creator in helping to bring about a better world.

➤ Science has been enriched by the brilliance of numerous Jews who have helped us fathom the meaning of matter, the atom, and life itself.

➤ Atomic energy presents humankind with its greatest challenge for choosing either blessing or curse, peace or universal destruction.

➤ The Chagalls, Modiglianis, and other Jewish artists of international fame have helped us see far more than we could with our own eyes and help us to perceive the deeper beauty of the world.

➤ Jewish masters of "the word" have enriched world literature with their profound, stimulating, humorous, insightful, and inspirational works.

➤ Jewish philosophers explained to us the Hebrew view of man's role in the universe and helped pave the way for a time of mutual understanding and universal trust.

Shalom

Whenever Jews meet or depart from each other they say the word *shalom*. It means "peace," but can also mean "hello" and "goodbye." It is the ultimate prayer. Peace between nations. Peace within families. Peace of mind and serenity within oneself. As we complete this journey of Jewish history and culture, I wish you, dear reader, *SHALOM*.

Glossary

Adam   Name of the first man, from the Hebrew word *adamah*—dust, earth. It served to remind man of his humble origin.

Aggadah   Nonlegal rabbinic interpretation, or *midrash*, of the Bible, including homilies, stories elaborating Scripture, stories about rabbis, and other genres.

Aliyah   (1) Immigration to Israel, derived from the term for "going up" to Jerusalem. It refers to each wave of immigration, beginning in 1882. (2) "Going up" to the Torah when it is publicly read, an honor given to individuals during a synagogue service.

Ashkenaz   The Jewish name first applied in the ninth century to the area of Franco-Germany and later Poland, too. It is derived from the Bible. It is contrasted with Sepharad, the Jewish name for Spain, the other major community of European Jews.

Atonement, Day of   The solemn day for expurgating the sins of the Jewish people, observed on the tenth day of the New Year, known in Hebrew as Yom Kippur.

Auto-da-fé   The Portuguese term for "act of faith," referring to the exposure of Christian heretics, many of them converted Jews, during the Church's Inquisition.

Baal   From the Hebrew "master, lord, warrior," used as a generic word for a pagan god.

Ba'al T'shuva   Literally, a returnee, or a "master of repentance;" a Jew who returns to religious practice and observance.

Badhan   The Hebrew term for "jester," an entertainer at Jewish weddings and other festivities, from the Talmudic period on.

Bar   Aramaic for "son" (ben in Hebrew), used in the names of many Jews in Greco-Roman times.

Bar mitzvah   Coming of age for a Jewish boy at age 13, at which time he becomes fully responsible for performing the commandments (*mitzvot*).

Bat   Hebrew for "daughter," used in forming traditional Jewish names (e.g., Esther bat Avihayil).

Bat mitzvah   Coming of age for a Jewish girl, traditionally at age 12, at which time she becomes fully responsible for performing the commandments (*mitzvot*).

Ben   Hebrew for "son," used in forming traditional Jewish names (e.g., David ben Yishai).

Bet Din   The Hebrew term for a "house of judgment," a rabbinic court.

Bet ha-midrash   A traditional "house of study," harking back to Roman times.

Bilu   A movement of eastern European Jews in the first aliyah (immigration wave) to Israel in 1882 named for the initials of a Biblical phrase meaning "House of Jacob, come, let us go."

Bimah   A platform in the center or front of a synagogue on which the Torah is read.

Blood libel   Spurious accusation that Jews murder a Gentile child to obtain ritual blood, especially for Passover matzah.

Caliph   The Anglicized form of the Arabic term for a ruler, literally "deputy" of God.

Chalutzim   Singular *chalutz*, pioneers, specifically the earliest settlers of Israel in modern times.

Circumcision   The removal of the foreskin of the male organ, practiced in Judaism on all males, on the eighth day of birth or at the time of conversion, symbolizing the covenant between God and the Jewish people and accordingly called *berit milah* (covenant of circumcision).

Cohen (or *kohen*)   A priest descended from the tribe of Levi. In traditional Judaism, *kohanim* (pl.) serve certain ritual functions.

Conversos   Jews "converted" to Christianity in Spain and Portugal during the Middle Ages. Some continued to practice Judaism in secret.

Cossacks   A Ukrainian group of paramilitary horsemen who attacked Jews in Russia and Poland in the seventeenth century.

Council of the Four Lands   The Jewish self-governing body in Russia-Poland originating in the 16th century. Named for the four regions of Major Poland, Minor Poland, Red Russia, and Lithuania, it was called in Hebrew Va'ad Arba Aratzot.

Dead Sea Scrolls   Scrolls and fragments of parchment found in caves above the northwest shore of the Dead Sea. They contain texts of the Hebrew bible as well as original works preserved and copied by a community of Jews who lived there in Roman times.

Decalogue　From the Greek for "ten" and "word," referring to the Ten Commandments, which represent ten words or major principles.

Desecration of the Host　A libel leveled by medieval Christians against Jews alleging that Jews had desecrated the bread that Christians believed had become in the Eucharist the body of Jesus. As in cases of blood libel (see previously), Christians would often attack Jews on the basis of the charge.

Diaspora　An overall term designating the aggregate of Jewish communities living outside the land of Israel. Because such communities often originated through an expulsion from Israel, the term is Greek for "dispersion."

Disputation　An argument over doctrine, grounded in the interpretation of Scripture, between Christian groups or between Christians and Jews, especially in the medieval period.

Emancipation　The extension of fundamental civil rights to Jews in Europe beginning in the early nineteenth century.

Eretz Israel　The "Land of Israel," the biblical name for what is later sometimes called Palestine.

Ethics of the Fathers　A special section of the Talmud quoting the ethical, moral teachings and maxims of ancient sages.

Exilarch　The title of the appointed head of the Babylonian Jewish community in the first millennium C.E., *resh galuta* (head of the exile) in Aramaic. Tradition had it that the exilarch was descended from King David.

Final solution　The Nazi euphemism for the extermination of the Jewish people.

***Gaon*, geonic**　The *gaon*, or eminent one, was the head or dean of a rabbinical academy in Babylonia from the sixth through the eleventh centuries.

Gemara　The edited commentary on and discussion of the Mishnah incorporated into the Palestinian and Babylonian Talmuds. The term is Aramaic for "learning."

Gematria　An ancient method of interpretation by which the letters of a Hebrew word are decoded according to an assigned numerical value and then equated with another word of the same numerical value. The term is probably derived from the Greek "gamma = tria" (the third letter of the alphabet = three).

Genizah　The "store room" of a synagogue used since the early Middle Ages for discarding unused Hebrew books and documents. *The Genizah* is the rich mine of medieval source material discovered in the late nineteenth century in the synagogue of Old Cairo.

Ghetto　Originally a walled quarter of a city in which all Jews were compelled to live; the first such ghetto was that in Venice in 1516. Recently, it refers to any urban area with a particular ethnic concentration.

Habimah   "The Stage," Jewish theater group originating in 1917 and evolving into the national Israeli theater company, based in Tel Aviv.

Hadassah   The Women's Zionist Organization of America, founded in 1912 by Henrietta (Hadassah) Szold and named for her in 1914. Active in providing medical and educational services to Israel, it is the largest Zionist organization.

Haggadah   The "narration" of the Exodus at the Passover meal, the seder. The book incorporating the entire liturgy of the seder is called the *Haggadah*.

Halachah   Traditional Jewish law based on rabbinic interpretation (*midrash*) of the Bible and later decided on the basis of rabbinic codes and precedents.

Hanukkah   The Jewish holiday at the onset on winter commemorating the "rededication" of the Jerusalem Temple by the Maccabees in 165 B.C.E. It is observed by kindling lights for eight nights in thanksgiving to God for delivering the few and weak from the hand of the numerous and powerful.

Haskalah   European Jewish "enlightenment," which introduced Jews to modern ways of expression and thoughts from about 1750 to about 1880.

Hasmonean   The family of the second-century B.C.E. nationalist Jewish priest from Modin, Mattathias, father of Judas (Judah) the Macabee.

Hasidism   The Jewish religious revivalist movement originating in eastern Europe in the late eighteenth century. It maintains many characteristics of early modern Polish life, including its dress. There are diverse sects of Hasidim.

"Hatikvah"   The song of the Zionist movement and the national anthem of the State of Israel; Hebrew for "the hope."

Herem   A "ban" of excommunication from the Jewish community imposed occasionally in the Middle Ages.

Herut   The right-wing Israeli political party inspired by Zev Jabotinsky and formed in 1948.

High Holy Days   The English term for the Days of Awe, Rosh Hashanah (New Year), and Yom Kippur (Day of Atonement), a period of penitence falling around September.

Holocaust   The Western term meaning "fully burned" sacrifice, designating the destruction of European Jewry during World War II. The parallel Hebrew term, *Sho'ah*, means "annihilation."

Hoshana Rabbah   The seventh day of the fall festival of Sukkot (Booths), on which worshippers encircle the synagogue seven times carrying the four species—myrtle, willow, palm, and etrog—and reciting hosannas.

Hovevei Zion   "Lovers of Zion," the ninetheenth-century Russian Jewish Zionist movement.

Huppah   A Jewish wedding canopy, and by extension the wedding ceremony itself.

Inquisition   The investigation by Christian church officials into whether Jewish converts to Christianity were true to their new faith or were secretly practicing their former religion.

Jihad   The Muslim word for "holy war."

Kabbalah   The esoteric tradition passed on among Jewish mystics beginning in Roman times and continuing in diverse forms through the Middle Ages and into the modern era.

Kahal   Hebrew for "congregation," used to denote the organized Jewish community in eastern Europe in the pre-emancipation era.

Kehillah   The local communal organization of eastern European Jewry.

Kibbutz Galuyot   Hebrew for "in-gathering of the exiles."

Kiddush Ha-shem   Literally, sanctification of the name (of the Almighty) is the Hebrew term for the act of martyrdom.

Klezmer   From the Hebrew *k'ley zemer*—musical instruments—the term for professional Jewish musicians specializing in tunes that are part of Jewish heritage.

Kosher   The Hebrew term meaning "fit," referring to food that is permitted according to Jewish religious law. The term has entered modern English in the sense of "legitimate."

Landsmannschaften   The Yiddish name for associations of eastern European Jewish immigrants from the same town formed for the purpose of economic assistance.

Maccabee   In Hebrew, "hammer," describing the members of the family of Mattathias and his sons, heroes of the Hanukkah story.

Magen David   The "Shield of David," often called the "Star of David," a six-pointed star used as a symbol of Jewishness since the seventeenth century.

Magic Carpet   The operation in 1949–1950 to airlift about 30,000 Jews from Yemen to the newly independent State of Israel.

Marrano   The Christian name for Jews in Spain and Portugal who converted to Christianity but continued to practice Judaism in secret and their descendants; Spanish for "pig."

Maskil   A Jew participating in the Enlightenment (see Haskalah).

Matzo   Unleavened crackerlike bread eaten on the festival of Passover. According to the Torah, matzo commemorates the Israelites' exodus from Egypt when they were too hurried to let their bread rise.

Megillah   Hebrew for "scroll," one of the five biblical books that are read on special days; the Book of Esther is read on the festival of Purim from a parchment scroll and is accordingly known as *the* Megillah.

Menorah "Candelabrum," the seven-branched solid-gold lamp that, according to the Torah, stood in the inner sanctum of the Tabernacle in the wilderness after the Israelites left Egypt and in the first and second Temples. It was the main symbol of Judaism in antiquity and remains an important one. An eight-branched menorah is used on the holiday of Hanukkah.

Messiah The "anointed" king from the House of David, understood from the Hellenistic period on as a savior who would rule the community Israel in the end of days.

Mezuzah Literally "doorpost," it is a small case containing a parchment on which the Shema is inscribed, traditionally affixed beside the door of one's home and rooms in which one dwells.

Midrash The "searching" of Scripture to discover divinely encoded meaning. The term comes to refer to all classical rabbinic interpretations of the Bible and is used to designate collections of such interpretation.

Minyan A "quorum" for public prayer, traditionally comprising ten men (bar mitzvah age or above); more recently in some communities, it includes women, too.

Mishnah The edition of rabbinic legal traditions and teachings by Rabbi Judah ha-Nasi in Israel around 200 C.E. The Mishnah forms the basis of the Palestinian and Babylonian Talmudim, which take it as their starting point. The Hebrew term means "teaching."

Mishnah Torah Literally, a "second Torah;" the master work on Jewish Law written by Maimonides.

Mishpachah The Hebrew, as well as the Yiddish word for family.

Mitnagdim "Opponents" of the emerging Hasidic movement, formed after Rabbi Elijah the Gaon of Vilna placed the Hasidim under ban (see *Herem*) in 1772. The division into Hasidic and Mitnagdic camps persists among ultra-Orthodox Jews.

Mitzvah A "commandment" of the Torah, traditionally incumbent upon all Jews.

Mizrahi The Orthodox Zionist movement founded in Vilna in 1902. The name, meaning "eastern" (i.e., Zion-oriented), is abridged from Merkaz Ruhani (Spiritual Center).

Moses The name given to the Jewish leader by the daughter of Pharaoh, from the word "drawn," because she said, "From the water I have drawn him," when she saved him from the Nile.

Moshav (pl., *moshavim*) Cooperative agricultural "settlements," established in the land of Israel since 1921, in which land and large machinery are owned commonly.

Nasi Usually rendered "prince," the term refers in the Bible to the head of a tribe and in Roman times designates the chief of the rabbinic court or Sanhedrin.

Nazarene A Jewish follower of Jesus, named after Jesus' home in Nazareth.

Nazir From the Hebrew "to separate." A nazir is someone who chooses to voluntarily separate himself from wine and the cutting of hair in order to gain closer kinship with God because of his voluntary acceptance of greater strictures on his behavior.

Oral Law The rabbinic interpretation of the written Torah (Pentateuch), understood traditionally as having been revealed together with the written Torah to Moses and transmitted from generation to generation. In Hebrew, *Torah she-be'al peh.*

Pale of Settlement The area to which Jews were restricted to reside in czarist Russia.

Passover See *Pesah.*

Patriarchs Hebrew forefathers of the Israelite people about whom we read primarily in the Book of Genesis—Abraham, Isaac, Jacob, and the twelve sons of Jacob, most prominent among whom are Judah and Joseph. The wives of the patriarchs are the matriarchs, principally Sarah, Rebecca, Leah, and Rachel.

Pentateuch The Bible's Five Books of Moses, known in Judaism as the Torah.

***Pesah* (Passover)** The biblical festival celebrating the land's renewed fertility and the exodus of the Hebrews from Egyptian bondage.

Pharaoh Hebraized Egyptian title for the king.

Pharisees A party of Jews that originated in the second century B.C.E., affirming such doctrines as resurrection of the dead and a high degree of ritual purity. The rabbis of the late first and subsequent centuries C.E. are Pharisees, a term (Hebrew, *perushim*) referring to "separation" from the impure.

Pogrom A Russian term used to designate a violent, unprovoked attack on a Jewish community. Though the term took on this usage only in the nineteenth century, it has come to be applied to anti-Jewish attacks in earlier times, too.

Protocols of the Elders of Zion Spurious tract composed by an anti-semite in Russia at the turn of the twentieth century describing an international conspiracy for Jewish domination of the world. Confirming common anti-Jewish stereotypes, the work has fueled antisemitism and has remained in circulation among Arabs and even in the West until today.

Purim The late winter/early spring holiday celebrating the success of ancient Persian Jewry in overcoming an attempt to annihilate them by anti-Semites. The Scroll of Esther, narrating the biblical story, is read aloud, and merrymaking as well as charity are ordained.

Pyramid A monumental tomb constructed for Egyptian royalty.

Rebbe Yiddish for "rabbi," used by Hasidim. The leading rebbe of a Hasidic sect (also known as the zaddik) is often held to possess wondrous mediatory powers with the divine.

Rosh Hashanah The Jewish New Year, literally "Head of the Year," beginning the 10 Days of Repentance culminating in the Day of Atonement (Yom Kippur).

Sabra The name of a fruit that is tough on the outside and sweet on the inside; it is the most popular way to describe a native-born Israeli.

Sanhedrin The Hebraized Greek word for "council," applied to the chief judicial and legislative body of the Jews in the land of Israel in late Greek and Roman times. In 1807 it was the name given to the Jewish assembly convoked by Napoléon in Paris.

Seder The traditional ceremonial meal observed on Passover. The seder (order) involves an elaborate recitation of the exodus story (see Haggadah) and a number of symbols that recall the ancient temple practices and reflect the themes of the festival.

Sephardic Pertaining to the Jews whose ancestors lived in Spain and Portugal, most of whom were expelled in the 1490s, and their culture, which is distinguished from that of Ashkenaz (Franco-Germany; see previously).

Shema Three paragraphs from the Torah developing the theme of covenant obligations between God and Israel, a centerpiece of the daily morning and evening liturgy. The recitation begins with Deuteronomy 6:4 "Hear, O Israel, the Lord our God, the Lord is One."

Shivah The initial period of mourning the loss of an immediate relative, ordinarily "seven" days, beginning at the time of burial.

Shoa The Hebrew word for Holocaust.

Shofar The "horn" of an animal, usually a ram, made into a trumpet to announce the approaching New Year and to symbolize the call to repentance during services on Rosh Hashanah.

Shtetl "Little town" in Yiddish, the eastern European village in which many Jews lived in the early modern period.

Shtibl "Little house" in Yiddish, the small eastern European synagogue in early modern times, transported by Hasidim to their new communities in Israel and the West.

Shul The name commonly used to describe a synagogue, from the German/Yiddish word *shul*, or school, emphasizing its main function as a house of study.

Shulhan Arukh The code of Jewish law compiled by Rabbi Joseph Caro in Israel around 1542 and amended for use by European Jews by Rabbi Moses Isserles. It remains the standard source for traditional observance.

Siddur The "arrangement" of the Jewish liturgy, hence, the daily prayer book.

Sofer A scribe who writes religious texts.

Synagogue This Greek term for a house of "assembly," corresponding to the Hebrew *beit knesset* (house of assembly), designates the building in which Jews would gather to study, worship, or otherwise meet.

Tachrichin The religious garb placed on the dead; its color, white, is meant to symbolize purity.

Tallit Prayer "shawl" with fringes (*tzitziyot*) on the four corners, as ordained by the Torah.

Talmud The "teaching" of Jewish law and lore presented as the discussion of the Mishnah by rabbinic sages in the academies of Israel and Babylonia. The Palestinian Talmud was completed by the end of the 4th century C.E., the far more extensive Babylonian Talmud by the seventh century.

Temple The Latin-derived term for the ancient "house" of God (Hebrew, *beit ha-migdash*, "house of the holy") in Jerusalem serving as the central holy place of the ancient Israelites and the Jewish people. The Temple built by King Solomon in the late tenth century B.C.E. was destroyed by Babylonia in 587/586 B.C.E.; the second Temple, rebuilt in 515 B.C.E. and refurbished by King Herod around the turn of the era, was destroyed by Rome in 70 C.E. In the nineteenth century, Reform Jews began calling their synagogues temples. Jewish tradition looks forward to rebuilding the Jerusalem Temple in the messianic era.

Ten Commandments More properly, the "ten statements" comprise the set of positive and negative injunctions delivered by God to Israel at Mount Sinai and recorded in Exodus 20 and Deuteronomy 5.

Teraphim Pagan household idols of biblical times.

Tisha b'Av The "ninth of (the Hebrew month of Av)," the traditional date on which the first and second Temples were destroyed and on which these national and religious catastrophes as well as others are commemorated by a day-long fast.

Torah Literally, divine "instruction," Torah broadly embraces all religious sources and teaching; more narrowly, it refers to the written Torah revealed by God, traditionally to Moses, and embodied in the Pentateuch, as well as the oral Torah, believed traditionally to be the concurrent unwritten yet revealed interpretation of the written Torah.

TZAHAL An acronym for the Israel Defense Forces, or IDF.

Ulpan The name of the course to teach the Hebrew language to new immigrants in Israel.

Yad Va-Shem Hebrew for "memorial-monument," the name of the Israeli institution authorized to research and educate concerning the Sho'ah (Holocaust), memorialize the six million Jewish victims, and honor the Jewish resistance fighters and the "righteous Gentiles" who rescued Jews. Officially called the Israel Martyrs' and Heroes' Remembrance, Yad Va-Shem is a many-faceted museum and memorial in Jerusalem.

Yeshiva A school for training younger students in traditional Jewish sources and an academy for training older students in Talmud and codes to prepare them as rabbis.

Yiddish   A Jewish language that developed beginning in the Middle Ages as Jews who were pushed eastward from Germany wove many Hebrew and some Slavic terms into the Germanic base of the language that they preserved as their ethnic tongue. Yiddish was spoken among Jews in eastern Europe and in places to which they migrated.

Zaddik (or tzaddik)   A "righteous man," leader of a Hasidic sect. (*See also* Rebbe) More generally, a person who displays exceptional generosity and other personal qualities. Legend holds that the world exists by virtue of 36 zaddikim.

Zionism   The political movement, initiated in the mid-nineteenth century in Europe, to reestablish a Jewish state in the land of Israel, or "Zion" in one of its biblical names; more generally, support of the State of Israel.

Zohar   The major work of the Jewish mystical tradition, a commentary on the Torah incorporating traditional and innovative ideas of Kabbalah. Meaning "shining, splendor," the book is traditionally attributed to the second-century sage Simeon bar Yohai, but it is ascribed by historians to Moses de Leon in thirteenth-century Spain.

How Many Jews Are There? A Population Guide

World Jewry

United States	5,600,000	Georgia	13,000	Ecuador	1,000
Israel	4,700,000	Kazakhstan	12,000	Ethiopia	1,000
France	600,000	Austria	10,000	Monaco	1,000
Russia	450,000	Denmark	8,000	Portugal	900
Canada	360,000	Poland	8,000	Zimbabwe	900
Ukraine	310,000	Panama	7,000	Cuba	800
United Kingdom	300,000	Morocco	6,500	Turkmenistan	700
Argentina	230,000	Lithuania	6,000	Luxembourg	600
Brazil	130,000	Slovakia	6,000	Bolivia	500
Australia	95,000	Colombia	5,650	Bosnia and Herzegovina	500
South Africa	92,000	Czech Republic	5,000	Gibraltar	500
Hungary	70,000	Greece	5,000	Yemen	500
Germany	60,000	India	5,000	Kenya	400
Belarus	45,000	New Zealand	5,000	Netherlands Antilles	400
Mexico	40,700	Kyrgystan	3,500	Congo (Zaire)	320
Belgium	40,000	Bulgaria	3,000	Curacao	300

Italy	30,000	Peru	3,000	Jamaica	300
Netherlands	30,000	Puerto Rico	2,500	Singapore	300
Uruguay	30,000	Costa Rica	2,500	U.S.Virgin Islands	300
Venezuela	30,000	Estonia	2,500	Dominican Republic	250
Iran	25,000	Hong Kong	2,500	Philippines	250
Chile	21,000	Yugoslavia	2,500	Thailand	250
Azerbaijan	20,000	Croatia	2,000	Bahamas	200
Turkey	20,000	Japan	2,000	Suriname	200
Uzbekistan	20,000	Tunisia	1,900	South Korea	150
Moldova	18,000	Tajikistan	1,800	El Salvador	120
Sweden	18,000	Norway	1,500	Iraq	120
Switzerland	18,000	Ireland	1,300	Syria	120
Latvia	15,000	Guatemala	1,200	Tahiti	120
Romania	14,000	Finland	1,200	Armenia	110
Spain	14,000	Paraguay	1,000		

Locations With Fewer Than 100 Persons

Afghanistan	Cayman Islands	Honduras	Namibia
Albania	China	Indonesia	New Caledonia
Algeria	Cyprus	Lebanon	Nicaragua
Aruba	Egypt	Macedonia	Reunion
Bahrain	Fiji	Malta	Slovenia
Barbados	French Guyana	Martinique	Taiwan
Bermuda	Guadeloupe	Mozambique	Zambia
Botswana	Haiti	Myanmar (Burma)	

Cities* With Largest Jewish Population in the Diaspora

New York	1,900,000	Moscow	200,000
Los Angeles	585,000	Buenos Aires	180,000
Miami	535,000	Toronto	175,000
Paris	350,000	Washington, D.C.	165,000
Philadelphia	315,000	Kiev	110,000
Chicago	250,000	Baltimore	100,000
Boston	225,000	Montreal	100,000
San Francisco	210,000	St. Petersburg	100,000

*Greater metropolitan areas

If You Want To Be Even Smarter: Suggested Reading List

If you want more information on any of the people or major themes discussed in this book, I recommend that you turn first to *The Encyclopedia Judaica*.

For a deeper study of the Bible, the best Jewish translation is probably that of the *Jewish Publication Society*.

You'll also enjoy *The World's Greatest Story* and *Who's Who In The Bible*, both by Joan Comay.

Next, a good one-volume history of the Jews during the Biblical period is *A History Of Israel* by John Bright.

Understanding Jesus from a Jewish perspective is explored in *Revolution In Judaea* by Hyam Maccoby.

The historic period of Jesus is dealt with very well in *Judaism in the First Centuries of the Christian Era* by George Foote Moore.

Adin Steinsaltz has written a fine book on the *Talmud* called *The Essential Talmud*.

Highly enjoyable too is *The Book of Legends: Legends from the Talmud and Midrash* by Hyam Bialik and Yehoshua Ravnitzky.

Every Man's Talmud, by A. Cohen, is a wonderful guide and overview to the contents of the *Talmud*.

Insights: A Talmudic Treasury, by Sol Weiss, is a brilliant collection of *Talmudic* quotes and commentaries.

The Jews of Islam, by Bernard Lewis, is a fascinating work on Jews in the early medieval period.

A History of Jewish Literature, by Meyer Waxman and *Great Jewish Personalities in Ancient and Medieval Times*, by Simon Noveck are very enlightening.

A Maimonides Reader, by Isadore Twersky, is an excellent way to learn more about this great rabbi/physician.

The History of Anti-Semitism: From the Time of Christ to the Court Jews, by Leon Poliakov, describes the Jewish experience during the time of the Crusades.

The Spanish Inquisition, by Cecil Roth, tells the story in moving detail.

Major Trends in Jewish Mysticism, by Gershom Scholem, is a classic work on the *Kabbalah.*

Tales of the Hassidim, by Martin Buber and *The Romance of Hassidism* by Jacob Minkin are both excellent introductions to the Hasidic movement.

For modern Jewish history, *The Course of Modern Jewish History,* by Howard M. Sachar, is a very good overview.

The Golden Tradition: Jewish Life and Thought in Eastern Europe, by Lucy Dawidowicz, is an excellent anthology of Jewish life in Eastern Europe.

The Humor of Sholom Aleichem, by Shmuel Niger, is a great way to get to know this famous Jewish humorist.

Herzl, by Amos Elon, is a great biography of the founder of modern Zionism.

The Tongue of the Prophets, by Robert St. John, tells the amazing story of Eliezer Ben-Yehuda, and the revival of Hebrew as a modern language.

Ben-Gurion: Prophet of Fire, by Dan Kurzman, makes exciting reading.

The Arab-Israeli Wars, by Chaim Herzo, and *O, Jerusalem*, by Larry Collins and Dominique LaPierre describe the important battles of modern-day Israel.

My Life, by Golda Meir, is an extremely interesting autobiography.

Books on the Holocaust are a field unto themselves. See the entry in *The Encyclopedia Judaica* for a list of suggested readings. I can only single out the works by Elie Wiesel; Lucy Dawidowicz's *The War Against the Jews*; Yehuda Bauer's *A History of the Holocaust*; David Wyman's *The Abandonment: America and the Holocaust 1941-1945*; Martin Gilbert's *Auschwitz and the Allies*; Robert Lifton's *The Nazi Doctors: Medical Killing and the Psychology of Genocide*; and Yaffa Eliach's *Hassidic Tales of the Holocaust.*

For more about the Eichmann trial, read *Justice in Jerusalem*, by Gideon Hausner, and Isser Harel's *The House on Garibaldi Street.*

For more about Jews in America, see *Haven and Home: The History of the Jews in America*, by Abraham Karp; *World of our Fathers*, by Irving Howe; *Only In America*, by Harry Golden; and *Profiles in American Judaism*, by Marc Lee Raphael, for an overview of the different denominations in American Jewish life.

For a detailed and fascinating account of the Jewish winners of the Nobel Prize, read *The Laureates*, by Tina Levitan.

The role of Jews in Hollywood is fully discussed in *An Empire of Their Own: How the Jews Invented Hollywood*, by Neal Gabler.

The Gifts of the Jews: How a Tribe of Desert Nomads Changed the Way Everyone Thinks and Feels, by Thomas Cahill, is an almost awestruck exploration of the gifts of the Jewish people to Western civilization.

And finally, for a wonderful book on Judaism as a religion, you must read *Understanding Judaism*—not only because you'll really enjoy it, but because I wrote it!

Index

B